CLOSED

VOLUME 38

Gosho Aoyama

Case Briefing:

Subject:
Occupation:
Special Skills:
Equipment:

Jimmy Kudo, a.k.a. Conan Edogawa
High School Student/Detective
Analytical thinking and deductive reasoning, Soccer
Bow Tie Voice Transmitter, Super Sneakers,
Homing Glasses, Stretchy Suspenders

The subject is hot on the trail of a pair of suspicious men in black when he is attacked from behind and administered a strange substance which physically transforms him into a first grader. When the subject confides in the eccentric inventor Dr. Agasa, they decide to keep the subject's true identity a secret for the safety of everyone around him. Assuming the new identity of first-grader Conan Edogawa, the subject continues to assist the police force on their most baffling cases. The only problem is that most crime-solving professionals won't take a little kid's advice!

Table of Contents

CONFIDEN

CASE CLOSED
Volume 38
Shonen Sunday Edition

Story and Art by GOSHO AOYAMA

Translation
Tetsuichiro Miyaki

Touch-up & Lettering
Freeman Wong

Cover & Graphic Design
Andrea Rice

Editor
Shaenon K. Garrity

Printed in Canada

Published by VIZ Media, LLC
P.O. Box 77010
San Francisco, CA 94107

10 9 8 7 6 5 4 3 2 1
First printing, April 2011

WWW.SHONENSUNDAY.COM

RATED T+ FOR OLDER TEEN

PARENTAL ADVISORY
CASE CLOSED is rated T+ for Older Teen and is recommended for ages 16 and up. This volume contains realistic and graphic violence.

ratings.viz.com

www.viz.com

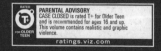

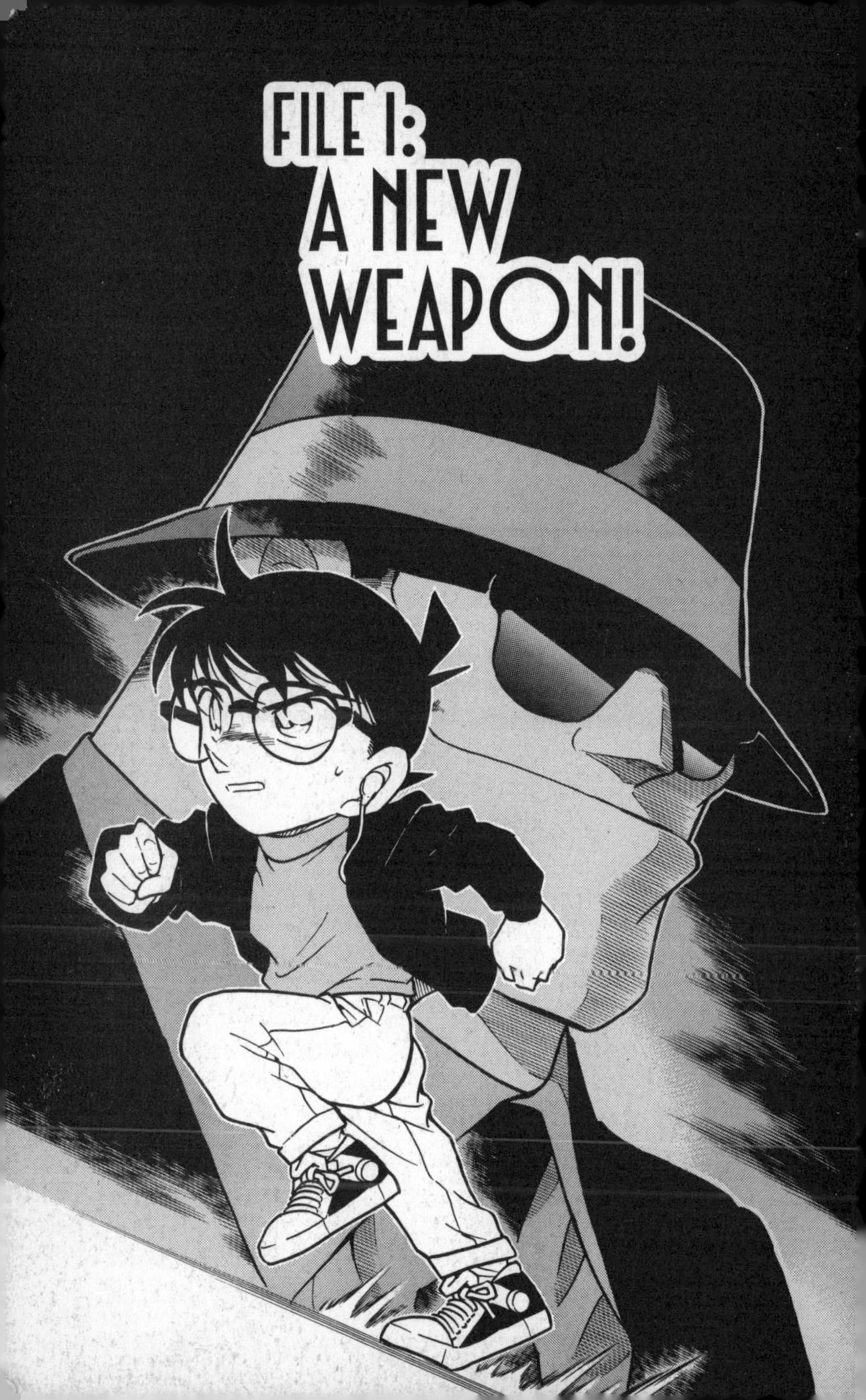
FILE 1:
A NEW WEAPON!

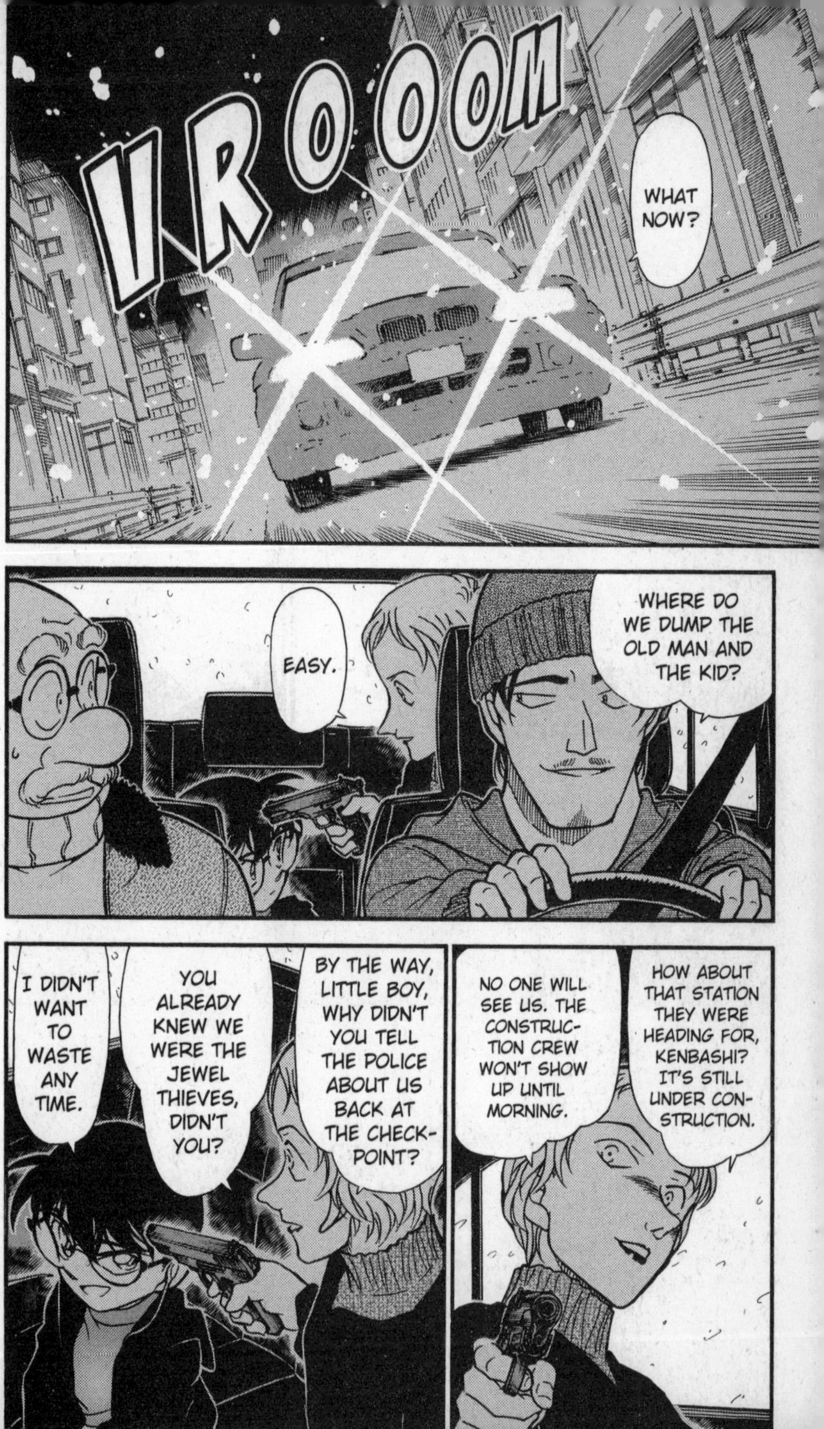
VROOOM
WHAT NOW?
WHERE DO WE DUMP THE OLD MAN AND THE KID?
EASY.
HOW ABOUT THAT STATION THEY WERE HEADING FOR, KENBASHI? IT'S STILL UNDER CONSTRUCTION.
NO ONE WILL SEE US. THE CONSTRUCTION CREW WON'T SHOW UP UNTIL MORNING.
BY THE WAY, LITTLE BOY, WHY DIDN'T YOU TELL THE POLICE ABOUT US BACK AT THE CHECKPOINT?
YOU ALREADY KNEW WE WERE THE JEWEL THIEVES, DIDN'T YOU?
I DIDN'T WANT TO WASTE ANY TIME.

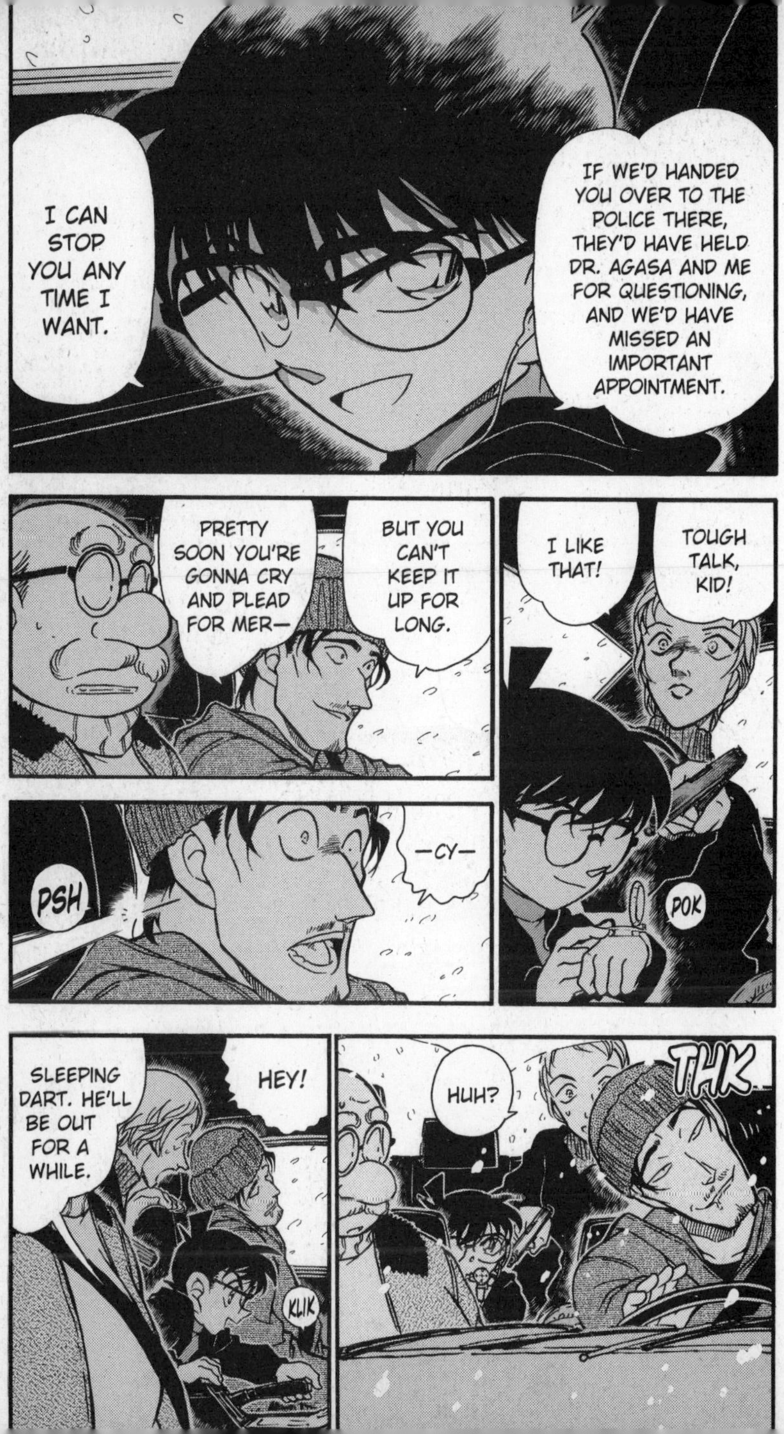
IF WE'D HANDED YOU OVER TO THE POLICE THERE, THEY'D HAVE HELD DR. AGASA AND ME FOR QUESTIONING, AND WE'D HAVE MISSED AN IMPORTANT APPOINTMENT.
I CAN STOP YOU ANY TIME I WANT.
TOUGH TALK, KID!
I LIKE THAT!
POK
BUT YOU CAN'T KEEP IT UP FOR LONG.
PRETTY SOON YOU'RE GONNA CRY AND PLEAD FOR MER—
—CY—
PSH
THK
HUH?
HEY!
SLEEPING DART. HE'LL BE OUT FOR A WHILE.
KLIK

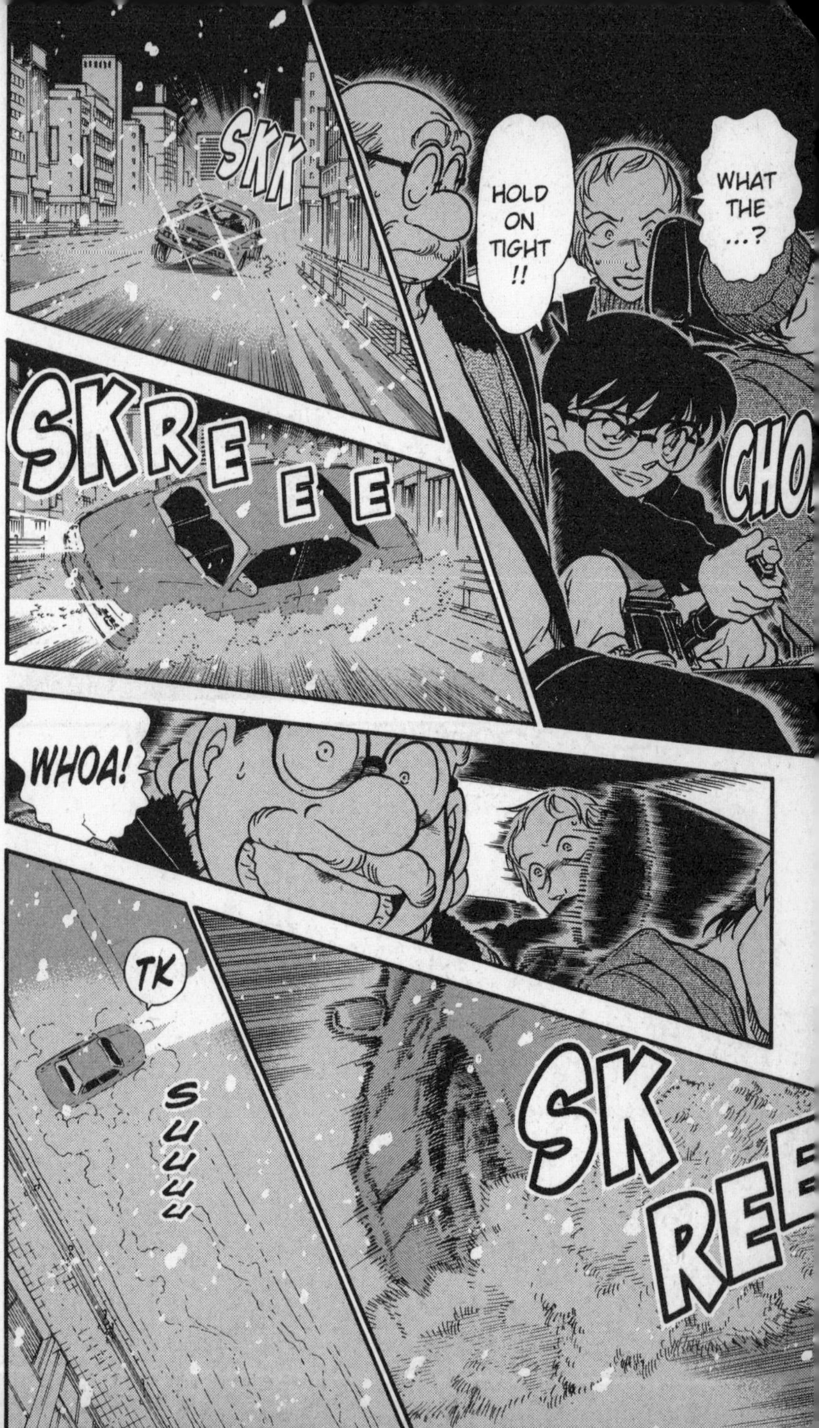
WHAT THE ...?
HOLD ON TIGHT!!
CHO
SKK
SKREEEE
WHOA!
SK REE
TK
SUUUUU

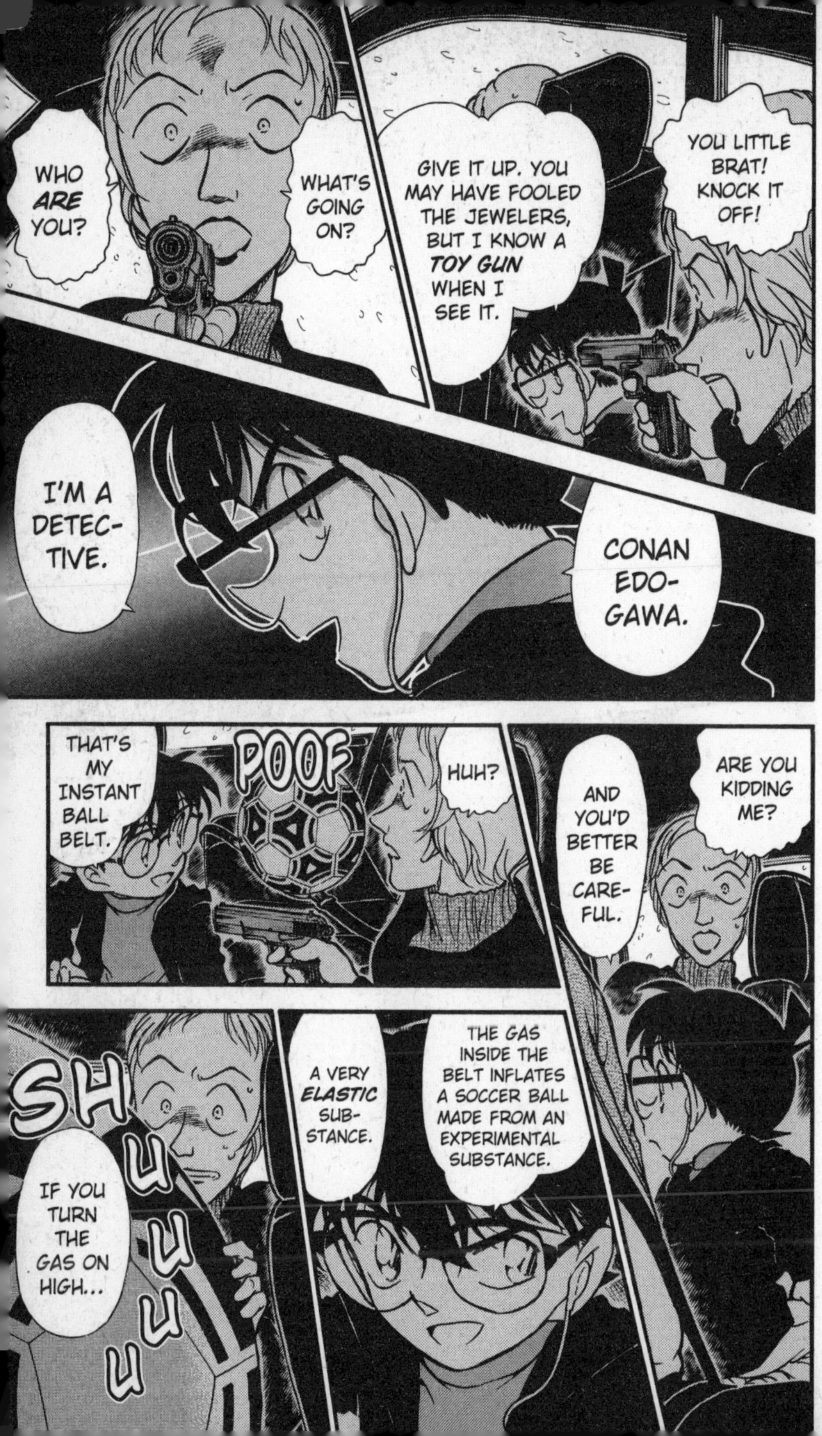
YOU LITTLE BRAT! KNOCK IT OFF!
GIVE IT UP. YOU MAY HAVE FOOLED THE JEWELERS, BUT I KNOW A **TOY GUN** WHEN I SEE IT.
WHAT'S GOING ON?
WHO **ARE** YOU?
CONAN EDO-GAWA.
I'M A DETEC-TIVE.
ARE YOU KIDDING ME?
AND YOU'D BETTER BE CARE-FUL.
HUH?
POOF
THAT'S MY INSTANT BALL BELT.
THE GAS INSIDE THE BELT INFLATES A SOCCER BALL MADE FROM AN EXPERIMENTAL SUBSTANCE.
A VERY **ELASTIC** SUB-STANCE.
SHUUUUU
IF YOU TURN THE GAS ON HIGH...

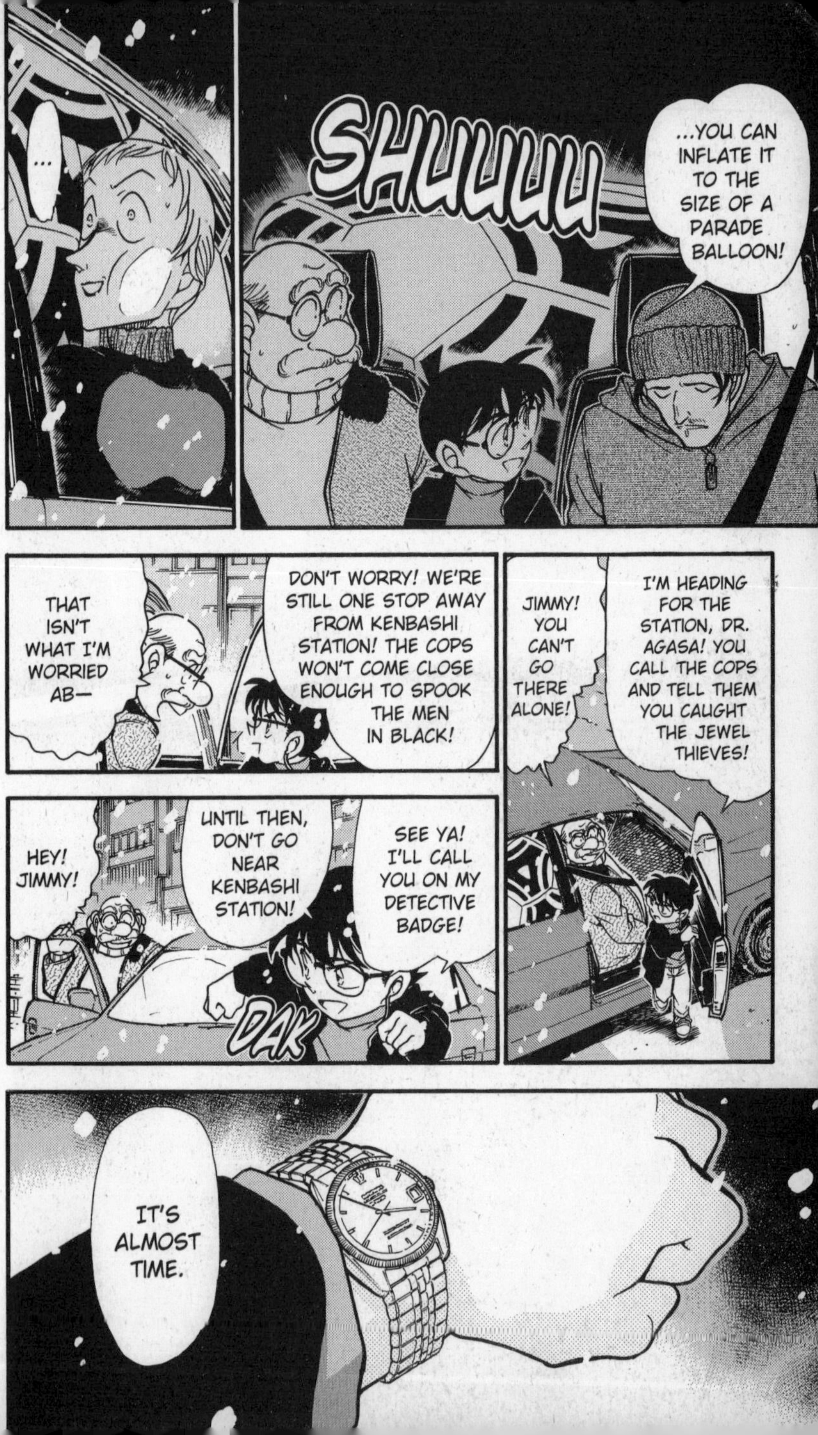
SHUUUU
...YOU CAN INFLATE IT TO THE SIZE OF A PARADE BALLOON!
...
I'M HEADING FOR THE STATION, DR. AGASA! YOU CALL THE COPS AND TELL THEM YOU CAUGHT THE JEWEL THIEVES!
JIMMY! YOU CAN'T GO THERE ALONE!
DON'T WORRY! WE'RE STILL ONE STOP AWAY FROM KENBASHI STATION! THE COPS WON'T COME CLOSE ENOUGH TO SPOOK THE MEN IN BLACK!
THAT ISN'T WHAT I'M WORRIED AB—
SEE YA! I'LL CALL YOU ON MY DETECTIVE BADGE!
UNTIL THEN, DON'T GO NEAR KENBASHI STATION!
HEY! JIMMY!
DAK
IT'S ALMOST TIME.

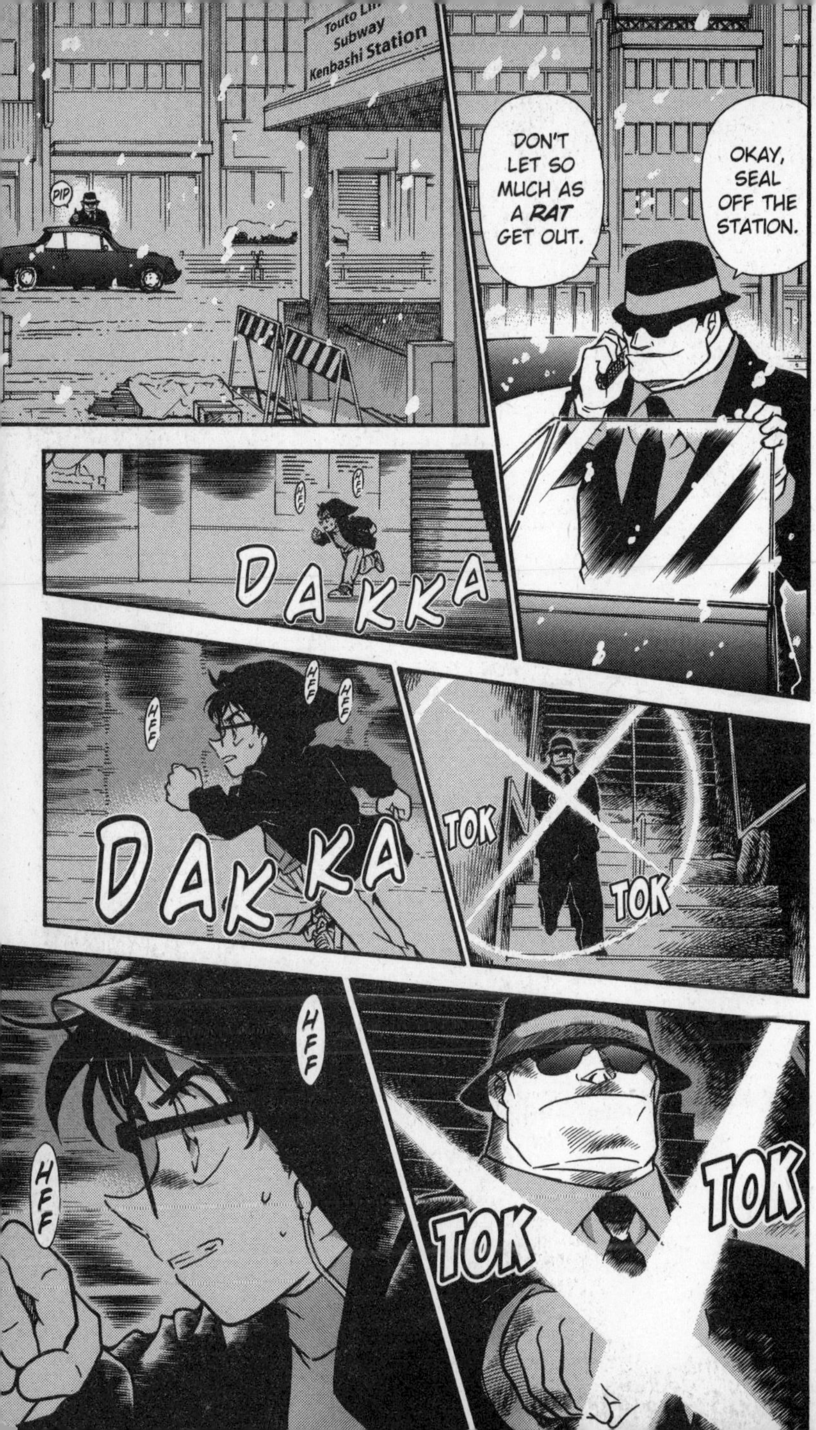
OKAY, SEAL OFF THE STATION.
DON'T LET SO MUCH AS A RAT GET OUT.
Subway
Kenbashi Station
PIP
HFF
DAKKA
TOK
TOK
HFF
HFF
HFF
DAKKA
TOK
TOK
HFF
HFF

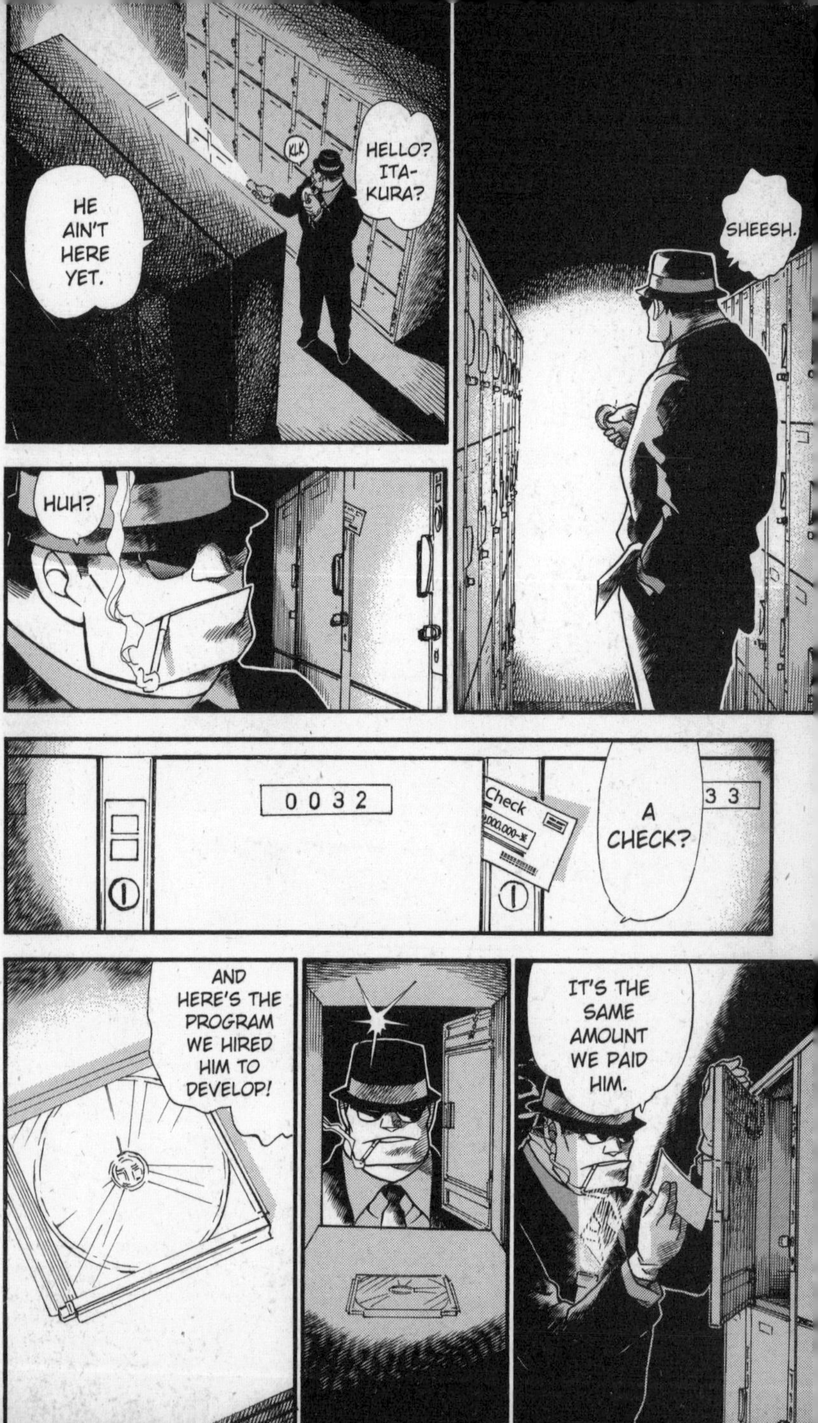
SHEESH.
HELLO? ITA-KURA?
KLK
HE AIN'T HERE YET.
HUH?
3 3
A CHECK?
Check
0 0 3 2
IT'S THE SAME AMOUNT WE PAID HIM.
AND HERE'S THE PROGRAM WE HIRED HIM TO DEVELOP!

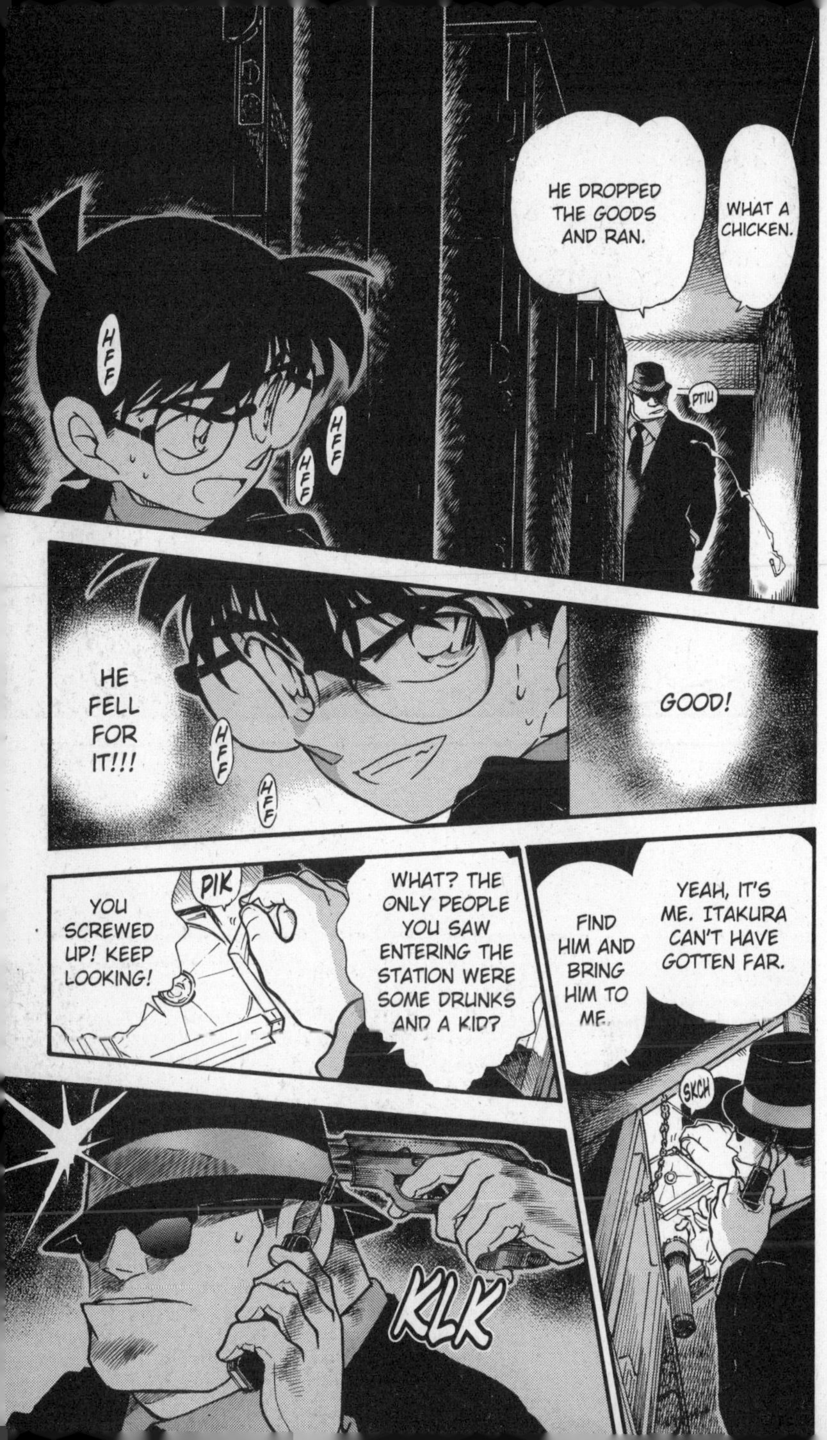
WHAT A CHICKEN.
HE DROPPED THE GOODS AND RAN.
PTIU
HFF
HFF
HFF
GOOD!
HE FELL FOR IT!!!
HFF
HFF
YEAH, IT'S ME. ITAKURA CAN'T HAVE GOTTEN FAR.
FIND HIM AND BRING HIM TO ME.
SKCH
WHAT? THE ONLY PEOPLE YOU SAW ENTERING THE STATION WERE SOME DRUNKS AND A KID?
PIK
YOU SCREWED UP! KEEP LOOKING!
KLK

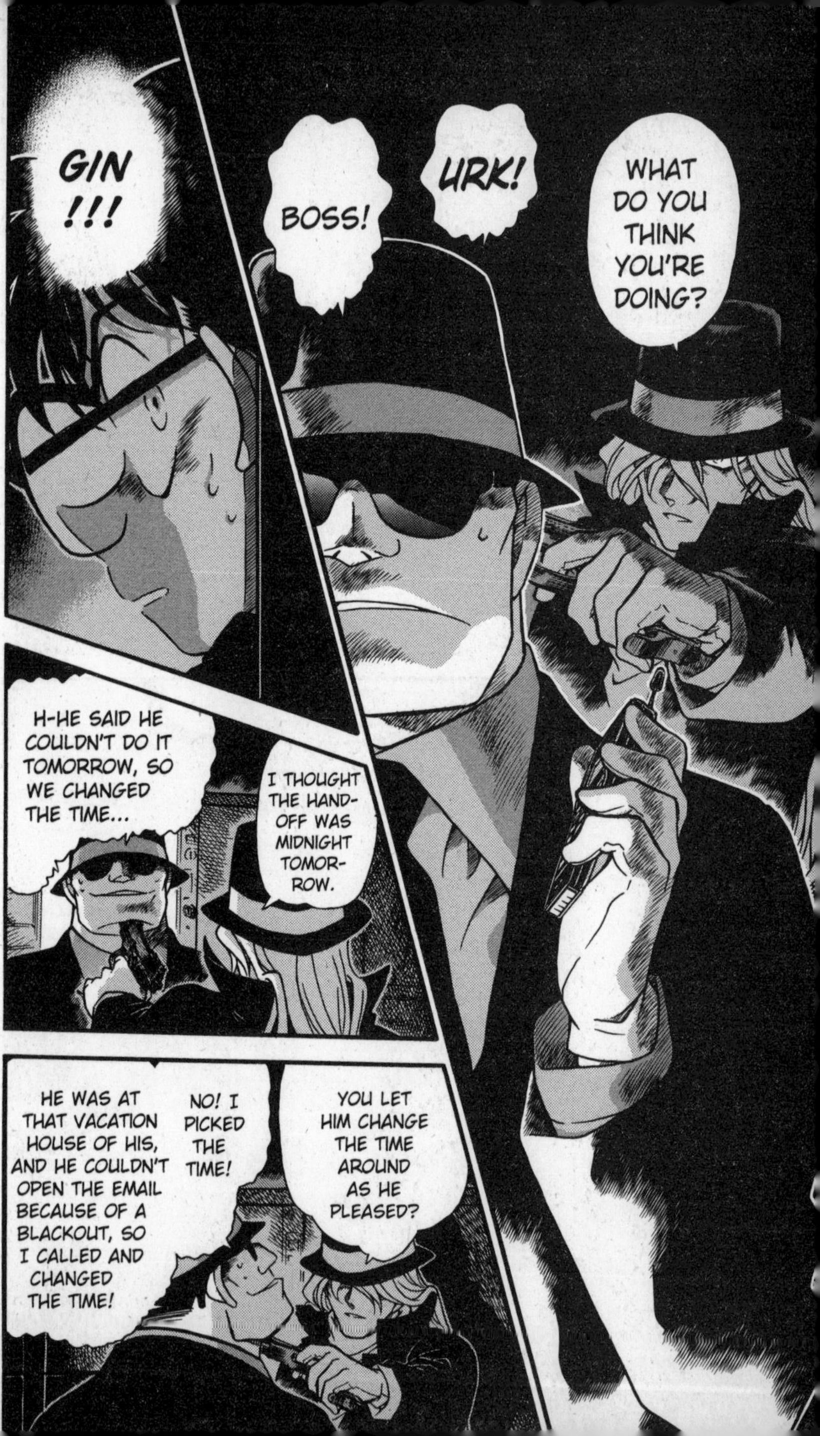
WHAT DO YOU THINK YOU'RE DOING?
URK!
BOSS!
GIN !!!
I THOUGHT THE HAND-OFF WAS MIDNIGHT TOMORROW.
H-HE SAID HE COULDN'T DO IT TOMORROW, SO WE CHANGED THE TIME...
YOU LET HIM CHANGE THE TIME AROUND AS HE PLEASED?
NO! I PICKED THE TIME!
HE WAS AT THAT VACATION HOUSE OF HIS, AND HE COULDN'T OPEN THE EMAIL BECAUSE OF A BLACKOUT, SO I CALLED AND CHANGED THE TIME!

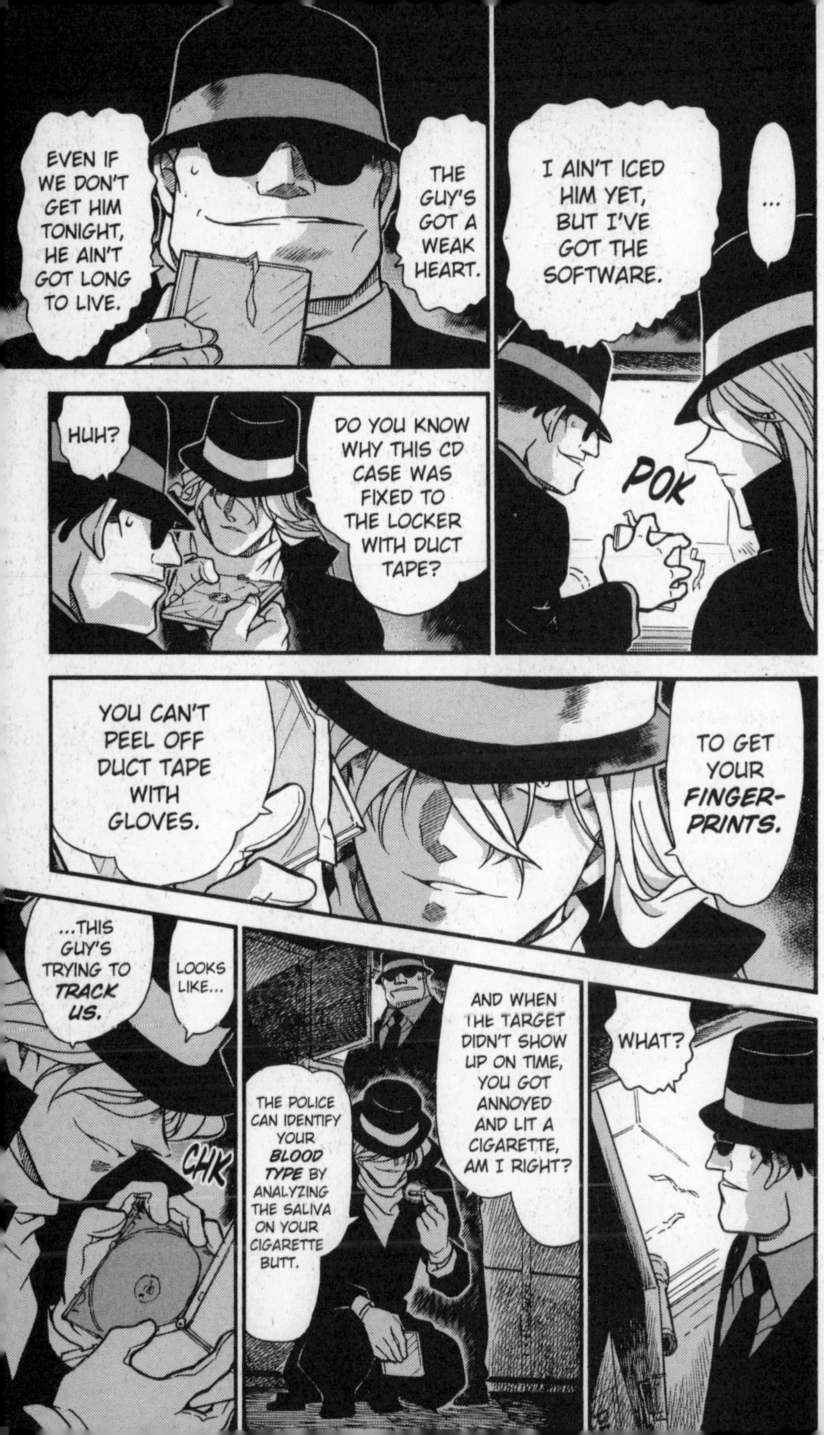
...
I AIN'T ICED HIM YET, BUT I'VE GOT THE SOFTWARE.
POK
THE GUY'S GOT A WEAK HEART.
EVEN IF WE DON'T GET HIM TONIGHT, HE AIN'T GOT LONG TO LIVE.
DO YOU KNOW WHY THIS CD CASE WAS FIXED TO THE LOCKER WITH DUCT TAPE?
HUH?
TO GET YOUR *FINGER-PRINTS.*
YOU CAN'T PEEL OFF DUCT TAPE WITH GLOVES.
WHAT?
AND WHEN THE TARGET DIDN'T SHOW UP ON TIME, YOU GOT ANNOYED AND LIT A CIGARETTE, AM I RIGHT?
THE POLICE CAN IDENTIFY YOUR *BLOOD TYPE* BY ANALYZING THE SALIVA ON YOUR CIGARETTE BUTT.
LOOKS LIKE...
...THIS GUY'S TRYING TO *TRACK US.*
CHK

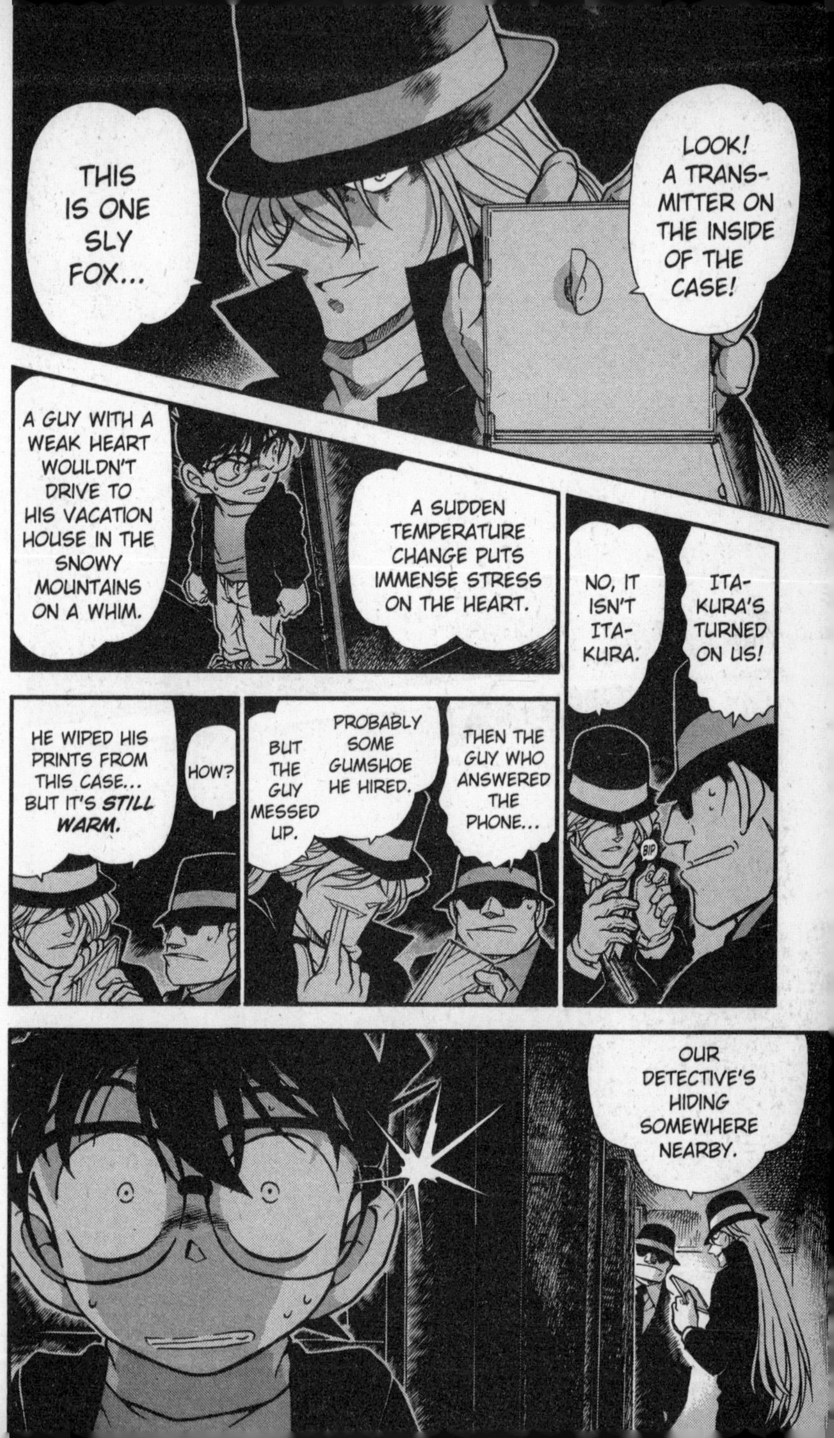
LOOK! A TRANSMITTER ON THE INSIDE OF THE CASE!
THIS IS ONE SLY FOX...
ITAKURA'S TURNED ON US!
NO, IT ISN'T ITAKURA.
BIP
A SUDDEN TEMPERATURE CHANGE PUTS IMMENSE STRESS ON THE HEART.
A GUY WITH A WEAK HEART WOULDN'T DRIVE TO HIS VACATION HOUSE IN THE SNOWY MOUNTAINS ON A WHIM.
THEN THE GUY WHO ANSWERED THE PHONE...
PROBABLY SOME GUMSHOE HE HIRED.
BUT THE GUY MESSED UP.
HOW?
HE WIPED HIS PRINTS FROM THIS CASE... BUT IT'S *STILL WARM.*
OUR DETECTIVE'S HIDING SOMEWHERE NEARBY.

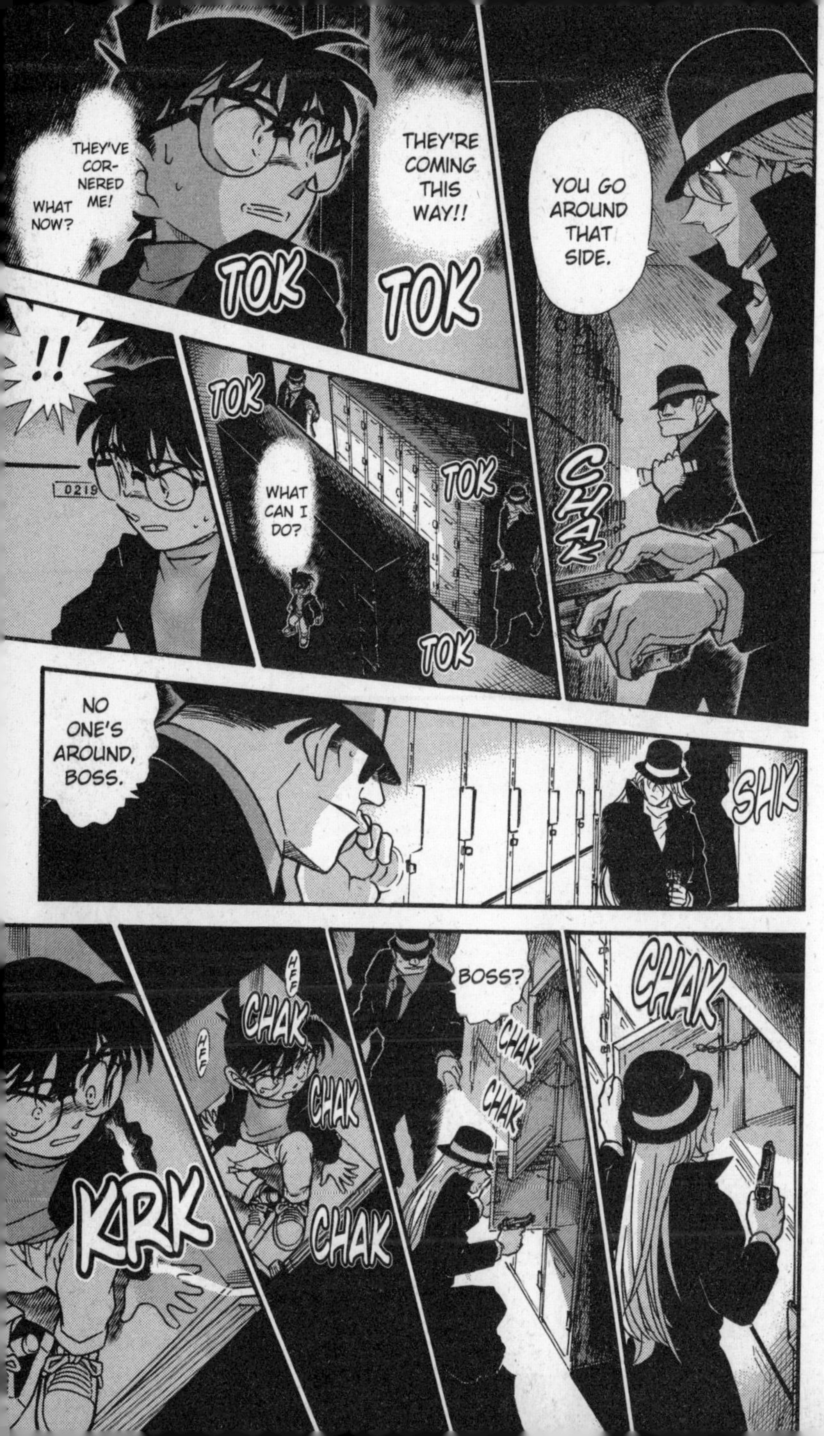
YOU GO AROUND THAT SIDE.
CHAK
THEY'RE COMING THIS WAY!!
TOK
THEY'VE CORNERED ME!
WHAT NOW?
TOK
TOK
WHAT CAN I DO?
TOK
TOK
!!
0219
SHK
NO ONE'S AROUND, BOSS.
CHAK
BOSS?
CHAK
CHAK
HFF
CHAK
HFF
CHAK
CHAK
KRK

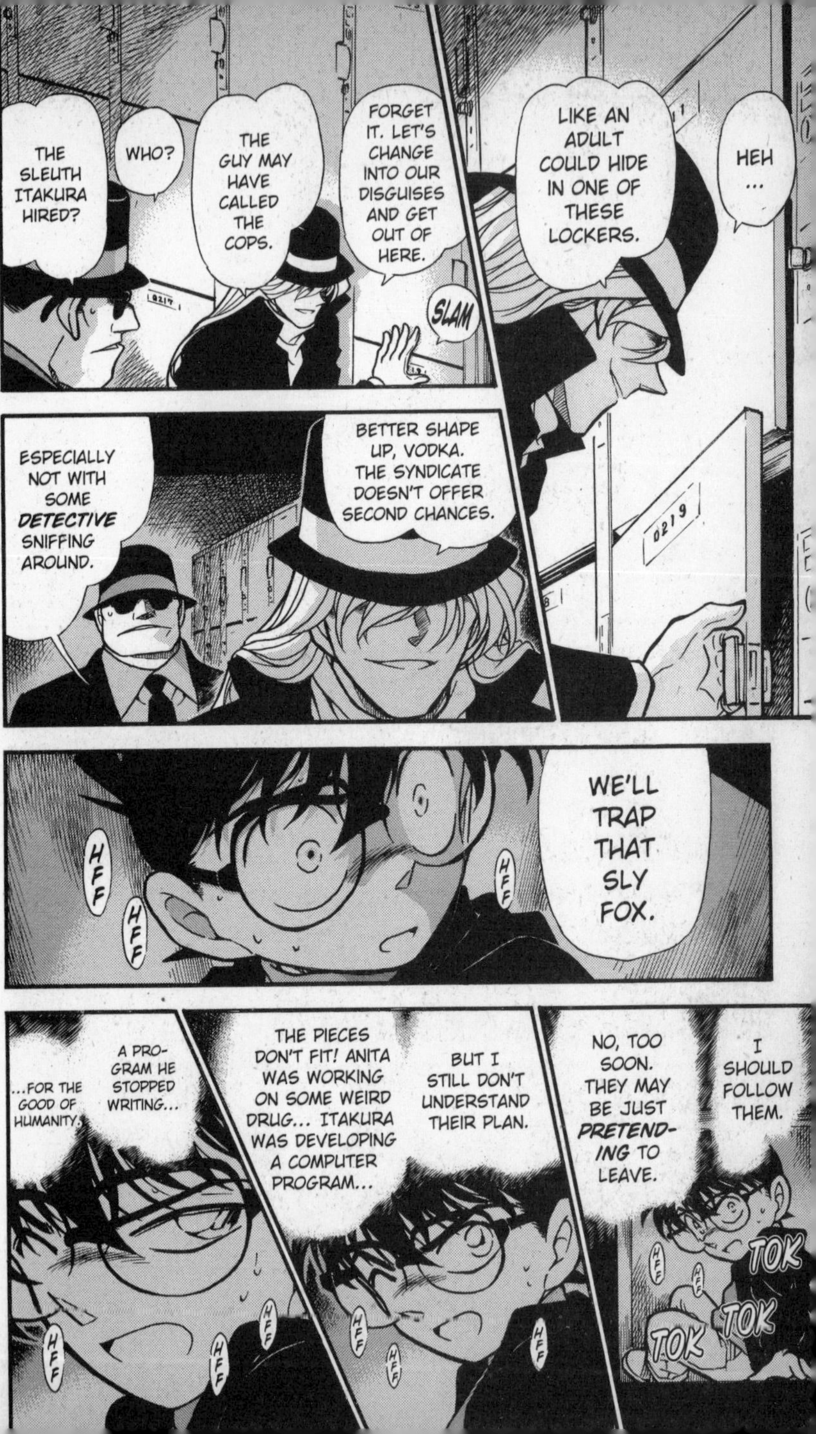
HEH ...
LIKE AN ADULT COULD HIDE IN ONE OF THESE LOCKERS.
FORGET IT. LET'S CHANGE INTO OUR DISGUISES AND GET OUT OF HERE.
SLAM
THE GUY MAY HAVE CALLED THE COPS.
WHO?
THE SLEUTH ITAKURA HIRED?
BETTER SHAPE UP, VODKA. THE SYNDICATE DOESN'T OFFER SECOND CHANCES.
ESPECIALLY NOT WITH SOME *DETECTIVE* SNIFFING AROUND.
WE'LL TRAP THAT SLY FOX.
HFF
HFF
HFF
I SHOULD FOLLOW THEM.
NO, TOO SOON. THEY MAY BE JUST *PRETEND-ING* TO LEAVE.
TOK
TOK
TOK
HFF
HFF
BUT I STILL DON'T UNDERSTAND THEIR PLAN.
THE PIECES DON'T FIT! ANITA WAS WORKING ON SOME WEIRD DRUG... ITAKURA WAS DEVELOPING A COMPUTER PROGRAM...
HFF
HFF
HFF
A PRO-GRAM HE STOPPED WRITING...
...FOR THE GOOD OF HUMANITY.
HFF
HFF

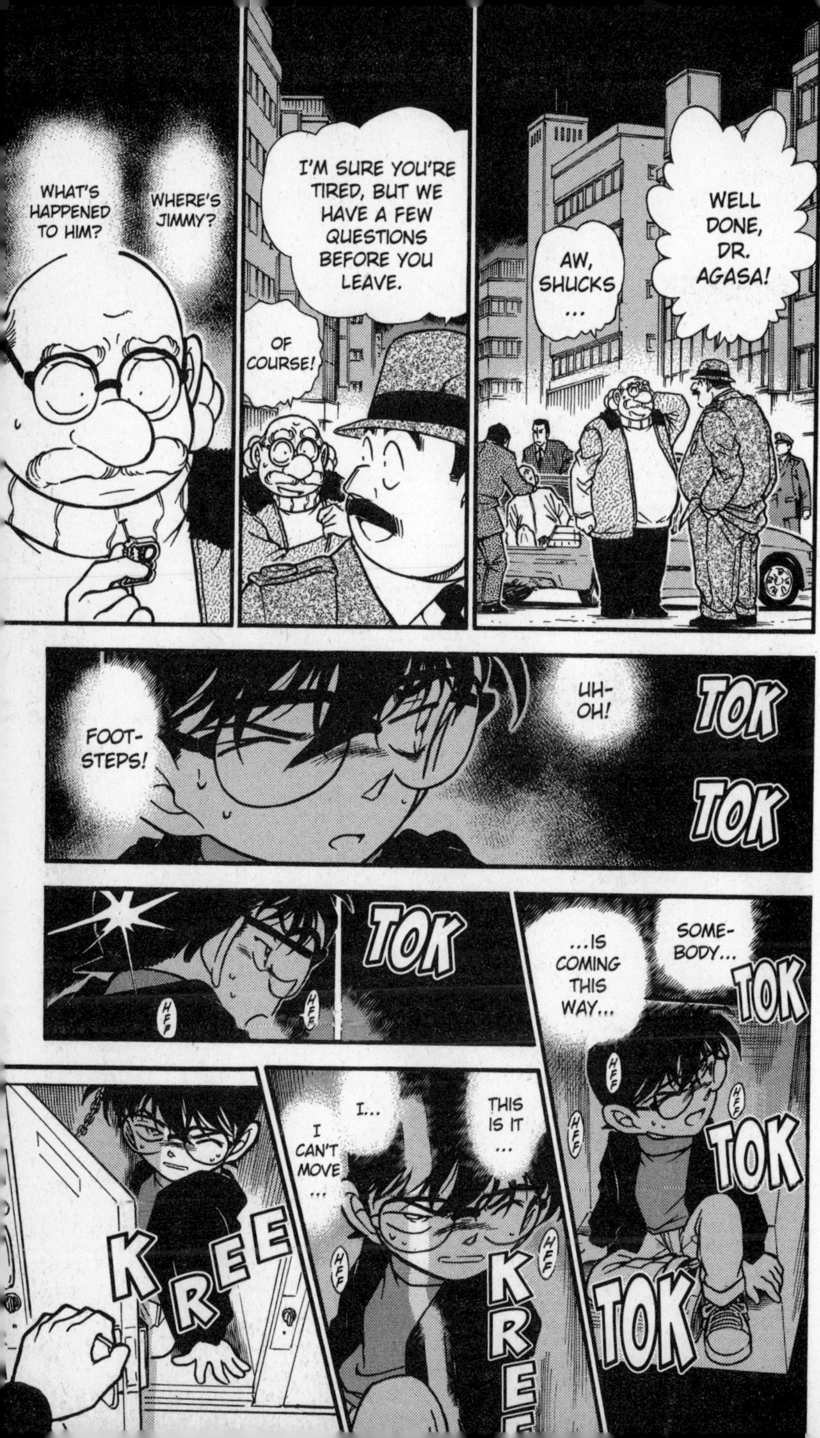
WELL DONE, DR. AGASA!
AW, SHUCKS...
I'M SURE YOU'RE TIRED, BUT WE HAVE A FEW QUESTIONS BEFORE YOU LEAVE.
OF COURSE!
WHERE'S JIMMY?
WHAT'S HAPPENED TO HIM?
TOK
TOK
UH-OH!
FOOT-STEPS!
SOMEBODY...
...IS COMING THIS WAY...
TOK
HFF
HFF
HFF
TOK
TOK
TOK
HFF
HFF
THIS IS IT...
I... I CAN'T MOVE...
HFF
HFF
KREE
KREE

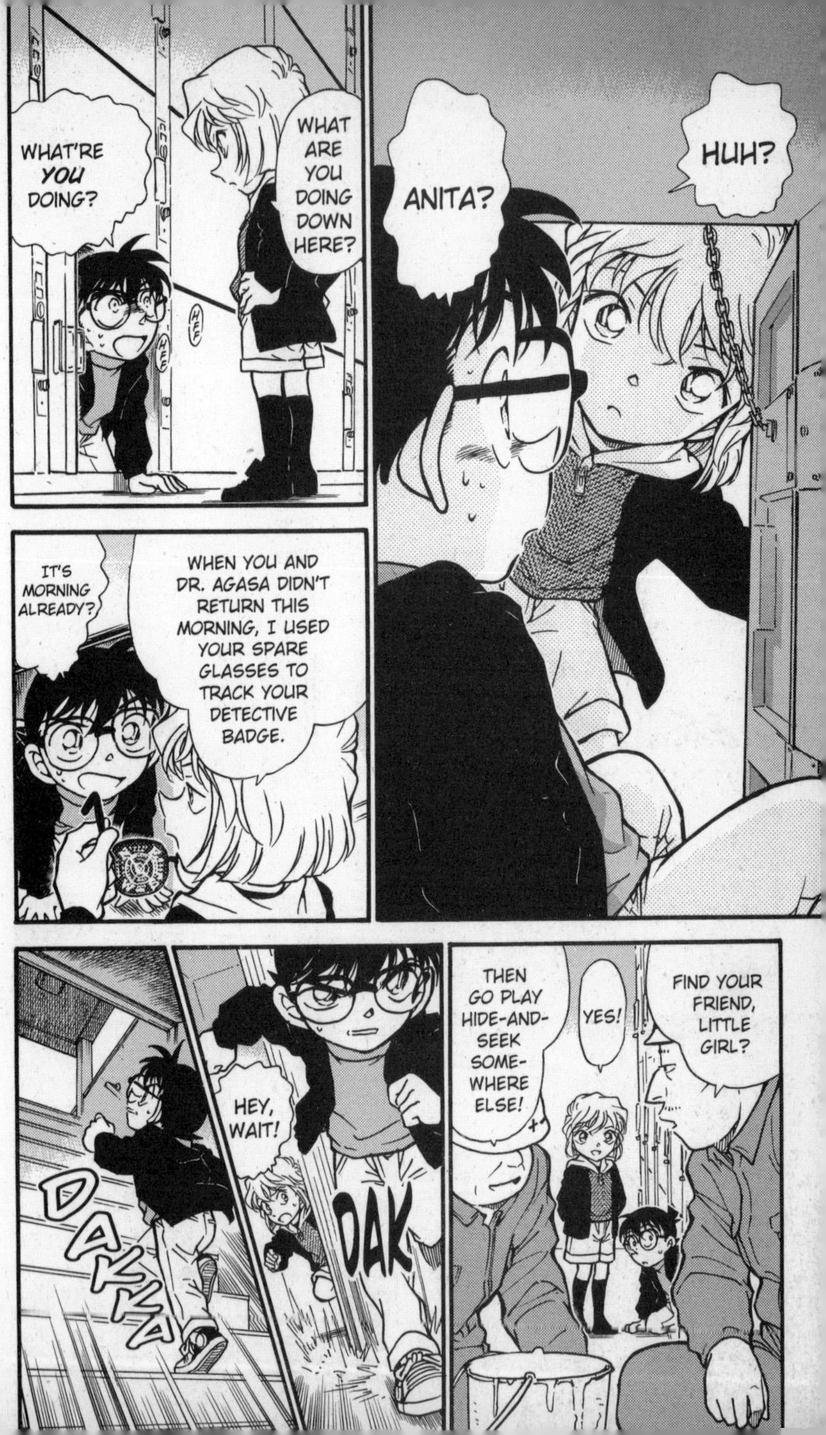
HUH?
ANITA?
WHAT ARE YOU DOING DOWN HERE?
WHAT'RE *YOU* DOING?
HEF HEF
WHEN YOU AND DR. AGASA DIDN'T RETURN THIS MORNING, I USED YOUR SPARE GLASSES TO TRACK YOUR DETECTIVE BADGE.
IT'S MORNING ALREADY?
FIND YOUR FRIEND, LITTLE GIRL?
YES!
THEN GO PLAY HIDE-AND-SEEK SOMEWHERE ELSE!
HEY, WAIT!
DAK
DAKKA

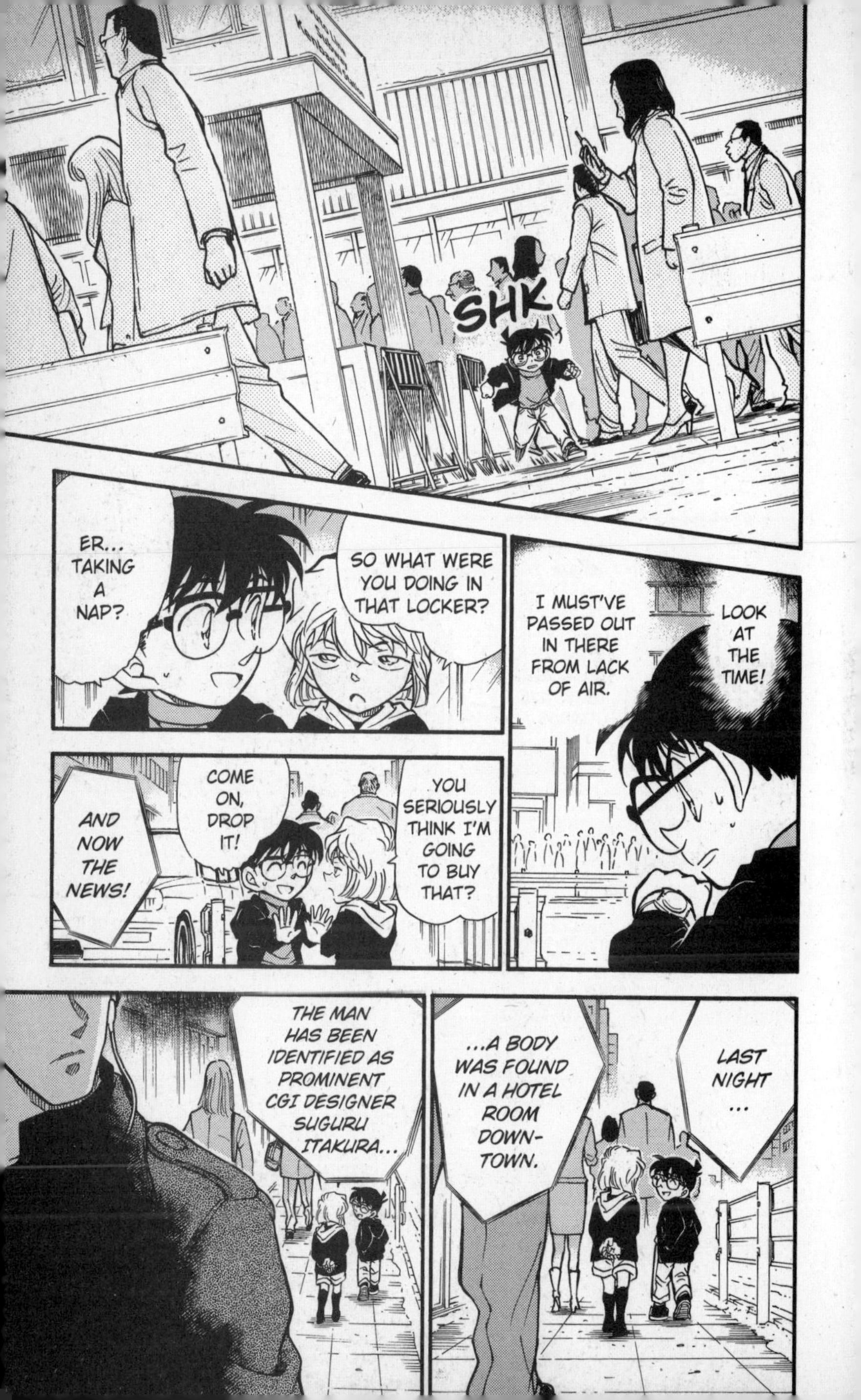
SHK
LOOK AT THE TIME!
I MUST'VE PASSED OUT IN THERE FROM LACK OF AIR.
SO WHAT WERE YOU DOING IN THAT LOCKER?
ER... TAKING A NAP?
YOU SERIOUSLY THINK I'M GOING TO BUY THAT?
COME ON, DROP IT!
AND NOW THE NEWS!
LAST NIGHT...
...A BODY WAS FOUND IN A HOTEL ROOM DOWNTOWN.
THE MAN HAS BEEN IDENTIFIED AS PROMINENT CGI DESIGNER SUGURU ITAKURA...

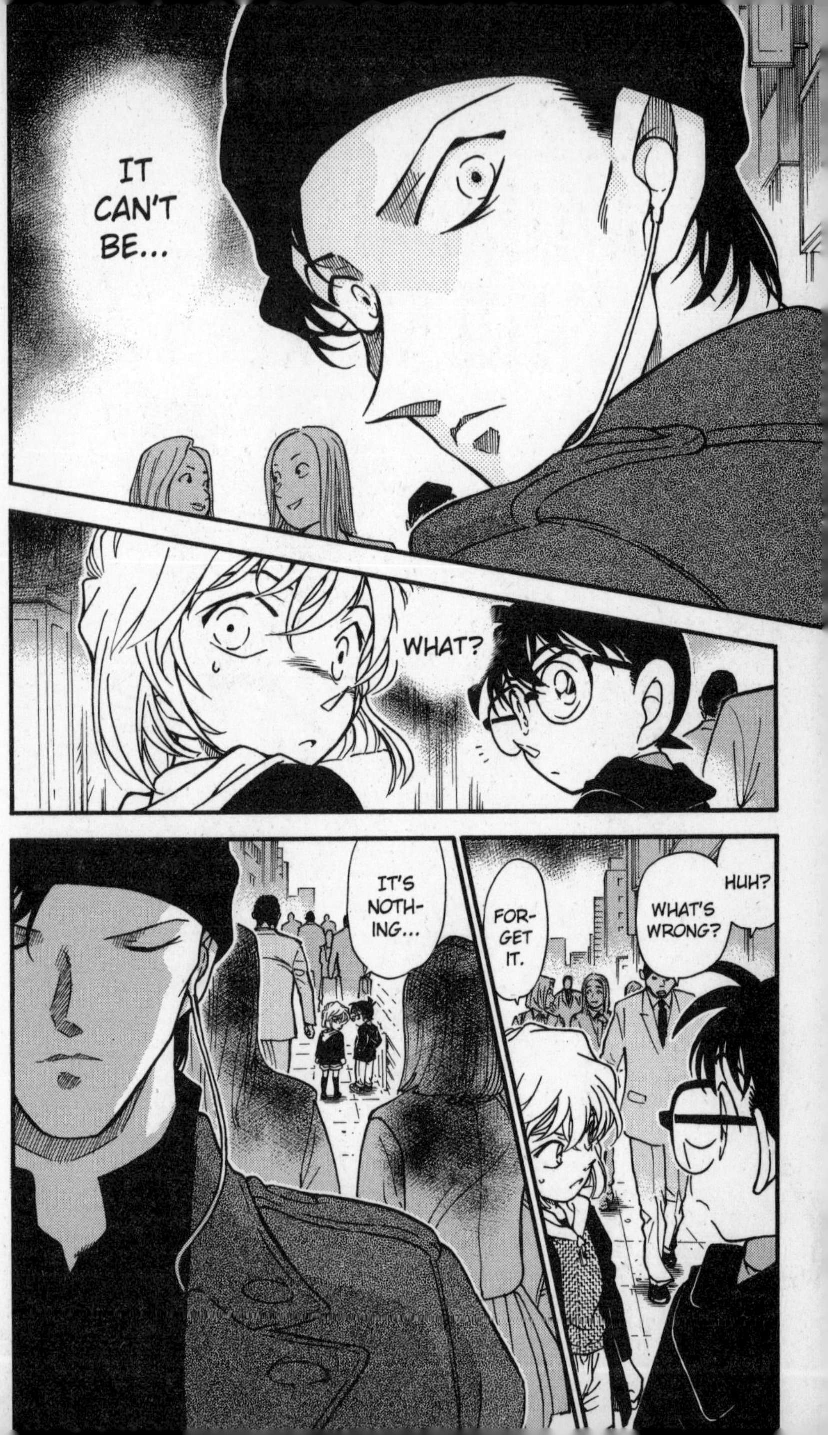
IT CAN'T BE...
WHAT?
HUH? WHAT'S WRONG?
FOR-GET IT.
IT'S NOTH-ING...

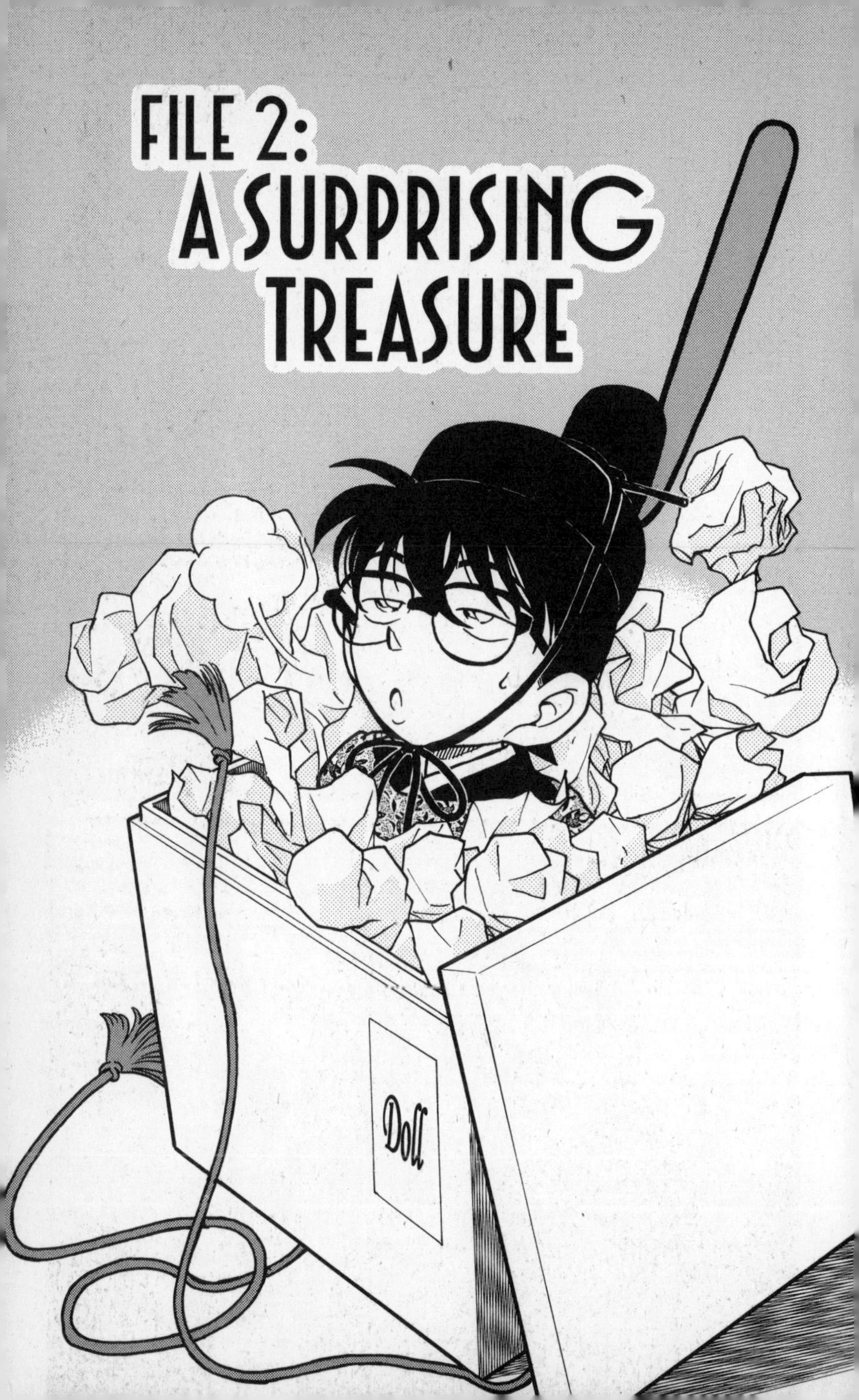
FILE 2:
A SURPRISING
TREASURE
Doll

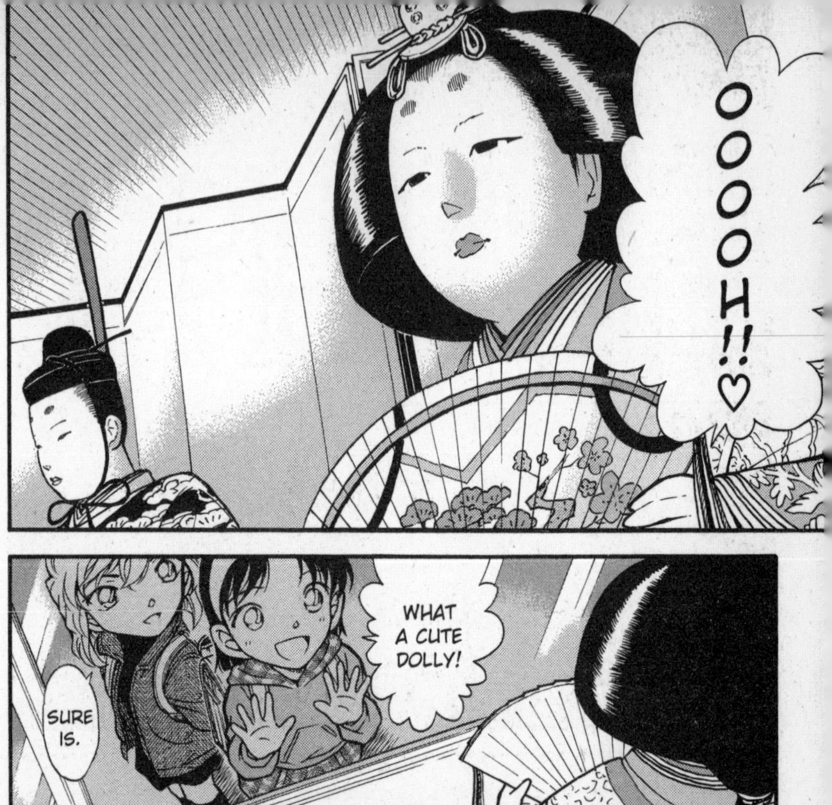
OOOOOH!!♥
WHAT A CUTE DOLLY!
SURE IS.

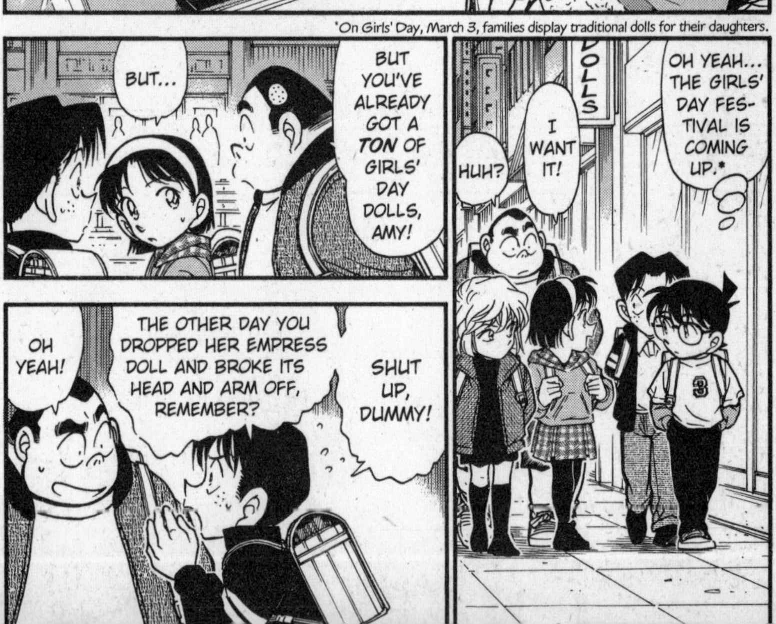
DOLLS
OH YEAH... THE GIRLS' DAY FES-TIVAL IS COMING UP.*
I WANT IT!
HUH?
BUT YOU'VE ALREADY GOT A *TON* OF GIRLS' DAY DOLLS, AMY!
BUT...
SHUT UP, DUMMY!
THE OTHER DAY YOU DROPPED HER EMPRESS DOLL AND BROKE ITS HEAD AND ARM OFF, REMEMBER?
OH YEAH!

*On Girls' Day, March 3, families display traditional dolls for their daughters.

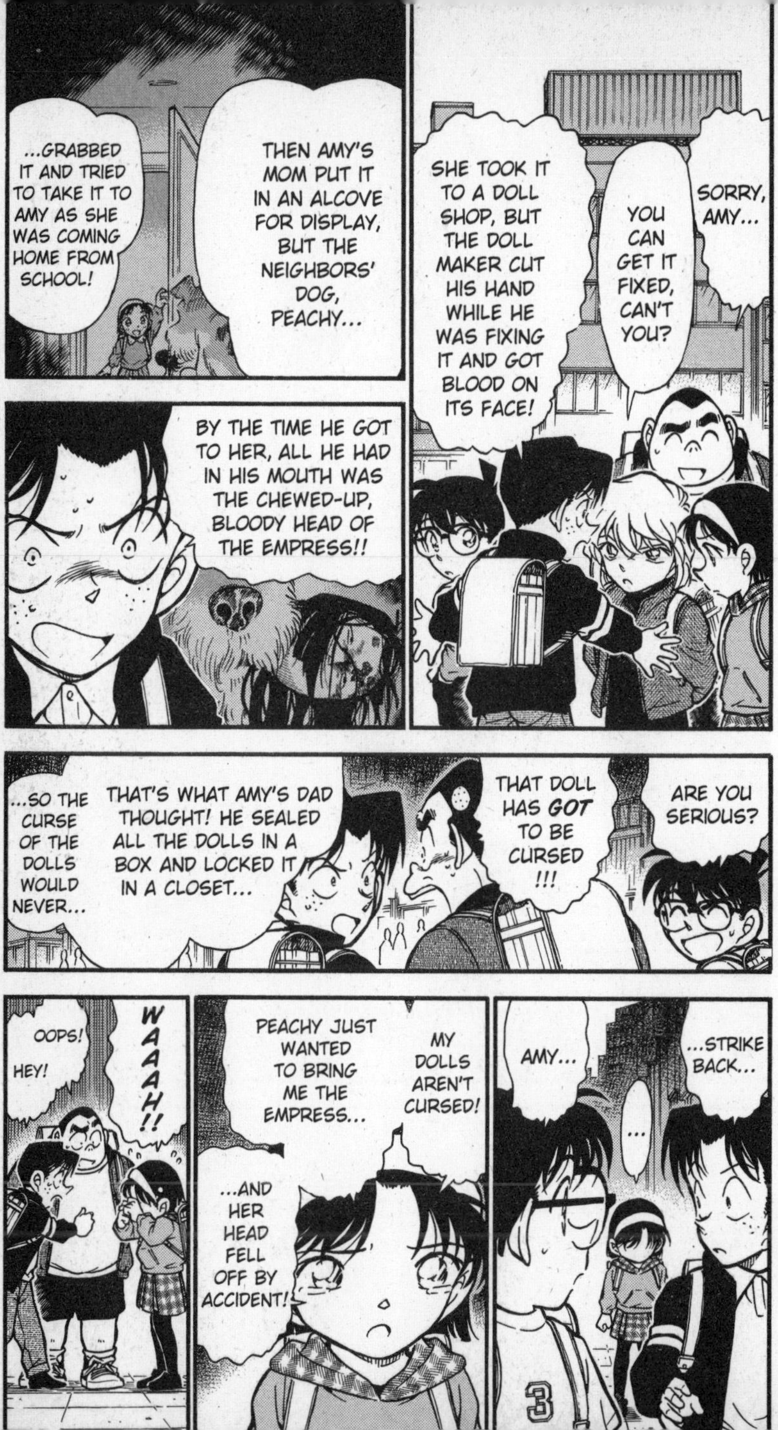
SORRY, AMY...
YOU CAN GET IT FIXED, CAN'T YOU?
SHE TOOK IT TO A DOLL SHOP, BUT THE DOLL MAKER CUT HIS HAND WHILE HE WAS FIXING IT AND GOT BLOOD ON ITS FACE!
THEN AMY'S MOM PUT IT IN AN ALCOVE FOR DISPLAY, BUT THE NEIGHBORS' DOG, PEACHY...
...GRABBED IT AND TRIED TO TAKE IT TO AMY AS SHE WAS COMING HOME FROM SCHOOL!
BY THE TIME HE GOT TO HER, ALL HE HAD IN HIS MOUTH WAS THE CHEWED-UP, BLOODY HEAD OF THE EMPRESS!!
ARE YOU SERIOUS?
THAT DOLL HAS *GOT* TO BE CURSED!!!
THAT'S WHAT AMY'S DAD THOUGHT! HE SEALED ALL THE DOLLS IN A BOX AND LOCKED IT IN A CLOSET...
...SO THE CURSE OF THE DOLLS WOULD NEVER...
...STRIKE BACK...
...
AMY...
MY DOLLS AREN'T CURSED!
PEACHY JUST WANTED TO BRING ME THE EMPRESS...
...AND HER HEAD FELL OFF BY ACCIDENT!
WAAAAH!!
OOPS!
HEY!

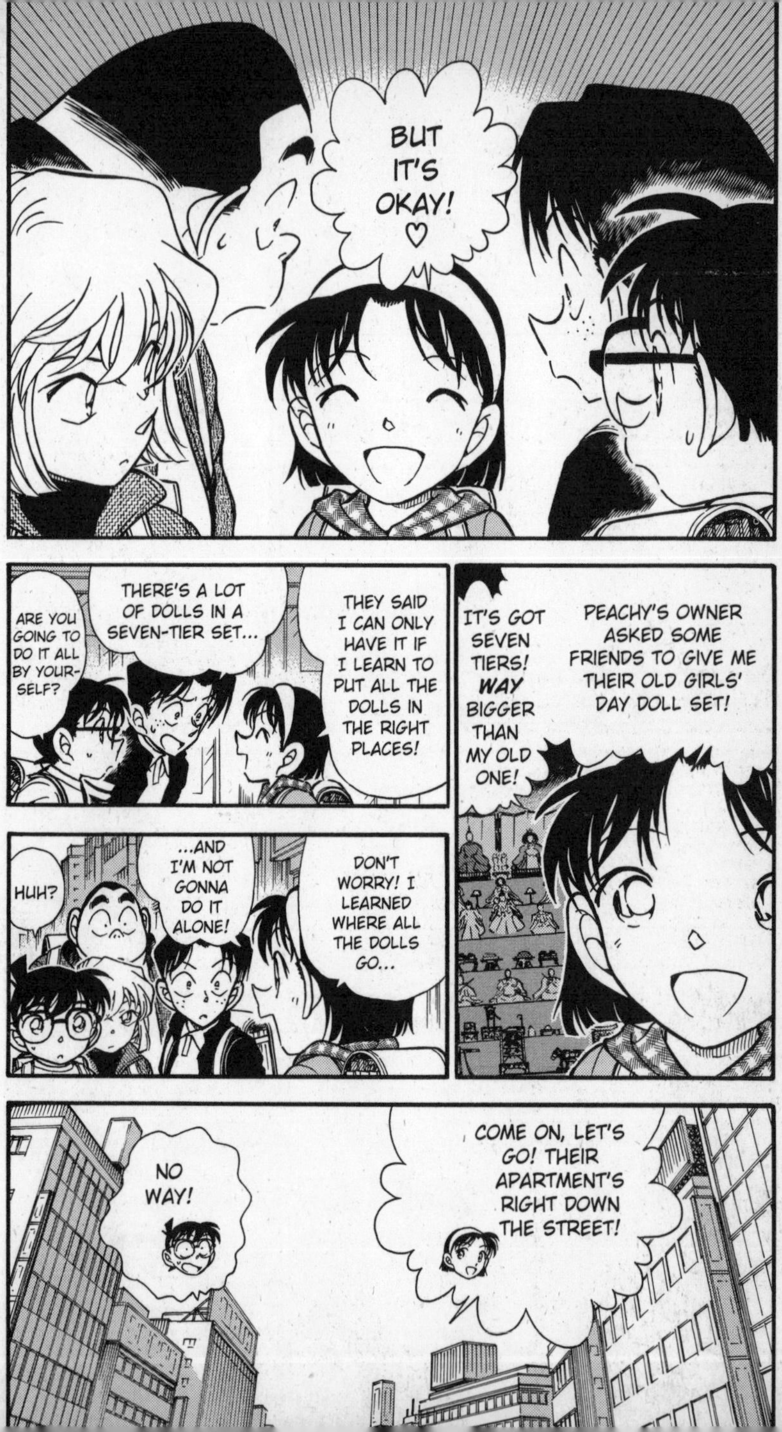
BUT IT'S OKAY! ♡
PEACHY'S OWNER ASKED SOME FRIENDS TO GIVE ME THEIR OLD GIRLS' DAY DOLL SET!
IT'S GOT SEVEN TIERS! *WAY* BIGGER THAN MY OLD ONE!
THEY SAID I CAN ONLY HAVE IT IF I LEARN TO PUT ALL THE DOLLS IN THE RIGHT PLACES!
THERE'S A LOT OF DOLLS IN A SEVEN-TIER SET...
ARE YOU GOING TO DO IT ALL BY YOURSELF?
DON'T WORRY! I LEARNED WHERE ALL THE DOLLS GO...
...AND I'M NOT GONNA DO IT ALONE!
HUH?
COME ON, LET'S GO! THEIR APARTMENT'S RIGHT DOWN THE STREET!
NO WAY!

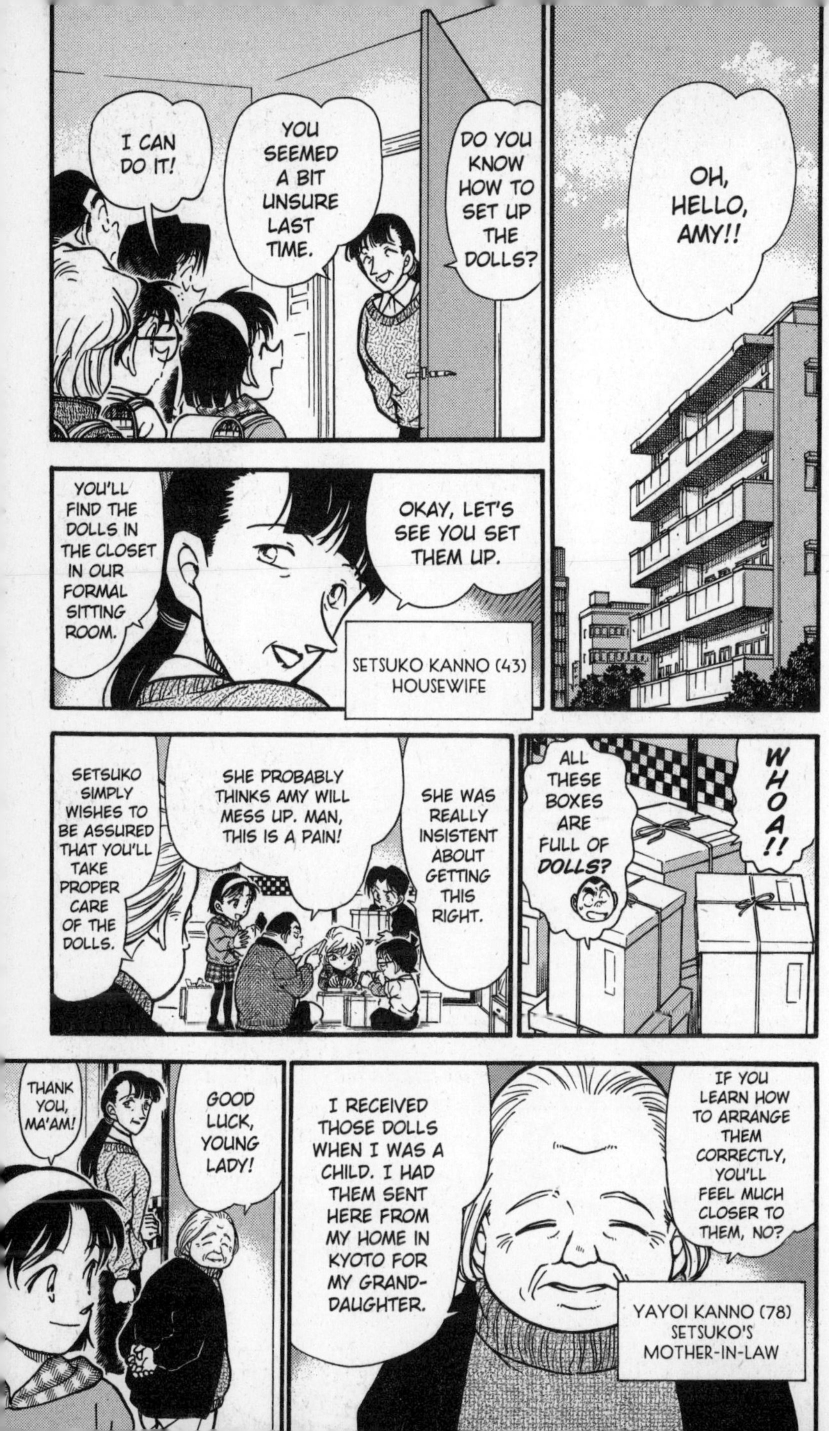
OH, HELLO, AMY!!
DO YOU KNOW HOW TO SET UP THE DOLLS?
YOU SEEMED A BIT UNSURE LAST TIME.
I CAN DO IT!
OKAY, LET'S SEE YOU SET THEM UP.
YOU'LL FIND THE DOLLS IN THE CLOSET IN OUR FORMAL SITTING ROOM.
SETSUKO KANNO (43) HOUSEWIFE
WHOA!!
ALL THESE BOXES ARE FULL OF DOLLS?
SHE WAS REALLY INSISTENT ABOUT GETTING THIS RIGHT.
SHE PROBABLY THINKS AMY WILL MESS UP. MAN, THIS IS A PAIN!
SETSUKO SIMPLY WISHES TO BE ASSURED THAT YOU'LL TAKE PROPER CARE OF THE DOLLS.
IF YOU LEARN HOW TO ARRANGE THEM CORRECTLY, YOU'LL FEEL MUCH CLOSER TO THEM, NO?
I RECEIVED THOSE DOLLS WHEN I WAS A CHILD. I HAD THEM SENT HERE FROM MY HOME IN KYOTO FOR MY GRAND-DAUGHTER.
YAYOI KANNO (78) SETSUKO'S MOTHER-IN-LAW
GOOD LUCK, YOUNG LADY!
THANK YOU, MA'AM!

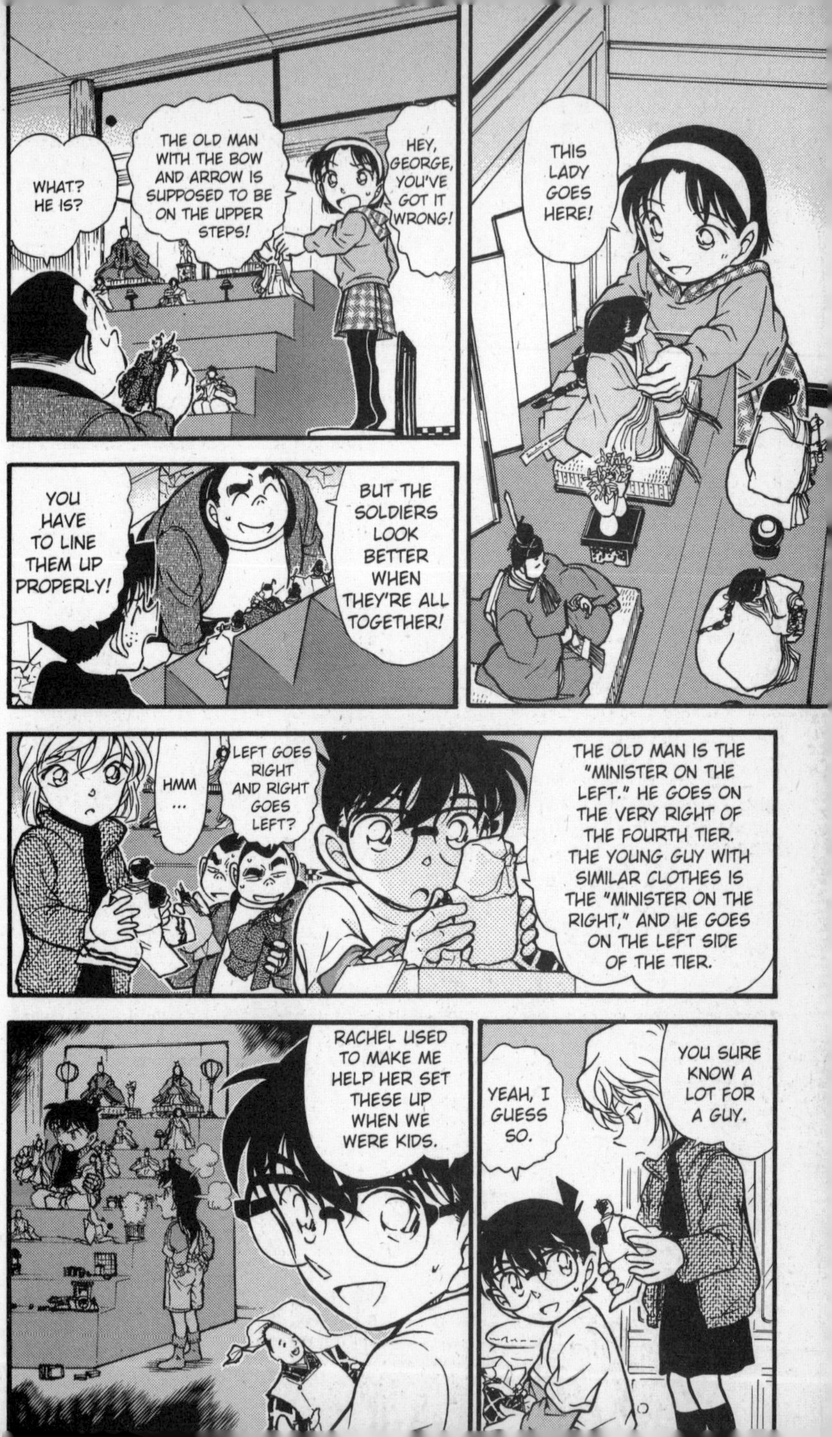
THIS LADY GOES HERE!
HEY, GEORGE, YOU'VE GOT IT WRONG!
THE OLD MAN WITH THE BOW AND ARROW IS SUPPOSED TO BE ON THE UPPER STEPS!
WHAT? HE IS?
BUT THE SOLDIERS LOOK BETTER WHEN THEY'RE ALL TOGETHER!
YOU HAVE TO LINE THEM UP PROPERLY!
THE OLD MAN IS THE "MINISTER ON THE LEFT." HE GOES ON THE VERY RIGHT OF THE FOURTH TIER. THE YOUNG GUY WITH SIMILAR CLOTHES IS THE "MINISTER ON THE RIGHT," AND HE GOES ON THE LEFT SIDE OF THE TIER.
LEFT GOES RIGHT AND RIGHT GOES LEFT?
HMM ...
YOU SURE KNOW A LOT FOR A GUY.
YEAH, I GUESS SO.
RACHEL USED TO MAKE ME HELP HER SET THESE UP WHEN WE WERE KIDS.

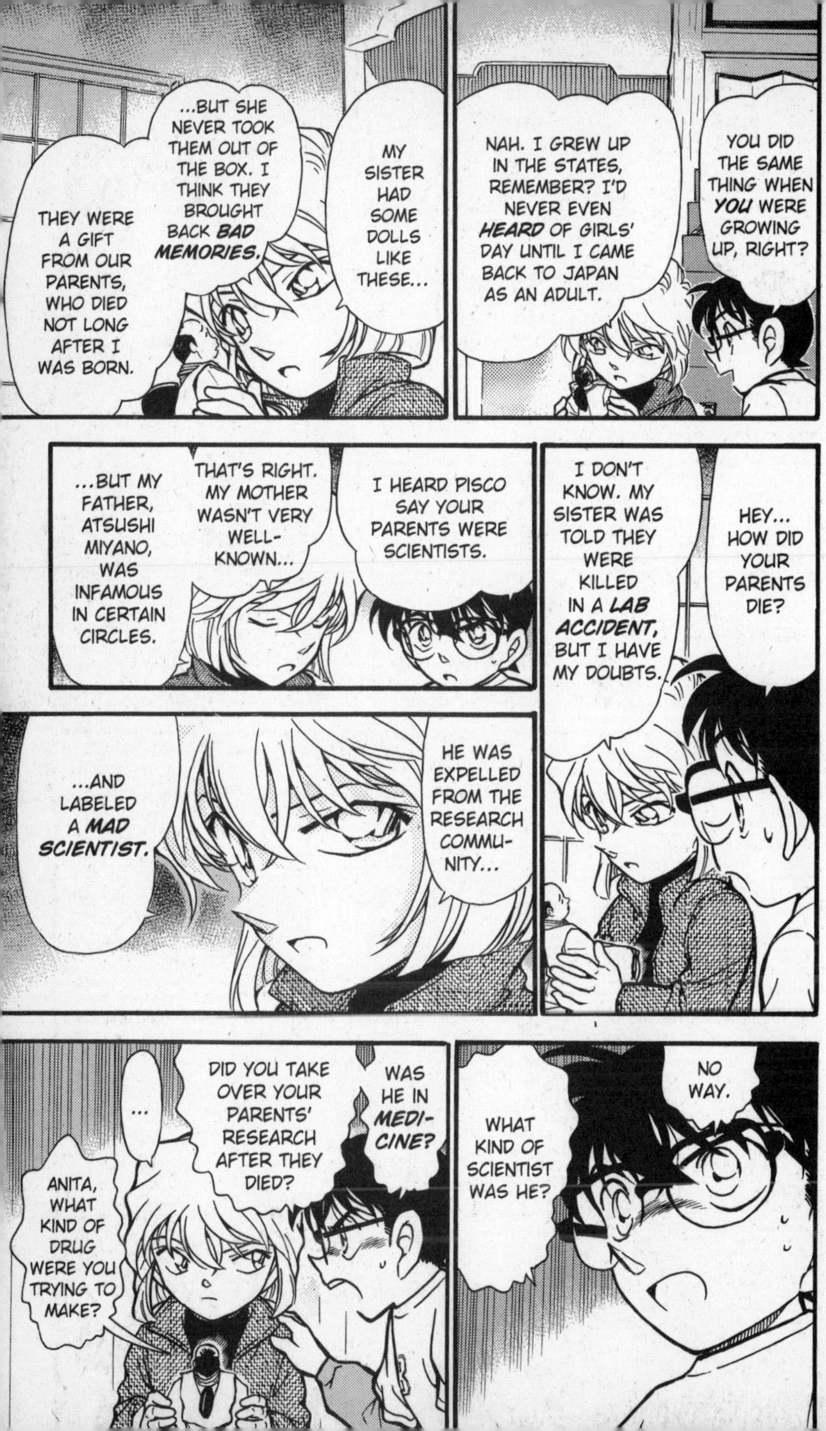
YOU DID THE SAME THING WHEN YOU WERE GROWING UP, RIGHT?
NAH. I GREW UP IN THE STATES, REMEMBER? I'D NEVER EVEN HEARD OF GIRLS' DAY UNTIL I CAME BACK TO JAPAN AS AN ADULT.
MY SISTER HAD SOME DOLLS LIKE THESE...
...BUT SHE NEVER TOOK THEM OUT OF THE BOX. I THINK THEY BROUGHT BACK BAD MEMORIES.
THEY WERE A GIFT FROM OUR PARENTS, WHO DIED NOT LONG AFTER I WAS BORN.
HEY... HOW DID YOUR PARENTS DIE?
I DON'T KNOW. MY SISTER WAS TOLD THEY WERE KILLED IN A LAB ACCIDENT, BUT I HAVE MY DOUBTS.
I HEARD PISCO SAY YOUR PARENTS WERE SCIENTISTS.
THAT'S RIGHT. MY MOTHER WASN'T VERY WELL-KNOWN...
...BUT MY FATHER, ATSUSHI MIYANO, WAS INFAMOUS IN CERTAIN CIRCLES.
HE WAS EXPELLED FROM THE RESEARCH COMMUNITY...
...AND LABELED A MAD SCIENTIST.
NO WAY.
WHAT KIND OF SCIENTIST WAS HE?
WAS HE IN MEDICINE?
DID YOU TAKE OVER YOUR PARENTS' RESEARCH AFTER THEY DIED?
...
ANITA, WHAT KIND OF DRUG WERE YOU TRYING TO MAKE?

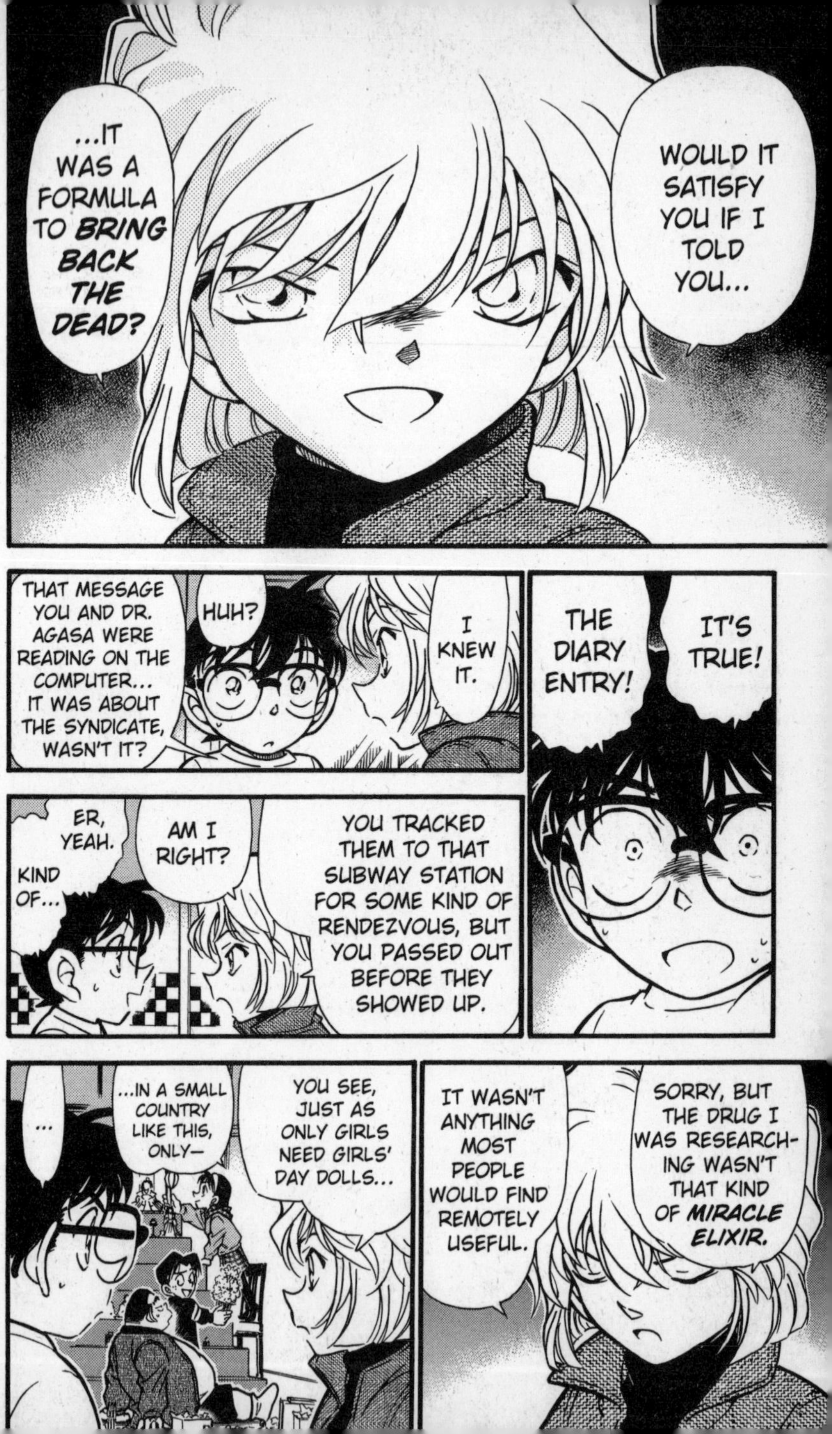

WOULD IT SATISFY YOU IF I TOLD YOU...
...IT WAS A FORMULA TO BRING BACK THE DEAD?
IT'S TRUE!
THE DIARY ENTRY!
I KNEW IT.
HUH?
THAT MESSAGE YOU AND DR. AGASA WERE READING ON THE COMPUTER... IT WAS ABOUT THE SYNDICATE, WASN'T IT?
YOU TRACKED THEM TO THAT SUBWAY STATION FOR SOME KIND OF RENDEZVOUS, BUT YOU PASSED OUT BEFORE THEY SHOWED UP.
AM I RIGHT?
ER, YEAH.
KIND OF...
SORRY, BUT THE DRUG I WAS RESEARCHING WASN'T THAT KIND OF MIRACLE ELIXIR.
IT WASN'T ANYTHING MOST PEOPLE WOULD FIND REMOTELY USEFUL.
YOU SEE, JUST AS ONLY GIRLS NEED GIRLS' DAY DOLLS...
...IN A SMALL COUNTRY LIKE THIS, ONLY—
...

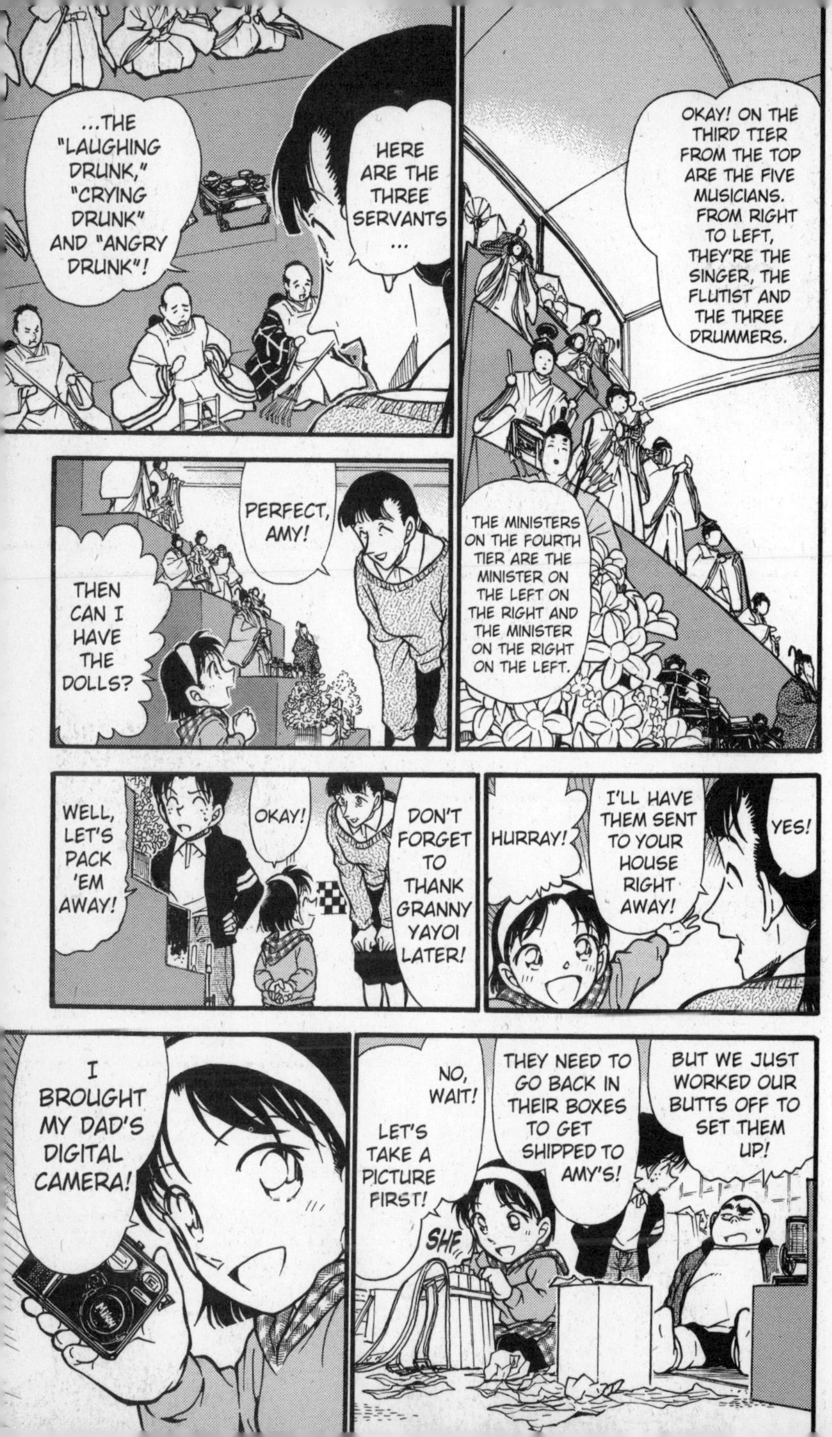
OKAY! ON THE THIRD TIER FROM THE TOP ARE THE FIVE MUSICIANS. FROM RIGHT TO LEFT, THEY'RE THE SINGER, THE FLUTIST AND THE THREE DRUMMERS.
THE MINISTERS ON THE FOURTH TIER ARE THE MINISTER ON THE LEFT ON THE RIGHT AND THE MINISTER ON THE RIGHT ON THE LEFT.
HERE ARE THE THREE SERVANTS...
...THE "LAUGHING DRUNK," "CRYING DRUNK" AND "ANGRY DRUNK"!
PERFECT, AMY!
THEN CAN I HAVE THE DOLLS?
YES!
I'LL HAVE THEM SENT TO YOUR HOUSE RIGHT AWAY!
HURRAY!
DON'T FORGET TO THANK GRANNY YAYOI LATER!
OKAY!
WELL, LET'S PACK 'EM AWAY!
BUT WE JUST WORKED OUR BUTTS OFF TO SET THEM UP!
THEY NEED TO GO BACK IN THEIR BOXES TO GET SHIPPED TO AMY'S!
NO, WAIT!
LET'S TAKE A PICTURE FIRST!
SHF
I BROUGHT MY DAD'S DIGITAL CAMERA!

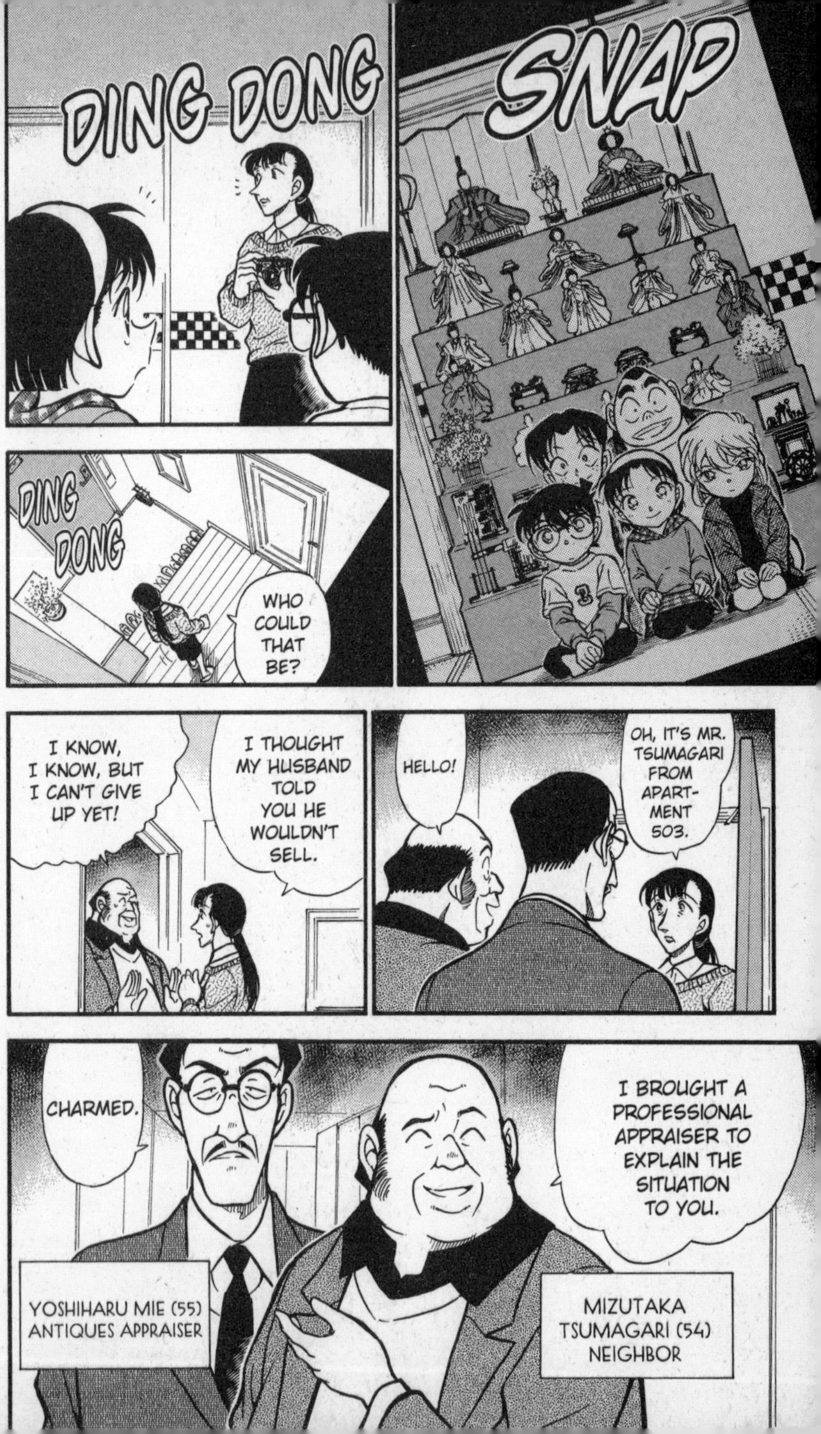
SNAP
DING DONG
DING DONG
WHO COULD THAT BE?
OH, IT'S MR. TSUMAGARI FROM APARTMENT 503.
HELLO!
I THOUGHT MY HUSBAND TOLD YOU HE WOULDN'T SELL.
I KNOW, I KNOW, BUT I CAN'T GIVE UP YET!
I BROUGHT A PROFESSIONAL APPRAISER TO EXPLAIN THE SITUATION TO YOU.
CHARMED.
MIZUTAKA TSUMAGARI (54) NEIGHBOR
YOSHIHARU MIE (55) ANTIQUES APPRAISER

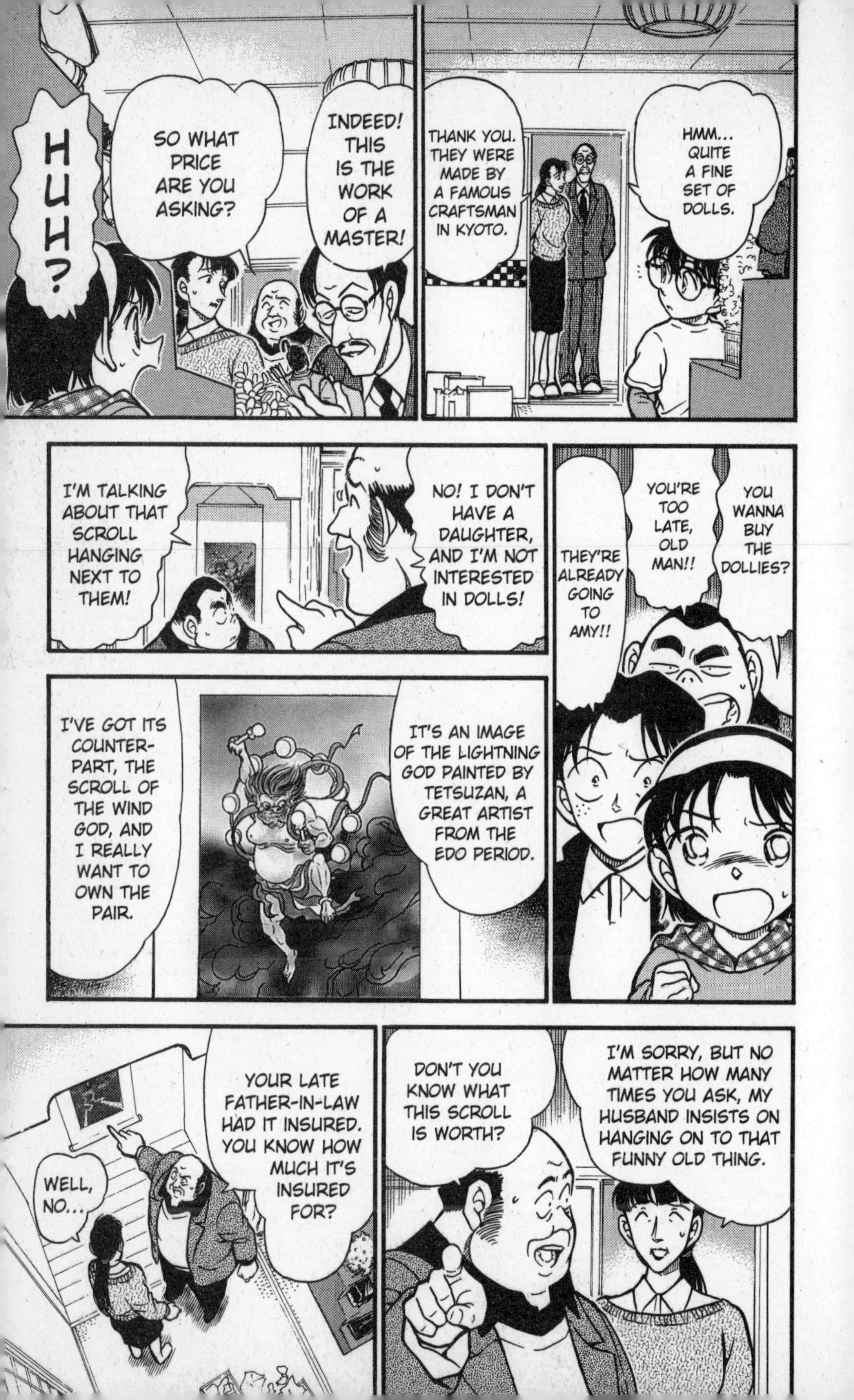
HMM... QUITE A FINE SET OF DOLLS.
THANK YOU. THEY WERE MADE BY A FAMOUS CRAFTSMAN IN KYOTO.
INDEED! THIS IS THE WORK OF A MASTER!
SO WHAT PRICE ARE YOU ASKING?
HUH?
YOU WANNA BUY THE DOLLIES?
YOU'RE TOO LATE, OLD MAN!!
THEY'RE ALREADY GOING TO AMY!!
NO! I DON'T HAVE A DAUGHTER, AND I'M NOT INTERESTED IN DOLLS!
I'M TALKING ABOUT THAT SCROLL HANGING NEXT TO THEM!
IT'S AN IMAGE OF THE LIGHTNING GOD PAINTED BY TETSUZAN, A GREAT ARTIST FROM THE EDO PERIOD.
I'VE GOT ITS COUNTERPART, THE SCROLL OF THE WIND GOD, AND I REALLY WANT TO OWN THE PAIR.
I'M SORRY, BUT NO MATTER HOW MANY TIMES YOU ASK, MY HUSBAND INSISTS ON HANGING ON TO THAT FUNNY OLD THING.
DON'T YOU KNOW WHAT THIS SCROLL IS WORTH?
YOUR LATE FATHER-IN-LAW HAD IT INSURED. YOU KNOW HOW MUCH IT'S INSURED FOR?
WELL, NO...

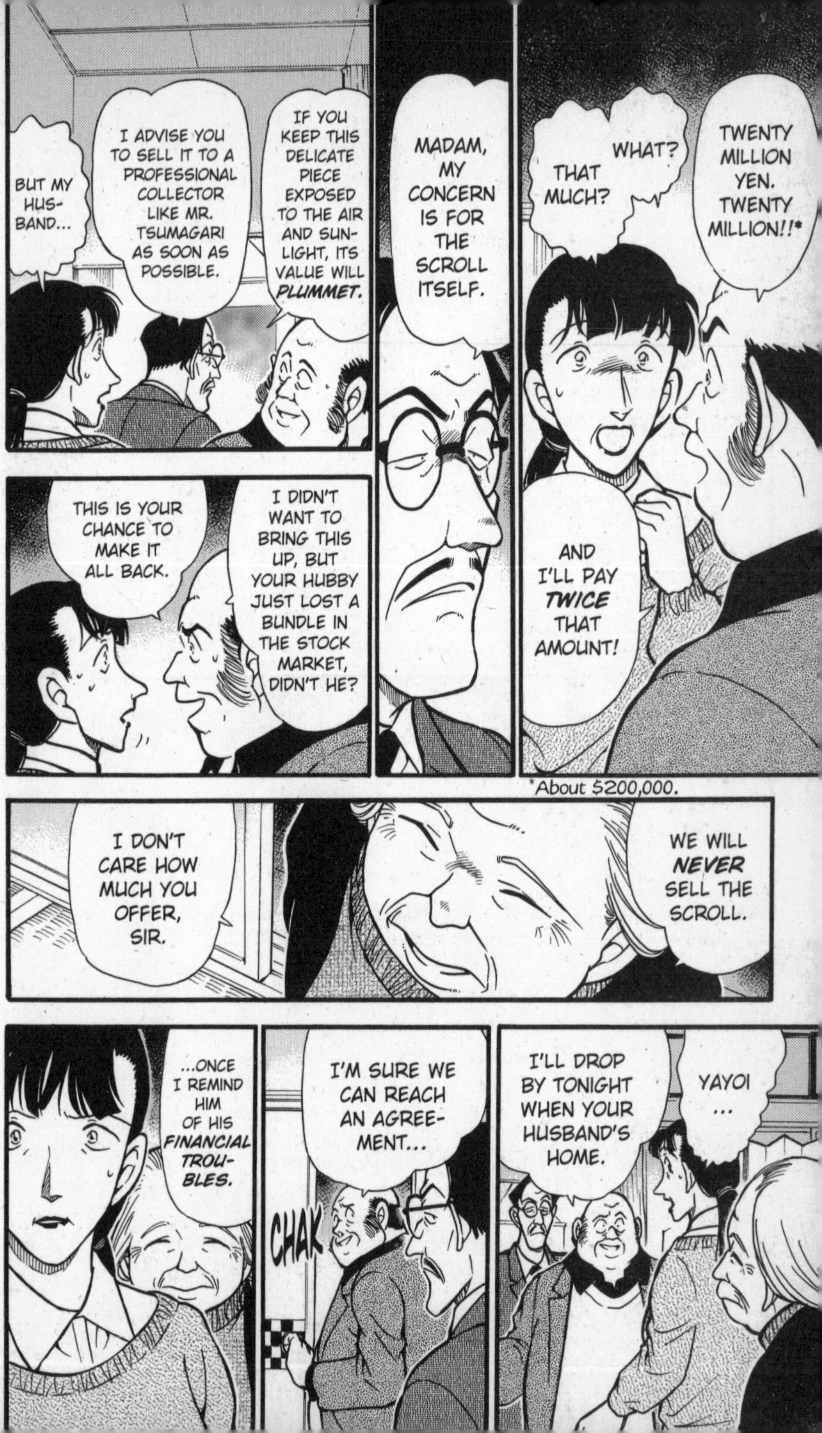
WHAT?
THAT MUCH?
TWENTY MILLION YEN. TWENTY MILLION!!*
AND I'LL PAY TWICE THAT AMOUNT!
MADAM, MY CONCERN IS FOR THE SCROLL ITSELF.
IF YOU KEEP THIS DELICATE PIECE EXPOSED TO THE AIR AND SUN-LIGHT, ITS VALUE WILL PLUMMET.
I ADVISE YOU TO SELL IT TO A PROFESSIONAL COLLECTOR LIKE MR. TSUMAGARI AS SOON AS POSSIBLE.
BUT MY HUS-BAND...
I DIDN'T WANT TO BRING THIS UP, BUT YOUR HUBBY JUST LOST A BUNDLE IN THE STOCK MARKET, DIDN'T HE?
THIS IS YOUR CHANCE TO MAKE IT ALL BACK.
WE WILL NEVER SELL THE SCROLL.
I DON'T CARE HOW MUCH YOU OFFER, SIR.
YAYOI ...
I'LL DROP BY TONIGHT WHEN YOUR HUSBAND'S HOME.
I'M SURE WE CAN REACH AN AGREE-MENT...
CHAK
...ONCE I REMIND HIM OF HIS FINANCIAL TROU-BLES.

*About $200,000.

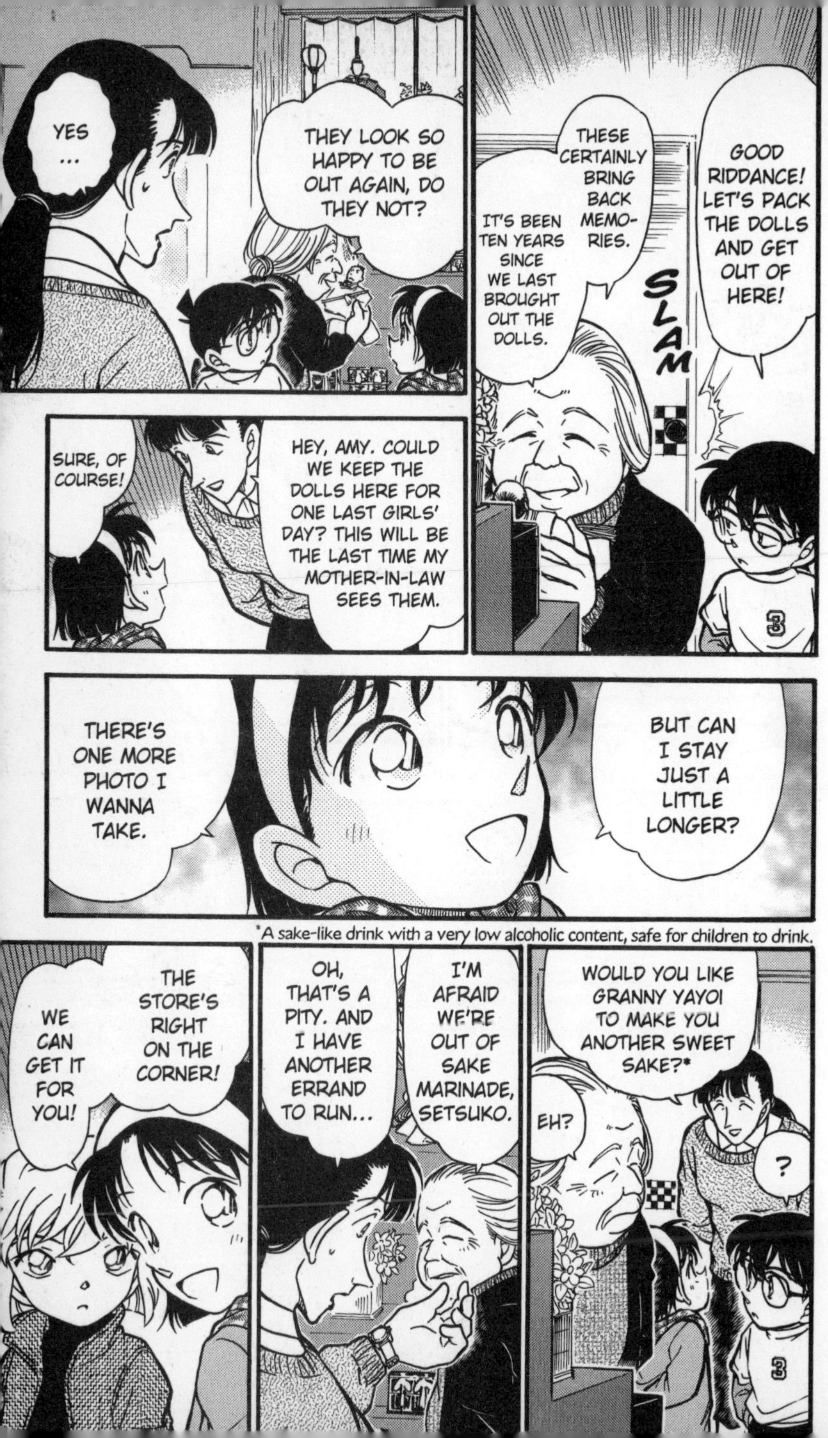
GOOD RIDDANCE! LET'S PACK THE DOLLS AND GET OUT OF HERE!
SLAM
THESE CERTAINLY BRING BACK MEMORIES.
IT'S BEEN TEN YEARS SINCE WE LAST BROUGHT OUT THE DOLLS.
THEY LOOK SO HAPPY TO BE OUT AGAIN, DO THEY NOT?
YES ...
HEY, AMY. COULD WE KEEP THE DOLLS HERE FOR ONE LAST GIRLS' DAY? THIS WILL BE THE LAST TIME MY MOTHER-IN-LAW SEES THEM.
SURE, OF COURSE!
BUT CAN I STAY JUST A LITTLE LONGER?
THERE'S ONE MORE PHOTO I WANNA TAKE.
WOULD YOU LIKE GRANNY YAYOI TO MAKE YOU ANOTHER SWEET SAKE?*
?
EH?
I'M AFRAID WE'RE OUT OF SAKE MARINADE, SETSUKO.
OH, THAT'S A PITY. AND I HAVE ANOTHER ERRAND TO RUN...
THE STORE'S RIGHT ON THE CORNER!
WE CAN GET IT FOR YOU!

*A sake-like drink with a very low alcoholic content, safe for children to drink.

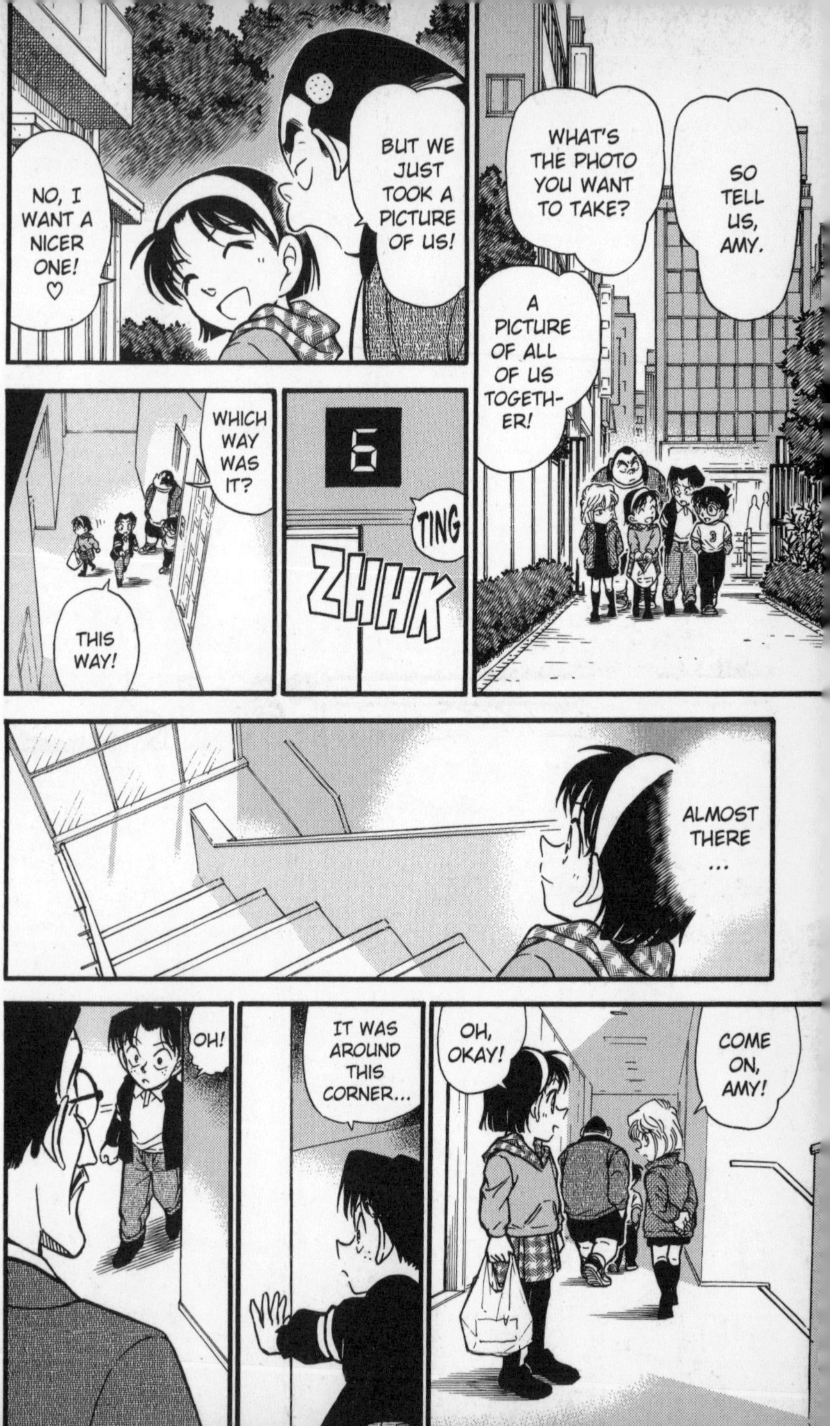
SO TELL US, AMY.
WHAT'S THE PHOTO YOU WANT TO TAKE?
A PICTURE OF ALL OF US TOGETHER!
BUT WE JUST TOOK A PICTURE OF US!
NO, I WANT A NICER ONE! ♡
6
TING
ZHHK
WHICH WAY WAS IT?
THIS WAY!
ALMOST THERE...
COME ON, AMY!
OH, OKAY!
IT WAS AROUND THIS CORNER...
OH!

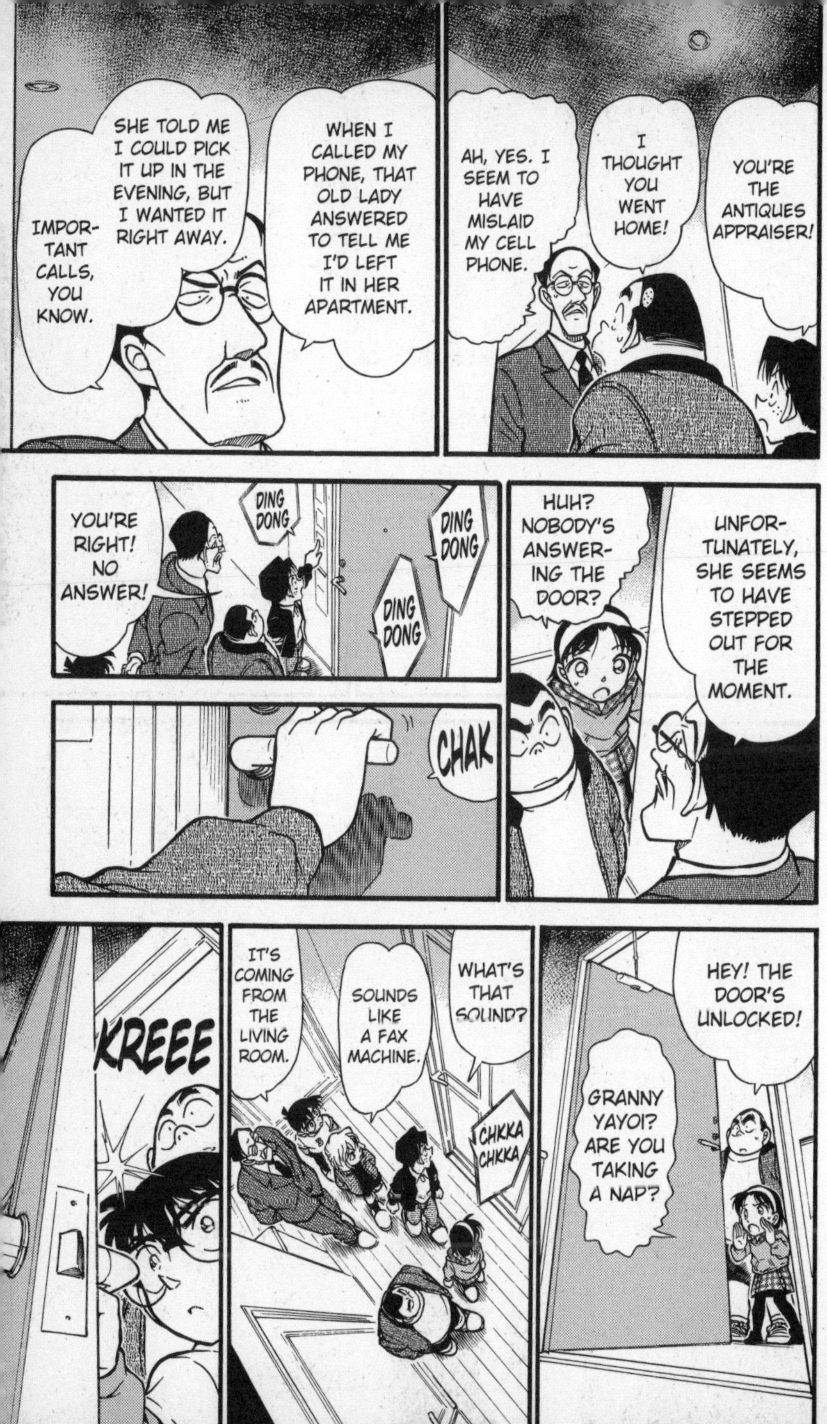
YOU'RE THE ANTIQUES APPRAISER!
I THOUGHT YOU WENT HOME!
AH, YES. I SEEM TO HAVE MISLAID MY CELL PHONE.
WHEN I CALLED MY PHONE, THAT OLD LADY ANSWERED TO TELL ME I'D LEFT IT IN HER APARTMENT.
SHE TOLD ME I COULD PICK IT UP IN THE EVENING, BUT I WANTED IT RIGHT AWAY.
IMPORTANT CALLS, YOU KNOW.
UNFORTUNATELY, SHE SEEMS TO HAVE STEPPED OUT FOR THE MOMENT.
HUH? NOBODY'S ANSWERING THE DOOR?
DING DONG
DING DONG
DING DONG
YOU'RE RIGHT! NO ANSWER!
CHAK
HEY! THE DOOR'S UNLOCKED!
GRANNY YAYOI? ARE YOU TAKING A NAP?
WHAT'S THAT SOUND?
CHKKA CHKKA
SOUNDS LIKE A FAX MACHINE.
IT'S COMING FROM THE LIVING ROOM.
KREEE

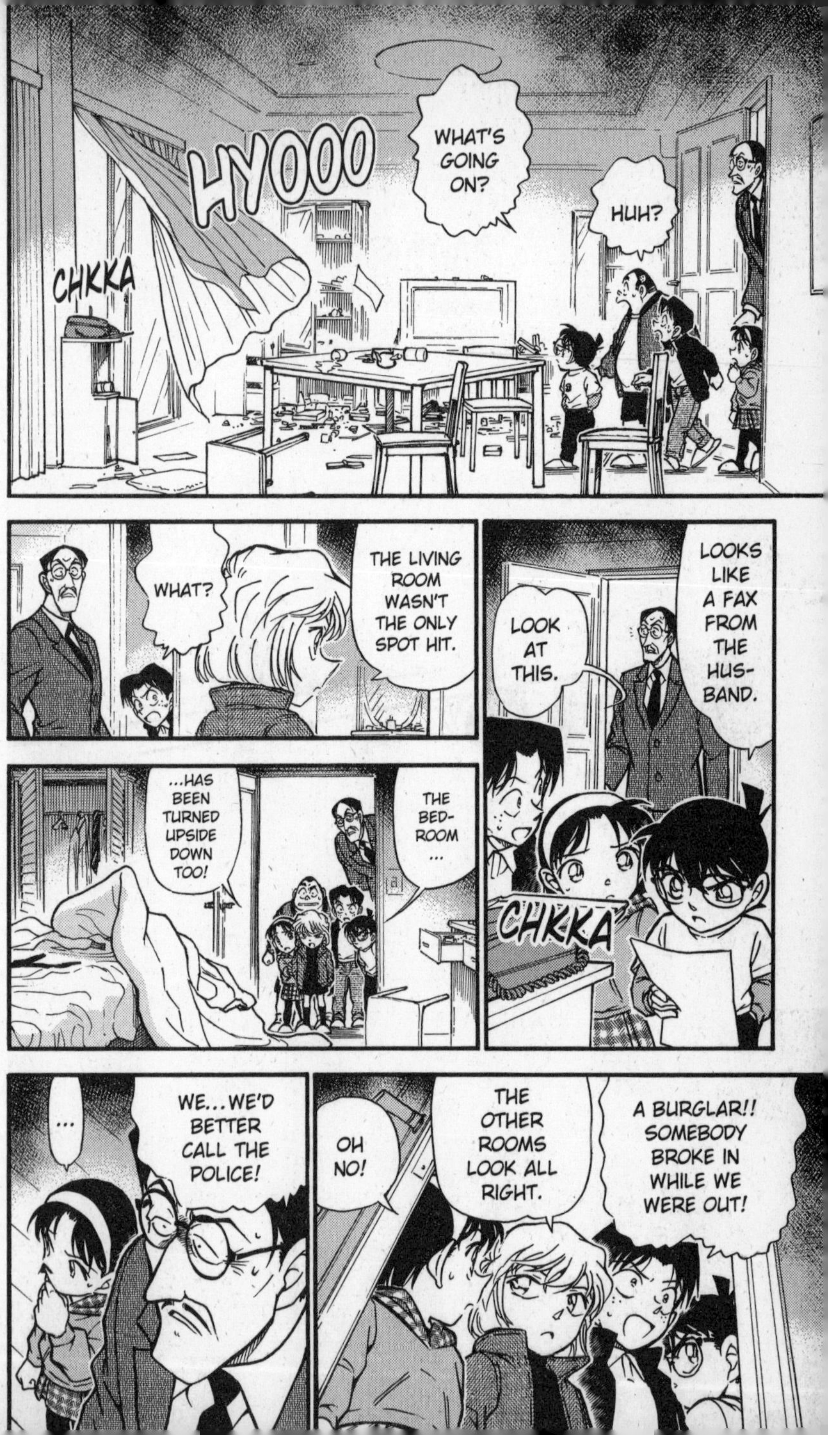
WHAT'S GOING ON?
HUH?
HYOOO
CHKKA
LOOKS LIKE A FAX FROM THE HUS-BAND.
LOOK AT THIS.
CHKKA
THE LIVING ROOM WASN'T THE ONLY SPOT HIT.
WHAT?
THE BED-ROOM ...
...HAS BEEN TURNED UPSIDE DOWN TOO!
A BURGLAR!! SOMEBODY BROKE IN WHILE WE WERE OUT!
THE OTHER ROOMS LOOK ALL RIGHT.
OH NO!
WE...WE'D BETTER CALL THE POLICE!
...

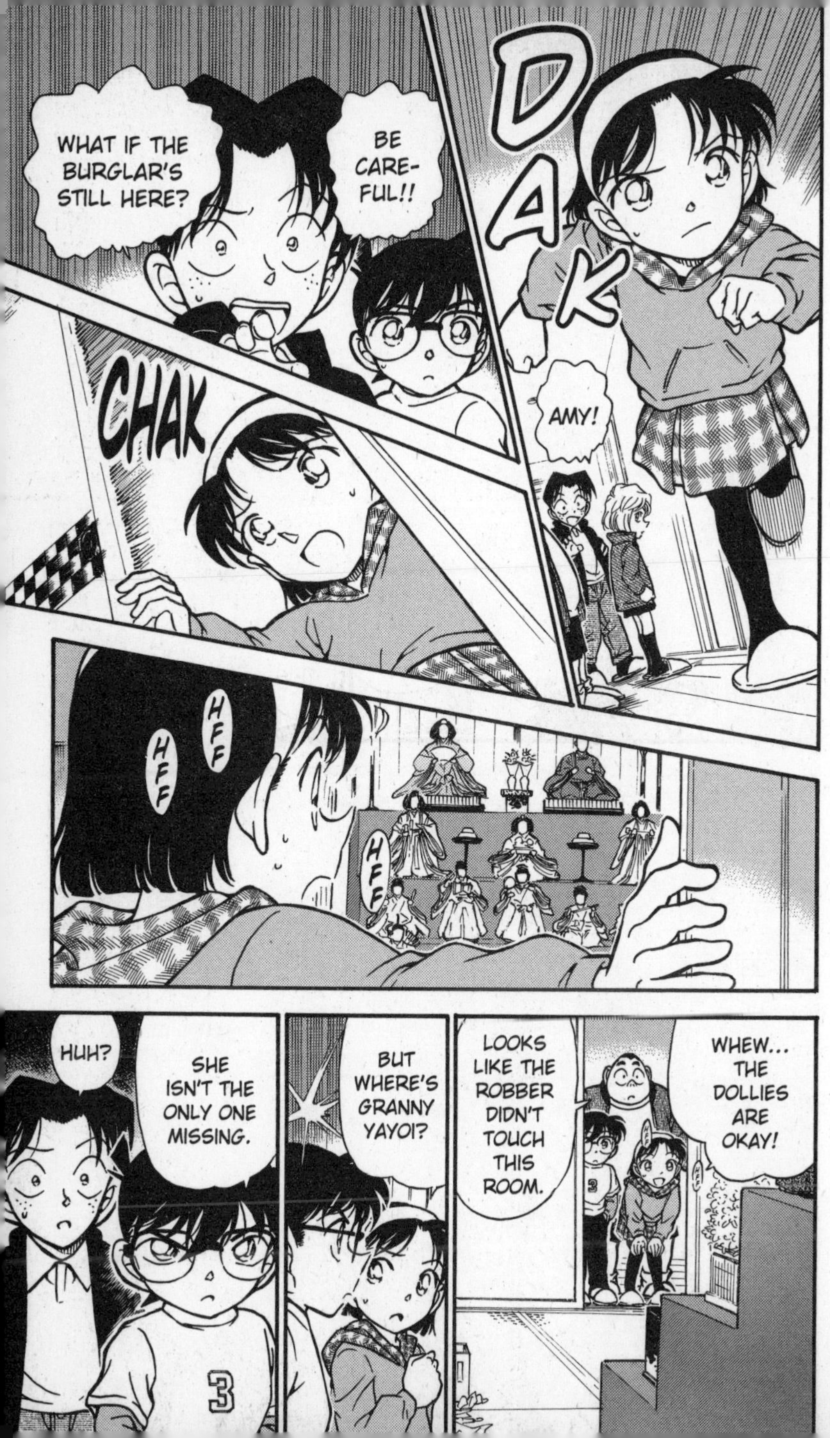
DAK
AMY!
BE CARE-FUL!!
WHAT IF THE BURGLAR'S STILL HERE?
CHAK
HFF
HFF
HFF
WHEW... THE DOLLIES ARE OKAY!
LOOKS LIKE THE ROBBER DIDN'T TOUCH THIS ROOM.
BUT WHERE'S GRANNY YAYOI?
SHE ISN'T THE ONLY ONE MISSING.
HUH?

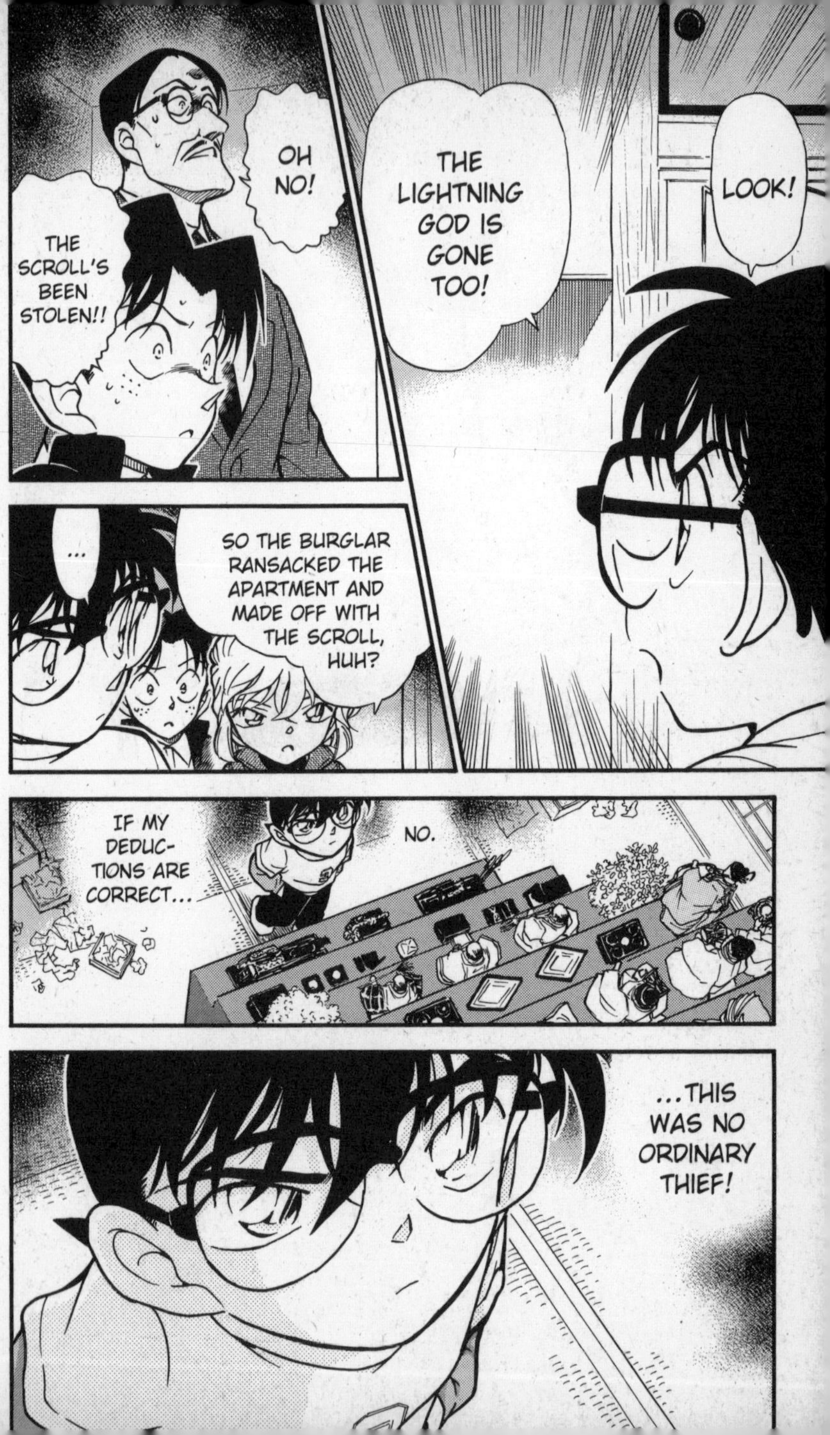
LOOK!
THE LIGHTNING GOD IS GONE TOO!
OH NO!
THE SCROLL'S BEEN STOLEN!!
SO THE BURGLAR RANSACKED THE APARTMENT AND MADE OFF WITH THE SCROLL, HUH?
...
NO.
IF MY DEDUC-TIONS ARE CORRECT...
...THIS WAS NO ORDINARY THIEF!

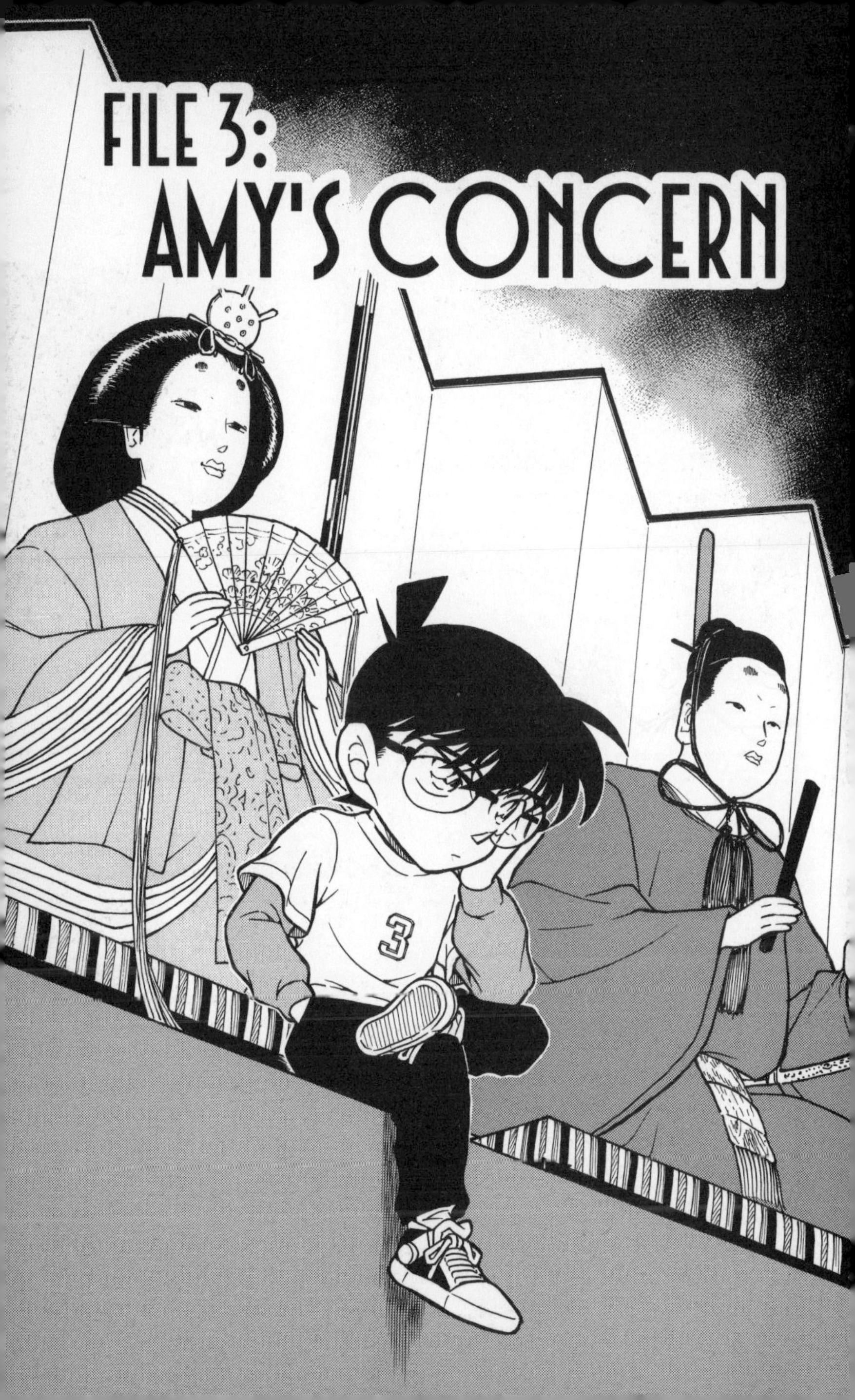
FILE 3:
AMY'S CONCERN
3

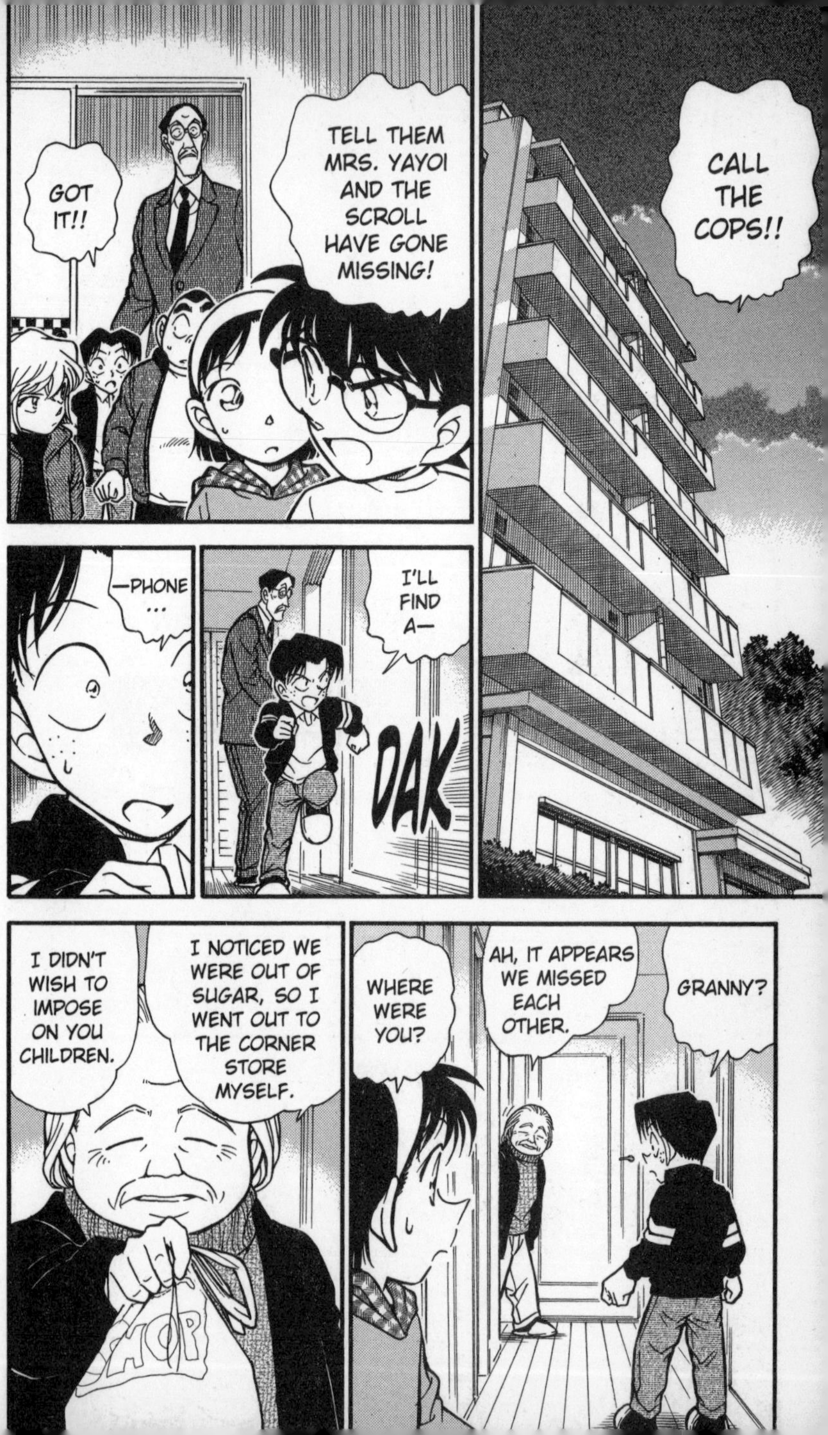

CALL THE COPS!!
TELL THEM MRS. YAYOI AND THE SCROLL HAVE GONE MISSING!
GOT IT!!
I'LL FIND A—
DAK
—PHONE ...
GRANNY?
AH, IT APPEARS WE MISSED EACH OTHER.
WHERE WERE YOU?
I NOTICED WE WERE OUT OF SUGAR, SO I WENT OUT TO THE CORNER STORE MYSELF.
I DIDN'T WISH TO IMPOSE ON YOU CHILDREN.
SHOP

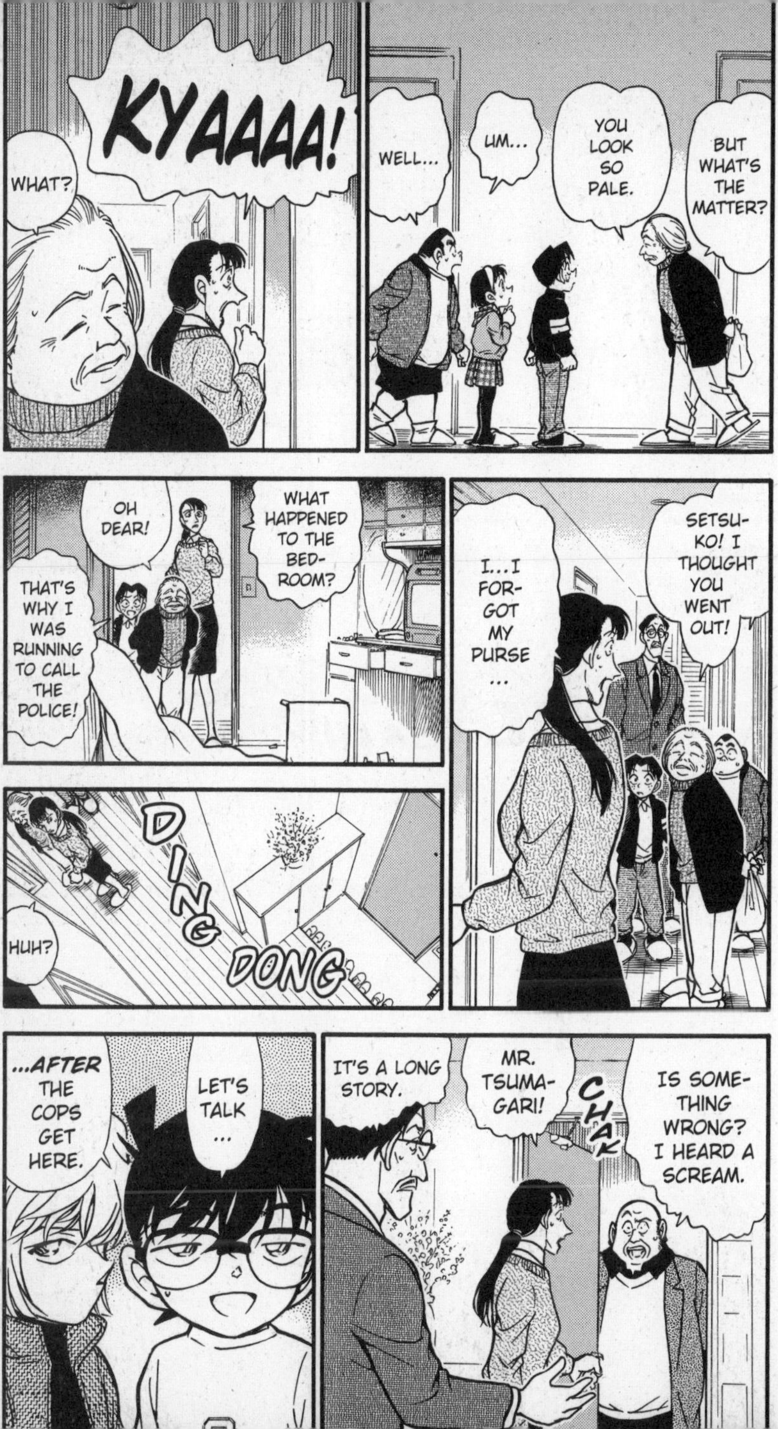
BUT WHAT'S THE MATTER?
YOU LOOK SO PALE.
UM...
WELL...
KYAAAA!
WHAT?
SETSU-KO! I THOUGHT YOU WENT OUT!
I...I FOR-GOT MY PURSE ...
WHAT HAPPENED TO THE BED-ROOM?
OH DEAR!
THAT'S WHY I WAS RUNNING TO CALL THE POLICE!
DING DONG
HUH?
IS SOME-THING WRONG? I HEARD A SCREAM.
CHAK
MR. TSUMA-GARI!
IT'S A LONG STORY.
LET'S TALK ...
...AFTER THE COPS GET HERE.

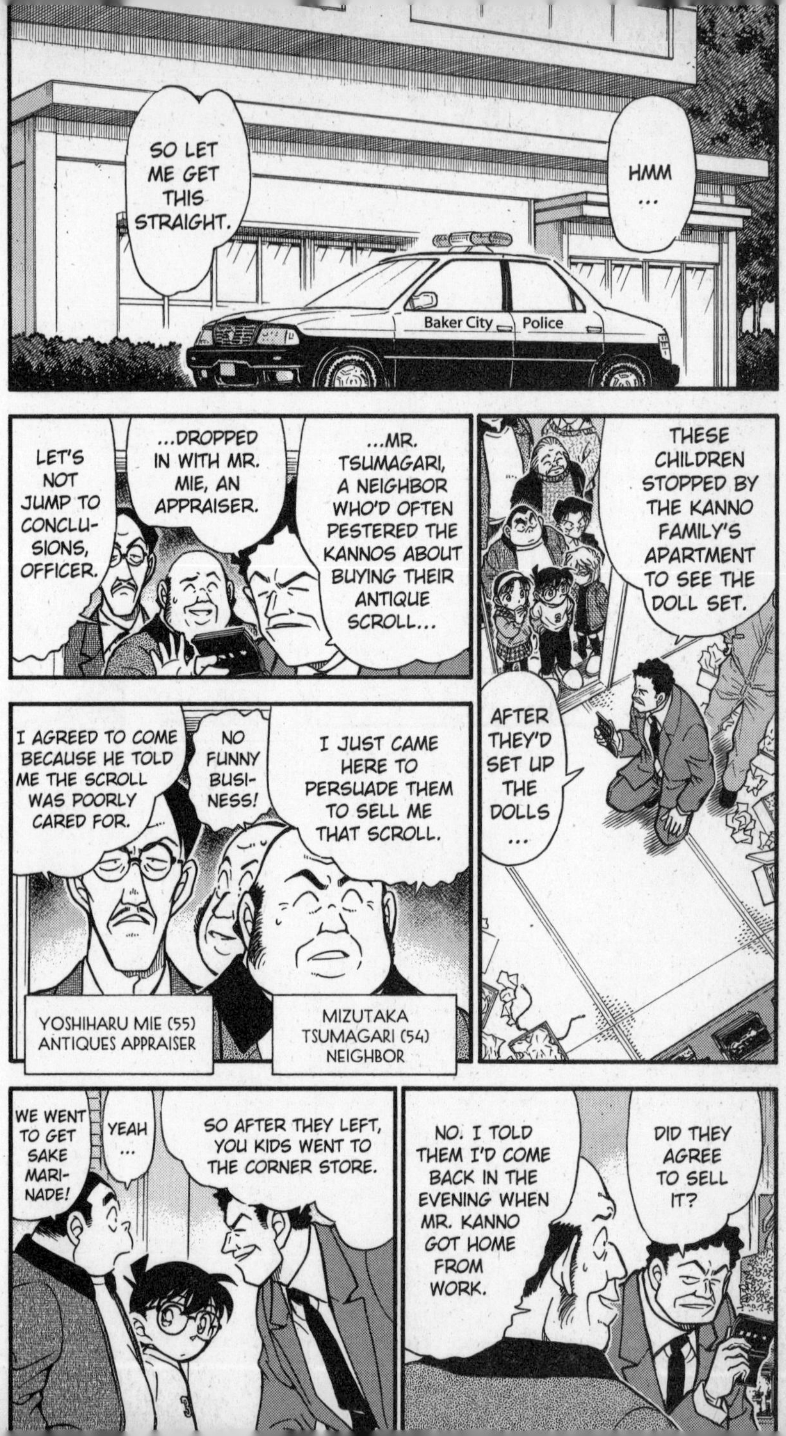
HMM ...
SO LET ME GET THIS STRAIGHT.
Baker City Police
THESE CHILDREN STOPPED BY THE KANNO FAMILY'S APARTMENT TO SEE THE DOLL SET.
AFTER THEY'D SET UP THE DOLLS ...
...MR. TSUMAGARI, A NEIGHBOR WHO'D OFTEN PESTERED THE KANNOS ABOUT BUYING THEIR ANTIQUE SCROLL...
...DROPPED IN WITH MR. MIE, AN APPRAISER.
LET'S NOT JUMP TO CONCLUSIONS, OFFICER.
I JUST CAME HERE TO PERSUADE THEM TO SELL ME THAT SCROLL.
NO FUNNY BUSINESS!
I AGREED TO COME BECAUSE HE TOLD ME THE SCROLL WAS POORLY CARED FOR.
MIZUTAKA TSUMAGARI (54) NEIGHBOR
YOSHIHARU MIE (55) ANTIQUES APPRAISER
DID THEY AGREE TO SELL IT?
NO. I TOLD THEM I'D COME BACK IN THE EVENING WHEN MR. KANNO GOT HOME FROM WORK.
SO AFTER THEY LEFT, YOU KIDS WENT TO THE CORNER STORE.
YEAH ...
WE WENT TO GET SAKE MARINADE!

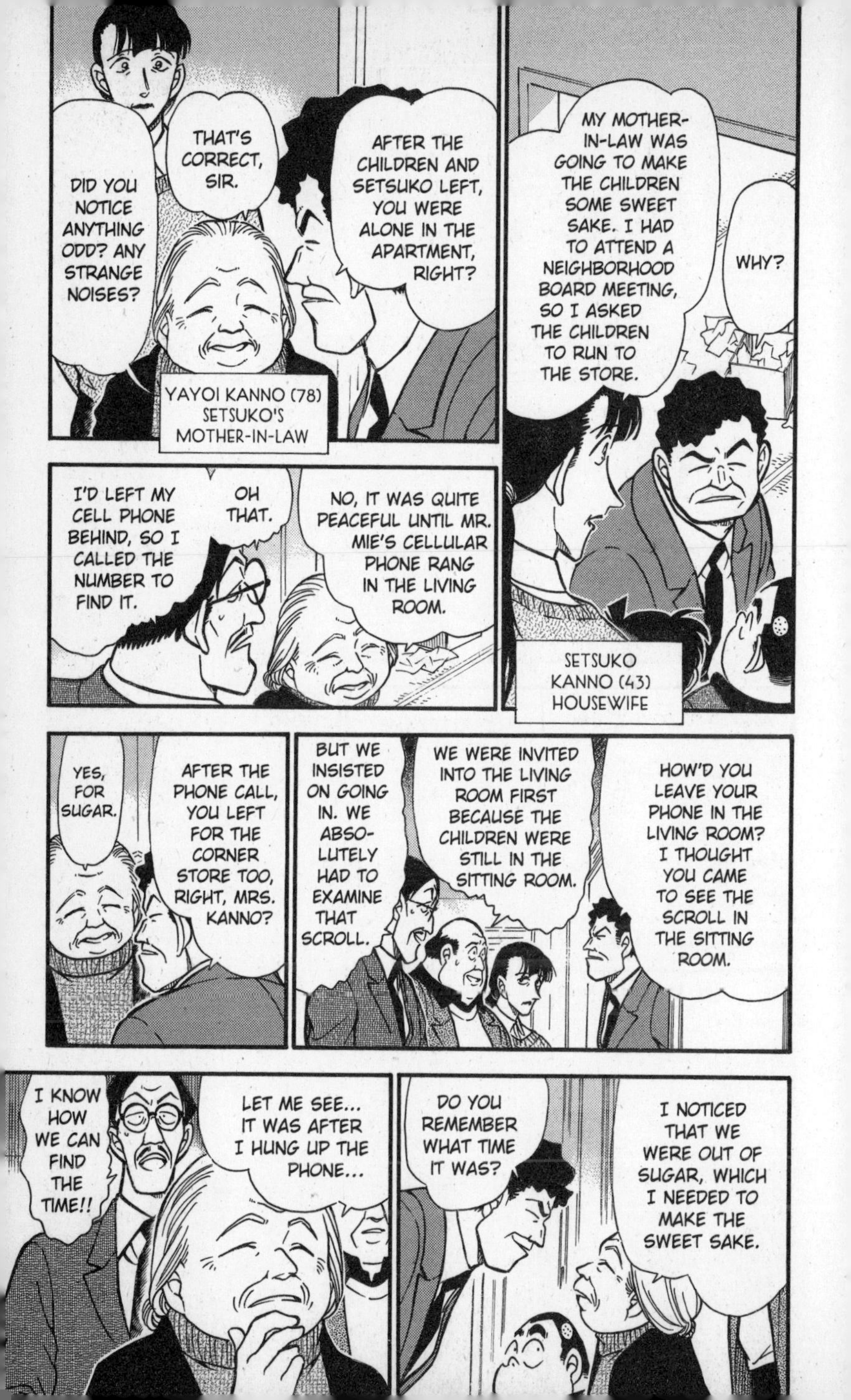
WHY?
MY MOTHER-IN-LAW WAS GOING TO MAKE THE CHILDREN SOME SWEET SAKE. I HAD TO ATTEND A NEIGHBORHOOD BOARD MEETING, SO I ASKED THE CHILDREN TO RUN TO THE STORE.
SETSUKO KANNO (43) HOUSEWIFE
AFTER THE CHILDREN AND SETSUKO LEFT, YOU WERE ALONE IN THE APARTMENT, RIGHT?
THAT'S CORRECT, SIR.
DID YOU NOTICE ANYTHING ODD? ANY STRANGE NOISES?
YAYOI KANNO (78) SETSUKO'S MOTHER-IN-LAW
NO, IT WAS QUITE PEACEFUL UNTIL MR. MIE'S CELLULAR PHONE RANG IN THE LIVING ROOM.
OH THAT.
I'D LEFT MY CELL PHONE BEHIND, SO I CALLED THE NUMBER TO FIND IT.
HOW'D YOU LEAVE YOUR PHONE IN THE LIVING ROOM? I THOUGHT YOU CAME TO SEE THE SCROLL IN THE SITTING ROOM.
WE WERE INVITED INTO THE LIVING ROOM FIRST BECAUSE THE CHILDREN WERE STILL IN THE SITTING ROOM.
BUT WE INSISTED ON GOING IN. WE ABSO-LUTELY HAD TO EXAMINE THAT SCROLL.
AFTER THE PHONE CALL, YOU LEFT FOR THE CORNER STORE TOO, RIGHT, MRS. KANNO?
YES, FOR SUGAR.
I NOTICED THAT WE WERE OUT OF SUGAR, WHICH I NEEDED TO MAKE THE SWEET SAKE.
DO YOU REMEMBER WHAT TIME IT WAS?
LET ME SEE... IT WAS AFTER I HUNG UP THE PHONE...
I KNOW HOW WE CAN FIND THE TIME!!

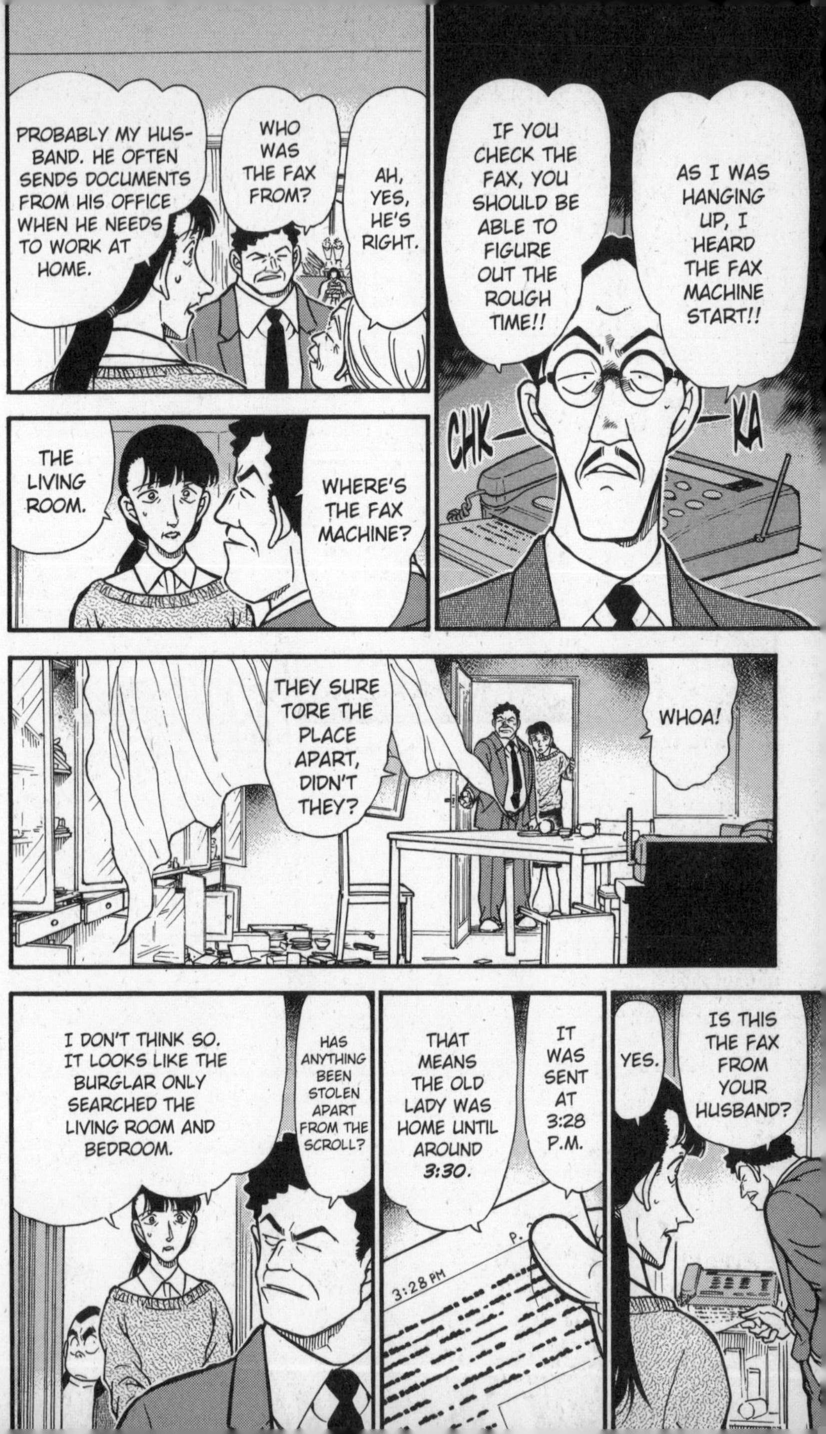
AS I WAS HANGING UP, I HEARD THE FAX MACHINE START!!
IF YOU CHECK THE FAX, YOU SHOULD BE ABLE TO FIGURE OUT THE ROUGH TIME!!
CHK—KA
AH, YES, HE'S RIGHT.
WHO WAS THE FAX FROM?
PROBABLY MY HUSBAND. HE OFTEN SENDS DOCUMENTS FROM HIS OFFICE WHEN HE NEEDS TO WORK AT HOME.
WHERE'S THE FAX MACHINE?
THE LIVING ROOM.
WHOA!
THEY SURE TORE THE PLACE APART, DIDN'T THEY?
IS THIS THE FAX FROM YOUR HUSBAND?
YES.
IT WAS SENT AT 3:28 P.M.
THAT MEANS THE OLD LADY WAS HOME UNTIL AROUND 3:30.
3:28 PM
HAS ANYTHING BEEN STOLEN APART FROM THE SCROLL?
I DON'T THINK SO. IT LOOKS LIKE THE BURGLAR ONLY SEARCHED THE LIVING ROOM AND BEDROOM.

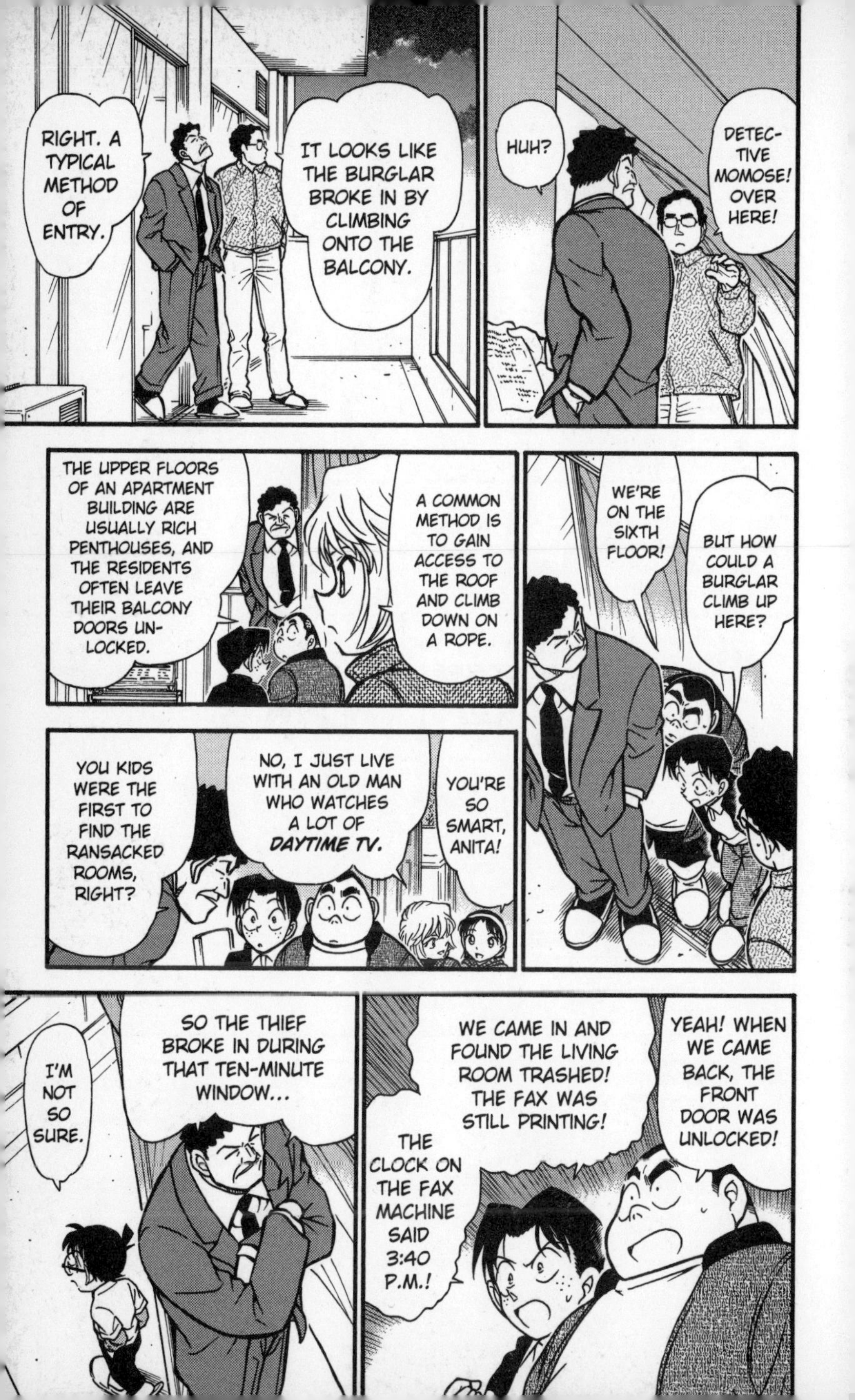
DETECTIVE MOMOSE! OVER HERE!
HUH?
IT LOOKS LIKE THE BURGLAR BROKE IN BY CLIMBING ONTO THE BALCONY.
RIGHT. A TYPICAL METHOD OF ENTRY.
WE'RE ON THE SIXTH FLOOR!
BUT HOW COULD A BURGLAR CLIMB UP HERE?
A COMMON METHOD IS TO GAIN ACCESS TO THE ROOF AND CLIMB DOWN ON A ROPE.
THE UPPER FLOORS OF AN APARTMENT BUILDING ARE USUALLY RICH PENTHOUSES, AND THE RESIDENTS OFTEN LEAVE THEIR BALCONY DOORS UNLOCKED.
YOU'RE SO SMART, ANITA!
NO, I JUST LIVE WITH AN OLD MAN WHO WATCHES A LOT OF *DAYTIME TV*.
YOU KIDS WERE THE FIRST TO FIND THE RANSACKED ROOMS, RIGHT?
YEAH! WHEN WE CAME BACK, THE FRONT DOOR WAS UNLOCKED!
WE CAME IN AND FOUND THE LIVING ROOM TRASHED! THE FAX WAS STILL PRINTING!
THE CLOCK ON THE FAX MACHINE SAID 3:40 P.M.!
SO THE THIEF BROKE IN DURING THAT TEN-MINUTE WINDOW...
I'M NOT SO SURE.

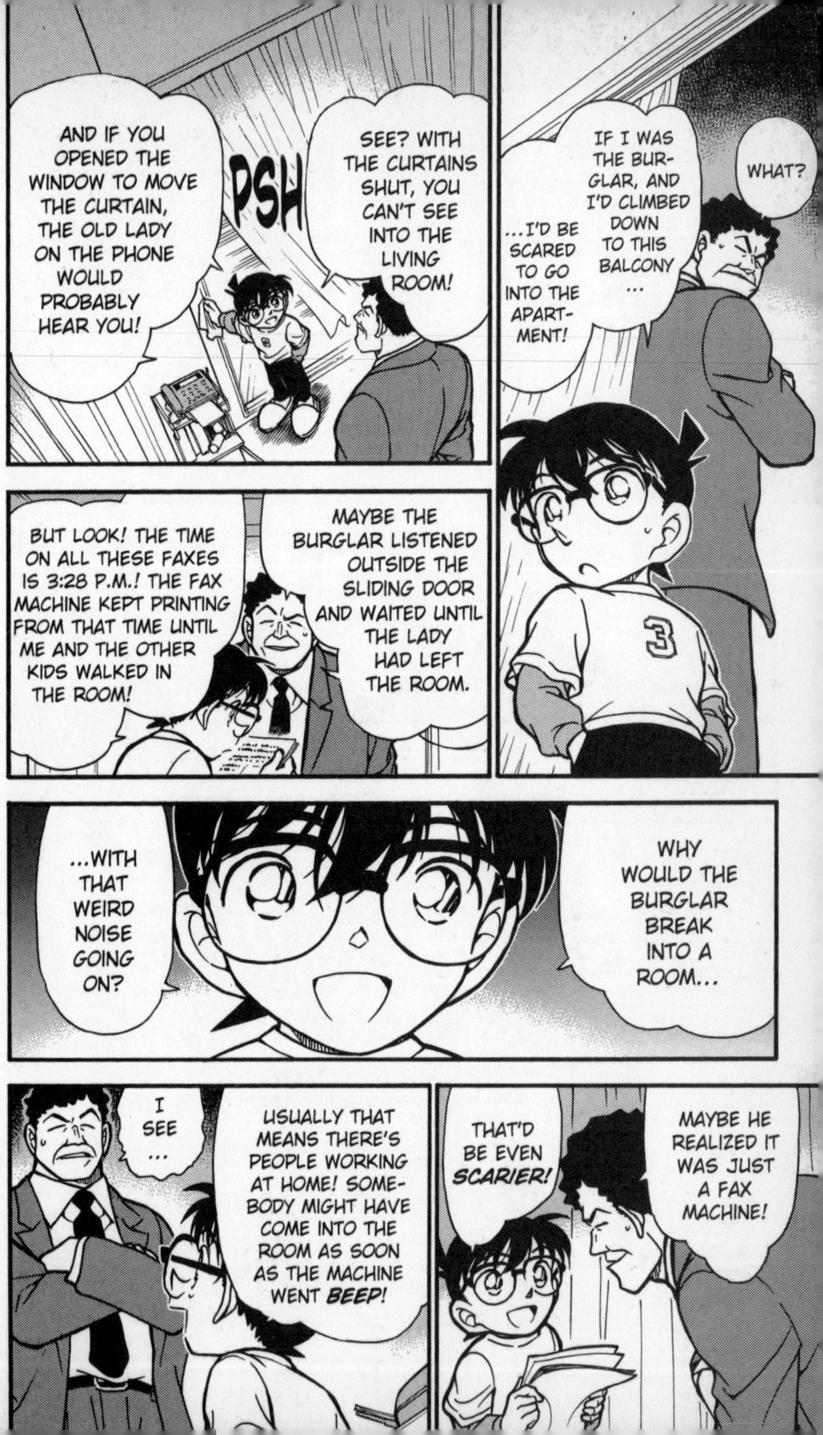
WHAT?
IF I WAS THE BURGLAR, AND I'D CLIMBED DOWN TO THIS BALCONY ...
...I'D BE SCARED TO GO INTO THE APARTMENT!
SEE? WITH THE CURTAINS SHUT, YOU CAN'T SEE INTO THE LIVING ROOM!
PSH
AND IF YOU OPENED THE WINDOW TO MOVE THE CURTAIN, THE OLD LADY ON THE PHONE WOULD PROBABLY HEAR YOU!
MAYBE THE BURGLAR LISTENED OUTSIDE THE SLIDING DOOR AND WAITED UNTIL THE LADY HAD LEFT THE ROOM.
BUT LOOK! THE TIME ON ALL THESE FAXES IS 3:28 P.M.! THE FAX MACHINE KEPT PRINTING FROM THAT TIME UNTIL ME AND THE OTHER KIDS WALKED IN THE ROOM!
WHY WOULD THE BURGLAR BREAK INTO A ROOM...
...WITH THAT WEIRD NOISE GOING ON?
MAYBE HE REALIZED IT WAS JUST A FAX MACHINE!
THAT'D BE EVEN *SCARIER!*
USUALLY THAT MEANS THERE'S PEOPLE WORKING AT HOME! SOMEBODY MIGHT HAVE COME INTO THE ROOM AS SOON AS THE MACHINE WENT *BEEP!*
I SEE ...

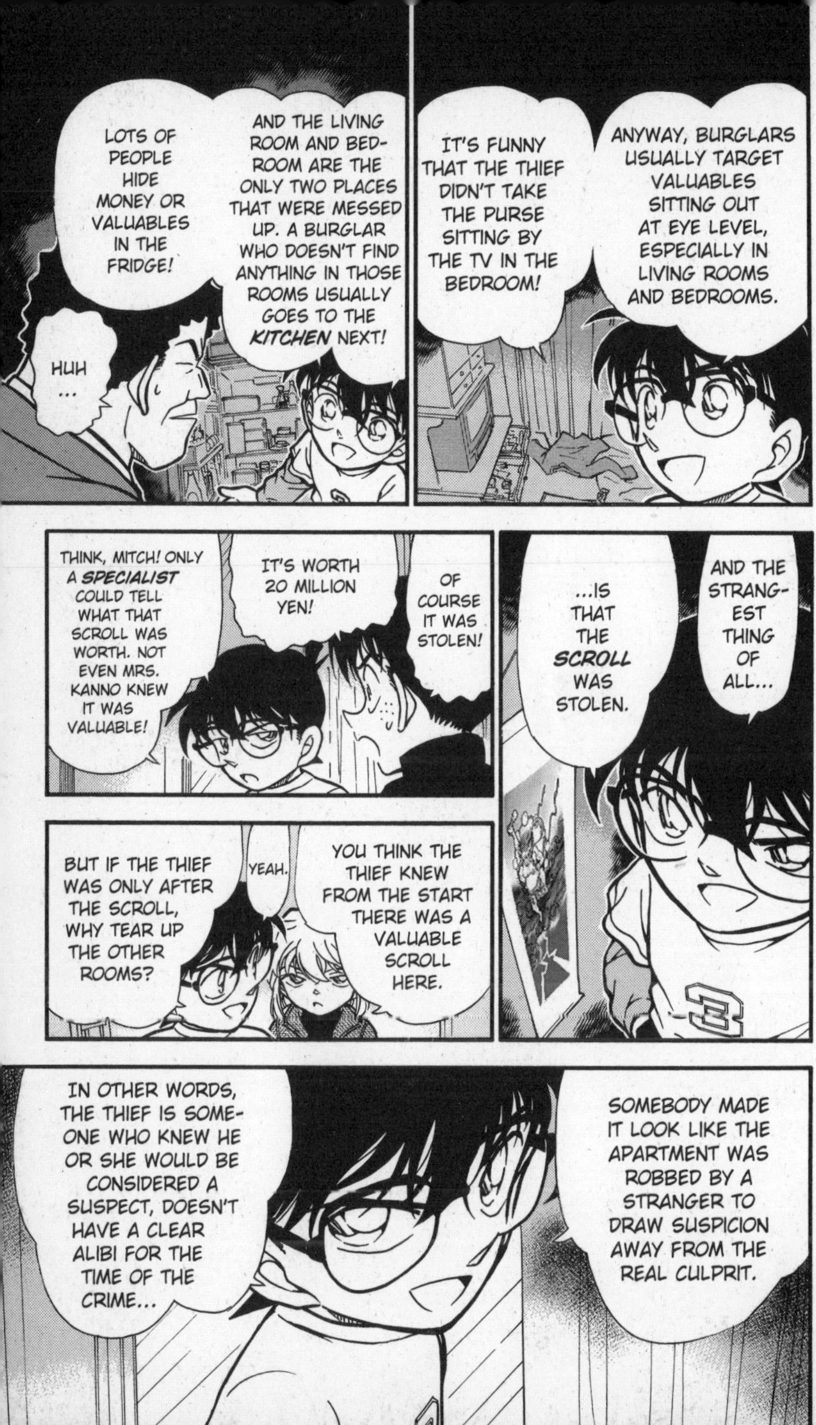
ANYWAY, BURGLARS USUALLY TARGET VALUABLES SITTING OUT AT EYE LEVEL, ESPECIALLY IN LIVING ROOMS AND BEDROOMS.
IT'S FUNNY THAT THE THIEF DIDN'T TAKE THE PURSE SITTING BY THE TV IN THE BEDROOM!
AND THE LIVING ROOM AND BED-ROOM ARE THE ONLY TWO PLACES THAT WERE MESSED UP. A BURGLAR WHO DOESN'T FIND ANYTHING IN THOSE ROOMS USUALLY GOES TO THE *KITCHEN* NEXT!
LOTS OF PEOPLE HIDE MONEY OR VALUABLES IN THE FRIDGE!
HUH ...
AND THE STRANG-EST THING OF ALL...
...IS THAT THE *SCROLL* WAS STOLEN.
OF COURSE IT WAS STOLEN!
IT'S WORTH 20 MILLION YEN!
THINK, MITCH! ONLY A *SPECIALIST* COULD TELL WHAT THAT SCROLL WAS WORTH. NOT EVEN MRS. KANNO KNEW IT WAS VALUABLE!
YOU THINK THE THIEF KNEW FROM THE START THERE WAS A VALUABLE SCROLL HERE.
YEAH.
BUT IF THE THIEF WAS ONLY AFTER THE SCROLL, WHY TEAR UP THE OTHER ROOMS?
SOMEBODY MADE IT LOOK LIKE THE APARTMENT WAS ROBBED BY A STRANGER TO DRAW SUSPICION AWAY FROM THE REAL CULPRIT.
IN OTHER WORDS, THE THIEF IS SOME-ONE WHO KNEW HE OR SHE WOULD BE CONSIDERED A SUSPECT, DOESN'T HAVE A CLEAR ALIBI FOR THE TIME OF THE CRIME...

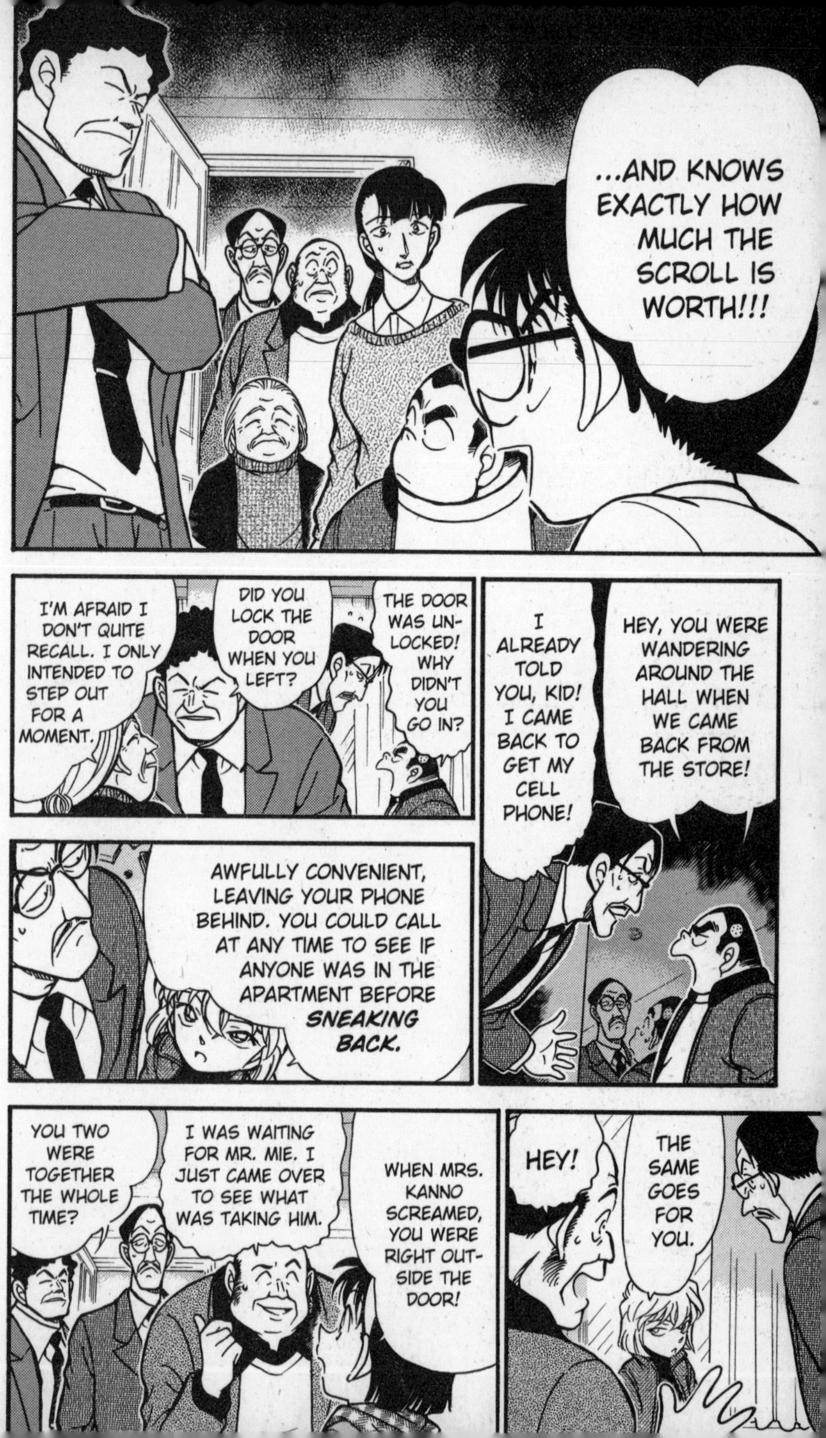
...AND KNOWS EXACTLY HOW MUCH THE SCROLL IS WORTH!!!
HEY, YOU WERE WANDERING AROUND THE HALL WHEN WE CAME BACK FROM THE STORE!
I ALREADY TOLD YOU, KID! I CAME BACK TO GET MY CELL PHONE!
THE DOOR WAS UN-LOCKED! WHY DIDN'T YOU GO IN?
DID YOU LOCK THE DOOR WHEN YOU LEFT?
I'M AFRAID I DON'T QUITE RECALL. I ONLY INTENDED TO STEP OUT FOR A MOMENT.
AWFULLY CONVENIENT, LEAVING YOUR PHONE BEHIND. YOU COULD CALL AT ANY TIME TO SEE IF ANYONE WAS IN THE APARTMENT BEFORE ***SNEAKING BACK.***
THE SAME GOES FOR YOU.
HEY!
WHEN MRS. KANNO SCREAMED, YOU WERE RIGHT OUT-SIDE THE DOOR!
I WAS WAITING FOR MR. MIE. I JUST CAME OVER TO SEE WHAT WAS TAKING HIM.
YOU TWO WERE TOGETHER THE WHOLE TIME?

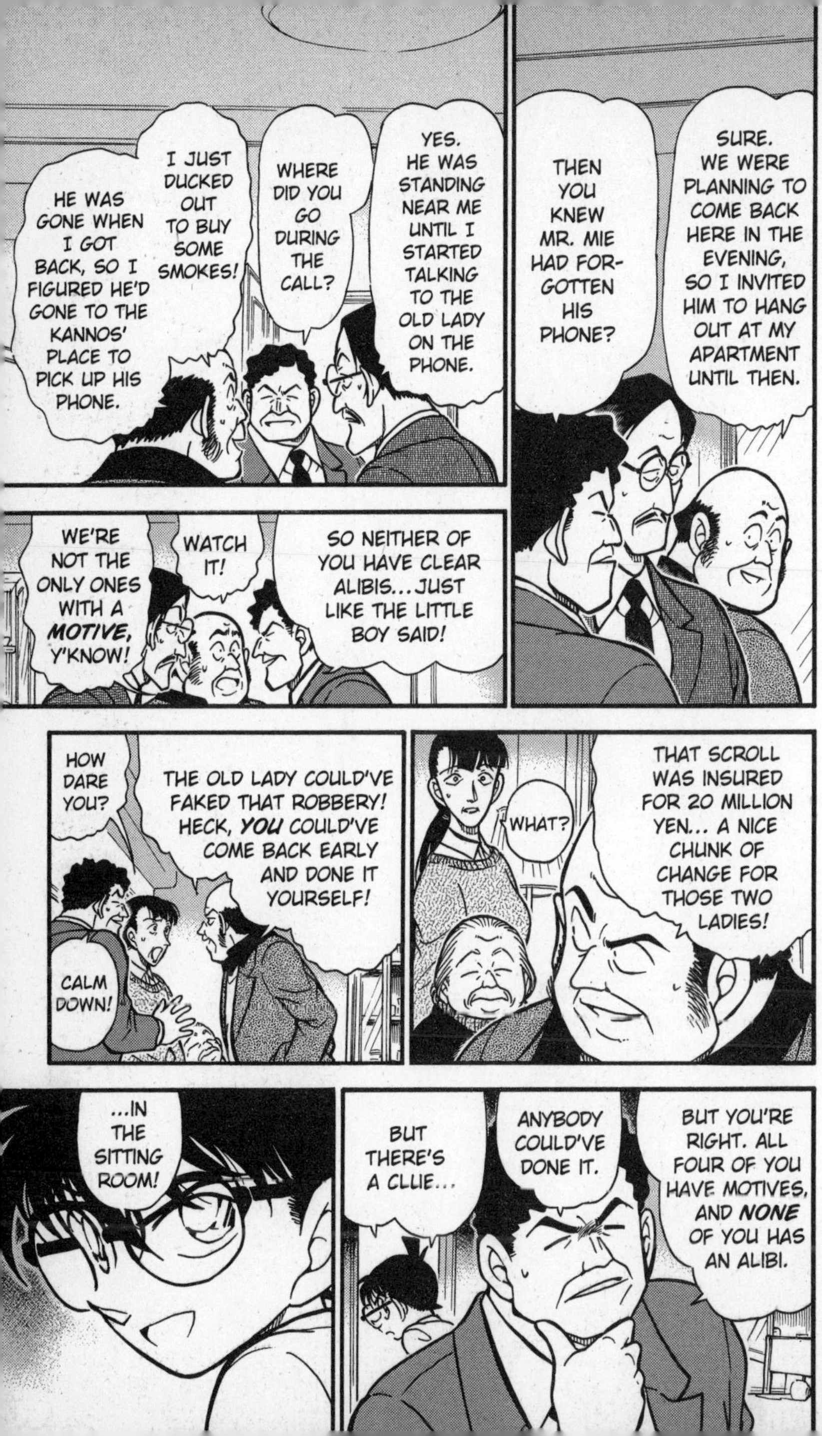
SURE. WE WERE PLANNING TO COME BACK HERE IN THE EVENING, SO I INVITED HIM TO HANG OUT AT MY APARTMENT UNTIL THEN.
THEN YOU KNEW MR. MIE HAD FOR-GOTTEN HIS PHONE?
YES. HE WAS STANDING NEAR ME UNTIL I STARTED TALKING TO THE OLD LADY ON THE PHONE.
WHERE DID YOU GO DURING THE CALL?
I JUST DUCKED OUT TO BUY SOME SMOKES!
HE WAS GONE WHEN I GOT BACK, SO I FIGURED HE'D GONE TO THE KANNOS' PLACE TO PICK UP HIS PHONE.
SO NEITHER OF YOU HAVE CLEAR ALIBIS... JUST LIKE THE LITTLE BOY SAID!
WATCH IT!
WE'RE NOT THE ONLY ONES WITH A ***MOTIVE,*** Y'KNOW!
THAT SCROLL WAS INSURED FOR 20 MILLION YEN... A NICE CHUNK OF CHANGE FOR THOSE TWO LADIES!
WHAT?
THE OLD LADY COULD'VE FAKED THAT ROBBERY! HECK, ***YOU*** COULD'VE COME BACK EARLY AND DONE IT YOURSELF!
HOW DARE YOU?
CALM DOWN!
BUT YOU'RE RIGHT. ALL FOUR OF YOU HAVE MOTIVES, AND ***NONE*** OF YOU HAS AN ALIBI.
ANYBODY COULD'VE DONE IT.
BUT THERE'S A CLUE...
...IN THE SITTING ROOM!

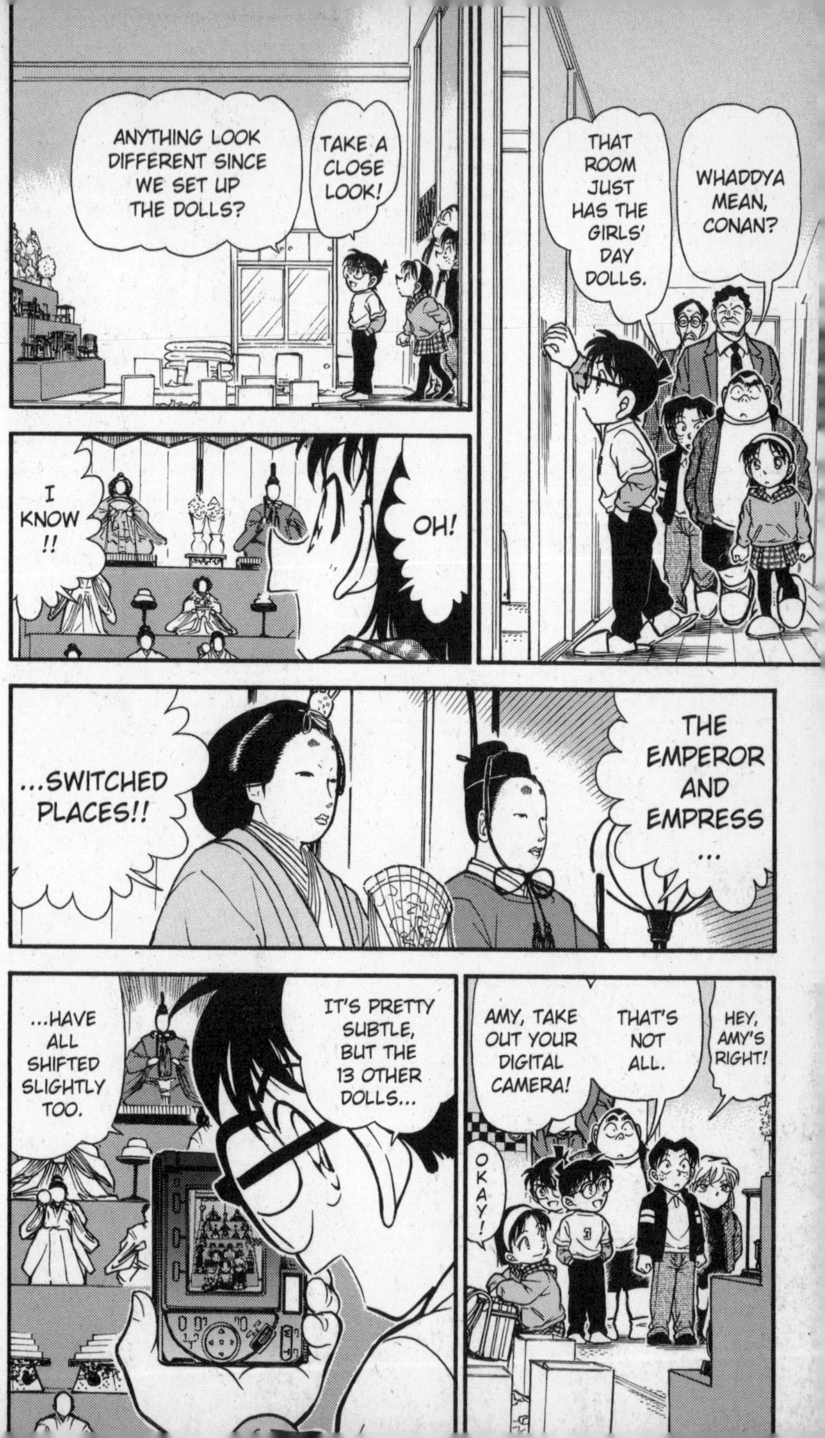
WHADDYA MEAN, CONAN?
THAT ROOM JUST HAS THE GIRLS' DAY DOLLS.
TAKE A CLOSE LOOK!
ANYTHING LOOK DIFFERENT SINCE WE SET UP THE DOLLS?
OH!
I KNOW!!
THE EMPEROR AND EMPRESS ...
...SWITCHED PLACES!!
HEY, AMY'S RIGHT!
THAT'S NOT ALL.
AMY, TAKE OUT YOUR DIGITAL CAMERA!
OKAY!
IT'S PRETTY SUBTLE, BUT THE 13 OTHER DOLLS...
...HAVE ALL SHIFTED SLIGHTLY TOO.

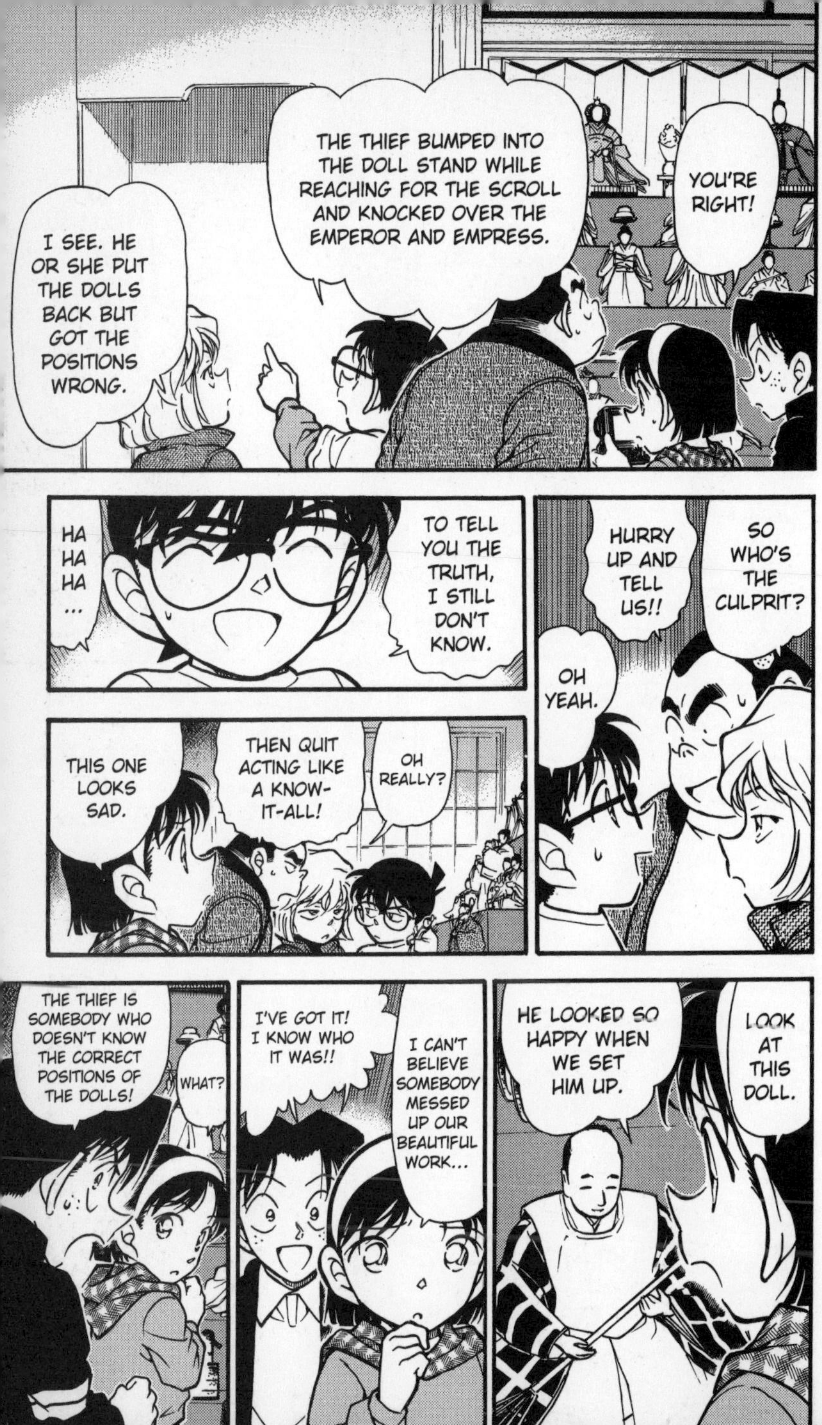
THE THIEF BUMPED INTO THE DOLL STAND WHILE REACHING FOR THE SCROLL AND KNOCKED OVER THE EMPEROR AND EMPRESS.
YOU'RE RIGHT!
I SEE. HE OR SHE PUT THE DOLLS BACK BUT GOT THE POSITIONS WRONG.
SO WHO'S THE CULPRIT?
HURRY UP AND TELL US!!
OH YEAH.
TO TELL YOU THE TRUTH, I STILL DON'T KNOW.
HA HA HA ...
OH REALLY?
THEN QUIT ACTING LIKE A KNOW-IT-ALL!
THIS ONE LOOKS SAD.
LOOK AT THIS DOLL.
HE LOOKED SO HAPPY WHEN WE SET HIM UP.
I CAN'T BELIEVE SOMEBODY MESSED UP OUR BEAUTIFUL WORK...
I'VE GOT IT! I KNOW WHO IT WAS!!
WHAT?
THE THIEF IS SOMEBODY WHO DOESN'T KNOW THE CORRECT POSITIONS OF THE DOLLS!

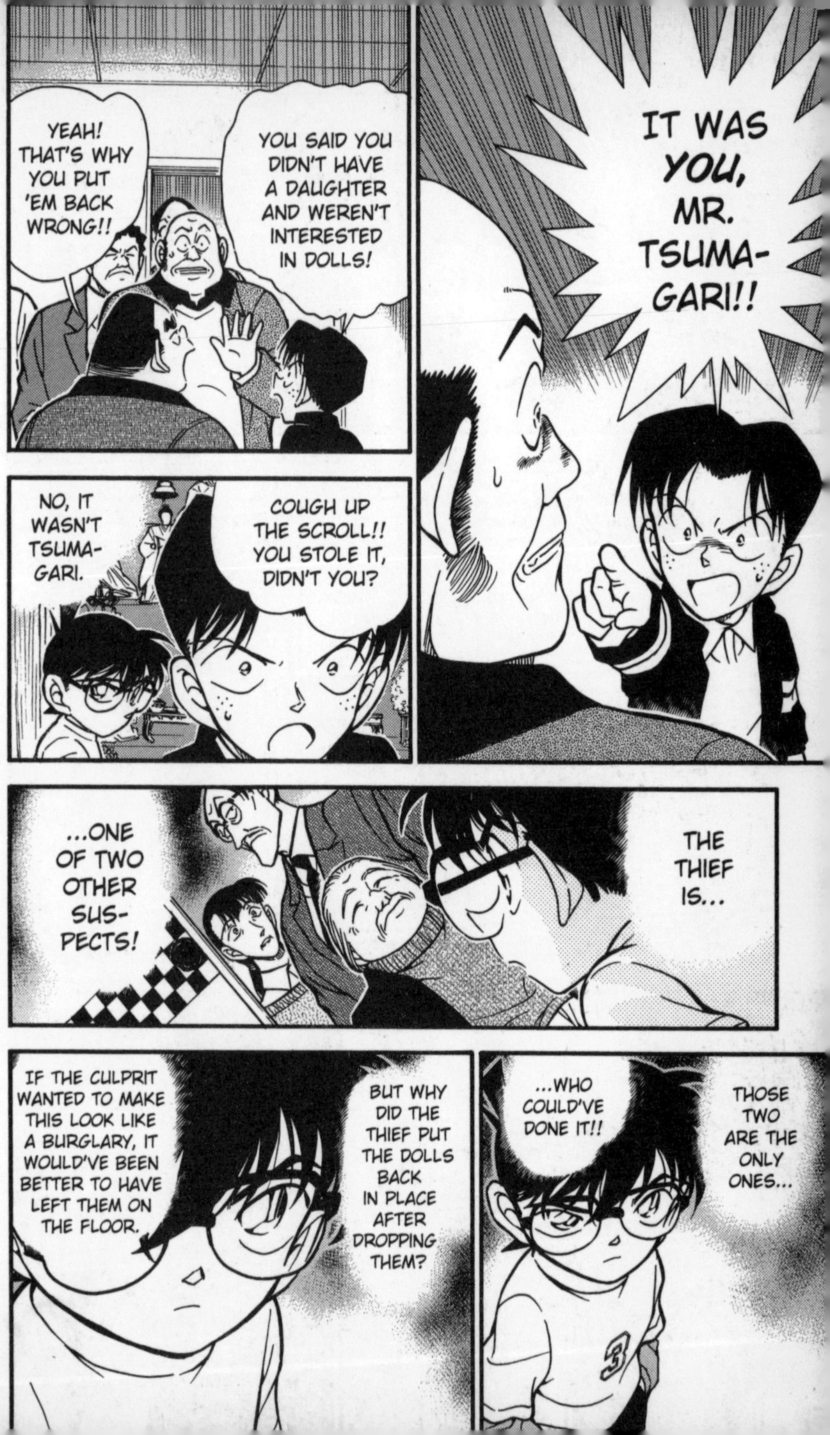
IT WAS YOU, MR. TSUMAGARI!!
YOU SAID YOU DIDN'T HAVE A DAUGHTER AND WEREN'T INTERESTED IN DOLLS!
YEAH! THAT'S WHY YOU PUT 'EM BACK WRONG!!
COUGH UP THE SCROLL!! YOU STOLE IT, DIDN'T YOU?
NO, IT WASN'T TSUMAGARI.
THE THIEF IS...
...ONE OF TWO OTHER SUSPECTS!
THOSE TWO ARE THE ONLY ONES...
...WHO COULD'VE DONE IT!!
BUT WHY DID THE THIEF PUT THE DOLLS BACK IN PLACE AFTER DROPPING THEM?
IF THE CULPRIT WANTED TO MAKE THIS LOOK LIKE A BURGLARY, IT WOULD'VE BEEN BETTER TO HAVE LEFT THEM ON THE FLOOR.

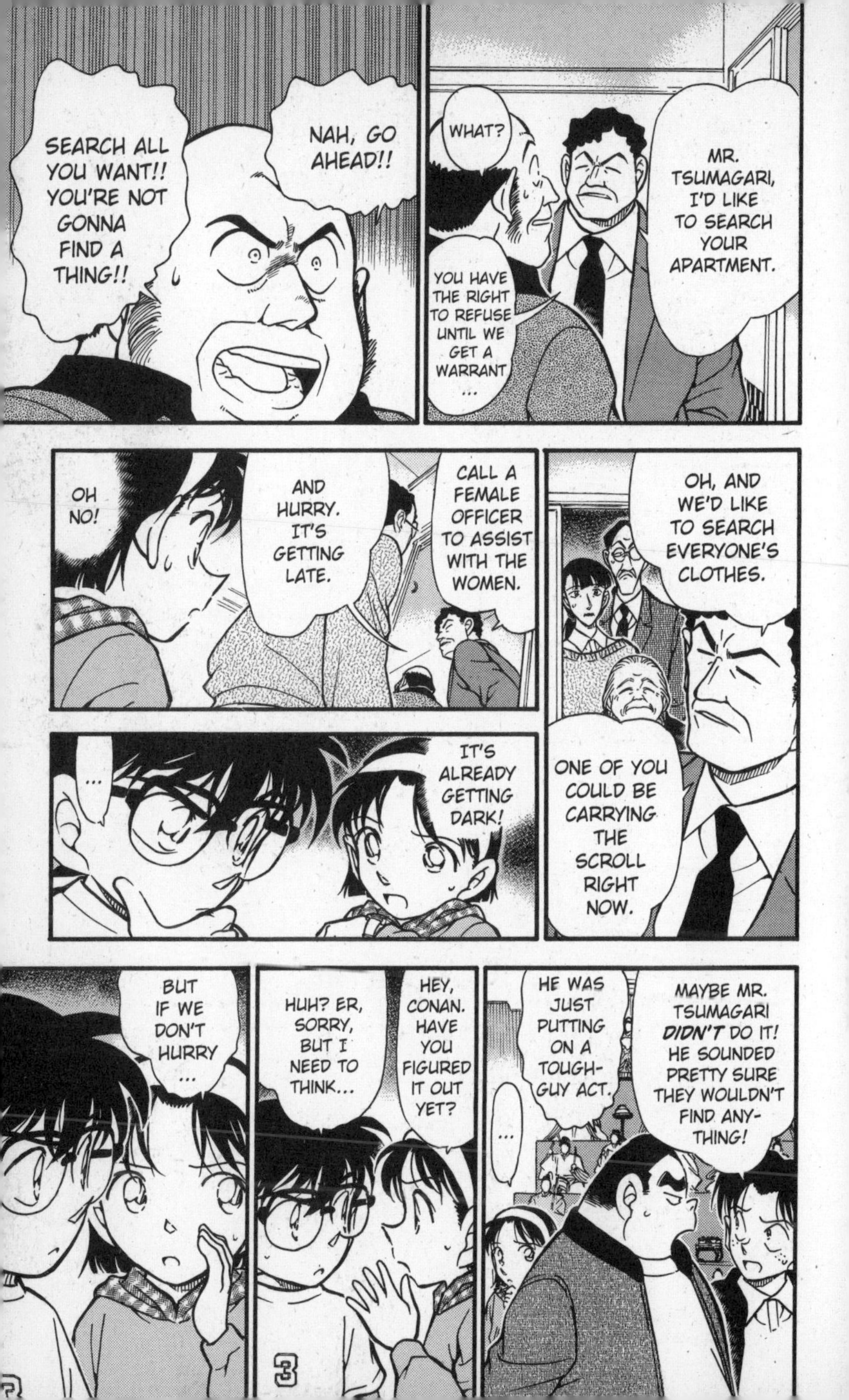
MR. TSUMAGARI, I'D LIKE TO SEARCH YOUR APARTMENT.
WHAT?
YOU HAVE THE RIGHT TO REFUSE UNTIL WE GET A WARRANT...
NAH, GO AHEAD!!
SEARCH ALL YOU WANT!! YOU'RE NOT GONNA FIND A THING!!
OH, AND WE'D LIKE TO SEARCH EVERYONE'S CLOTHES.
CALL A FEMALE OFFICER TO ASSIST WITH THE WOMEN.
AND HURRY. IT'S GETTING LATE.
OH NO!
ONE OF YOU COULD BE CARRYING THE SCROLL RIGHT NOW.
IT'S ALREADY GETTING DARK!
...
MAYBE MR. TSUMAGARI **DIDN'T** DO IT! HE SOUNDED PRETTY SURE THEY WOULDN'T FIND ANY-THING!
HE WAS JUST PUTTING ON A TOUGH-GUY ACT.
...
HEY, CONAN. HAVE YOU FIGURED IT OUT YET?
HUH? ER, SORRY, BUT I NEED TO THINK...
BUT IF WE DON'T HURRY...

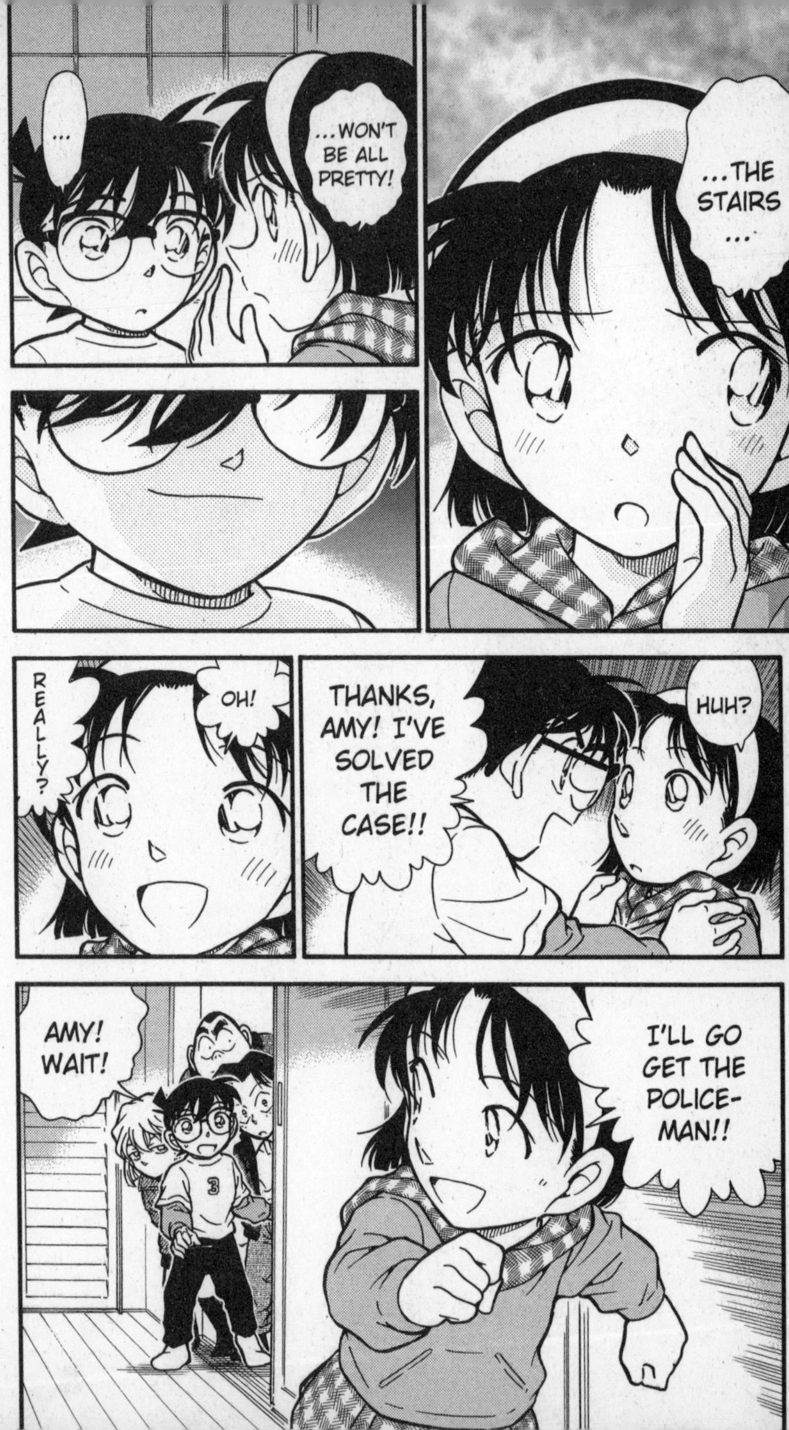

...THE STAIRS ...
...WON'T BE ALL PRETTY!
...
HUH?
THANKS, AMY! I'VE SOLVED THE CASE!!
OH!
REALLY?
I'LL GO GET THE POLICE-MAN!!
AMY! WAIT!

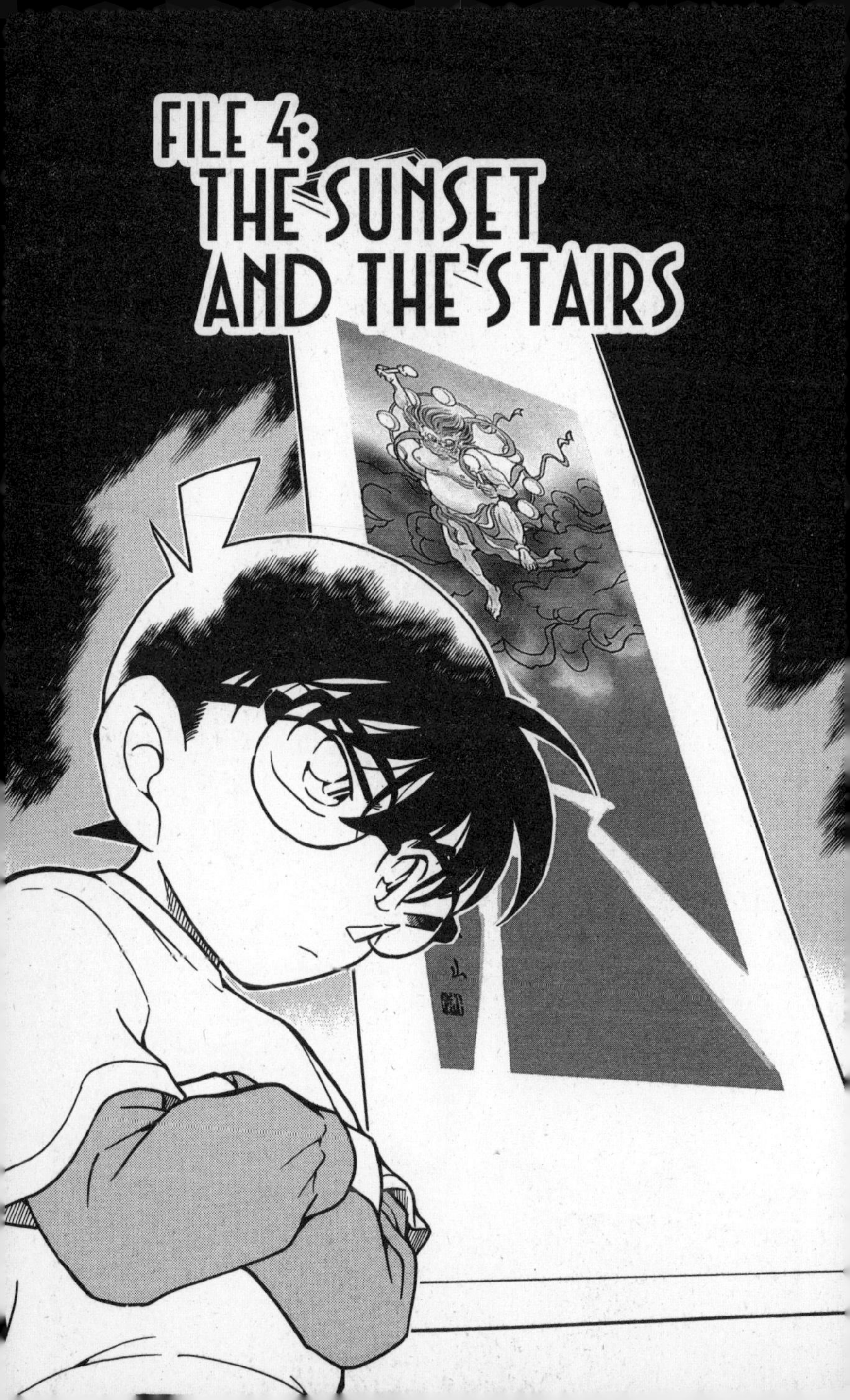
FILE 4:
THE SUNSET AND THE STAIRS

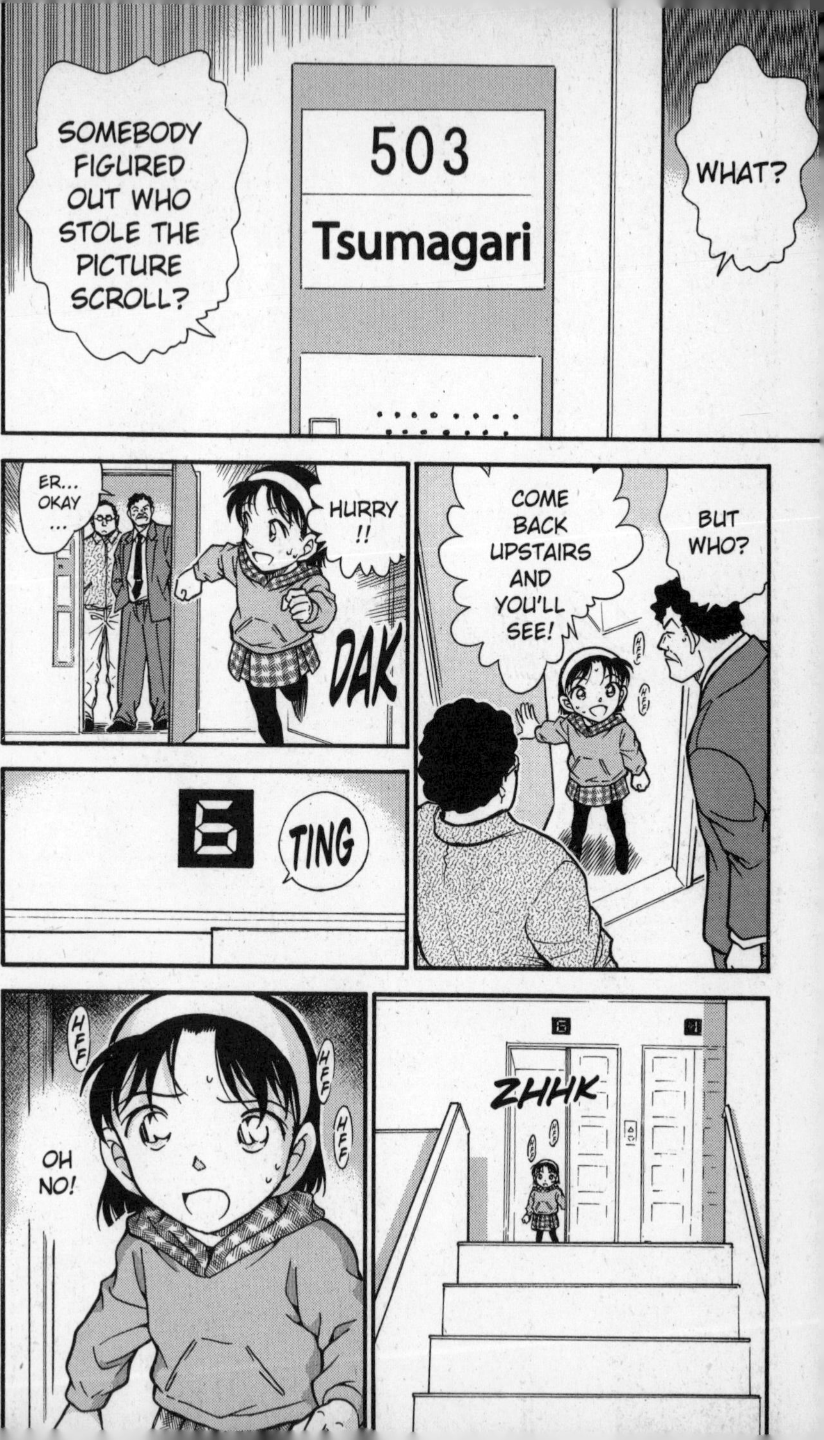
WHAT?
SOMEBODY FIGURED OUT WHO STOLE THE PICTURE SCROLL?
503
Tsumagari
BUT WHO?
COME BACK UPSTAIRS AND YOU'LL SEE!
HEF
HEF
HURRY!!
ER... OKAY ...
DAK
6
TING
ZHHK
HEF
HEF
HFF
HFF
HFF
OH NO!

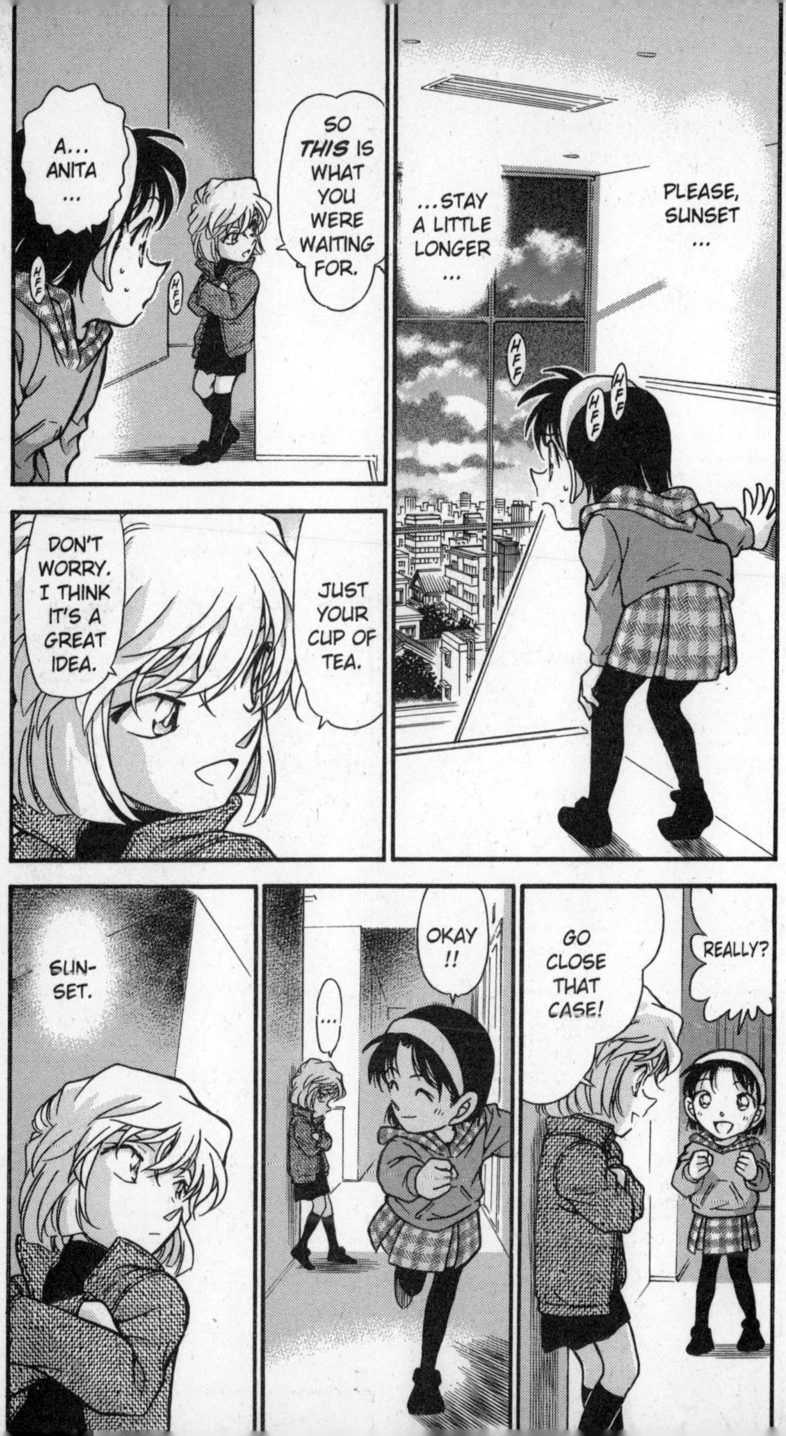
PLEASE, SUNSET ...
...STAY A LITTLE LONGER ...
HFF
HFF
HFF
SO *THIS* IS WHAT YOU WERE WAITING FOR.
A... ANITA ...
HFF
HFF
JUST YOUR CUP OF TEA.
DON'T WORRY. I THINK IT'S A GREAT IDEA.
REALLY?
GO CLOSE THAT CASE!
OKAY !!
...
SUN-SET.

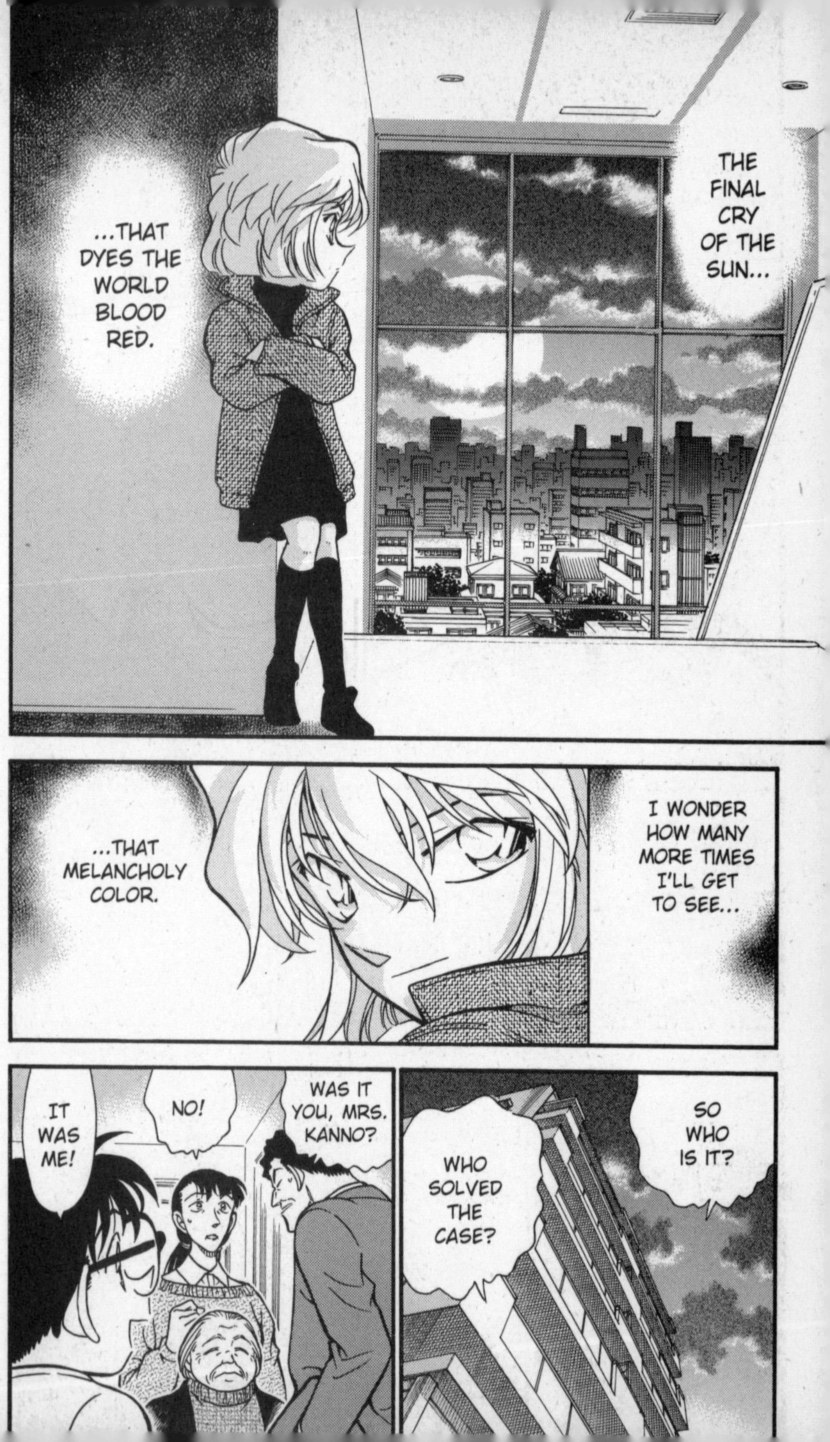
THE FINAL CRY OF THE SUN...
...THAT DYES THE WORLD BLOOD RED.
I WONDER HOW MANY MORE TIMES I'LL GET TO SEE...
...THAT MELANCHOLY COLOR.
SO WHO IS IT?
WHO SOLVED THE CASE?
WAS IT YOU, MRS. KANNO?
NO!
IT WAS ME!

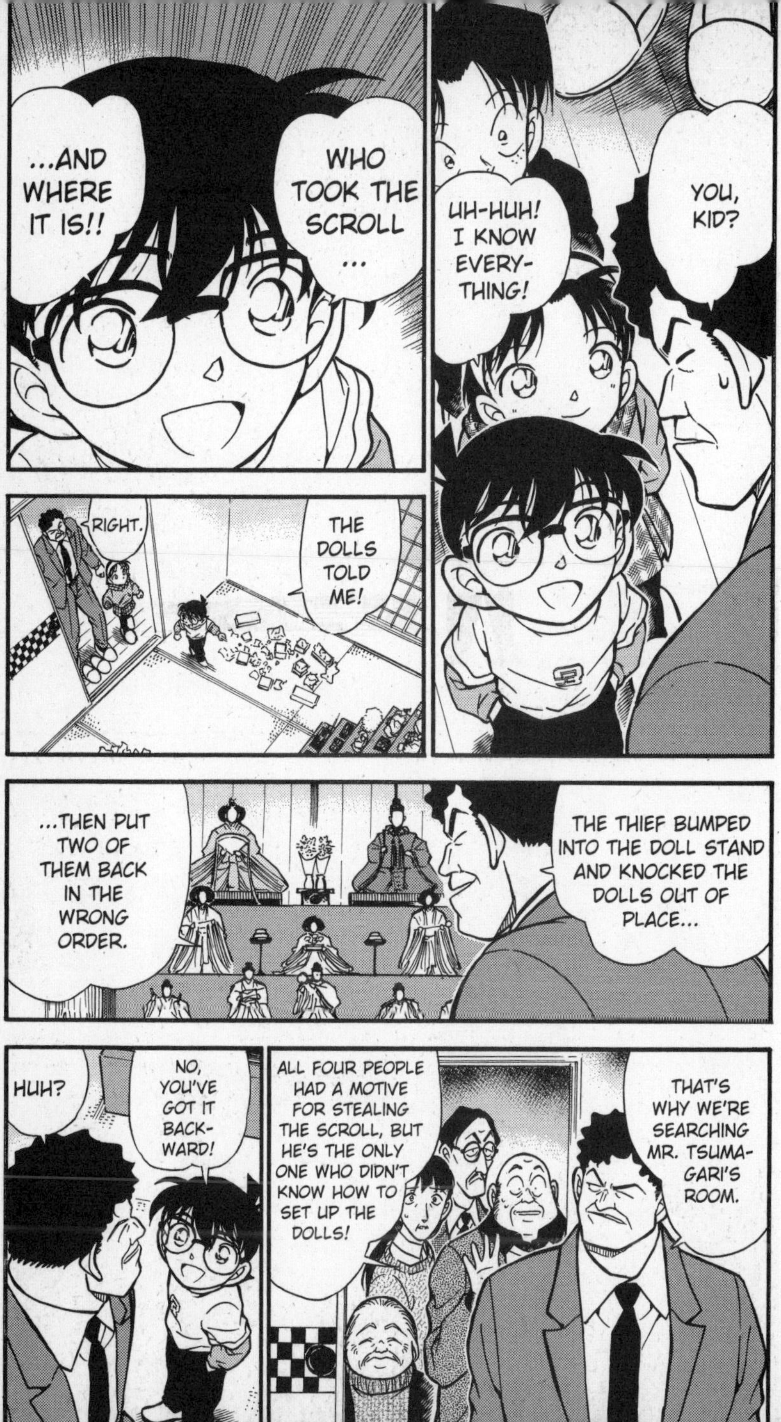
WHO TOOK THE SCROLL ...
...AND WHERE IT IS!!
YOU, KID?
UH-HUH! I KNOW EVERY-THING!
THE DOLLS TOLD ME!
RIGHT.
THE THIEF BUMPED INTO THE DOLL STAND AND KNOCKED THE DOLLS OUT OF PLACE...
...THEN PUT TWO OF THEM BACK IN THE WRONG ORDER.
THAT'S WHY WE'RE SEARCHING MR. TSUMA-GARI'S ROOM.
ALL FOUR PEOPLE HAD A MOTIVE FOR STEALING THE SCROLL, BUT HE'S THE ONLY ONE WHO DIDN'T KNOW HOW TO SET UP THE DOLLS!
NO, YOU'VE GOT IT BACK-WARD!
HUH?

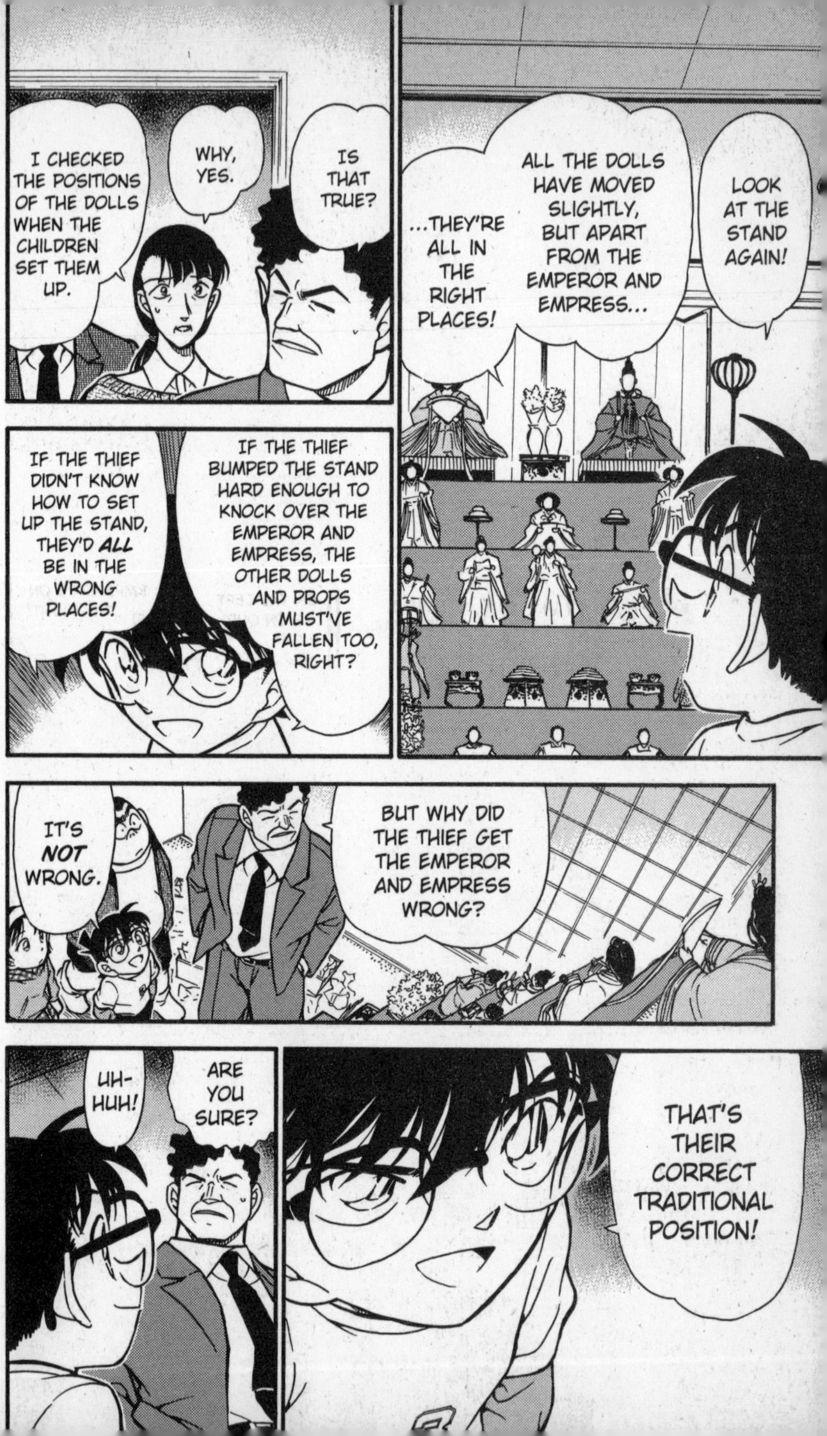
LOOK AT THE STAND AGAIN!
ALL THE DOLLS HAVE MOVED SLIGHTLY, BUT APART FROM THE EMPEROR AND EMPRESS...
...THEY'RE ALL IN THE RIGHT PLACES!
IS THAT TRUE?
WHY, YES.
I CHECKED THE POSITIONS OF THE DOLLS WHEN THE CHILDREN SET THEM UP.
IF THE THIEF BUMPED THE STAND HARD ENOUGH TO KNOCK OVER THE EMPEROR AND EMPRESS, THE OTHER DOLLS AND PROPS MUST'VE FALLEN TOO, RIGHT?
IF THE THIEF DIDN'T KNOW HOW TO SET UP THE STAND, THEY'D ***ALL*** BE IN THE WRONG PLACES!
BUT WHY DID THE THIEF GET THE EMPEROR AND EMPRESS WRONG?
IT'S ***NOT*** WRONG.
THAT'S THEIR CORRECT TRADITIONAL POSITION!
ARE YOU SURE?
UH-HUH!

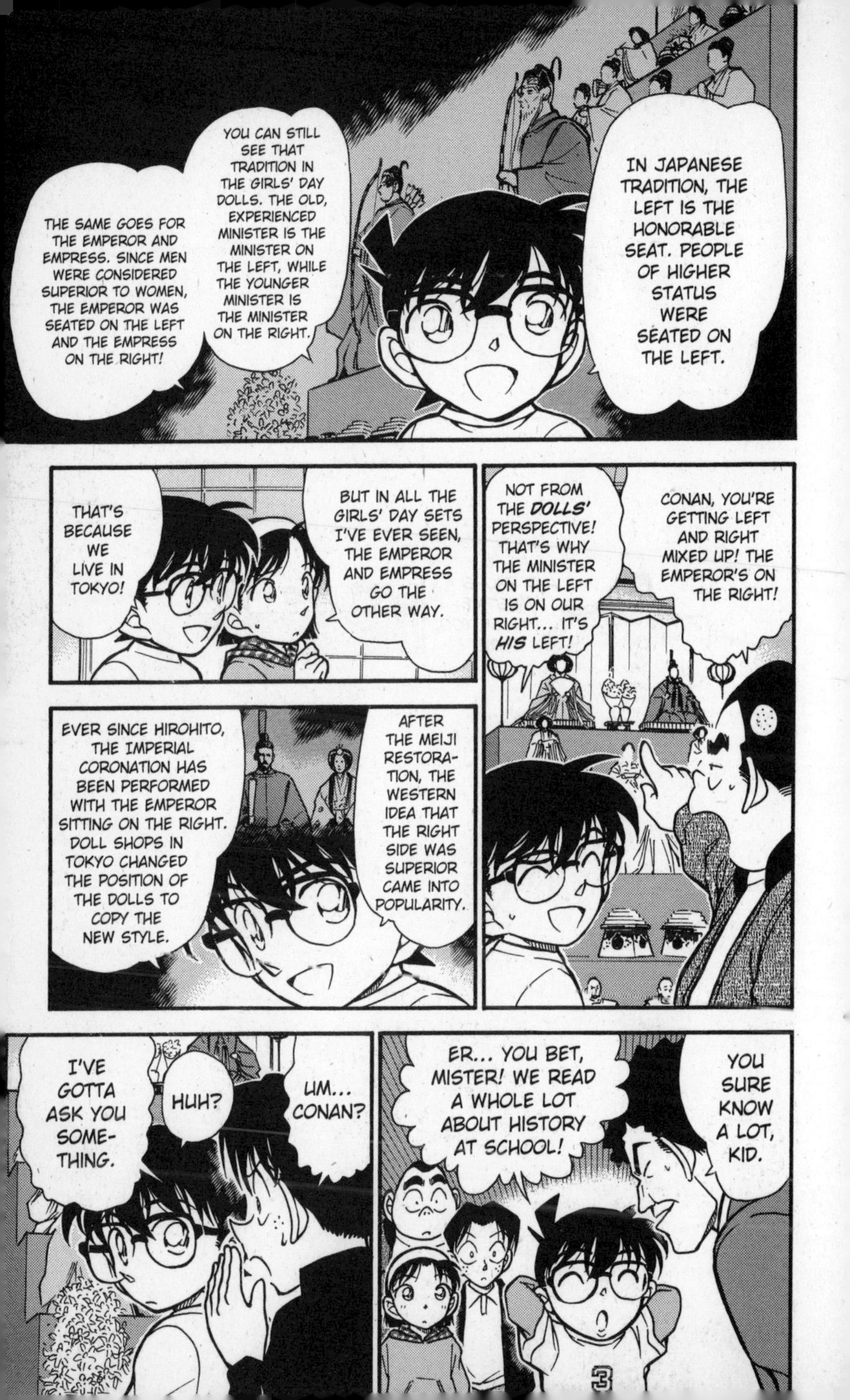

IN JAPANESE TRADITION, THE LEFT IS THE HONORABLE SEAT. PEOPLE OF HIGHER STATUS WERE SEATED ON THE LEFT.
YOU CAN STILL SEE THAT TRADITION IN THE GIRLS' DAY DOLLS. THE OLD, EXPERIENCED MINISTER IS THE MINISTER ON THE LEFT, WHILE THE YOUNGER MINISTER IS THE MINISTER ON THE RIGHT.
THE SAME GOES FOR THE EMPEROR AND EMPRESS. SINCE MEN WERE CONSIDERED SUPERIOR TO WOMEN, THE EMPEROR WAS SEATED ON THE LEFT AND THE EMPRESS ON THE RIGHT!
CONAN, YOU'RE GETTING LEFT AND RIGHT MIXED UP! THE EMPEROR'S ON THE RIGHT!
NOT FROM THE ***DOLLS'*** PERSPECTIVE! THAT'S WHY THE MINISTER ON THE LEFT IS ON OUR RIGHT... IT'S ***HIS*** LEFT!
BUT IN ALL THE GIRLS' DAY SETS I'VE EVER SEEN, THE EMPEROR AND EMPRESS GO THE OTHER WAY.
THAT'S BECAUSE WE LIVE IN TOKYO!
AFTER THE MEIJI RESTORATION, THE WESTERN IDEA THAT THE RIGHT SIDE WAS SUPERIOR CAME INTO POPULARITY.
EVER SINCE HIROHITO, THE IMPERIAL CORONATION HAS BEEN PERFORMED WITH THE EMPEROR SITTING ON THE RIGHT. DOLL SHOPS IN TOKYO CHANGED THE POSITION OF THE DOLLS TO COPY THE NEW STYLE.
YOU SURE KNOW A LOT, KID.
ER... YOU BET, MISTER! WE READ A WHOLE LOT ABOUT HISTORY AT SCHOOL!
UM... CONAN?
HUH?
I'VE GOTTA ASK YOU SOMETHING.

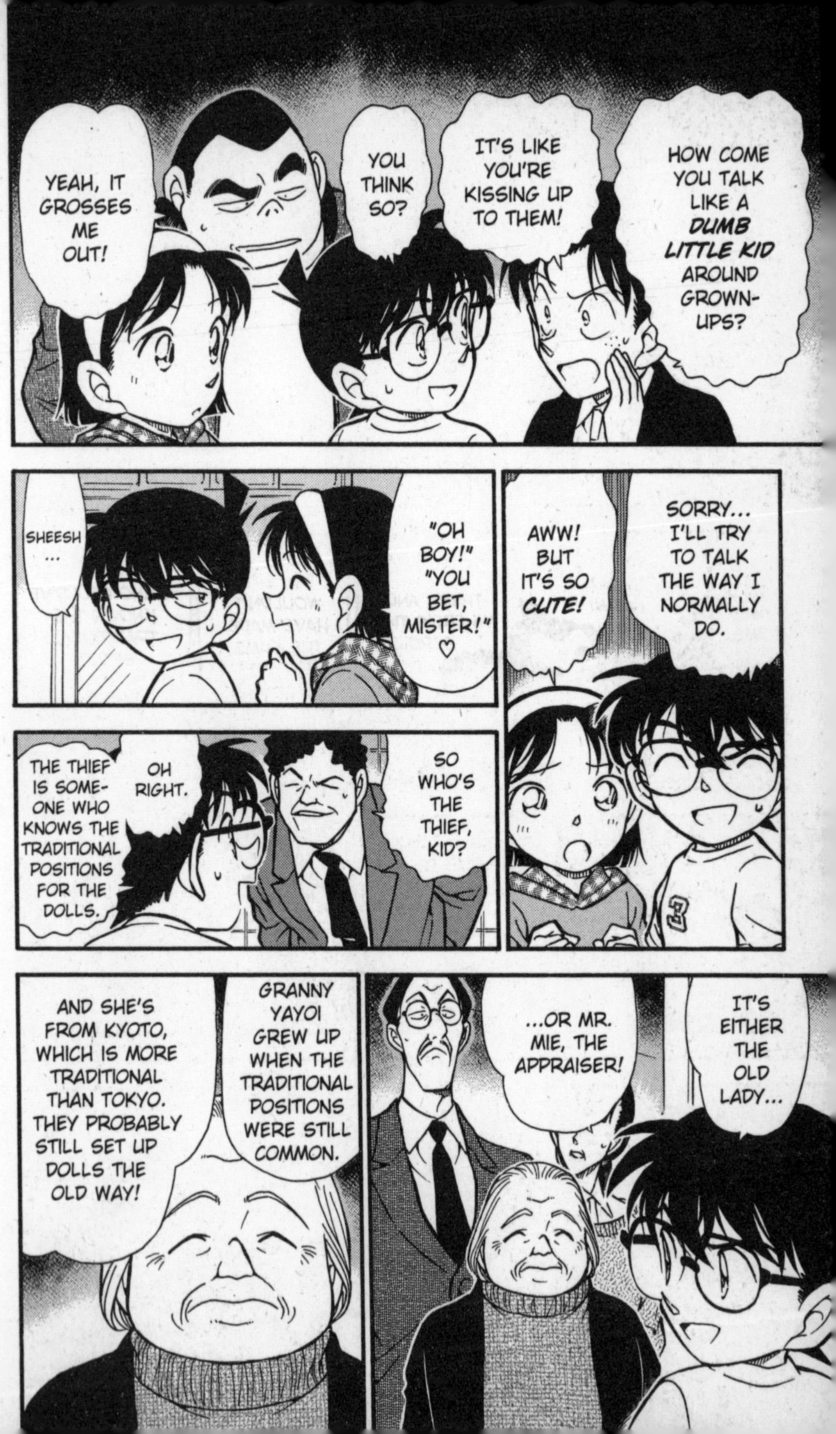
HOW COME YOU TALK LIKE A **DUMB LITTLE KID** AROUND GROWN-UPS?
IT'S LIKE YOU'RE KISSING UP TO THEM!
YOU THINK SO?
YEAH, IT GROSSES ME OUT!
SORRY... I'LL TRY TO TALK THE WAY I NORMALLY DO.
AWW! BUT IT'S SO **CUTE!**
"OH BOY!" "YOU BET, MISTER!" ♡
SHEESH...
SO WHO'S THE THIEF, KID?
OH RIGHT.
THE THIEF IS SOMEONE WHO KNOWS THE TRADITIONAL POSITIONS FOR THE DOLLS.
IT'S EITHER THE OLD LADY...
...OR MR. MIE, THE APPRAISER!
GRANNY YAYOI GREW UP WHEN THE TRADITIONAL POSITIONS WERE STILL COMMON.
AND SHE'S FROM KYOTO, WHICH IS MORE TRADITIONAL THAN TOKYO. THEY PROBABLY STILL SET UP DOLLS THE OLD WAY!

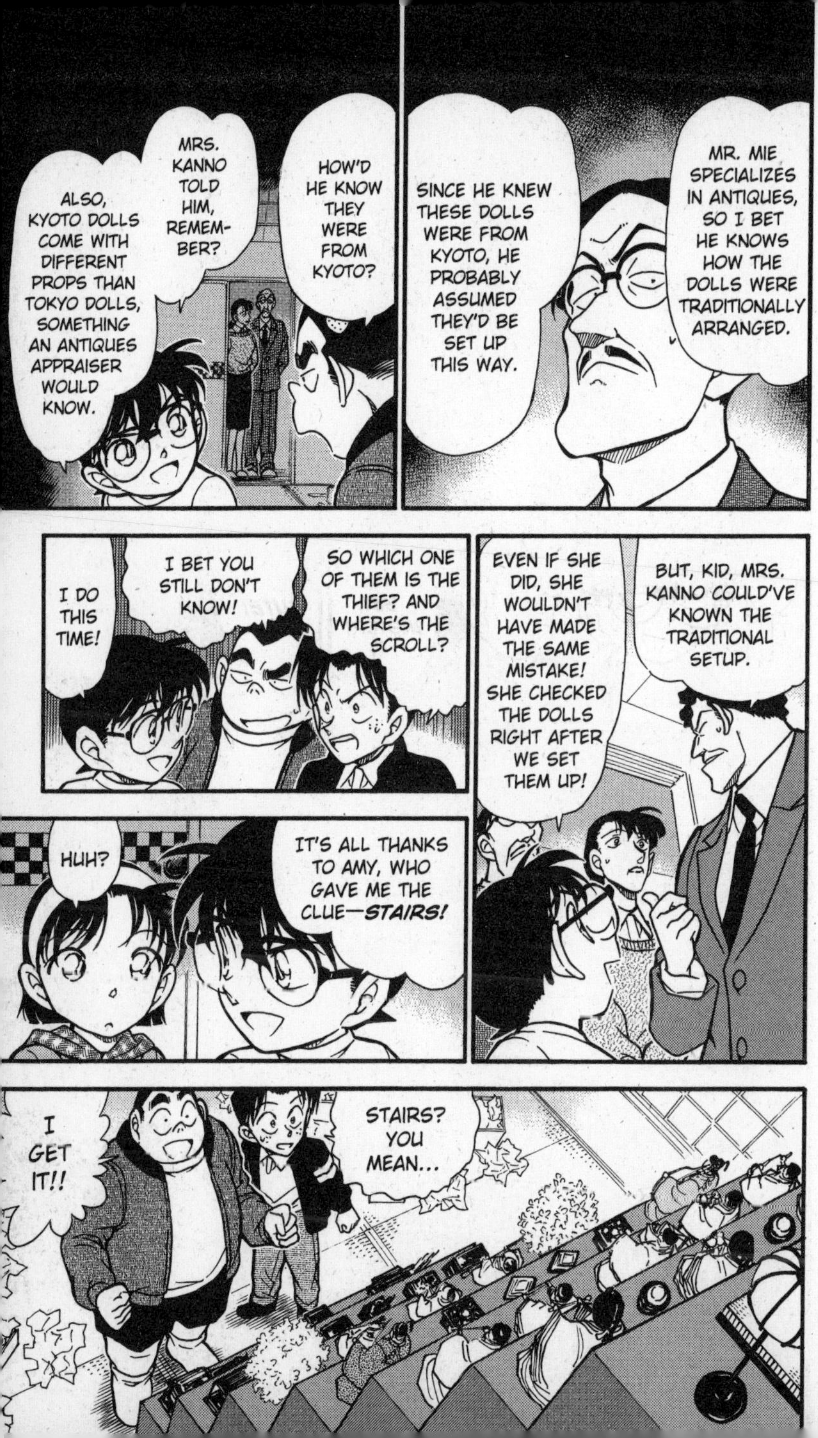
MR. MIE SPECIALIZES IN ANTIQUES, SO I BET HE KNOWS HOW THE DOLLS WERE TRADITIONALLY ARRANGED.
SINCE HE KNEW THESE DOLLS WERE FROM KYOTO, HE PROBABLY ASSUMED THEY'D BE SET UP THIS WAY.
HOW'D HE KNOW THEY WERE FROM KYOTO?
MRS. KANNO TOLD HIM, REMEMBER?
ALSO, KYOTO DOLLS COME WITH DIFFERENT PROPS THAN TOKYO DOLLS, SOMETHING AN ANTIQUES APPRAISER WOULD KNOW.
BUT, KID, MRS. KANNO COULD'VE KNOWN THE TRADITIONAL SETUP.
EVEN IF SHE DID, SHE WOULDN'T HAVE MADE THE SAME MISTAKE! SHE CHECKED THE DOLLS RIGHT AFTER WE SET THEM UP!
SO WHICH ONE OF THEM IS THE THIEF? AND WHERE'S THE SCROLL?
I BET YOU STILL DON'T KNOW!
I DO THIS TIME!
IT'S ALL THANKS TO AMY, WHO GAVE ME THE CLUE—*STAIRS!*
HUH?
STAIRS? YOU MEAN...
I GET IT!!

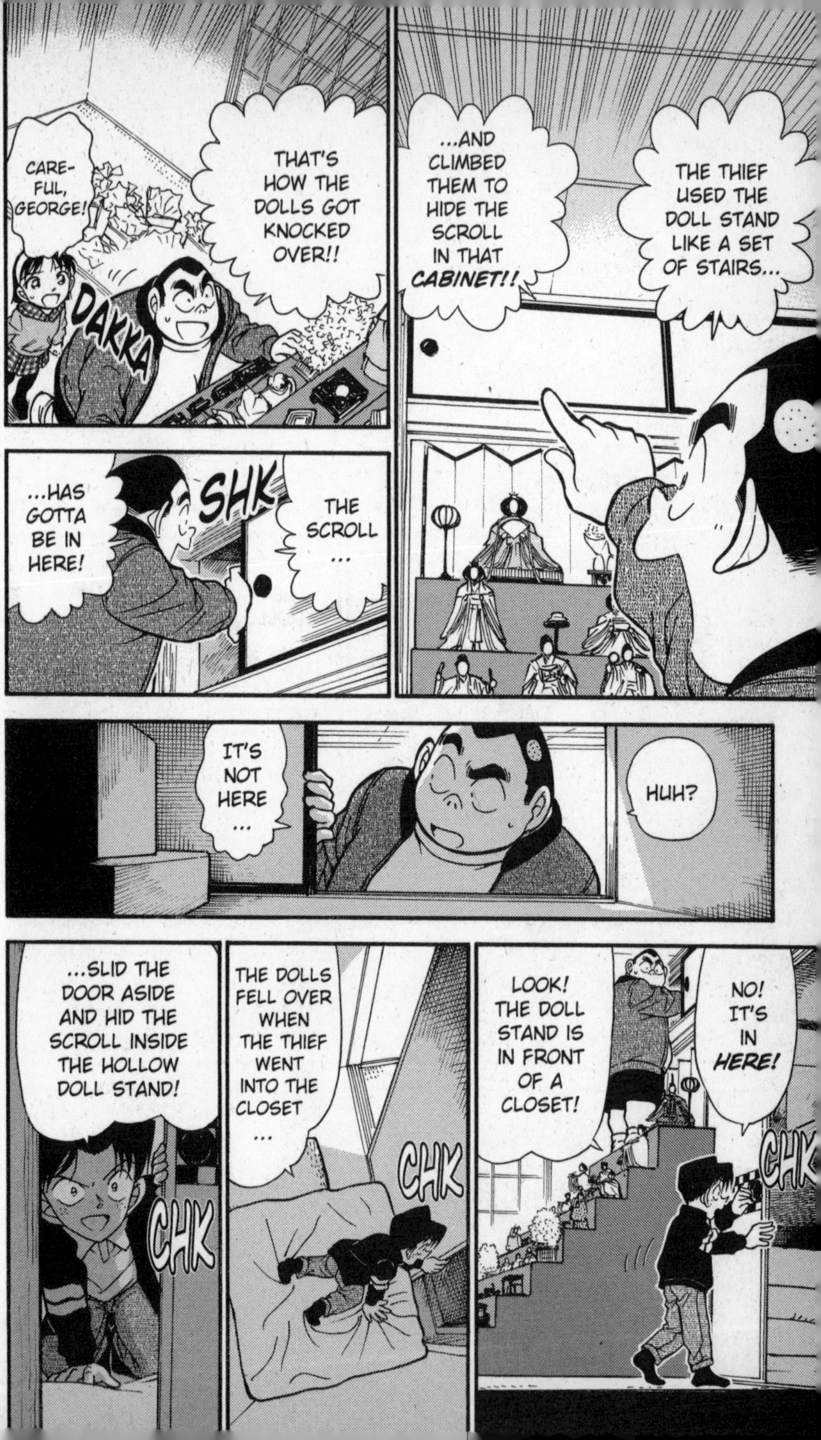
THE THIEF USED THE DOLL STAND LIKE A SET OF STAIRS...
...AND CLIMBED THEM TO HIDE THE SCROLL IN THAT *CABINET!!*
THAT'S HOW THE DOLLS GOT KNOCKED OVER!!
CARE-FUL, GEORGE!
DAKKA
THE SCROLL...
SHK
...HAS GOTTA BE IN HERE!
HUH?
IT'S NOT HERE...
NO! IT'S IN *HERE!*
CHK
LOOK! THE DOLL STAND IS IN FRONT OF A CLOSET!
THE DOLLS FELL OVER WHEN THE THIEF WENT INTO THE CLOSET...
CHK
...SLID THE DOOR ASIDE AND HID THE SCROLL INSIDE THE HOLLOW DOLL STAND!
CHK

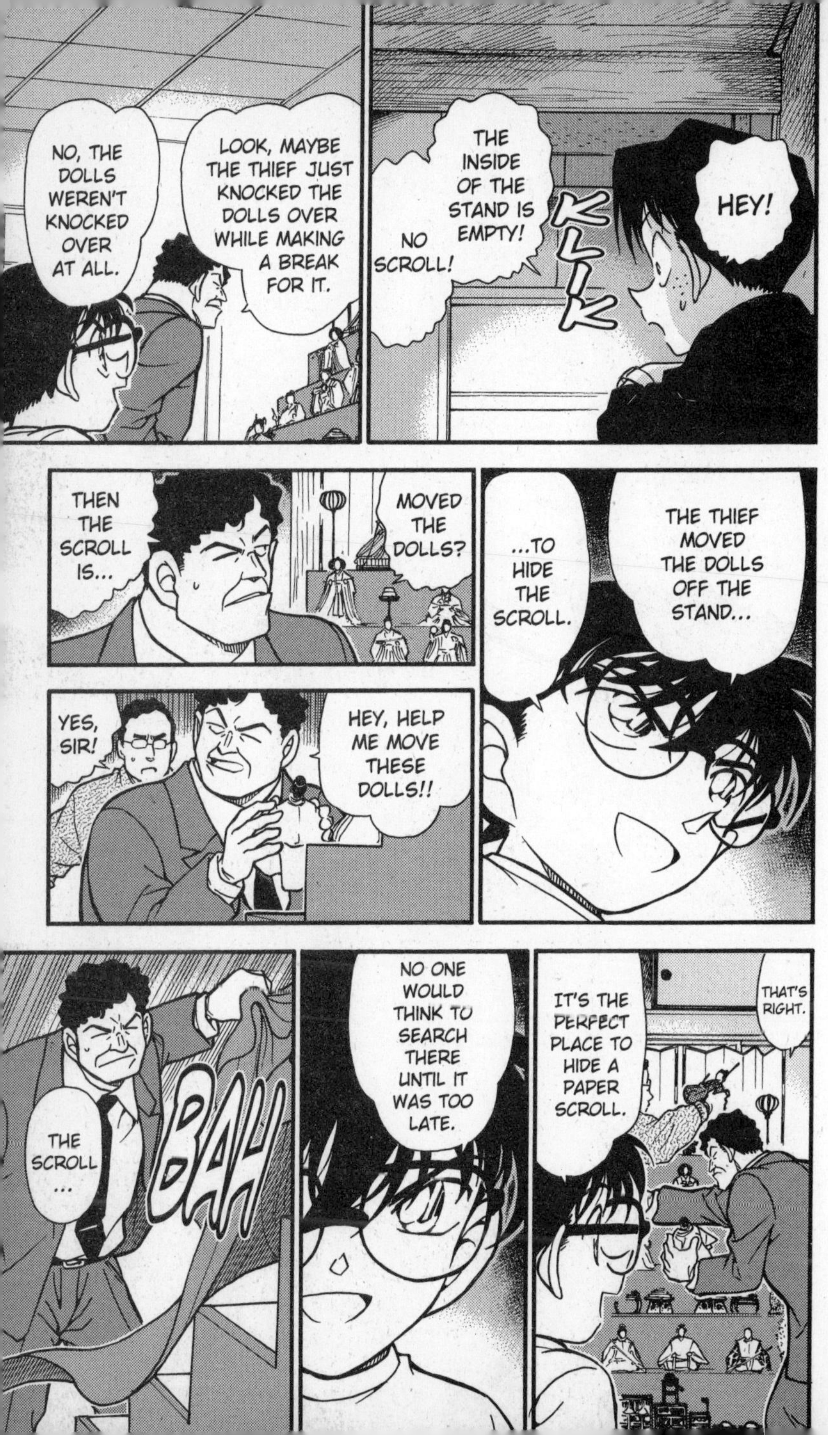
HEY!
THE INSIDE OF THE STAND IS EMPTY!
NO SCROLL!
KLIK
LOOK, MAYBE THE THIEF JUST KNOCKED THE DOLLS OVER WHILE MAKING A BREAK FOR IT.
NO, THE DOLLS WEREN'T KNOCKED OVER AT ALL.
THE THIEF MOVED THE DOLLS OFF THE STAND...
...TO HIDE THE SCROLL.
MOVED THE DOLLS?
THEN THE SCROLL IS...
HEY, HELP ME MOVE THESE DOLLS!!
YES, SIR!
THAT'S RIGHT.
IT'S THE PERFECT PLACE TO HIDE A PAPER SCROLL.
NO ONE WOULD THINK TO SEARCH THERE UNTIL IT WAS TOO LATE.
BAH
THE SCROLL...

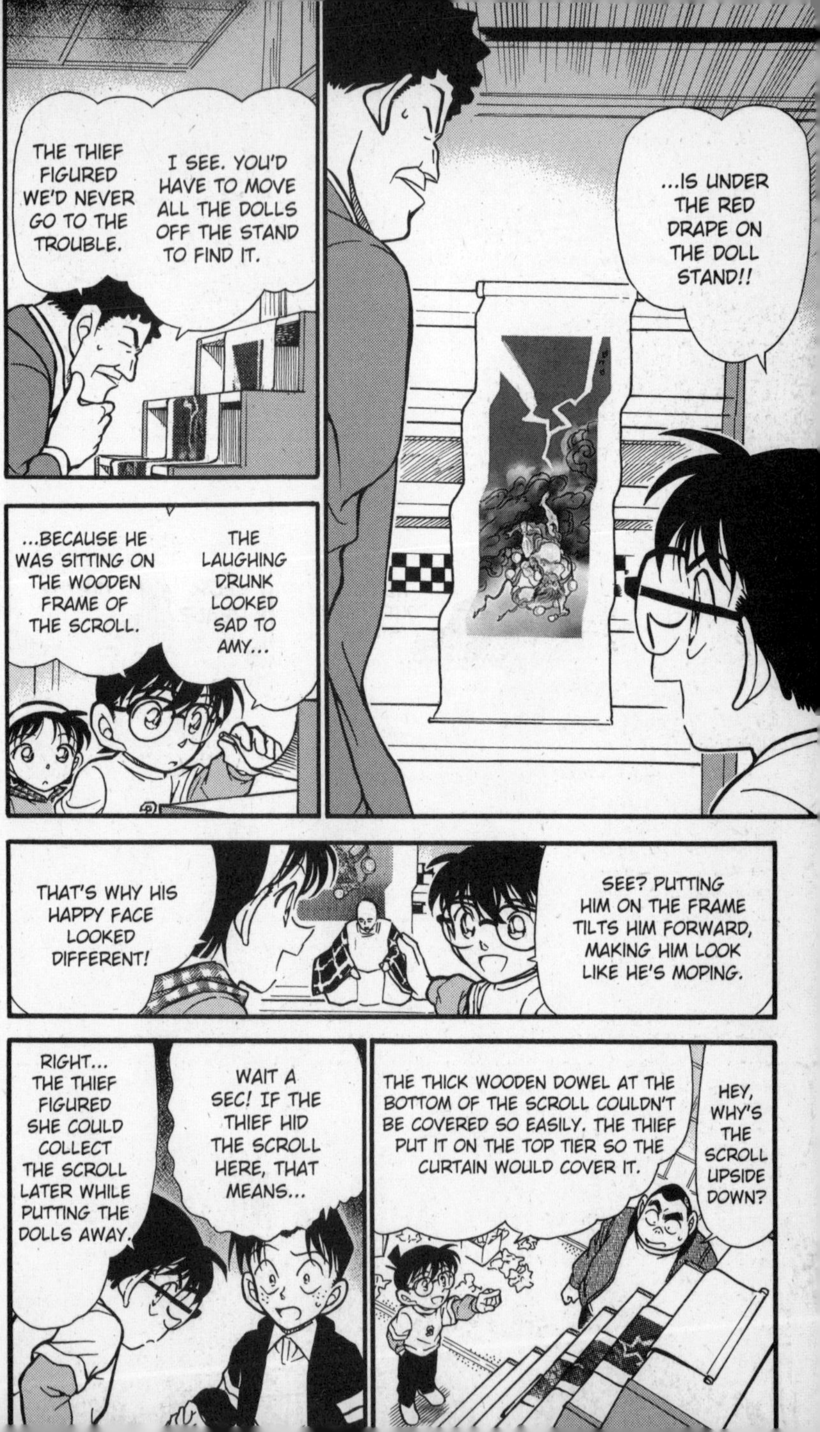
...IS UNDER THE RED DRAPE ON THE DOLL STAND!!
I SEE. YOU'D HAVE TO MOVE ALL THE DOLLS OFF THE STAND TO FIND IT.
THE THIEF FIGURED WE'D NEVER GO TO THE TROUBLE.
THE LAUGHING DRUNK LOOKED SAD TO AMY...
...BECAUSE HE WAS SITTING ON THE WOODEN FRAME OF THE SCROLL.
SEE? PUTTING HIM ON THE FRAME TILTS HIM FORWARD, MAKING HIM LOOK LIKE HE'S MOPING.
THAT'S WHY HIS HAPPY FACE LOOKED DIFFERENT!
HEY, WHY'S THE SCROLL UPSIDE DOWN?
THE THICK WOODEN DOWEL AT THE BOTTOM OF THE SCROLL COULDN'T BE COVERED SO EASILY. THE THIEF PUT IT ON THE TOP TIER SO THE CURTAIN WOULD COVER IT.
WAIT A SEC! IF THE THIEF HID THE SCROLL HERE, THAT MEANS...
RIGHT... THE THIEF FIGURED SHE COULD COLLECT THE SCROLL LATER WHILE PUTTING THE DOLLS AWAY.

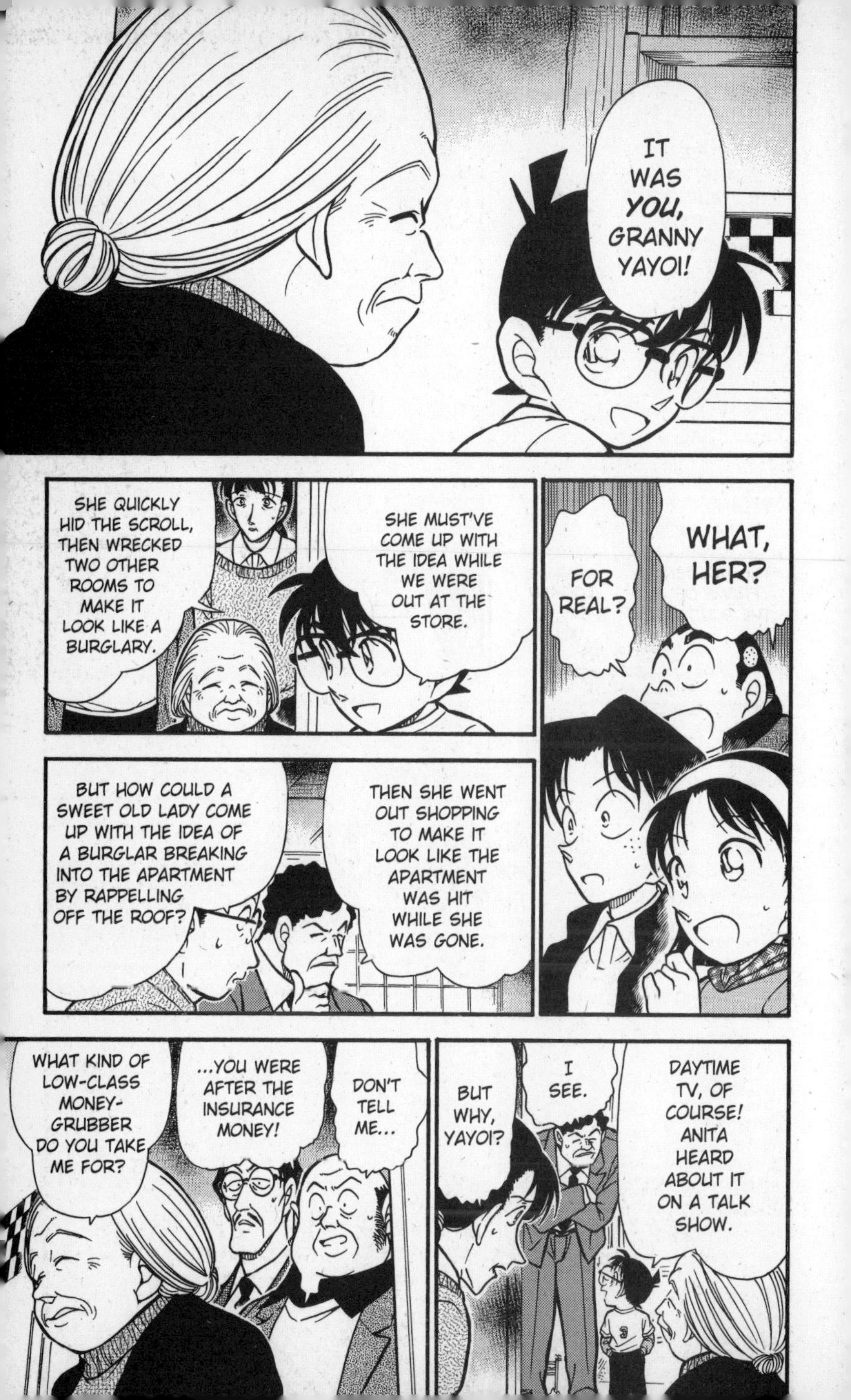
IT WAS *YOU*, GRANNY YAYOI!
WHAT, HER?
FOR REAL?
SHE MUST'VE COME UP WITH THE IDEA WHILE WE WERE OUT AT THE STORE.
SHE QUICKLY HID THE SCROLL, THEN WRECKED TWO OTHER ROOMS TO MAKE IT LOOK LIKE A BURGLARY.
THEN SHE WENT OUT SHOPPING TO MAKE IT LOOK LIKE THE APARTMENT WAS HIT WHILE SHE WAS GONE.
BUT HOW COULD A SWEET OLD LADY COME UP WITH THE IDEA OF A BURGLAR BREAKING INTO THE APARTMENT BY RAPPELLING OFF THE ROOF?
DAYTIME TV, OF COURSE! ANITA HEARD ABOUT IT ON A TALK SHOW.
I SEE.
BUT WHY, YAYOI?
DON'T TELL ME...
...YOU WERE AFTER THE INSURANCE MONEY!
WHAT KIND OF LOW-CLASS MONEY-GRUBBER DO YOU TAKE ME FOR?

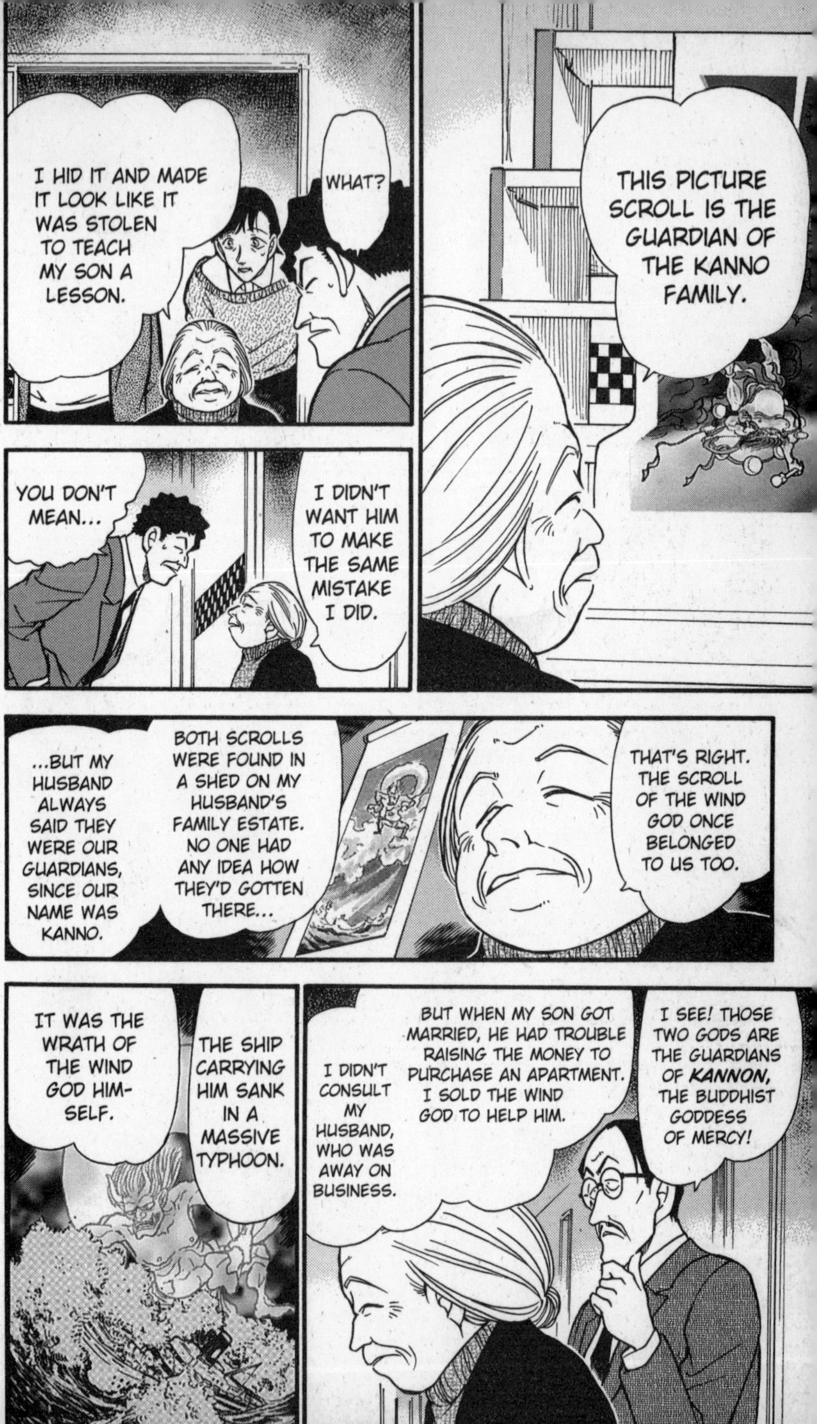
THIS PICTURE SCROLL IS THE GUARDIAN OF THE KANNO FAMILY.
WHAT?
I HID IT AND MADE IT LOOK LIKE IT WAS STOLEN TO TEACH MY SON A LESSON.
I DIDN'T WANT HIM TO MAKE THE SAME MISTAKE I DID.
YOU DON'T MEAN...
THAT'S RIGHT. THE SCROLL OF THE WIND GOD ONCE BELONGED TO US TOO.
BOTH SCROLLS WERE FOUND IN A SHED ON MY HUSBAND'S FAMILY ESTATE. NO ONE HAD ANY IDEA HOW THEY'D GOTTEN THERE...
...BUT MY HUSBAND ALWAYS SAID THEY WERE OUR GUARDIANS, SINCE OUR NAME WAS KANNO.
I SEE! THOSE TWO GODS ARE THE GUARDIANS OF ***KANNON,*** THE BUDDHIST GODDESS OF MERCY!
BUT WHEN MY SON GOT MARRIED, HE HAD TROUBLE RAISING THE MONEY TO PURCHASE AN APARTMENT. I SOLD THE WIND GOD TO HELP HIM.
I DIDN'T CONSULT MY HUSBAND, WHO WAS AWAY ON BUSINESS.
THE SHIP CARRYING HIM SANK IN A MASSIVE TYPHOON.
IT WAS THE WRATH OF THE WIND GOD HIM-SELF.

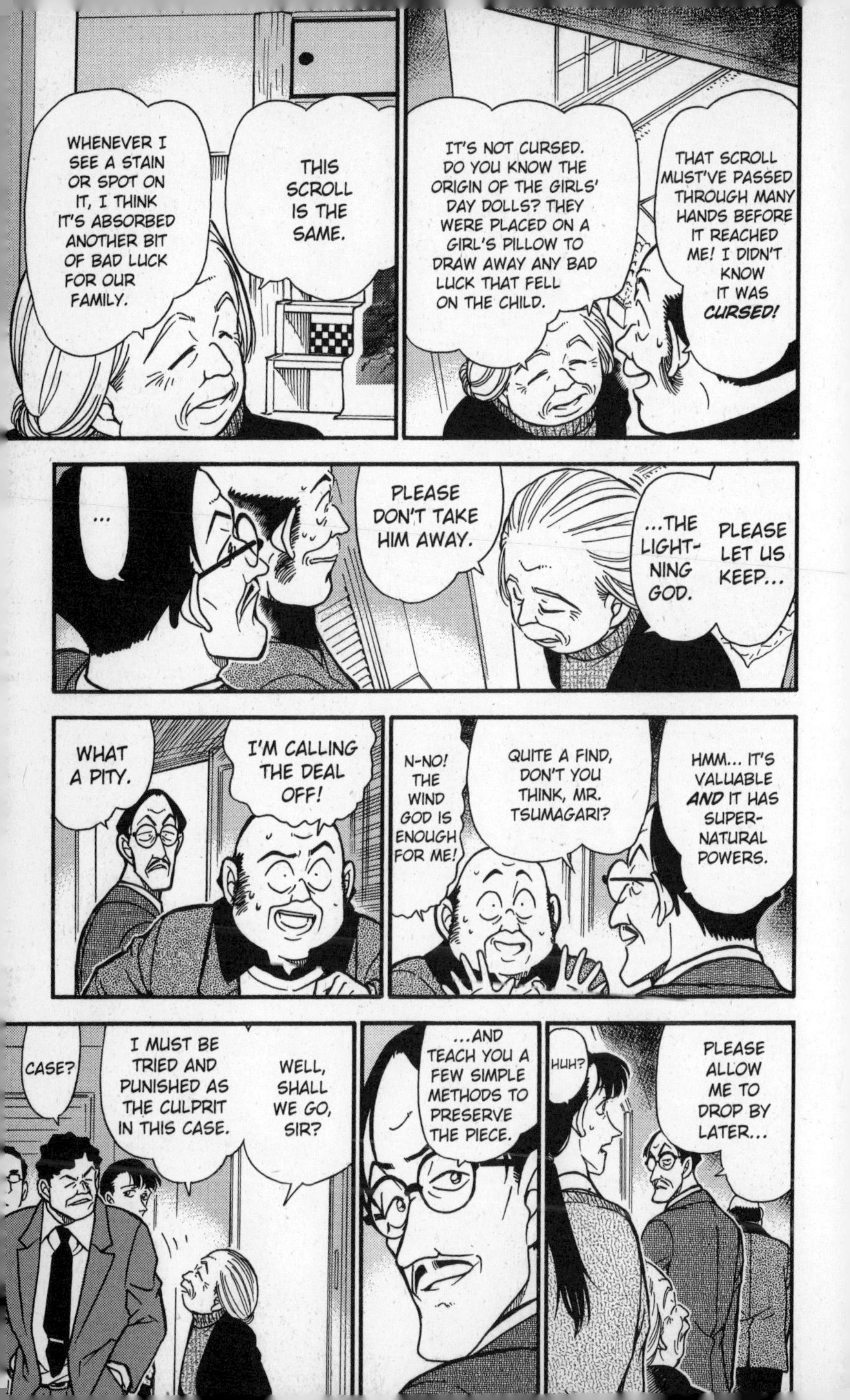
THAT SCROLL MUST'VE PASSED THROUGH MANY HANDS BEFORE IT REACHED ME! I DIDN'T KNOW IT WAS *CURSED!*
IT'S NOT CURSED. DO YOU KNOW THE ORIGIN OF THE GIRLS' DAY DOLLS? THEY WERE PLACED ON A GIRL'S PILLOW TO DRAW AWAY ANY BAD LUCK THAT FELL ON THE CHILD.
THIS SCROLL IS THE SAME.
WHENEVER I SEE A STAIN OR SPOT ON IT, I THINK IT'S ABSORBED ANOTHER BIT OF BAD LUCK FOR OUR FAMILY.
PLEASE LET US KEEP...
...THE LIGHTNING GOD.
PLEASE DON'T TAKE HIM AWAY.
...
HMM... IT'S VALUABLE ***AND*** IT HAS SUPERNATURAL POWERS.
QUITE A FIND, DON'T YOU THINK, MR. TSUMAGARI?
N-NO! THE WIND GOD IS ENOUGH FOR ME!
I'M CALLING THE DEAL OFF!
WHAT A PITY.
PLEASE ALLOW ME TO DROP BY LATER...
HUH?
...AND TEACH YOU A FEW SIMPLE METHODS TO PRESERVE THE PIECE.
WELL, SHALL WE GO, SIR?
I MUST BE TRIED AND PUNISHED AS THE CULPRIT IN THIS CASE.
CASE?

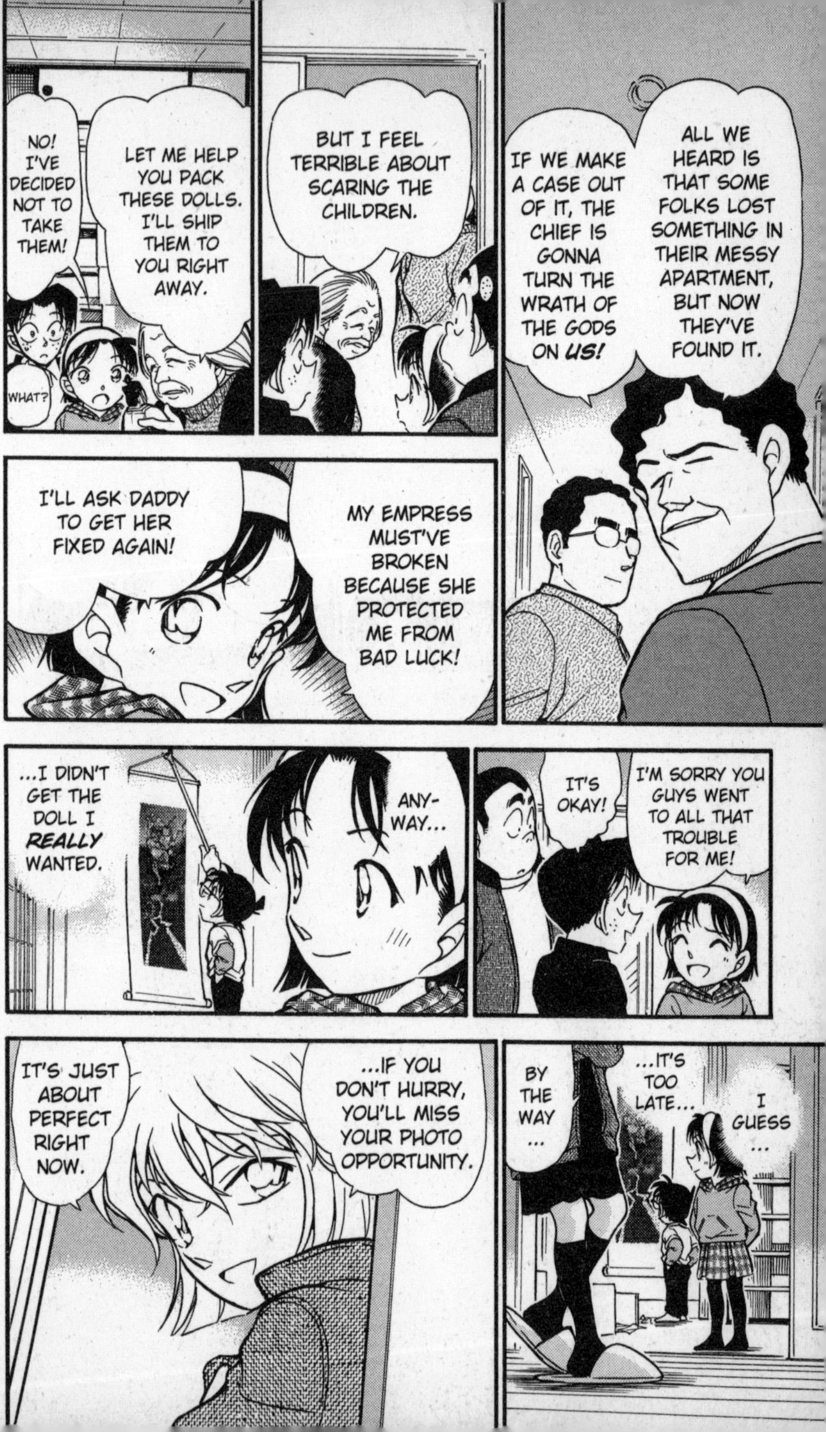
ALL WE HEARD IS THAT SOME FOLKS LOST SOMETHING IN THEIR MESSY APARTMENT, BUT NOW THEY'VE FOUND IT.
IF WE MAKE A CASE OUT OF IT, THE CHIEF IS GONNA TURN THE WRATH OF THE GODS ON *US!*
BUT I FEEL TERRIBLE ABOUT SCARING THE CHILDREN.
LET ME HELP YOU PACK THESE DOLLS. I'LL SHIP THEM TO YOU RIGHT AWAY.
NO! I'VE DECIDED NOT TO TAKE THEM!
WHAT?
MY EMPRESS MUST'VE BROKEN BECAUSE SHE PROTECTED ME FROM BAD LUCK!
I'LL ASK DADDY TO GET HER FIXED AGAIN!
I'M SORRY YOU GUYS WENT TO ALL THAT TROUBLE FOR ME!
IT'S OKAY!
ANY-WAY...
...I DIDN'T GET THE DOLL I *REALLY* WANTED.
...IT'S TOO LATE...
I GUESS...
BY THE WAY...
...IF YOU DON'T HURRY, YOU'LL MISS YOUR PHOTO OPPORTUNITY.
IT'S JUST ABOUT PERFECT RIGHT NOW.

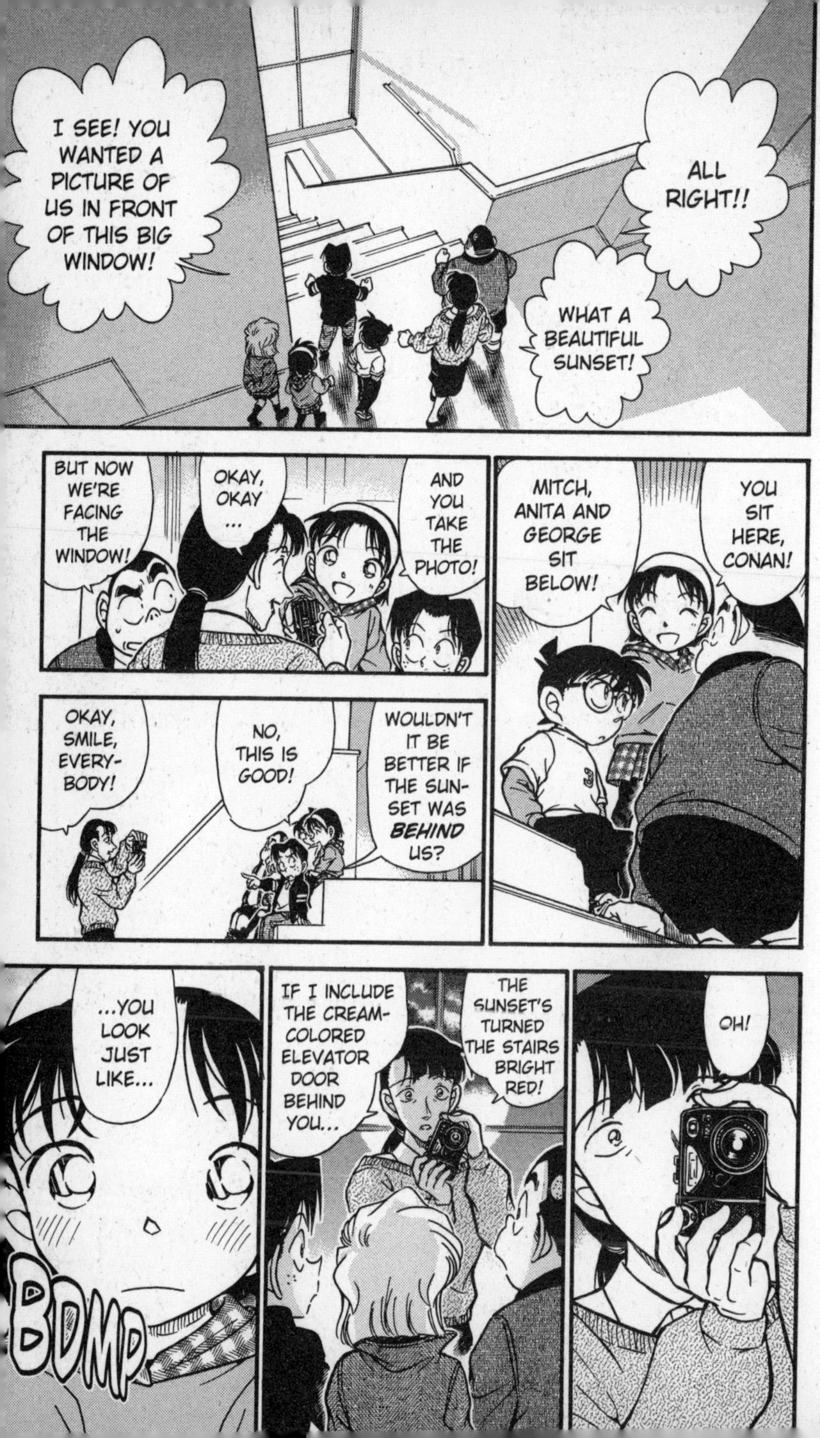
ALL RIGHT!!
WHAT A BEAUTIFUL SUNSET!
I SEE! YOU WANTED A PICTURE OF US IN FRONT OF THIS BIG WINDOW!
YOU SIT HERE, CONAN!
MITCH, ANITA AND GEORGE SIT BELOW!
AND YOU TAKE THE PHOTO!
OKAY, OKAY ...
BUT NOW WE'RE FACING THE WINDOW!
WOULDN'T IT BE BETTER IF THE SUNSET WAS *BEHIND* US?
NO, THIS IS GOOD!
OKAY, SMILE, EVERYBODY!
OH!
THE SUNSET'S TURNED THE STAIRS BRIGHT RED!
IF I INCLUDE THE CREAM-COLORED ELEVATOR DOOR BEHIND YOU...
...YOU LOOK JUST LIKE...
BDMP

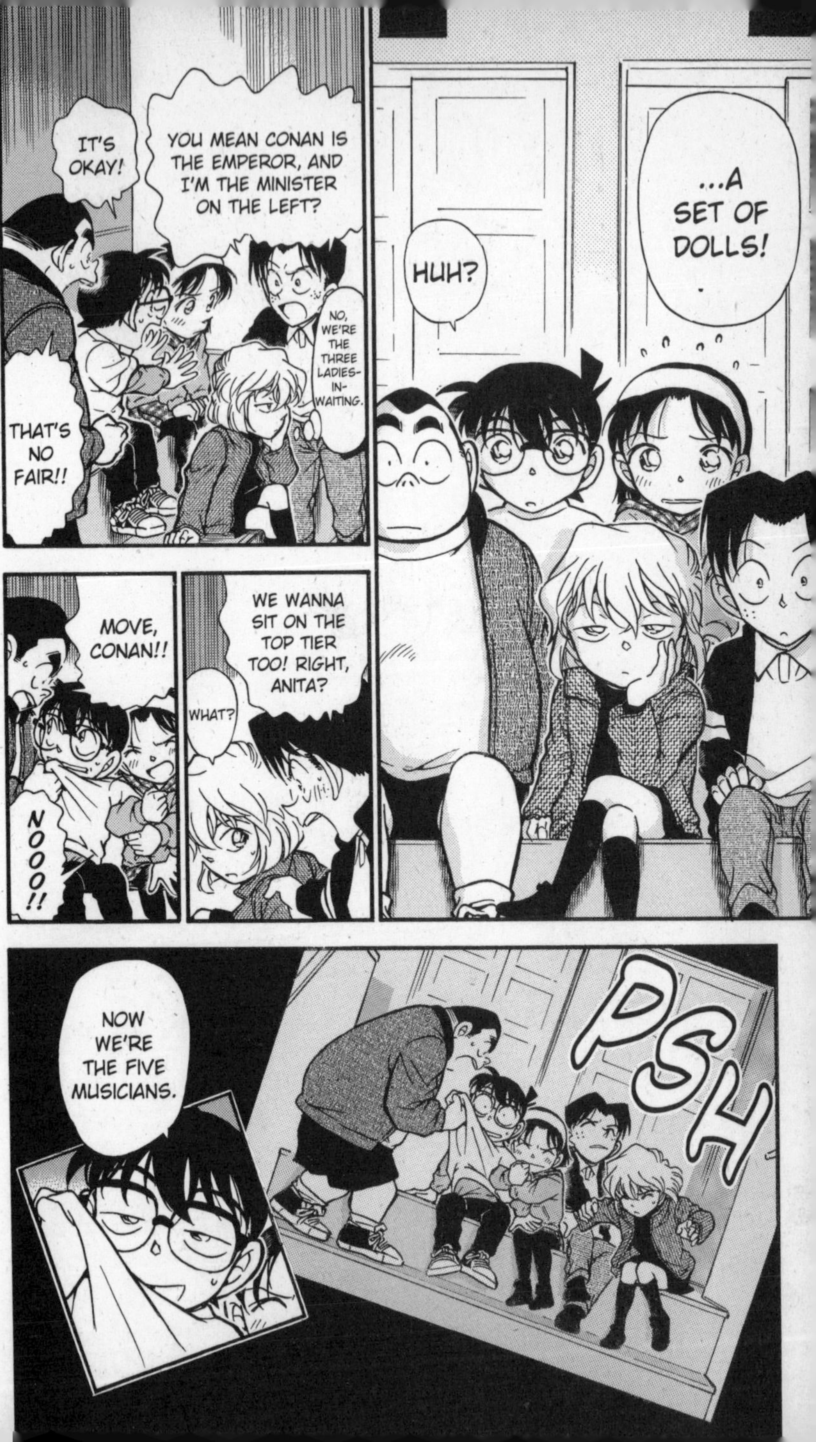
...A SET OF DOLLS!
HUH?
YOU MEAN CONAN IS THE EMPEROR, AND I'M THE MINISTER ON THE LEFT?
IT'S OKAY!
NO, WE'RE THE THREE LADIES-IN-WAITING.
THAT'S NO FAIR!!
WE WANNA SIT ON THE TOP TIER TOO! RIGHT, ANITA?
WHAT?
MOVE, CONAN!!
NOOOO!!
PSH
NOW WE'RE THE FIVE MUSICIANS.

FILE 5: TARNISHED HERO

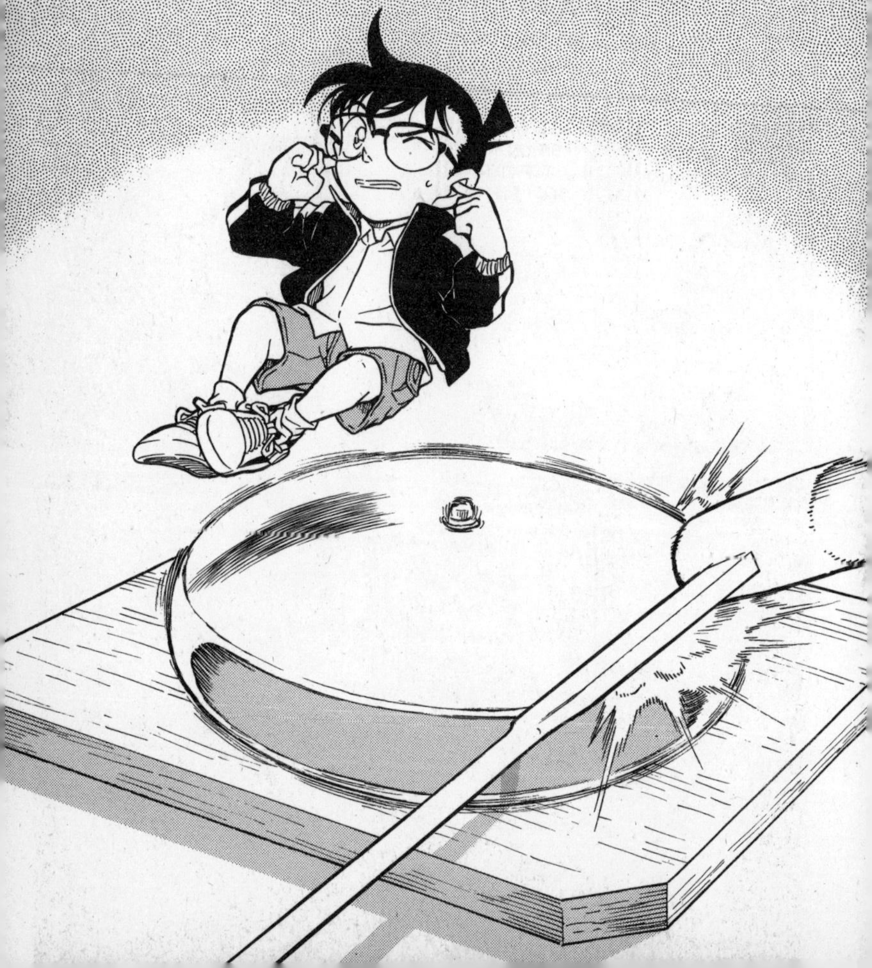

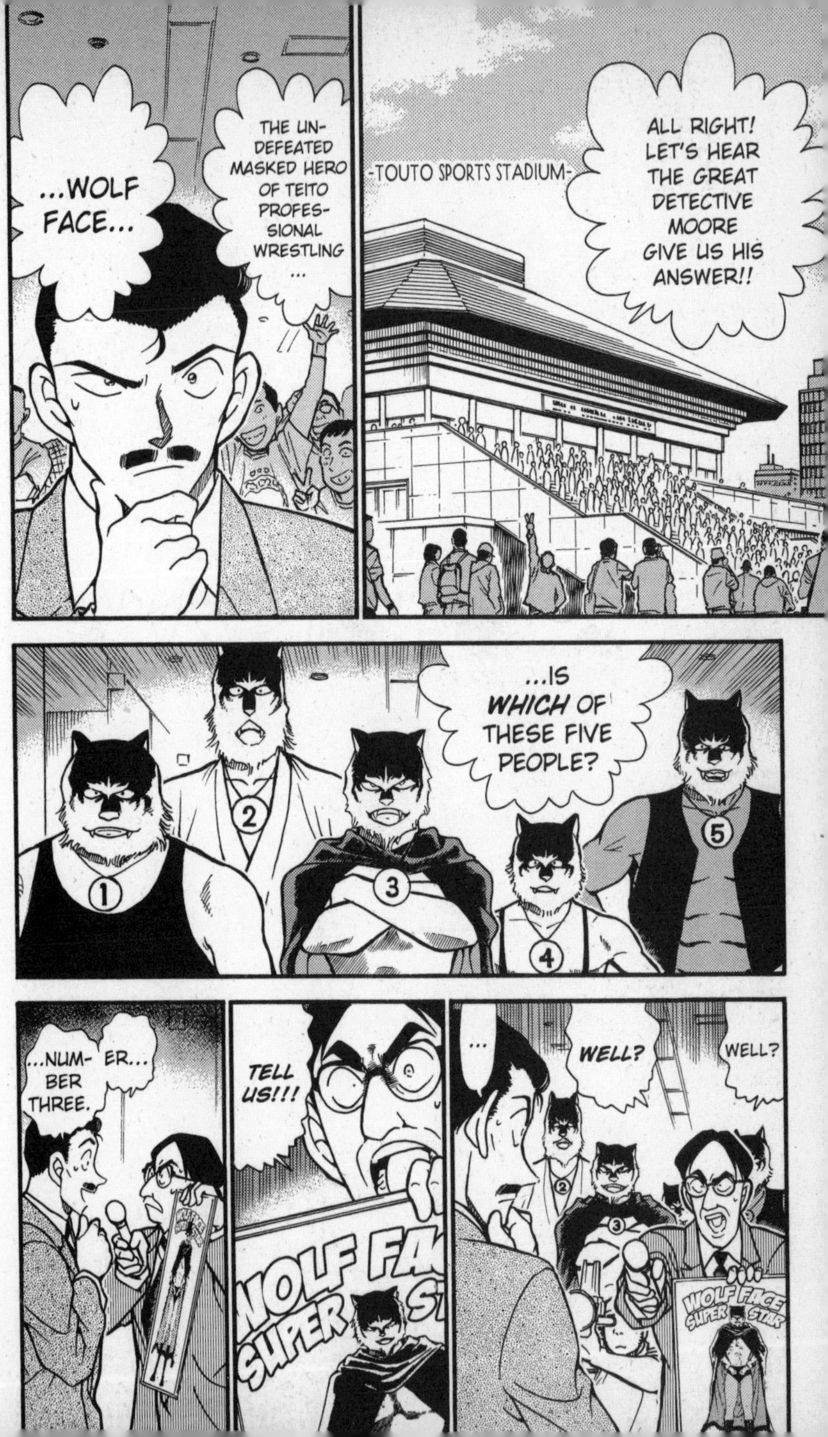
-TOUTO SPORTS STADIUM-
ALL RIGHT! LET'S HEAR THE GREAT DETECTIVE MOORE GIVE US HIS ANSWER!!
THE UN-DEFEATED MASKED HERO OF TEITO PROFES-SIONAL WRESTLING ...
...WOLF FACE...
...IS WHICH OF THESE FIVE PEOPLE?
WELL?
WELL?
...
WOLF FACE SUPER STAR
TELL US!!!
ER...
...NUM-BER THREE.

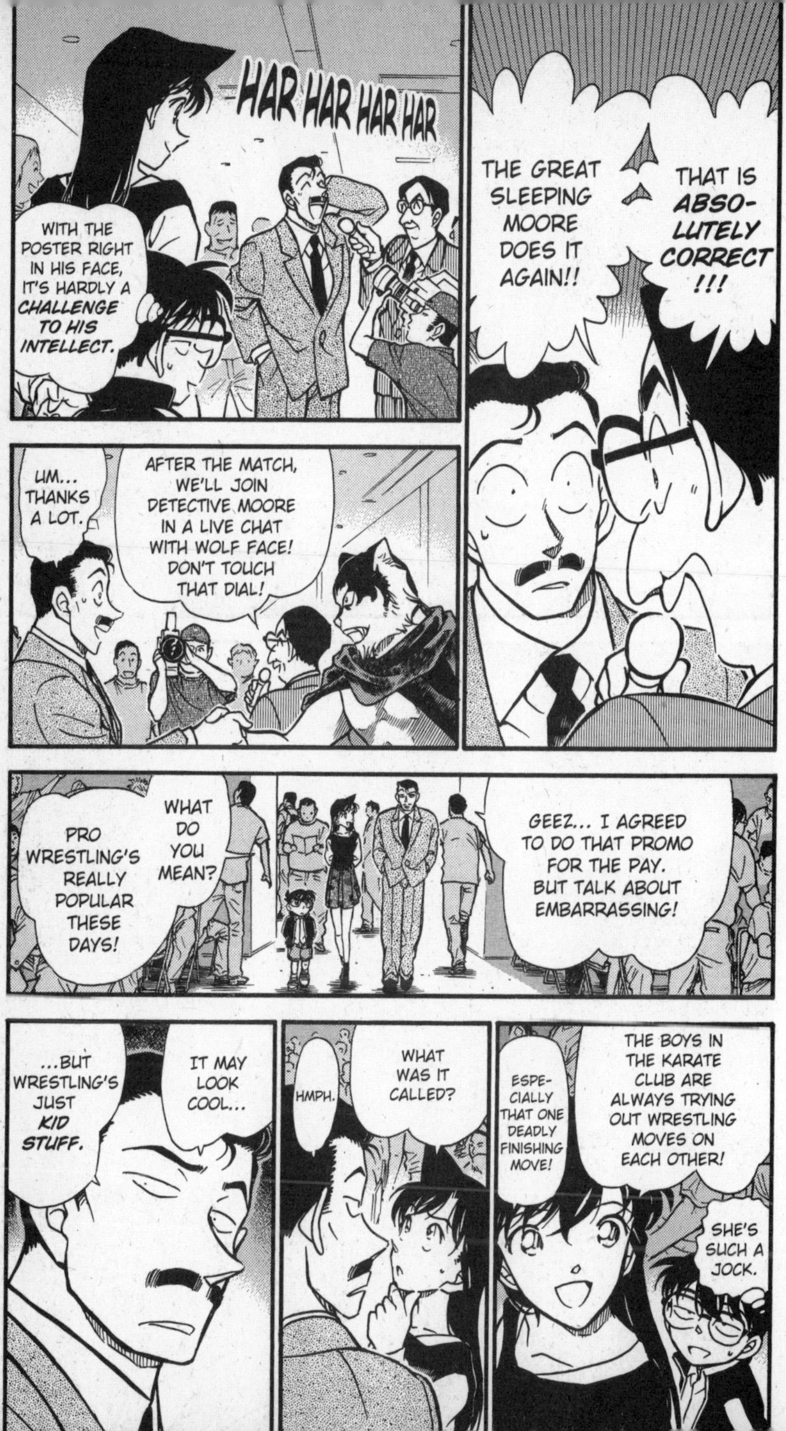
THAT IS ABSOLUTELY CORRECT!!!
THE GREAT SLEEPING MOORE DOES IT AGAIN!!
HAR HAR HAR HAR
WITH THE POSTER RIGHT IN HIS FACE, IT'S HARDLY A CHALLENGE TO HIS INTELLECT.
AFTER THE MATCH, WE'LL JOIN DETECTIVE MOORE IN A LIVE CHAT WITH WOLF FACE! DON'T TOUCH THAT DIAL!
UM... THANKS A LOT.
GEEZ... I AGREED TO DO THAT PROMO FOR THE PAY. BUT TALK ABOUT EMBARRASSING!
WHAT DO YOU MEAN?
PRO WRESTLING'S REALLY POPULAR THESE DAYS!
THE BOYS IN THE KARATE CLUB ARE ALWAYS TRYING OUT WRESTLING MOVES ON EACH OTHER!
ESPECIALLY THAT ONE DEADLY FINISHING MOVE!
SHE'S SUCH A JOCK.
WHAT WAS IT CALLED?
HMPH.
IT MAY LOOK COOL...
...BUT WRESTLING'S JUST KID STUFF.

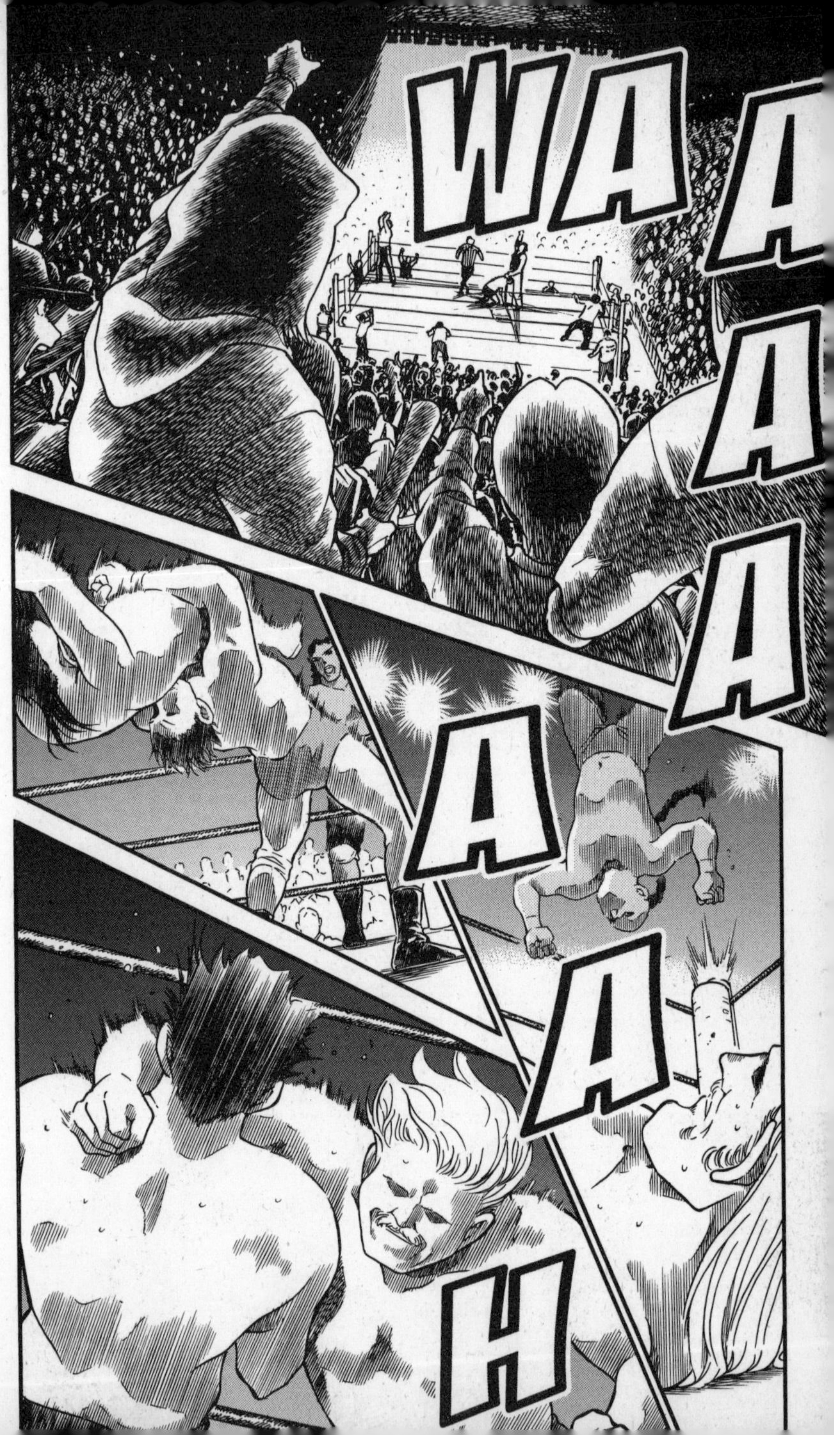
WAAAAAAH

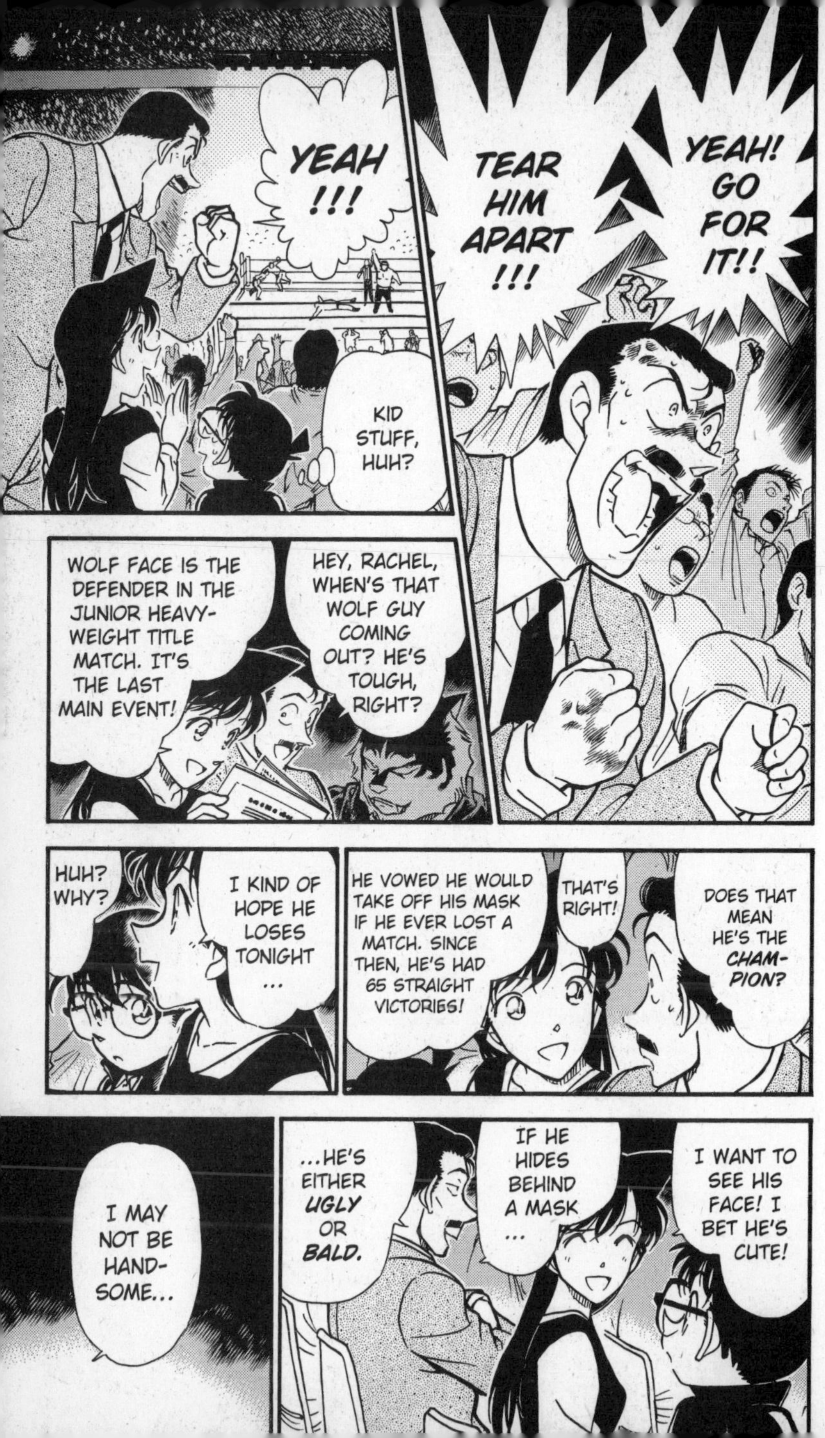
YEAH! GO FOR IT!!
TEAR HIM APART!!!
YEAH!!!
KID STUFF, HUH?
HEY, RACHEL, WHEN'S THAT WOLF GUY COMING OUT? HE'S TOUGH, RIGHT?
WOLF FACE IS THE DEFENDER IN THE JUNIOR HEAVY-WEIGHT TITLE MATCH. IT'S THE LAST MAIN EVENT!
DOES THAT MEAN HE'S THE CHAMPION?
THAT'S RIGHT!
HE VOWED HE WOULD TAKE OFF HIS MASK IF HE EVER LOST A MATCH. SINCE THEN, HE'S HAD 65 STRAIGHT VICTORIES!
I KIND OF HOPE HE LOSES TONIGHT...
HUH? WHY?
I WANT TO SEE HIS FACE! I BET HE'S CUTE!
IF HE HIDES BEHIND A MASK...
...HE'S EITHER UGLY OR BALD.
I MAY NOT BE HANDSOME...

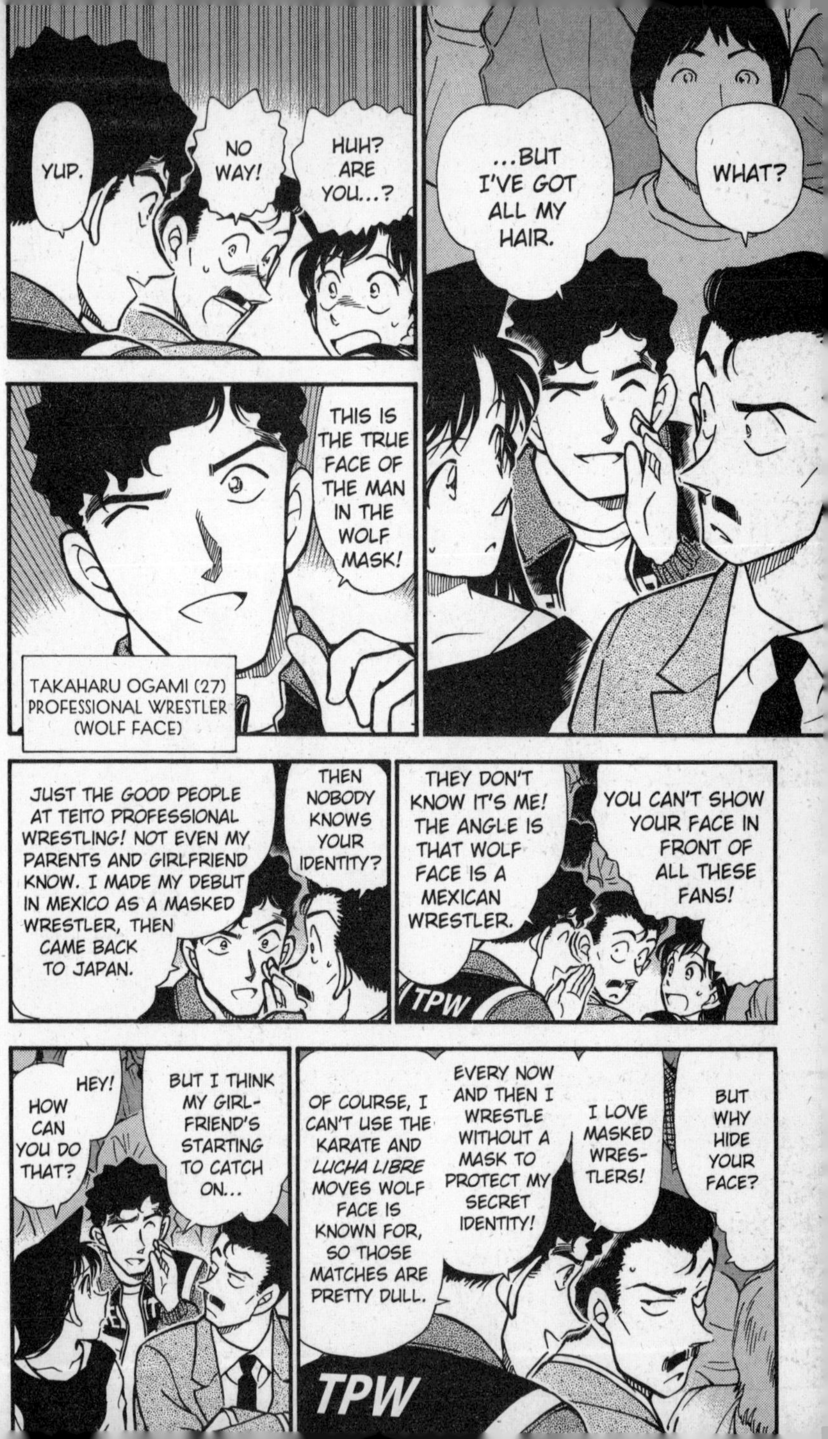
WHAT?
...BUT I'VE GOT ALL MY HAIR.
HUH? ARE YOU...?
NO WAY!
YUP.
THIS IS THE TRUE FACE OF THE MAN IN THE WOLF MASK!
TAKAHARU OGAMI (27) PROFESSIONAL WRESTLER (WOLF FACE)
YOU CAN'T SHOW YOUR FACE IN FRONT OF ALL THESE FANS!
THEY DON'T KNOW IT'S ME! THE ANGLE IS THAT WOLF FACE IS A MEXICAN WRESTLER.
TPW
THEN NOBODY KNOWS YOUR IDENTITY?
JUST THE GOOD PEOPLE AT TEITO PROFESSIONAL WRESTLING! NOT EVEN MY PARENTS AND GIRLFRIEND KNOW. I MADE MY DEBUT IN MEXICO AS A MASKED WRESTLER, THEN CAME BACK TO JAPAN.
BUT WHY HIDE YOUR FACE?
I LOVE MASKED WRES-TLERS!
EVERY NOW AND THEN I WRESTLE WITHOUT A MASK TO PROTECT MY SECRET IDENTITY!
OF COURSE, I CAN'T USE THE KARATE AND LUCHA LIBRE MOVES WOLF FACE IS KNOWN FOR, SO THOSE MATCHES ARE PRETTY DULL.
TPW
BUT I THINK MY GIRL-FRIEND'S STARTING TO CATCH ON...
HEY! HOW CAN YOU DO THAT?

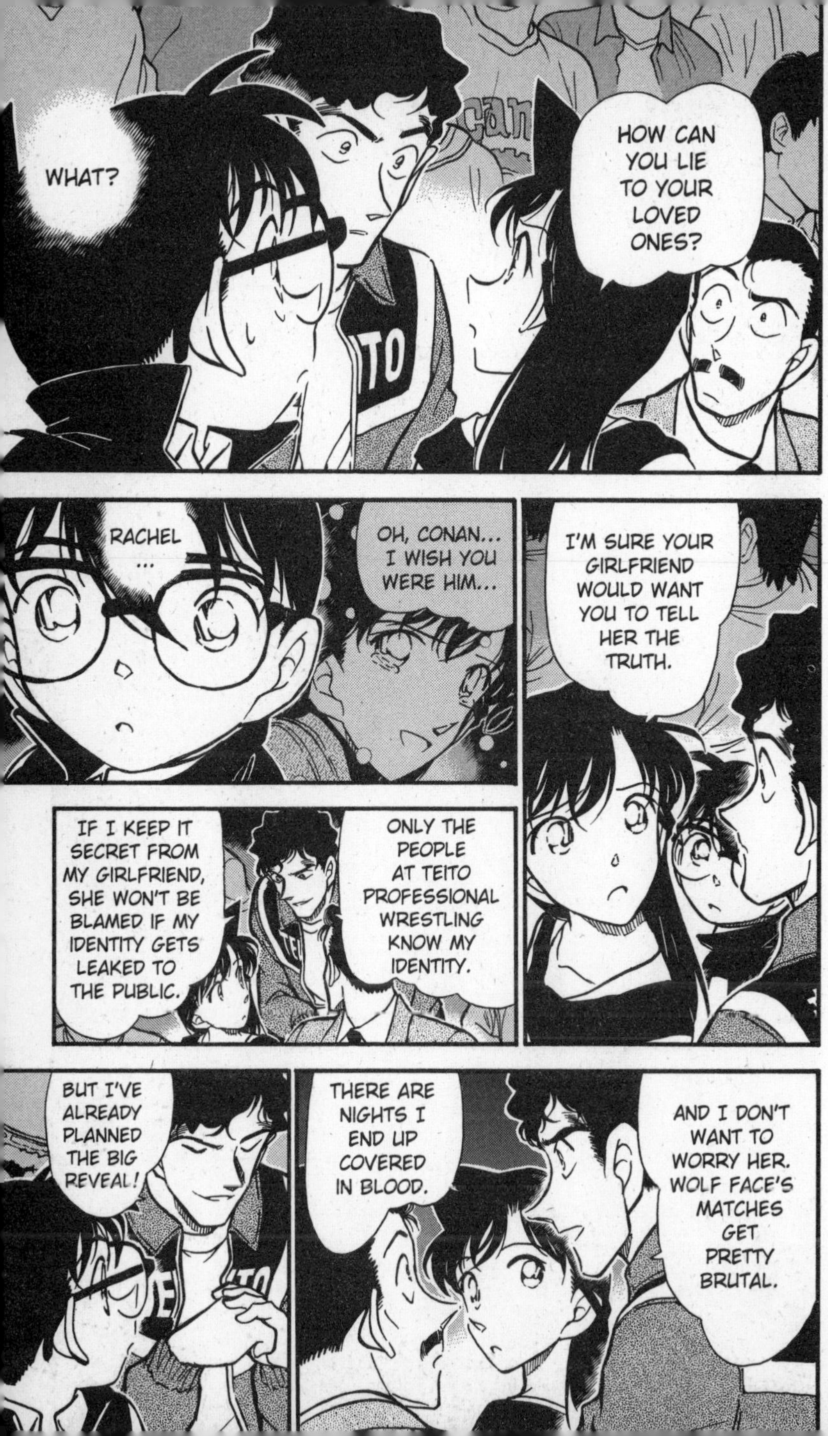
HOW CAN YOU LIE TO YOUR LOVED ONES?
WHAT?
I'M SURE YOUR GIRLFRIEND WOULD WANT YOU TO TELL HER THE TRUTH.
OH, CONAN... I WISH YOU WERE HIM...
RACHEL ...
ONLY THE PEOPLE AT TEITO PROFESSIONAL WRESTLING KNOW MY IDENTITY.
IF I KEEP IT SECRET FROM MY GIRLFRIEND, SHE WON'T BE BLAMED IF MY IDENTITY GETS LEAKED TO THE PUBLIC.
AND I DON'T WANT TO WORRY HER. WOLF FACE'S MATCHES GET PRETTY BRUTAL.
THERE ARE NIGHTS I END UP COVERED IN BLOOD.
BUT I'VE ALREADY PLANNED THE BIG REVEAL!

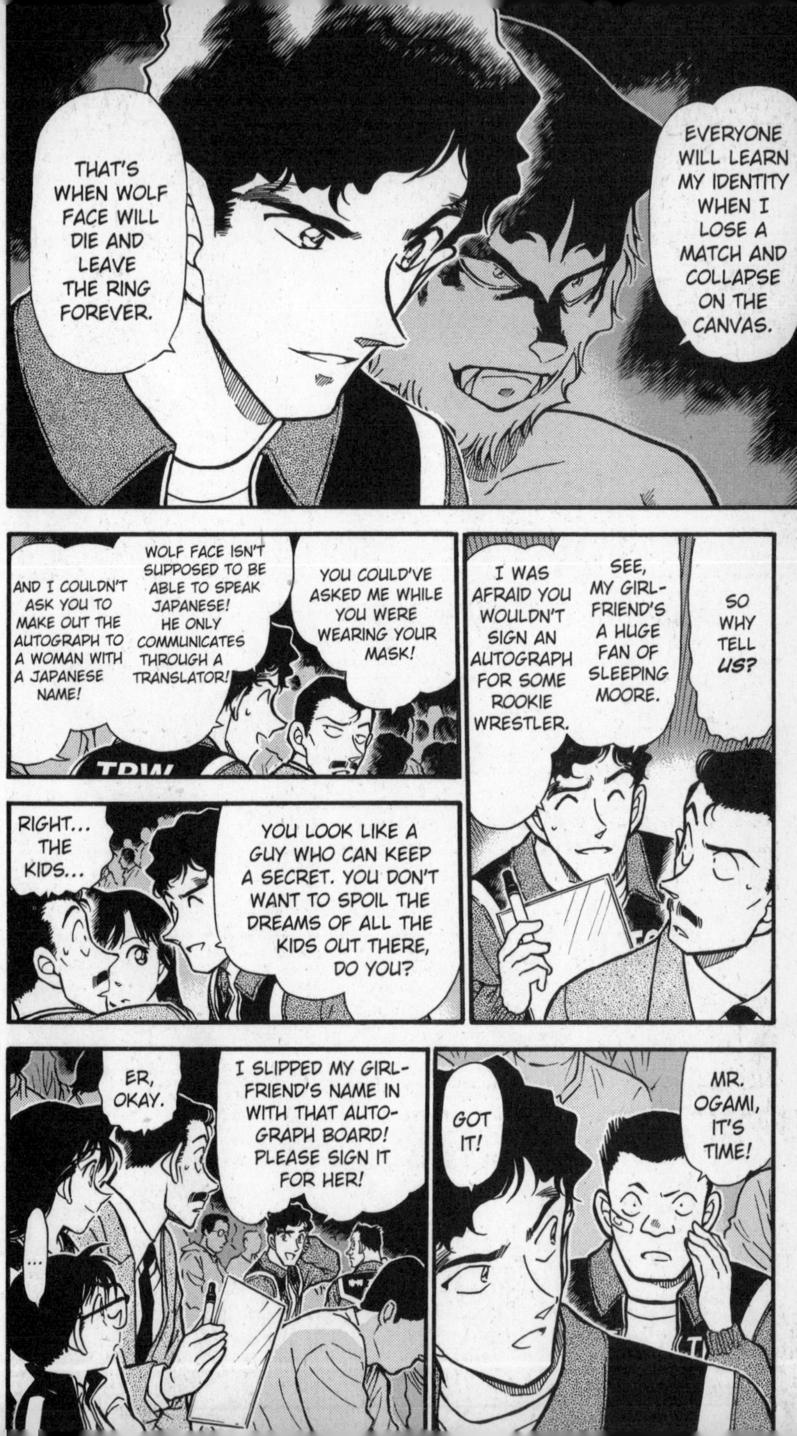
EVERYONE WILL LEARN MY IDENTITY WHEN I LOSE A MATCH AND COLLAPSE ON THE CANVAS.
THAT'S WHEN WOLF FACE WILL DIE AND LEAVE THE RING FOREVER.
SO WHY TELL *US?*
SEE, MY GIRL-FRIEND'S A HUGE FAN OF SLEEPING MOORE.
I WAS AFRAID YOU WOULDN'T SIGN AN AUTOGRAPH FOR SOME ROOKIE WRESTLER.
YOU COULD'VE ASKED ME WHILE YOU WERE WEARING YOUR MASK!
WOLF FACE ISN'T SUPPOSED TO BE ABLE TO SPEAK JAPANESE! HE ONLY COMMUNICATES THROUGH A TRANSLATOR!
AND I COULDN'T ASK YOU TO MAKE OUT THE AUTOGRAPH TO A WOMAN WITH A JAPANESE NAME!
YOU LOOK LIKE A GUY WHO CAN KEEP A SECRET. YOU DON'T WANT TO SPOIL THE DREAMS OF ALL THE KIDS OUT THERE, DO YOU?
RIGHT... THE KIDS...
MR. OGAMI, IT'S TIME!
GOT IT!
I SLIPPED MY GIRL-FRIEND'S NAME IN WITH THAT AUTO-GRAPH BOARD! PLEASE SIGN IT FOR HER!
ER, OKAY.
...

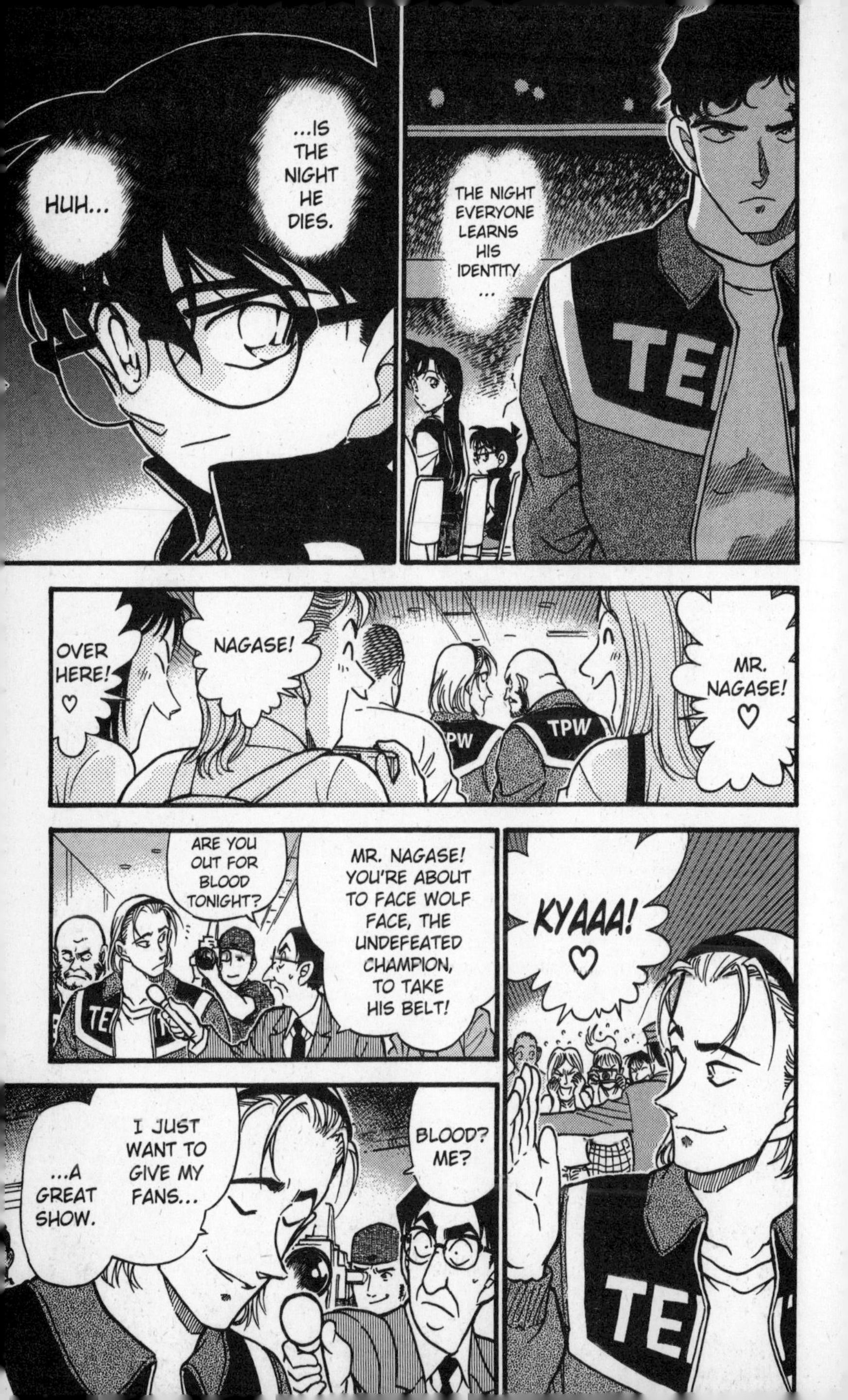
THE NIGHT EVERYONE LEARNS HIS IDENTITY ...
...IS THE NIGHT HE DIES.
HUH...
MR. NAGASE! ♡
NAGASE!
OVER HERE! ♡
KYAAA! ♡
MR. NAGASE! YOU'RE ABOUT TO FACE WOLF FACE, THE UNDEFEATED CHAMPION, TO TAKE HIS BELT!
ARE YOU OUT FOR BLOOD TONIGHT?
BLOOD? ME?
I JUST WANT TO GIVE MY FANS...
...A GREAT SHOW.

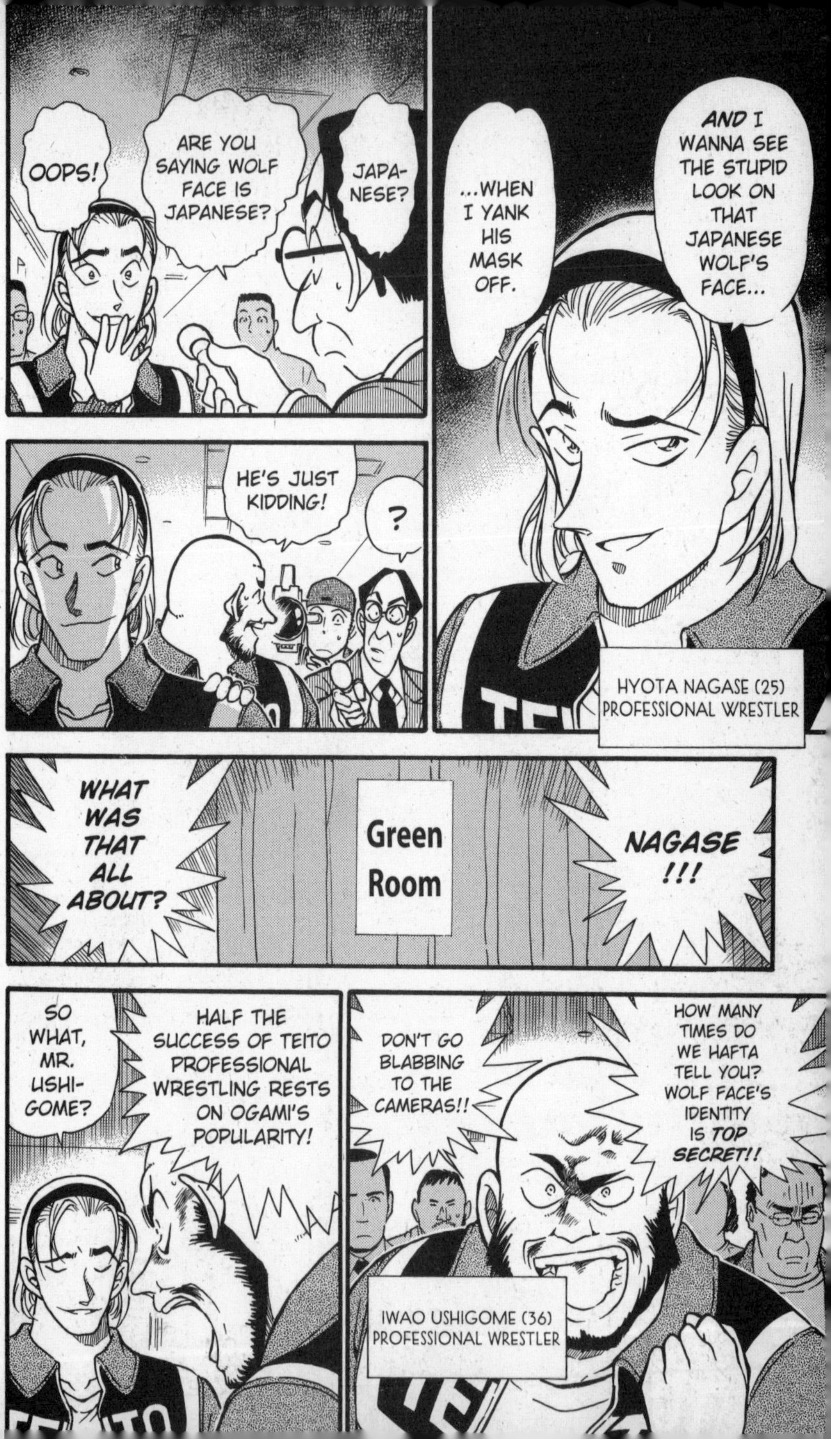
AND I WANNA SEE THE STUPID LOOK ON THAT JAPANESE WOLF'S FACE...
...WHEN I YANK HIS MASK OFF.
HYOTA NAGASE (25) PROFESSIONAL WRESTLER
JAPA-NESE?
ARE YOU SAYING WOLF FACE IS JAPANESE?
OOPS!
HE'S JUST KIDDING!
?
NAGASE!!!
Green Room
WHAT WAS THAT ALL ABOUT?
HOW MANY TIMES DO WE HAFTA TELL YOU? WOLF FACE'S IDENTITY IS TOP SECRET!!
DON'T GO BLABBING TO THE CAMERAS!!
IWAO USHIGOME (36) PROFESSIONAL WRESTLER
HALF THE SUCCESS OF TEITO PROFESSIONAL WRESTLING RESTS ON OGAMI'S POPULARITY!
SO WHAT, MR. USHI-GOME?

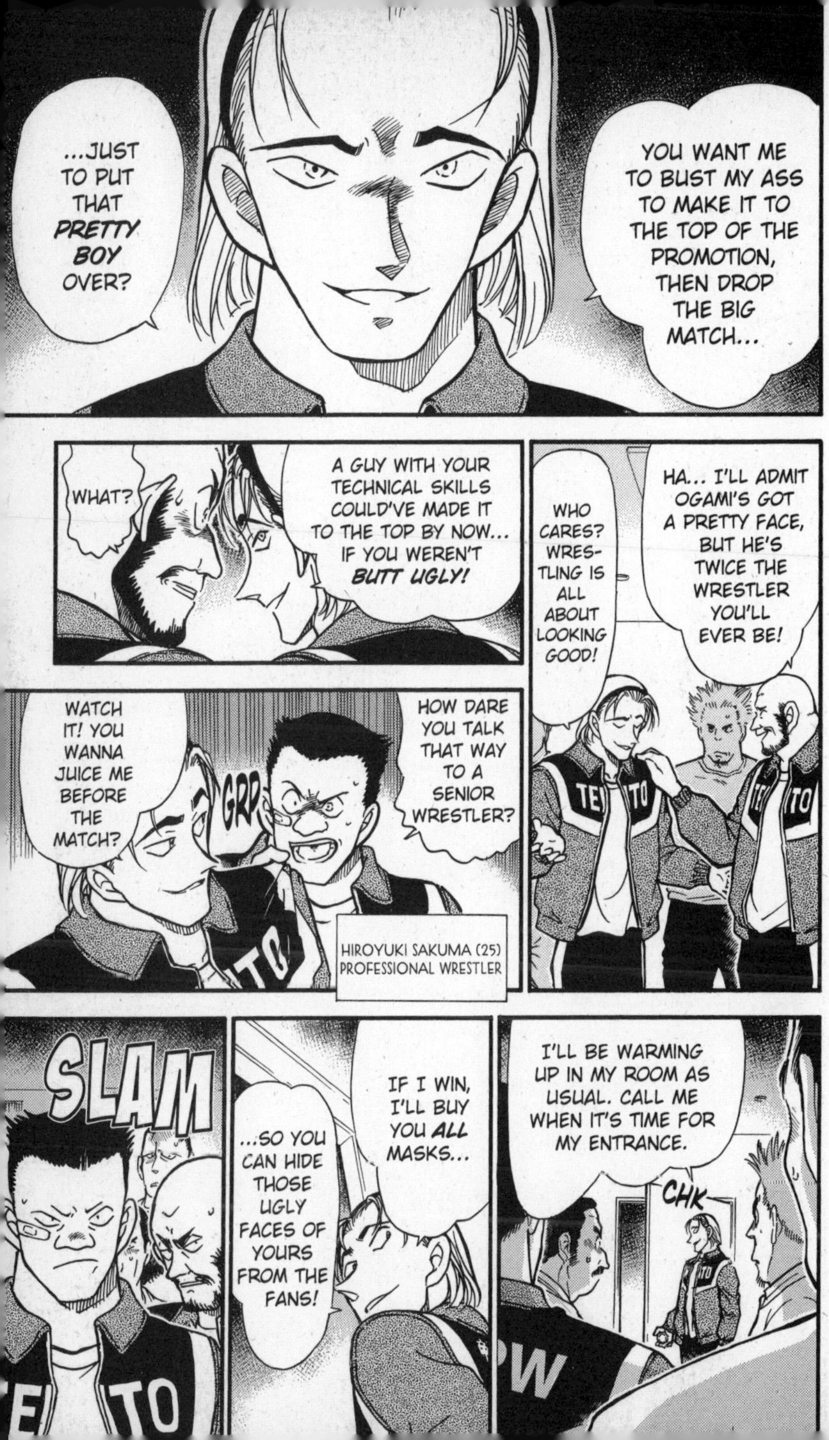
YOU WANT ME TO BUST MY ASS TO MAKE IT TO THE TOP OF THE PROMOTION, THEN DROP THE BIG MATCH...
...JUST TO PUT THAT *PRETTY BOY* OVER?
HA... I'LL ADMIT OGAMI'S GOT A PRETTY FACE, BUT HE'S TWICE THE WRESTLER YOU'LL EVER BE!
WHO CARES? WRES-TLING IS ALL ABOUT LOOKING GOOD!
A GUY WITH YOUR TECHNICAL SKILLS COULD'VE MADE IT TO THE TOP BY NOW... IF YOU WEREN'T *BUTT UGLY!*
WHAT?
HOW DARE YOU TALK THAT WAY TO A SENIOR WRESTLER?
GRP
WATCH IT! YOU WANNA JUICE ME BEFORE THE MATCH?
HIROYUKI SAKUMA (25) PROFESSIONAL WRESTLER
I'LL BE WARMING UP IN MY ROOM AS USUAL. CALL ME WHEN IT'S TIME FOR MY ENTRANCE.
CHK
IF I WIN, I'LL BUY YOU *ALL* MASKS...
...SO YOU CAN HIDE THOSE UGLY FACES OF YOURS FROM THE FANS!
SLAM

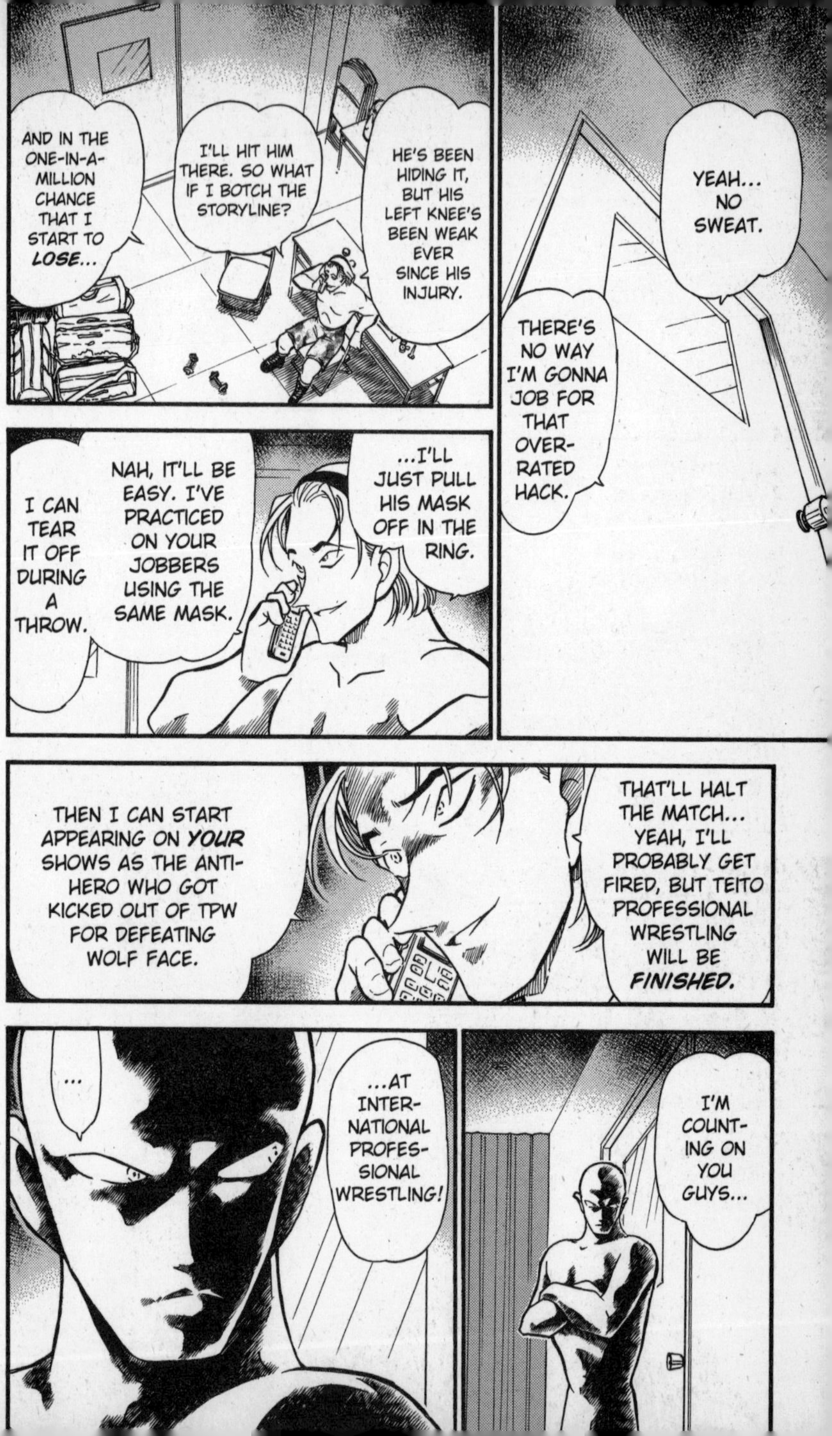
YEAH... NO SWEAT.
THERE'S NO WAY I'M GONNA JOB FOR THAT OVER-RATED HACK.
HE'S BEEN HIDING IT, BUT HIS LEFT KNEE'S BEEN WEAK EVER SINCE HIS INJURY.
I'LL HIT HIM THERE. SO WHAT IF I BOTCH THE STORYLINE?
AND IN THE ONE-IN-A-MILLION CHANCE THAT I START TO *LOSE*...
...I'LL JUST PULL HIS MASK OFF IN THE RING.
NAH, IT'LL BE EASY. I'VE PRACTICED ON YOUR JOBBERS USING THE SAME MASK.
I CAN TEAR IT OFF DURING A THROW.
THAT'LL HALT THE MATCH... YEAH, I'LL PROBABLY GET FIRED, BUT TEITO PROFESSIONAL WRESTLING WILL BE ***FINISHED.***
THEN I CAN START APPEARING ON ***YOUR*** SHOWS AS THE ANTI-HERO WHO GOT KICKED OUT OF TPW FOR DEFEATING WOLF FACE.
I'M COUNTING ON YOU GUYS...
...AT INTERNATIONAL PROFESSIONAL WRESTLING!
...

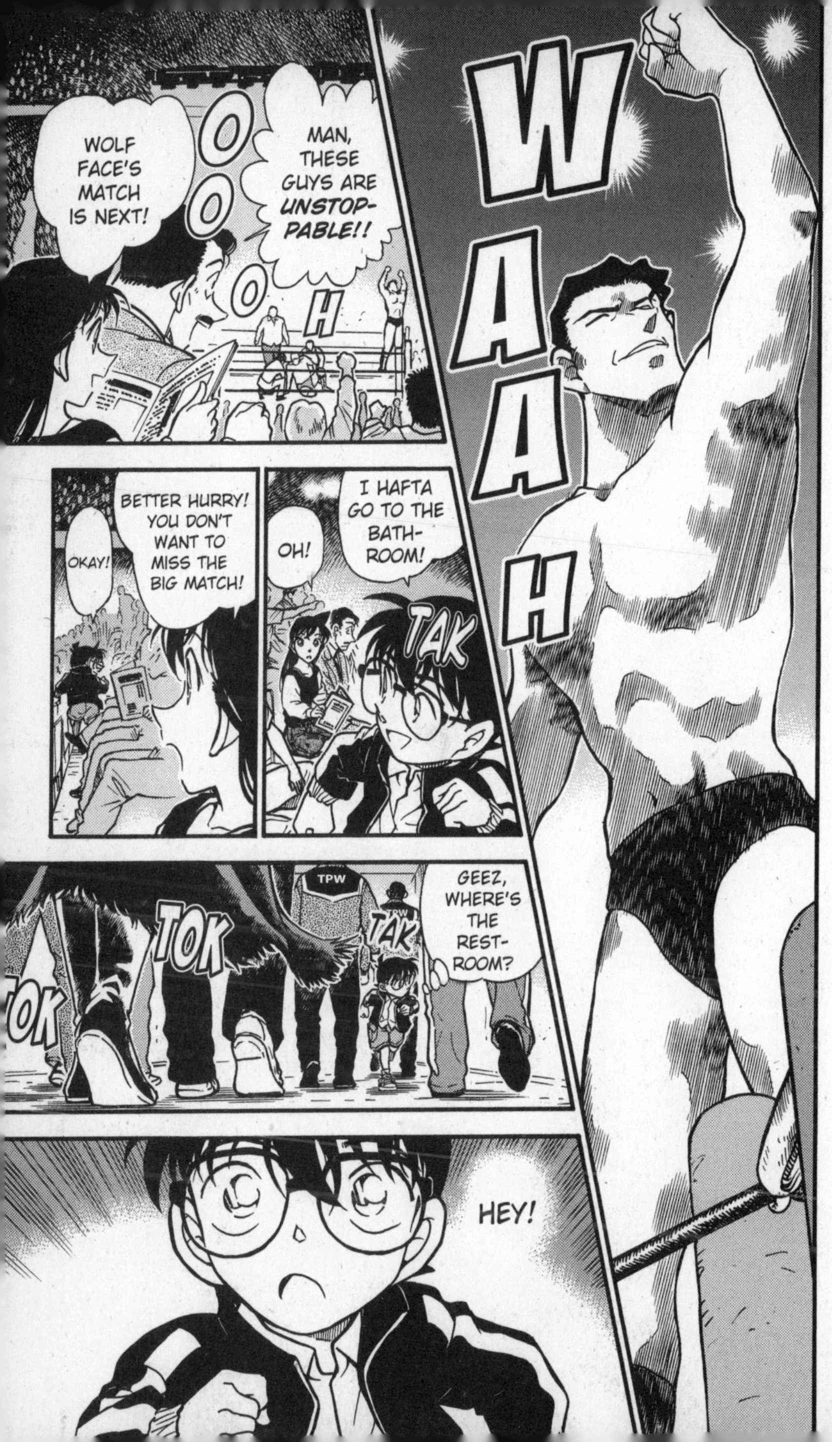
WAAAH
MAN, THESE GUYS ARE *UNSTOPPABLE!!*
OOOH
WOLF FACE'S MATCH IS NEXT!
I HAFTA GO TO THE BATHROOM!
OH!
TAK
BETTER HURRY! YOU DON'T WANT TO MISS THE BIG MATCH!
OKAY!
GEEZ, WHERE'S THE RESTROOM?
TAK
TOK
TOK
HEY!

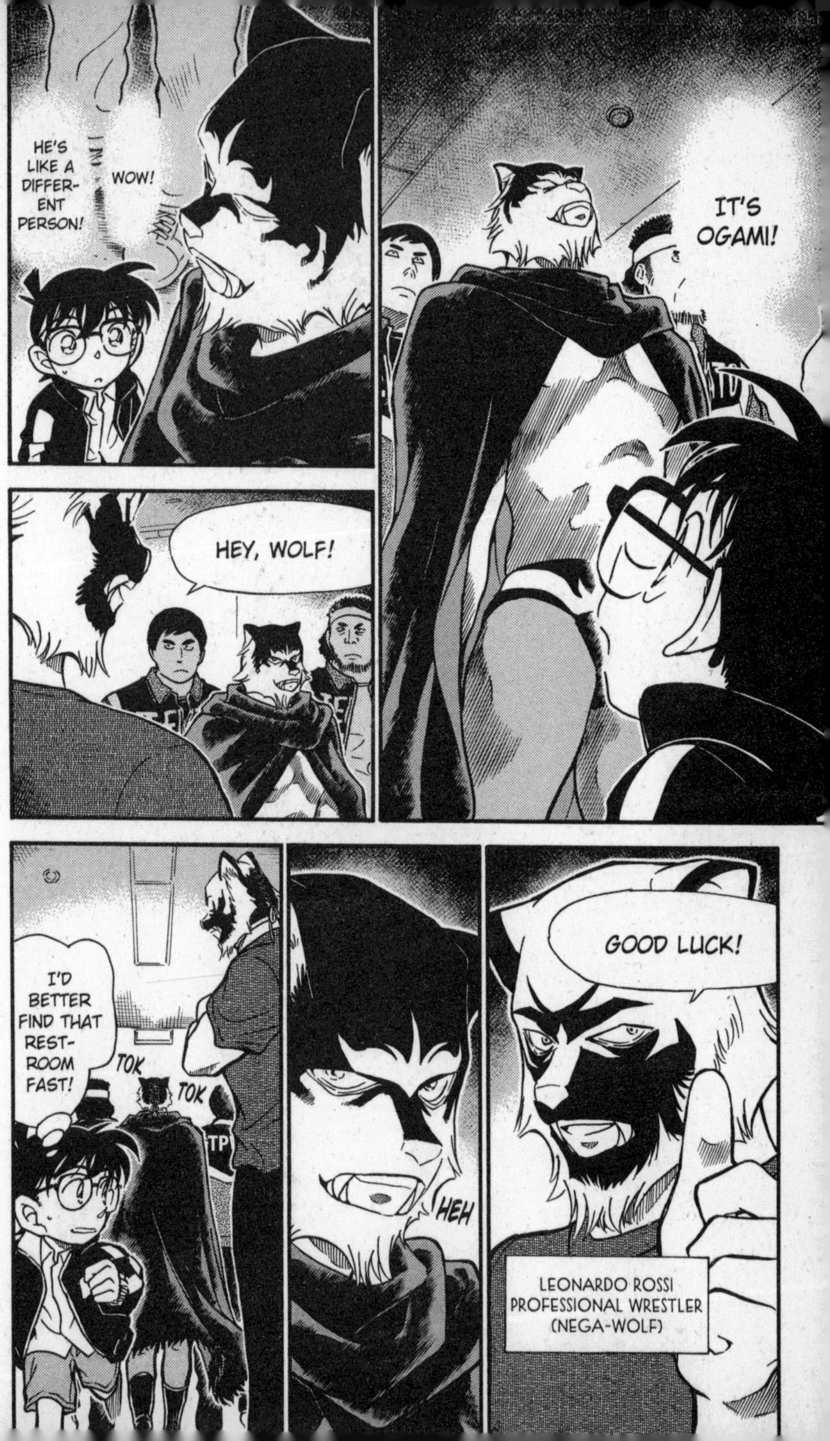

IT'S OGAMI!
WOW!
HE'S LIKE A DIFFER-ENT PERSON!
HEY, WOLF!
GOOD LUCK!
LEONARDO ROSSI
PROFESSIONAL WRESTLER
(NEGA-WOLF)
HEH
I'D BETTER FIND THAT REST-ROOM FAST!
TOK
TOK

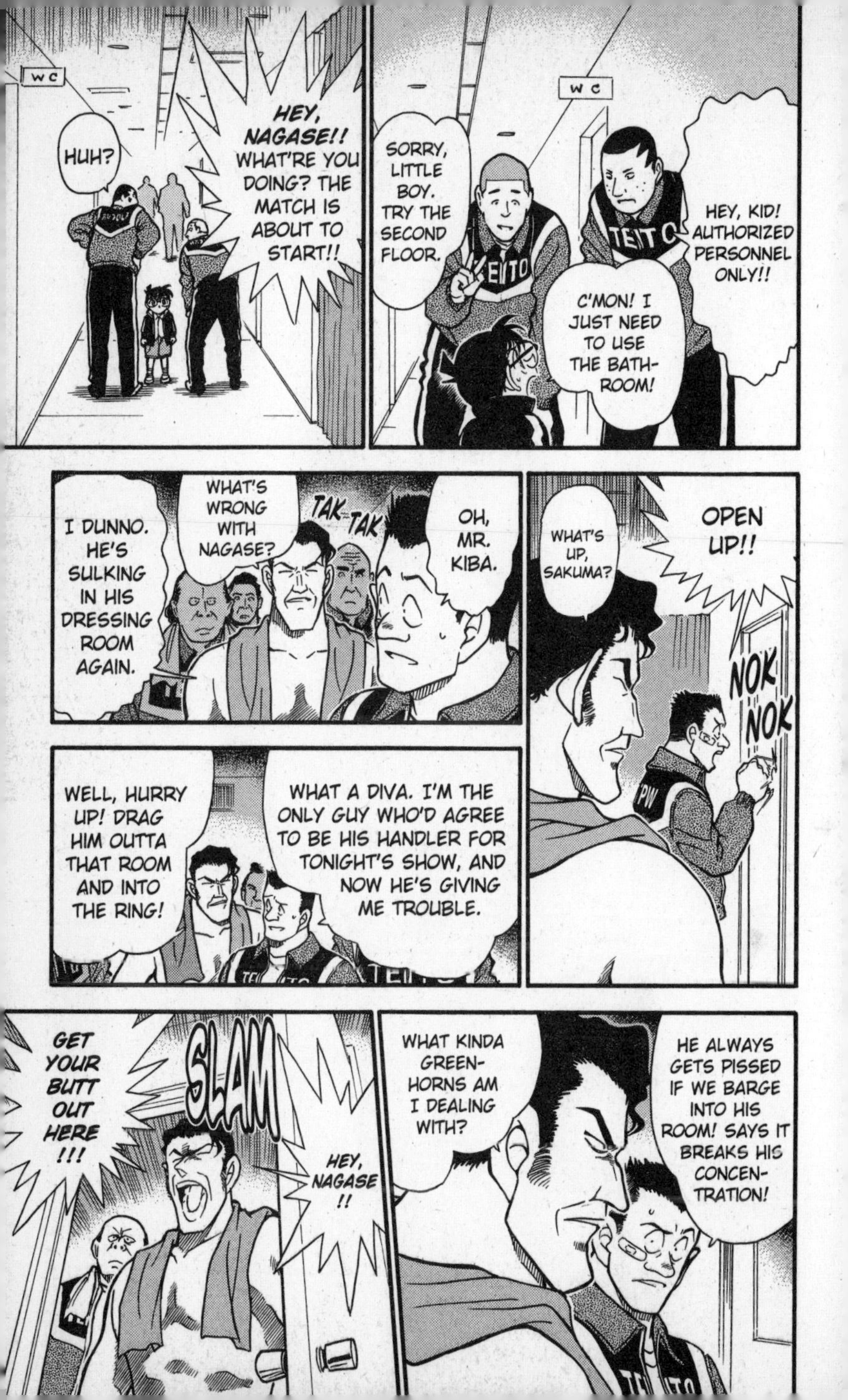
W C
HEY, KID! AUTHORIZED PERSONNEL ONLY!!
SORRY, LITTLE BOY. TRY THE SECOND FLOOR.
C'MON! I JUST NEED TO USE THE BATHROOM!
W C
HEY, NAGASE!! WHAT'RE YOU DOING? THE MATCH IS ABOUT TO START!!
HUH?
OPEN UP!!
WHAT'S UP, SAKUMA?
NOK NOK
OH, MR. KIBA.
TAK TAK
WHAT'S WRONG WITH NAGASE?
I DUNNO. HE'S SULKING IN HIS DRESSING ROOM AGAIN.
WHAT A DIVA. I'M THE ONLY GUY WHO'D AGREE TO BE HIS HANDLER FOR TONIGHT'S SHOW, AND NOW HE'S GIVING ME TROUBLE.
WELL, HURRY UP! DRAG HIM OUTTA THAT ROOM AND INTO THE RING!
HE ALWAYS GETS PISSED IF WE BARGE INTO HIS ROOM! SAYS IT BREAKS HIS CONCEN-TRATION!
WHAT KINDA GREEN-HORNS AM I DEALING WITH?
HEY, NAGASE!!
SLAM
GET YOUR BUTT OUT HERE!!!

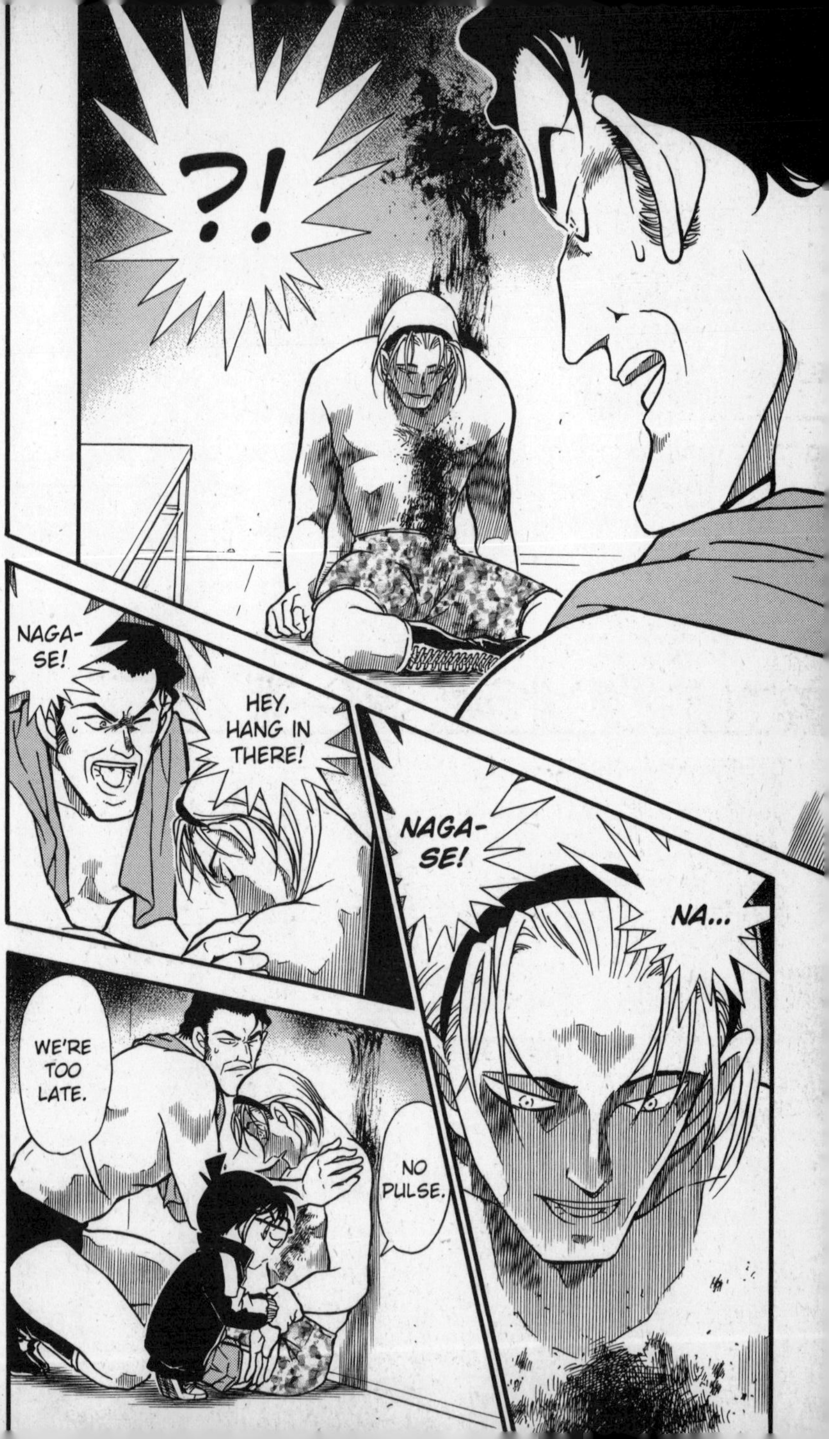
?!
NAGA-SE!
NA...
NAGA-SE!
HEY, HANG IN THERE!
NO PULSE.
WE'RE TOO LATE.

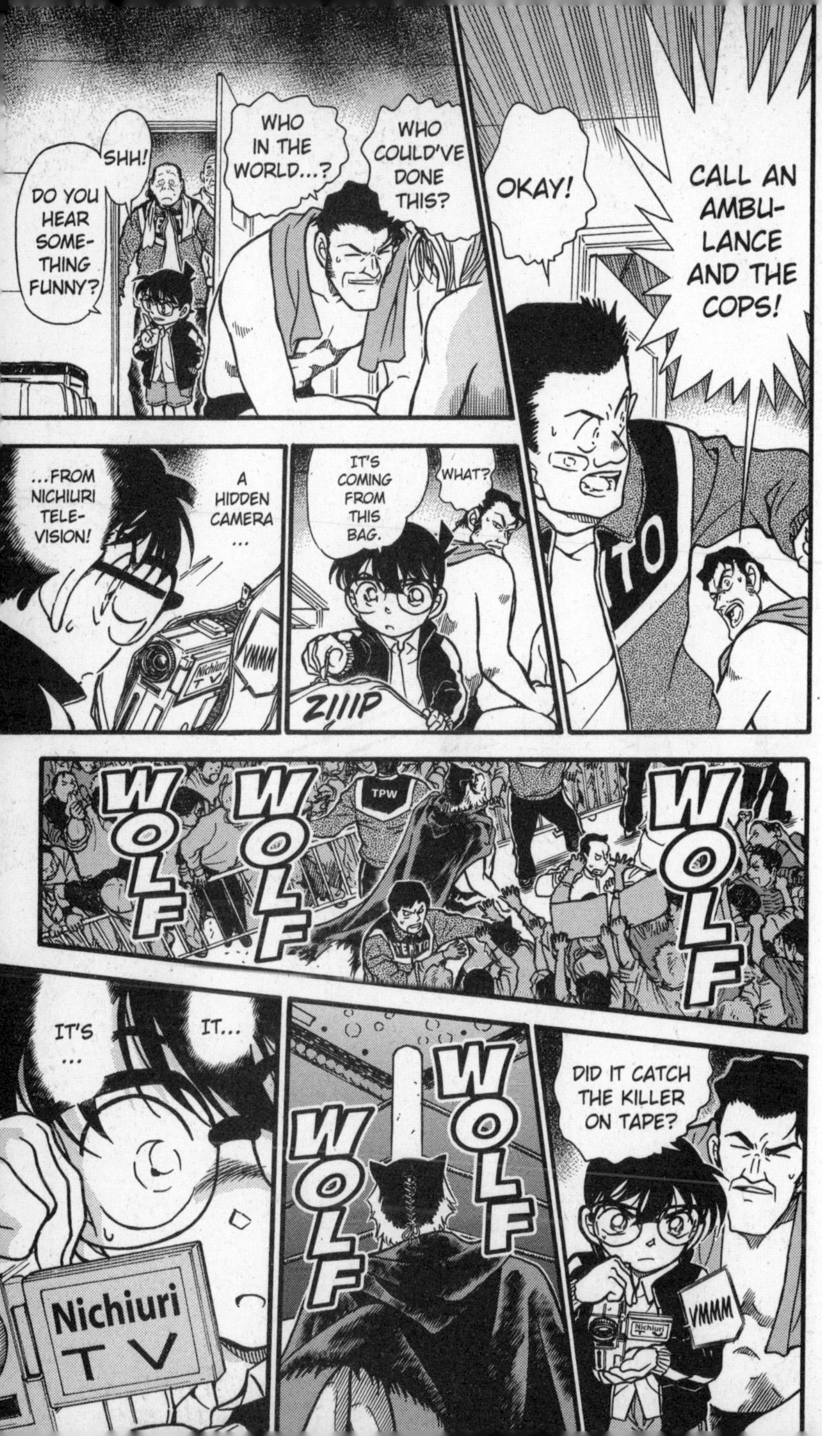
CALL AN AMBULANCE AND THE COPS!
OKAY!
WHO COULD'VE DONE THIS?
WHO IN THE WORLD...?
SHH!
DO YOU HEAR SOMETHING FUNNY?
TO
WHAT?
IT'S COMING FROM THIS BAG.
ZIIIP
A HIDDEN CAMERA...
...FROM NICHIURI TELEVISION!
VMMM
Nichiuri TV
WOLF
TPW
WOLF
WOLF
DID IT CATCH THE KILLER ON TAPE?
VMMM
Nichiuri
WOLF
WOLF
IT...
IT'S...
Nichiuri TV

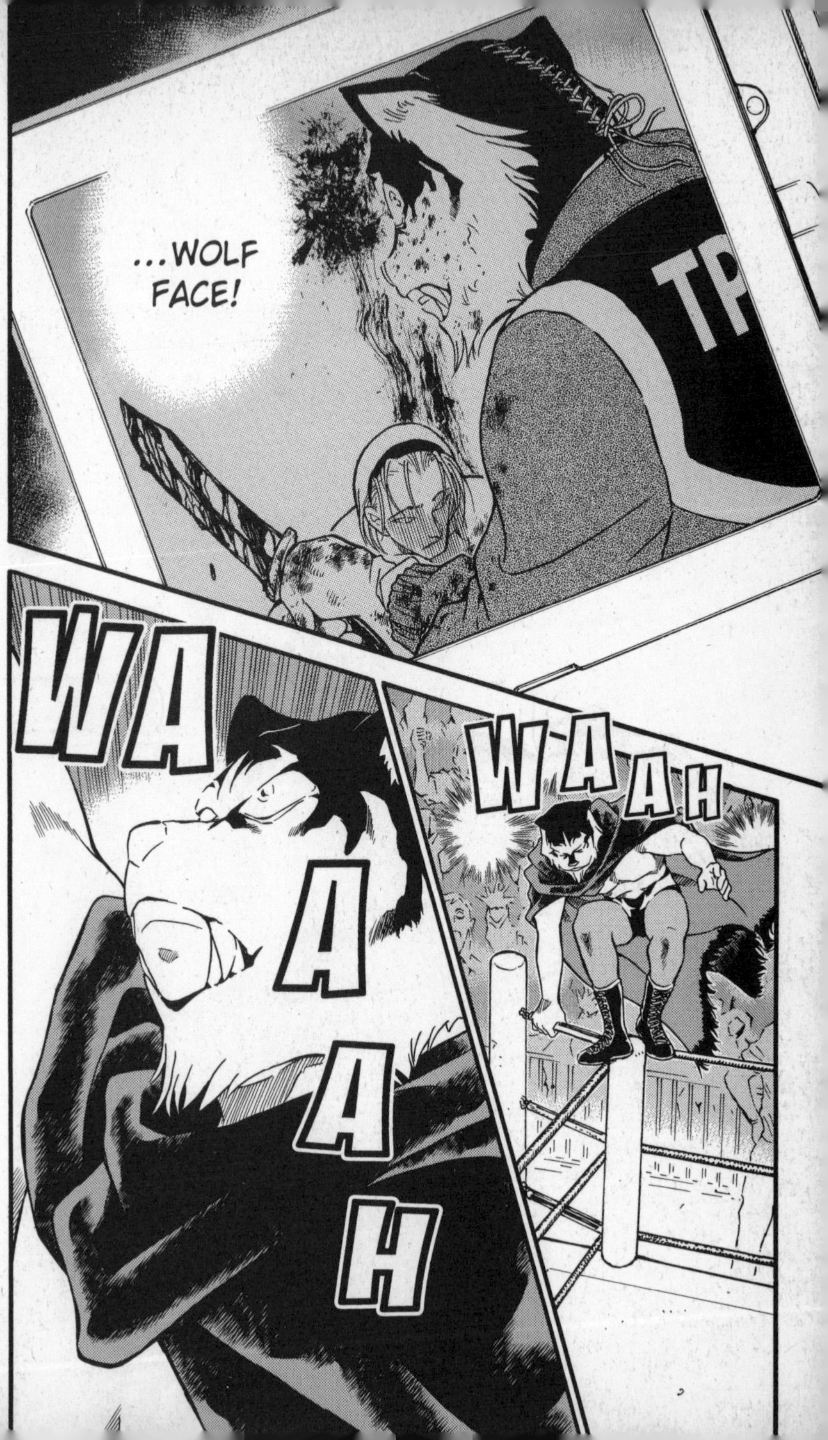
...WOLF FACE!
WAAH
WAAAH

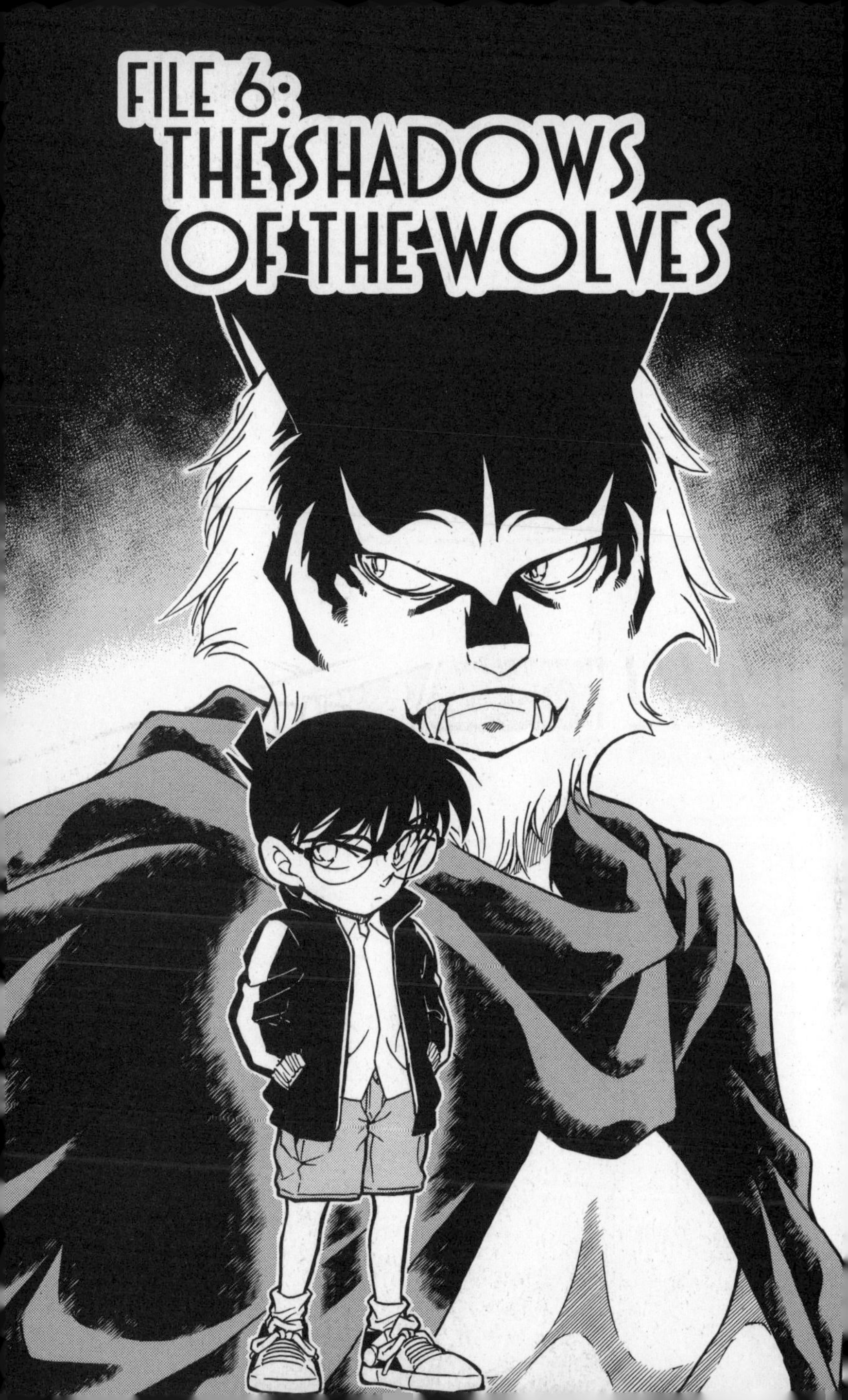
FILE 6:
THE SHADOWS OF THE WOLVES

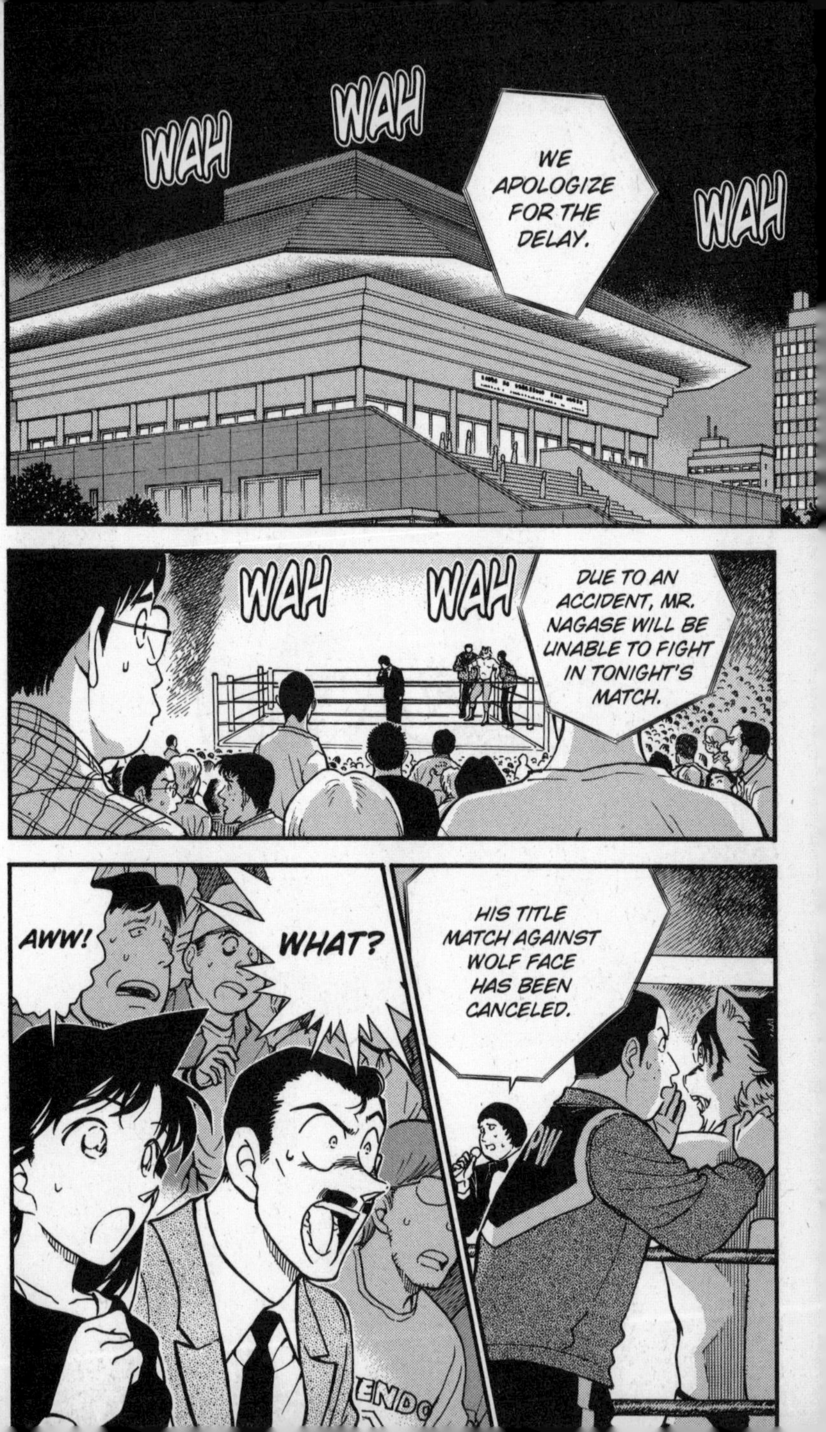
WAH
WE APOLOGIZE FOR THE DELAY.
WAH
WAH
DUE TO AN ACCIDENT, MR. NAGASE WILL BE UNABLE TO FIGHT IN TONIGHT'S MATCH.
WAH
WAH
HIS TITLE MATCH AGAINST WOLF FACE HAS BEEN CANCELED.
WHAT?
AWW!

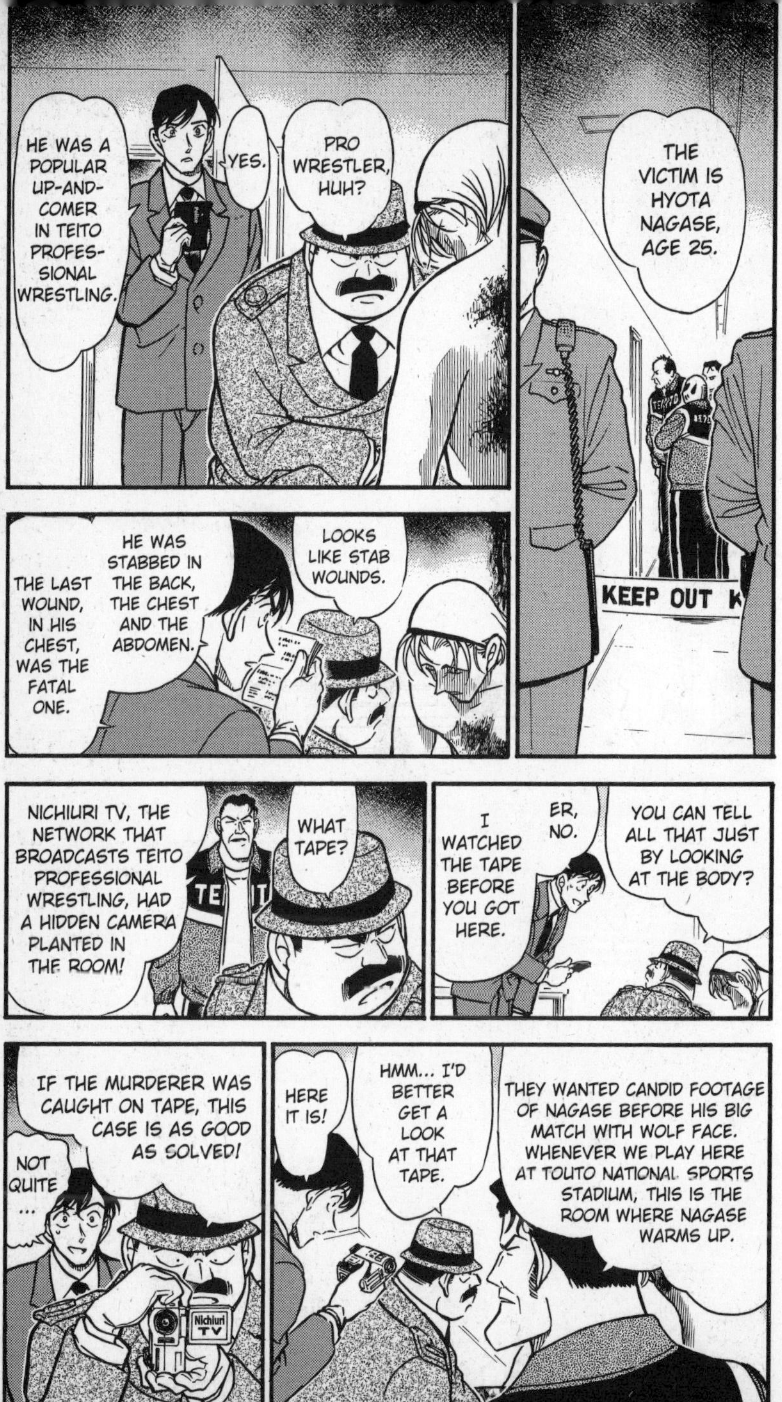
THE VICTIM IS HYOTA NAGASE, AGE 25.
KEEP OUT K
PRO WRESTLER, HUH?
YES.
HE WAS A POPULAR UP-AND-COMER IN TEITO PROFES-SIONAL WRESTLING.
LOOKS LIKE STAB WOUNDS.
HE WAS STABBED IN THE BACK, THE CHEST AND THE ABDOMEN.
THE LAST WOUND, IN HIS CHEST, WAS THE FATAL ONE.
YOU CAN TELL ALL THAT JUST BY LOOKING AT THE BODY?
ER, NO.
I WATCHED THE TAPE BEFORE YOU GOT HERE.
WHAT TAPE?
NICHIURI TV, THE NETWORK THAT BROADCASTS TEITO PROFESSIONAL WRESTLING, HAD A HIDDEN CAMERA PLANTED IN THE ROOM!
THEY WANTED CANDID FOOTAGE OF NAGASE BEFORE HIS BIG MATCH WITH WOLF FACE. WHENEVER WE PLAY HERE AT TOUTO NATIONAL SPORTS STADIUM, THIS IS THE ROOM WHERE NAGASE WARMS UP.
HMM... I'D BETTER GET A LOOK AT THAT TAPE.
HERE IT IS!
IF THE MURDERER WAS CAUGHT ON TAPE, THIS CASE IS AS GOOD AS SOLVED!
NOT QUITE...
Nichiuri TV

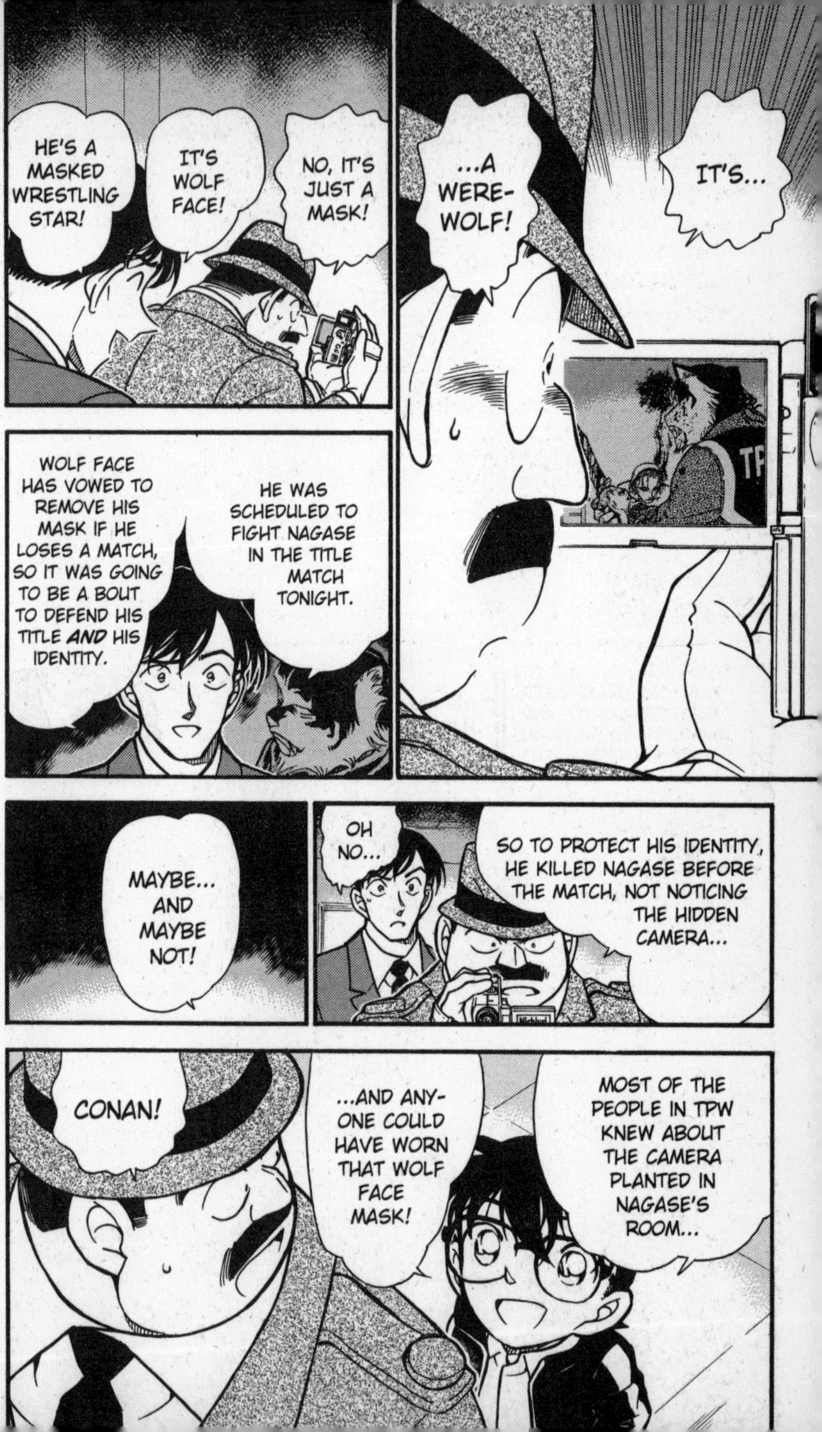
IT'S...
...A WERE-WOLF!
NO, IT'S JUST A MASK!
IT'S WOLF FACE!
HE'S A MASKED WRESTLING STAR!
HE WAS SCHEDULED TO FIGHT NAGASE IN THE TITLE MATCH TONIGHT.
WOLF FACE HAS VOWED TO REMOVE HIS MASK IF HE LOSES A MATCH, SO IT WAS GOING TO BE A BOUT TO DEFEND HIS TITLE *AND* HIS IDENTITY.
SO TO PROTECT HIS IDENTITY, HE KILLED NAGASE BEFORE THE MATCH, NOT NOTICING THE HIDDEN CAMERA...
OH NO...
MAYBE... AND MAYBE NOT!
MOST OF THE PEOPLE IN TPW KNEW ABOUT THE CAMERA PLANTED IN NAGASE'S ROOM...
...AND ANY-ONE COULD HAVE WORN THAT WOLF FACE MASK!
CONAN!

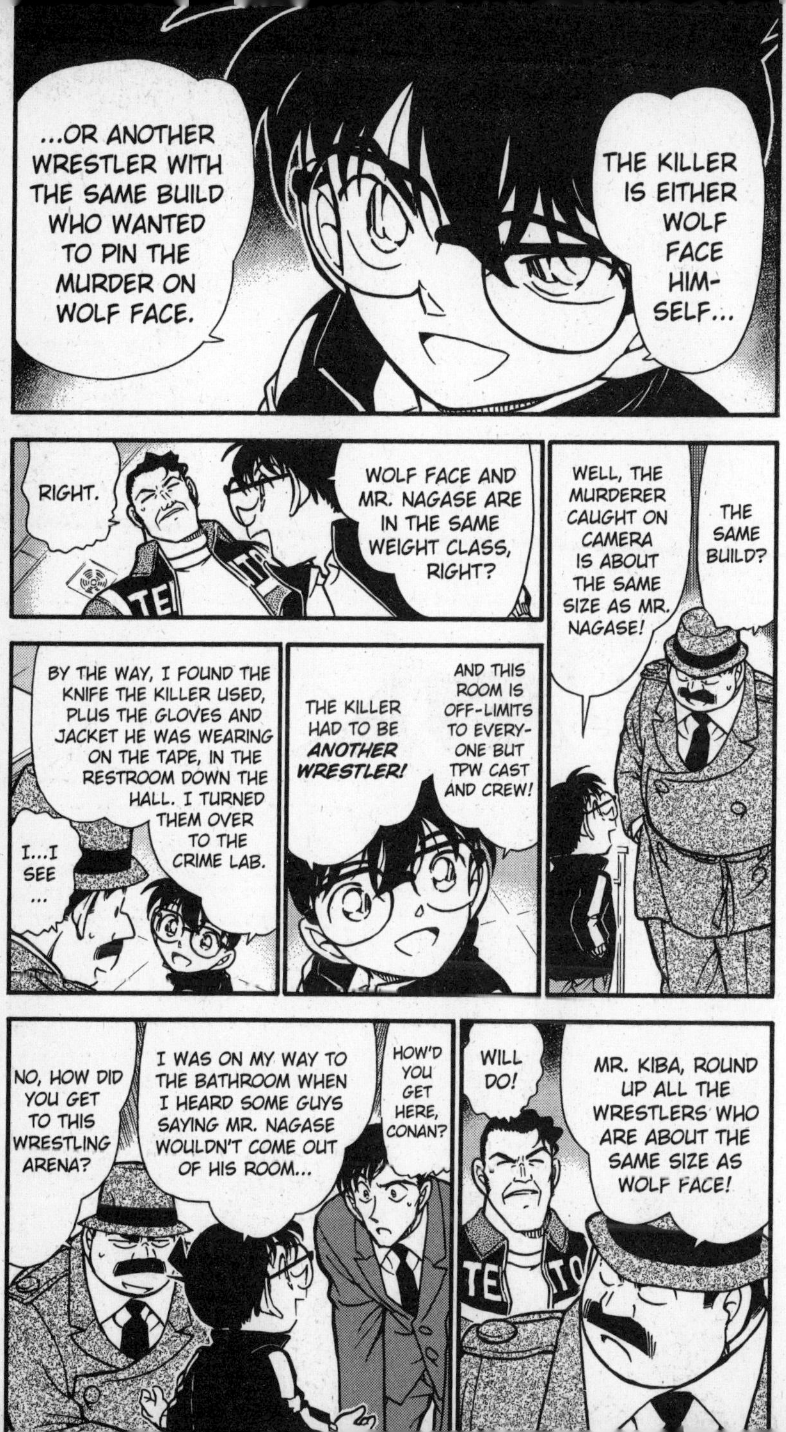
THE KILLER IS EITHER WOLF FACE HIMSELF...
...OR ANOTHER WRESTLER WITH THE SAME BUILD WHO WANTED TO PIN THE MURDER ON WOLF FACE.
THE SAME BUILD?
WELL, THE MURDERER CAUGHT ON CAMERA IS ABOUT THE SAME SIZE AS MR. NAGASE!
WOLF FACE AND MR. NAGASE ARE IN THE SAME WEIGHT CLASS, RIGHT?
RIGHT.
AND THIS ROOM IS OFF-LIMITS TO EVERYONE BUT TPW CAST AND CREW!
THE KILLER HAD TO BE *ANOTHER WRESTLER!*
BY THE WAY, I FOUND THE KNIFE THE KILLER USED, PLUS THE GLOVES AND JACKET HE WAS WEARING ON THE TAPE, IN THE RESTROOM DOWN THE HALL. I TURNED THEM OVER TO THE CRIME LAB.
I...I SEE...
MR. KIBA, ROUND UP ALL THE WRESTLERS WHO ARE ABOUT THE SAME SIZE AS WOLF FACE!
WILL DO!
HOW'D YOU GET HERE, CONAN?
I WAS ON MY WAY TO THE BATHROOM WHEN I HEARD SOME GUYS SAYING MR. NAGASE WOULDN'T COME OUT OF HIS ROOM...
NO, HOW DID YOU GET TO THIS WRESTLING ARENA?

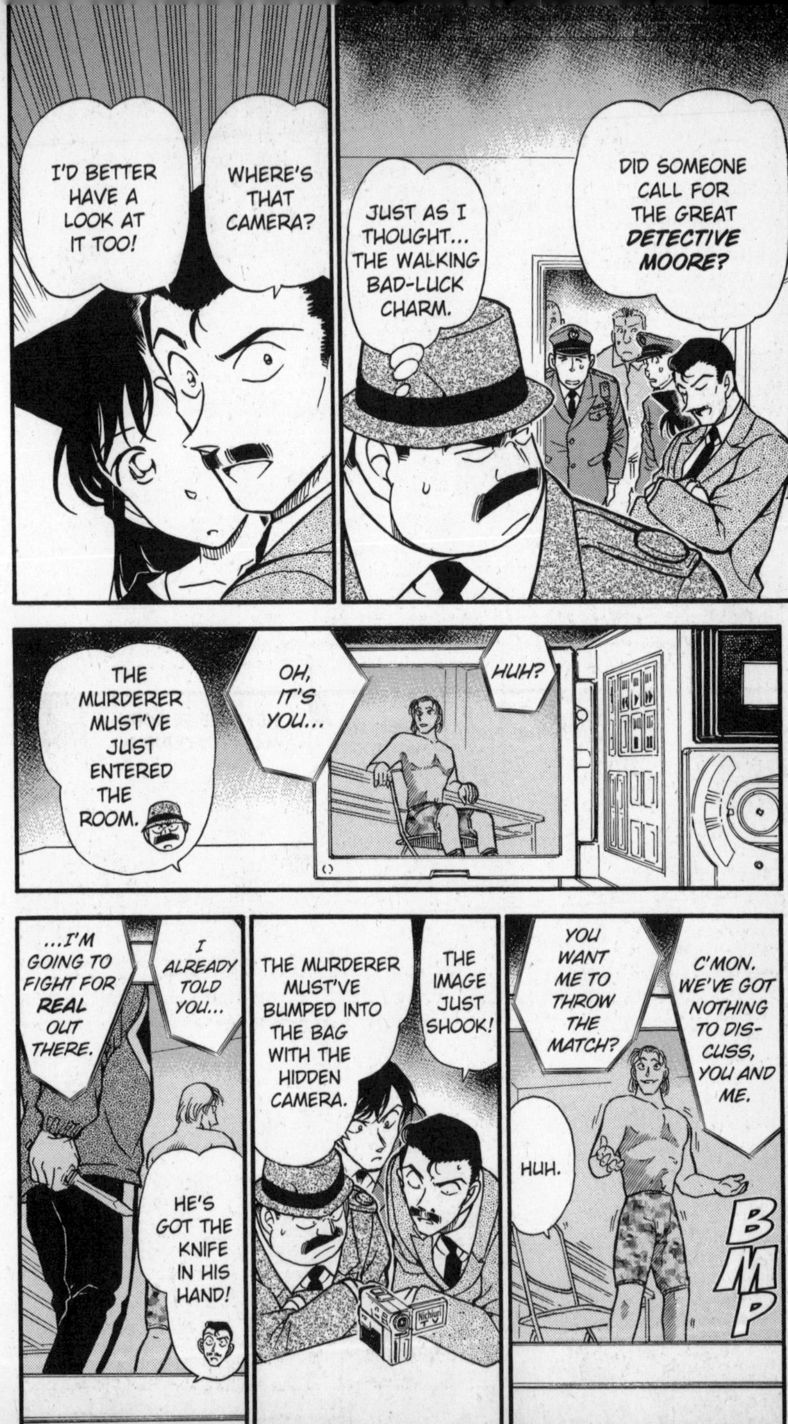
DID SOMEONE CALL FOR THE GREAT **DETECTIVE MOORE?**
JUST AS I THOUGHT... THE WALKING BAD-LUCK CHARM.
WHERE'S THAT CAMERA?
I'D BETTER HAVE A LOOK AT IT TOO!
HUH?
OH, IT'S YOU...
THE MURDERER MUST'VE JUST ENTERED THE ROOM.
C'MON. WE'VE GOT NOTHING TO DIS-CUSS, YOU AND ME.
YOU WANT ME TO THROW THE MATCH?
HUH.
BMP
THE IMAGE JUST SHOOK!
THE MURDERER MUST'VE BUMPED INTO THE BAG WITH THE HIDDEN CAMERA.
I ALREADY TOLD YOU...
...I'M GOING TO FIGHT FOR **REAL** OUT THERE.
HE'S GOT THE KNIFE IN HIS HAND!

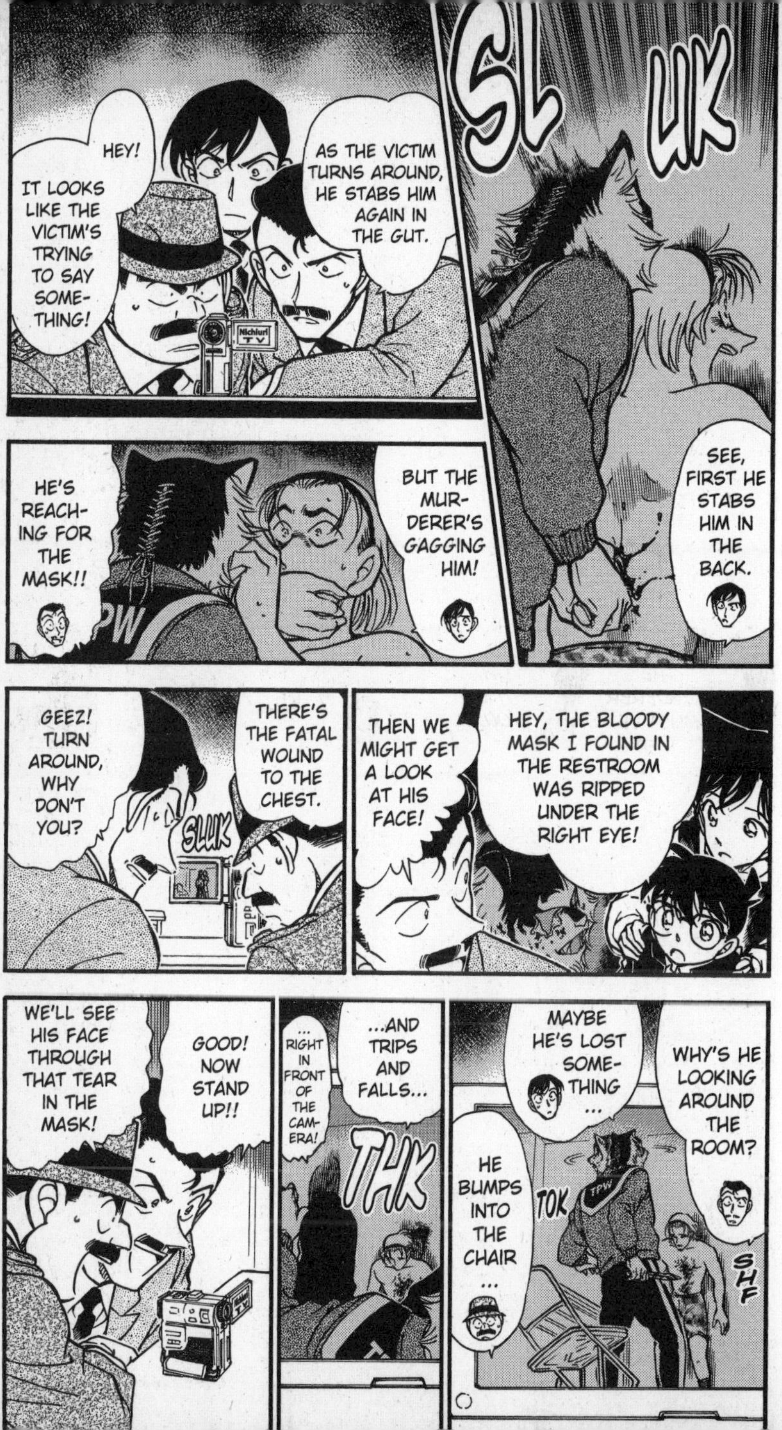

SL UK
SEE, FIRST HE STABS HIM IN THE BACK.
AS THE VICTIM TURNS AROUND, HE STABS HIM AGAIN IN THE GUT.
HEY! IT LOOKS LIKE THE VICTIM'S TRYING TO SAY SOME-THING!
Nichiuri TV
BUT THE MUR-DERER'S GAGGING HIM!
HE'S REACH-ING FOR THE MASK!!
HEY, THE BLOODY MASK I FOUND IN THE RESTROOM WAS RIPPED UNDER THE RIGHT EYE!
THEN WE MIGHT GET A LOOK AT HIS FACE!
THERE'S THE FATAL WOUND TO THE CHEST.
SLUK
GEEZ! TURN AROUND, WHY DON'T YOU?
WHY'S HE LOOKING AROUND THE ROOM?
SHF
MAYBE HE'S LOST SOME-THING ...
HE BUMPS INTO THE CHAIR ...
TOK
...AND TRIPS AND FALLS...
... RIGHT IN FRONT OF THE CAM-ERA!
THK
GOOD! NOW STAND UP!!
WE'LL SEE HIS FACE THROUGH THAT TEAR IN THE MASK!

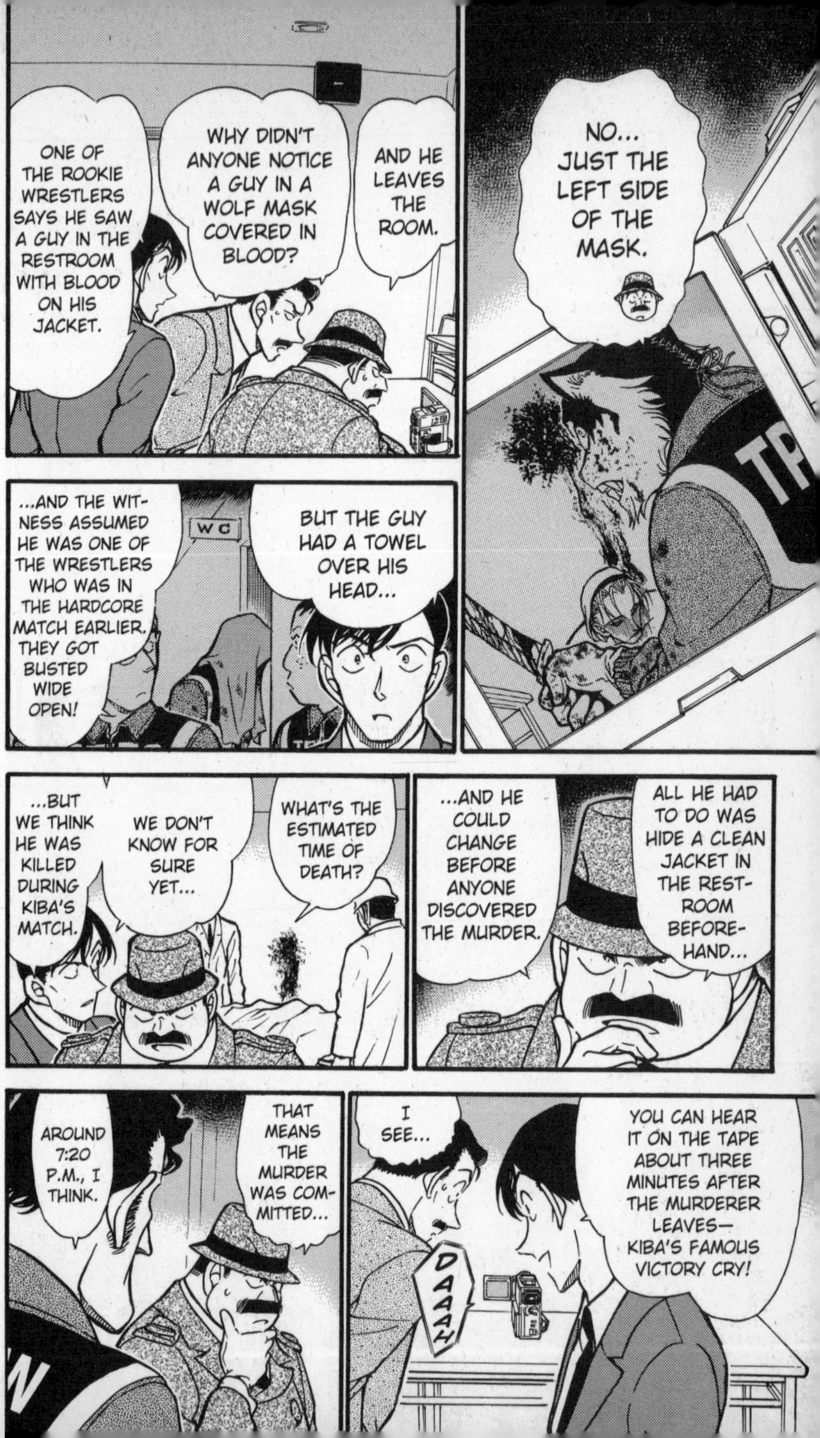
NO... JUST THE LEFT SIDE OF THE MASK.
AND HE LEAVES THE ROOM.
WHY DIDN'T ANYONE NOTICE A GUY IN A WOLF MASK COVERED IN BLOOD?
ONE OF THE ROOKIE WRESTLERS SAYS HE SAW A GUY IN THE RESTROOM WITH BLOOD ON HIS JACKET.
BUT THE GUY HAD A TOWEL OVER HIS HEAD...
WC
...AND THE WITNESS ASSUMED HE WAS ONE OF THE WRESTLERS WHO WAS IN THE HARDCORE MATCH EARLIER. THEY GOT BUSTED WIDE OPEN!
ALL HE HAD TO DO WAS HIDE A CLEAN JACKET IN THE RESTROOM BEFOREHAND...
...AND HE COULD CHANGE BEFORE ANYONE DISCOVERED THE MURDER.
WHAT'S THE ESTIMATED TIME OF DEATH?
WE DON'T KNOW FOR SURE YET...
...BUT WE THINK HE WAS KILLED DURING KIBA'S MATCH.
YOU CAN HEAR IT ON THE TAPE ABOUT THREE MINUTES AFTER THE MURDERER LEAVES—KIBA'S FAMOUS VICTORY CRY!
DAAAH
I SEE...
THAT MEANS THE MURDER WAS COMMITTED...
AROUND 7:20 P.M., I THINK.

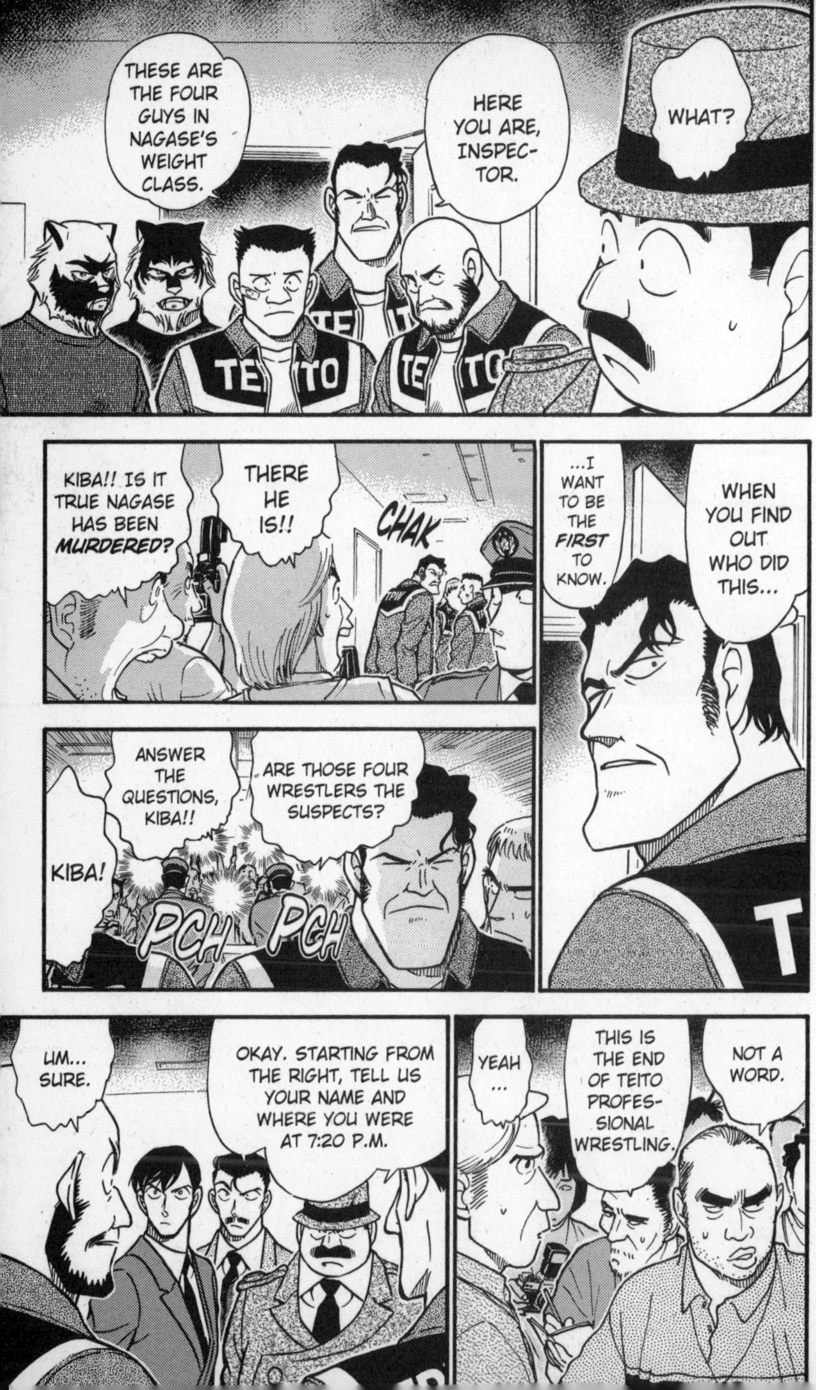
WHAT?
HERE YOU ARE, INSPECTOR.
THESE ARE THE FOUR GUYS IN NAGASE'S WEIGHT CLASS.
WHEN YOU FIND OUT WHO DID THIS...
...I WANT TO BE THE *FIRST* TO KNOW.
CHAK
THERE HE IS!!
KIBA!! IS IT TRUE NAGASE HAS BEEN ***MURDERED?***
ARE THOSE FOUR WRESTLERS THE SUSPECTS?
ANSWER THE QUESTIONS, KIBA!!
KIBA!
PCH PCH
NOT A WORD.
THIS IS THE END OF TEITO PROFESSIONAL WRESTLING.
YEAH ...
OKAY. STARTING FROM THE RIGHT, TELL US YOUR NAME AND WHERE YOU WERE AT 7:20 P.M.
UM... SURE.

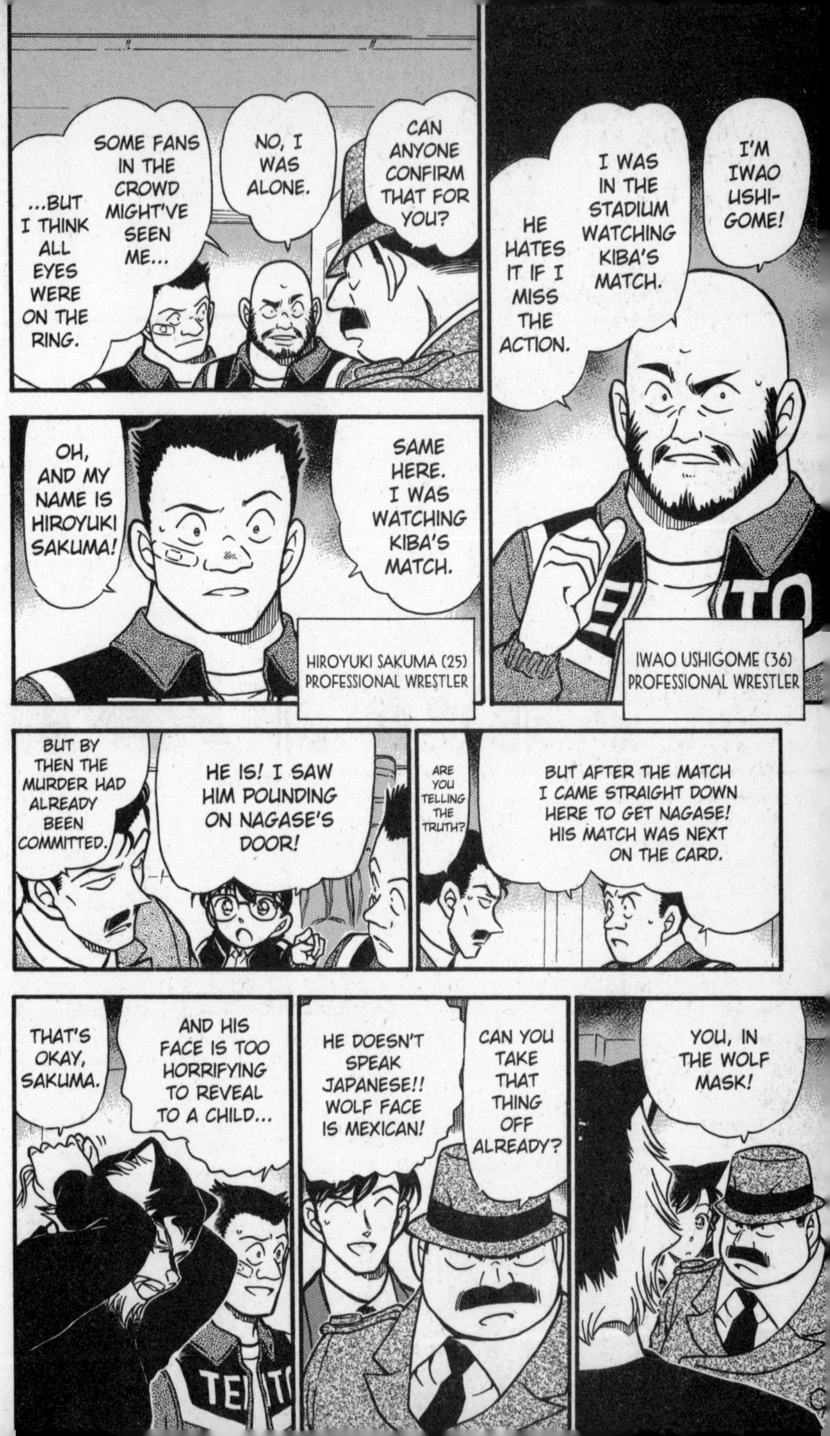
I'M IWAO USHI-GOME!
I WAS IN THE STADIUM WATCHING KIBA'S MATCH.
HE HATES IT IF I MISS THE ACTION.
IWAO USHIGOME (36) PROFESSIONAL WRESTLER
CAN ANYONE CONFIRM THAT FOR YOU?
NO, I WAS ALONE.
SOME FANS IN THE CROWD MIGHT'VE SEEN ME...
...BUT I THINK ALL EYES WERE ON THE RING.
SAME HERE. I WAS WATCHING KIBA'S MATCH.
OH, AND MY NAME IS HIROYUKI SAKUMA!
HIROYUKI SAKUMA (25) PROFESSIONAL WRESTLER
BUT AFTER THE MATCH I CAME STRAIGHT DOWN HERE TO GET NAGASE! HIS MATCH WAS NEXT ON THE CARD.
ARE YOU TELLING THE TRUTH?
HE IS! I SAW HIM POUNDING ON NAGASE'S DOOR!
BUT BY THEN THE MURDER HAD ALREADY BEEN COMMITTED.
YOU, IN THE WOLF MASK!
CAN YOU TAKE THAT THING OFF ALREADY?
HE DOESN'T SPEAK JAPANESE!! WOLF FACE IS MEXICAN!
AND HIS FACE IS TOO HORRIFYING TO REVEAL TO A CHILD...
THAT'S OKAY, SAKUMA.

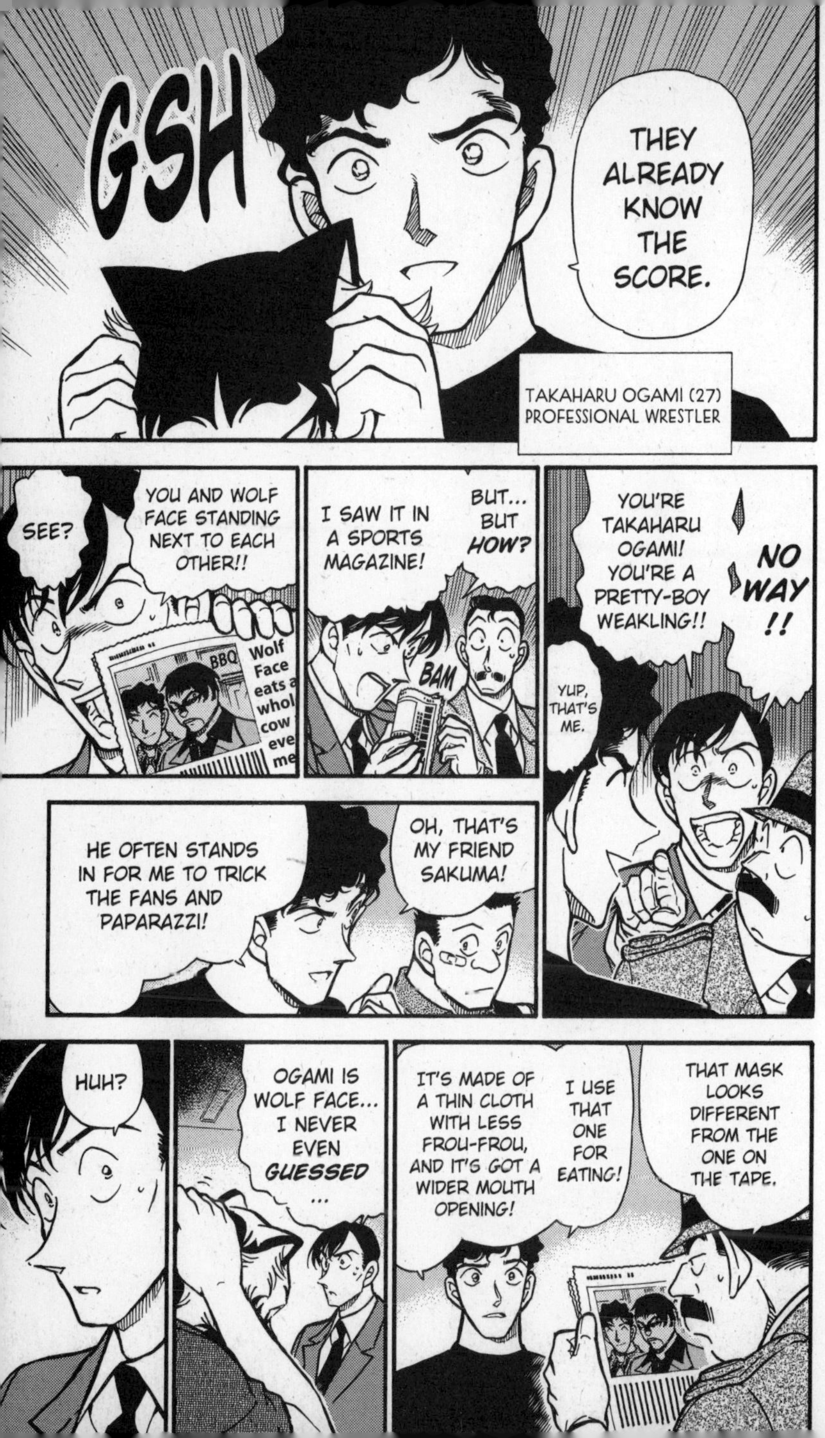
GSH
THEY ALREADY KNOW THE SCORE.
TAKAHARU OGAMI (27) PROFESSIONAL WRESTLER
NO WAY!!
YOU'RE TAKAHARU OGAMI! YOU'RE A PRETTY-BOY WEAKLING!!
YUP, THAT'S ME.
BUT... BUT HOW?
I SAW IT IN A SPORTS MAGAZINE!
BAM
YOU AND WOLF FACE STANDING NEXT TO EACH OTHER!!
SEE?
BBQ
Wolf Face eats a whol cow eve me
OH, THAT'S MY FRIEND SAKUMA!
HE OFTEN STANDS IN FOR ME TO TRICK THE FANS AND PAPARAZZI!
THAT MASK LOOKS DIFFERENT FROM THE ONE ON THE TAPE.
I USE THAT ONE FOR EATING!
IT'S MADE OF A THIN CLOTH WITH LESS FROU-FROU, AND IT'S GOT A WIDER MOUTH OPENING!
OGAMI IS WOLF FACE... I NEVER EVEN GUESSED ...
HUH?

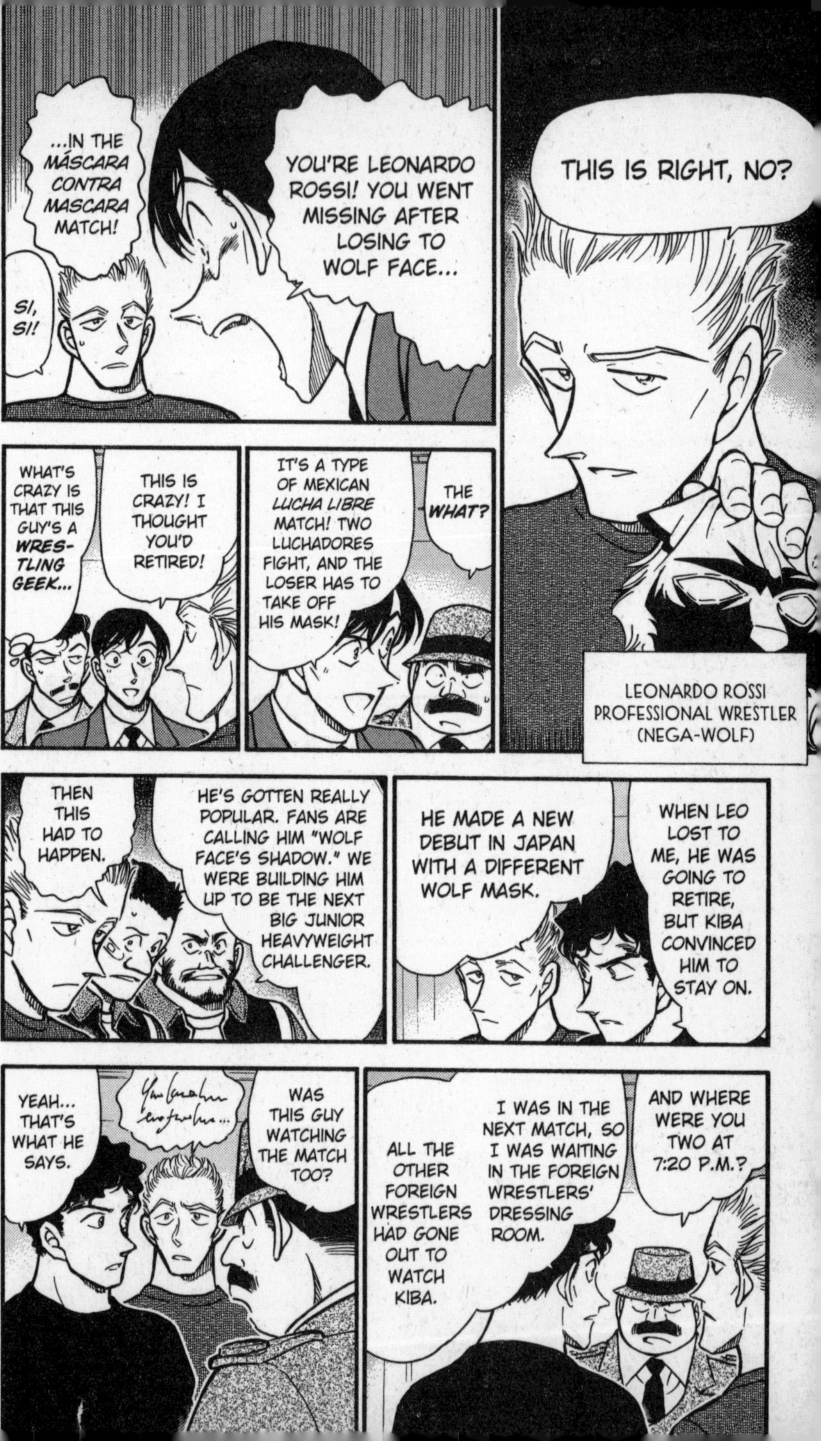
THIS IS RIGHT, NO?
LEONARDO ROSSI PROFESSIONAL WRESTLER (NEGA-WOLF)
YOU'RE LEONARDO ROSSI! YOU WENT MISSING AFTER LOSING TO WOLF FACE...
...IN THE MÁSCARA CONTRA MASCARA MATCH!
SI, SI!
THE WHAT?
IT'S A TYPE OF MEXICAN LUCHA LIBRE MATCH! TWO LUCHADORES FIGHT, AND THE LOSER HAS TO TAKE OFF HIS MASK!
THIS IS CRAZY! I THOUGHT YOU'D RETIRED!
WHAT'S CRAZY IS THAT THIS GUY'S A WRESTLING GEEK...
WHEN LEO LOST TO ME, HE WAS GOING TO RETIRE, BUT KIBA CONVINCED HIM TO STAY ON.
HE MADE A NEW DEBUT IN JAPAN WITH A DIFFERENT WOLF MASK.
HE'S GOTTEN REALLY POPULAR. FANS ARE CALLING HIM "WOLF FACE'S SHADOW." WE WERE BUILDING HIM UP TO BE THE NEXT BIG JUNIOR HEAVYWEIGHT CHALLENGER.
THEN THIS HAD TO HAPPEN.
AND WHERE WERE YOU TWO AT 7:20 P.M.?
I WAS IN THE NEXT MATCH, SO I WAS WAITING IN THE FOREIGN WRESTLERS' DRESSING ROOM.
ALL THE OTHER FOREIGN WRESTLERS HAD GONE OUT TO WATCH KIBA.
WAS THIS GUY WATCHING THE MATCH TOO?
YEAH... THAT'S WHAT HE SAYS.

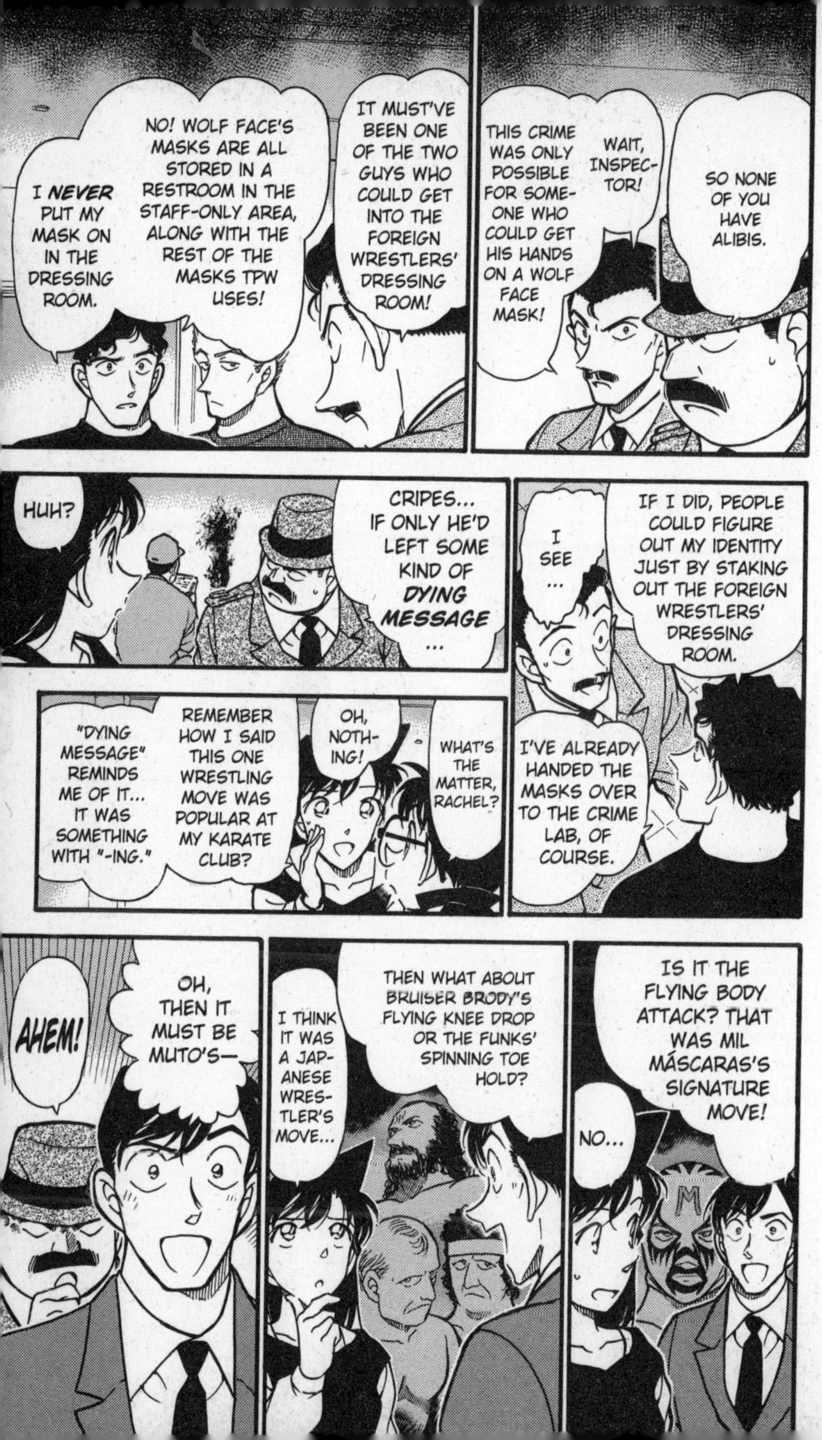
SO NONE OF YOU HAVE ALIBIS.
WAIT, INSPECTOR!
THIS CRIME WAS ONLY POSSIBLE FOR SOMEONE WHO COULD GET HIS HANDS ON A WOLF FACE MASK!
IT MUST'VE BEEN ONE OF THE TWO GUYS WHO COULD GET INTO THE FOREIGN WRESTLERS' DRESSING ROOM!
NO! WOLF FACE'S MASKS ARE ALL STORED IN A RESTROOM IN THE STAFF-ONLY AREA, ALONG WITH THE REST OF THE MASKS TPW USES!
I *NEVER* PUT MY MASK ON IN THE DRESSING ROOM.
IF I DID, PEOPLE COULD FIGURE OUT MY IDENTITY JUST BY STAKING OUT THE FOREIGN WRESTLERS' DRESSING ROOM.
I SEE...
I'VE ALREADY HANDED THE MASKS OVER TO THE CRIME LAB, OF COURSE.
CRIPES... IF ONLY HE'D LEFT SOME KIND OF ***DYING MESSAGE***...
HUH?
WHAT'S THE MATTER, RACHEL?
OH, NOTHING!
REMEMBER HOW I SAID THIS ONE WRESTLING MOVE WAS POPULAR AT MY KARATE CLUB?
"DYING MESSAGE" REMINDS ME OF IT... IT WAS SOMETHING WITH "-ING."
IS IT THE FLYING BODY ATTACK? THAT WAS MIL MÁSCARAS'S SIGNATURE MOVE!
NO...
THEN WHAT ABOUT BRUISER BRODY'S FLYING KNEE DROP OR THE FUNKS' SPINNING TOE HOLD?
I THINK IT WAS A JAPANESE WRESTLER'S MOVE...
OH, THEN IT MUST BE MUTO'S—
AHEM!

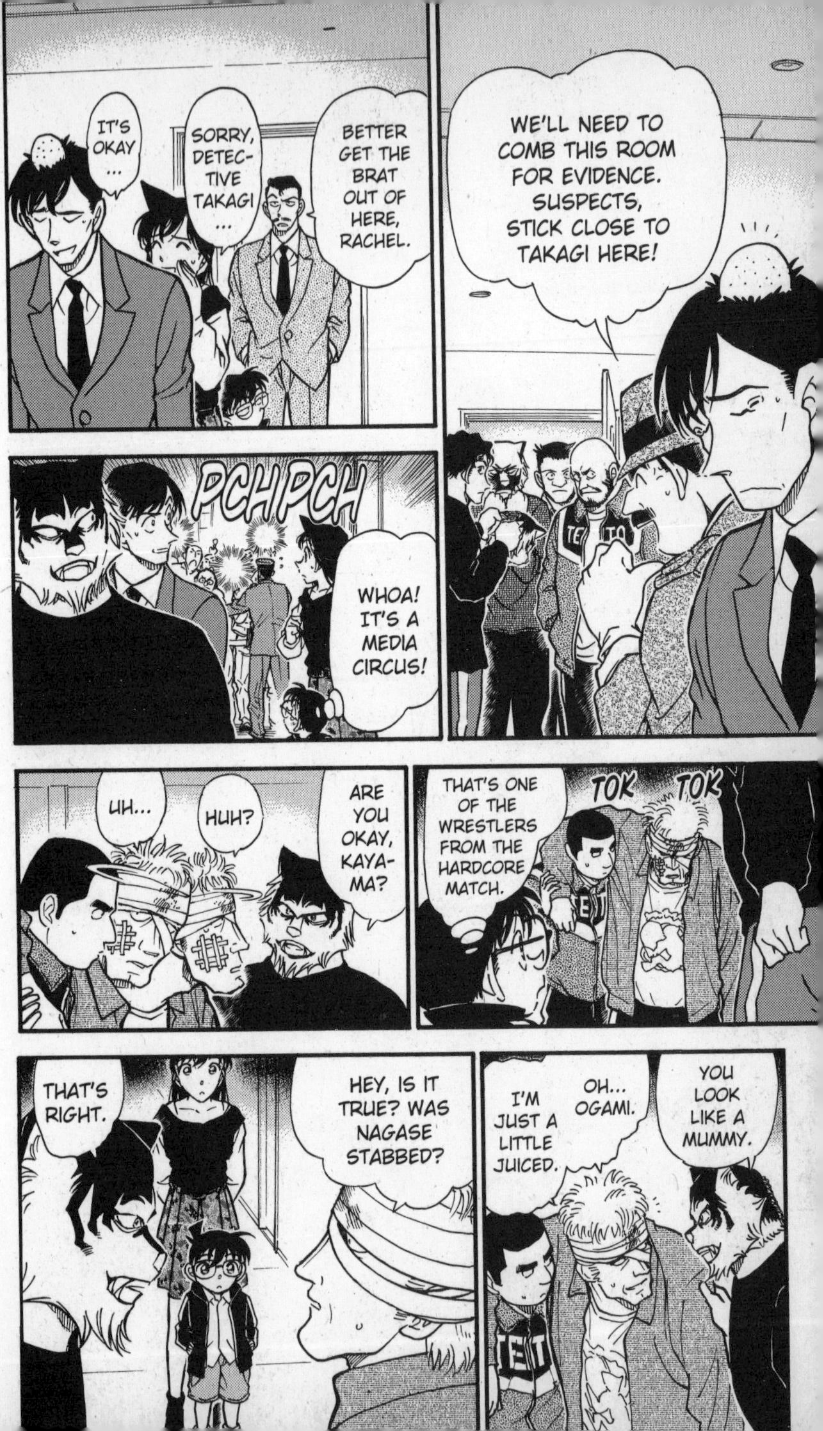
WE'LL NEED TO COMB THIS ROOM FOR EVIDENCE. SUSPECTS, STICK CLOSE TO TAKAGI HERE!
BETTER GET THE BRAT OUT OF HERE, RACHEL.
SORRY, DETEC-TIVE TAKAGI...
IT'S OKAY...
PCHPCH
WHOA! IT'S A MEDIA CIRCUS!
TOK TOK
THAT'S ONE OF THE WRESTLERS FROM THE HARDCORE MATCH.
ARE YOU OKAY, KAYA-MA?
HUH?
UH...
YOU LOOK LIKE A MUMMY.
OH... OGAMI.
I'M JUST A LITTLE JUICED.
HEY, IS IT TRUE? WAS NAGASE STABBED?
THAT'S RIGHT.

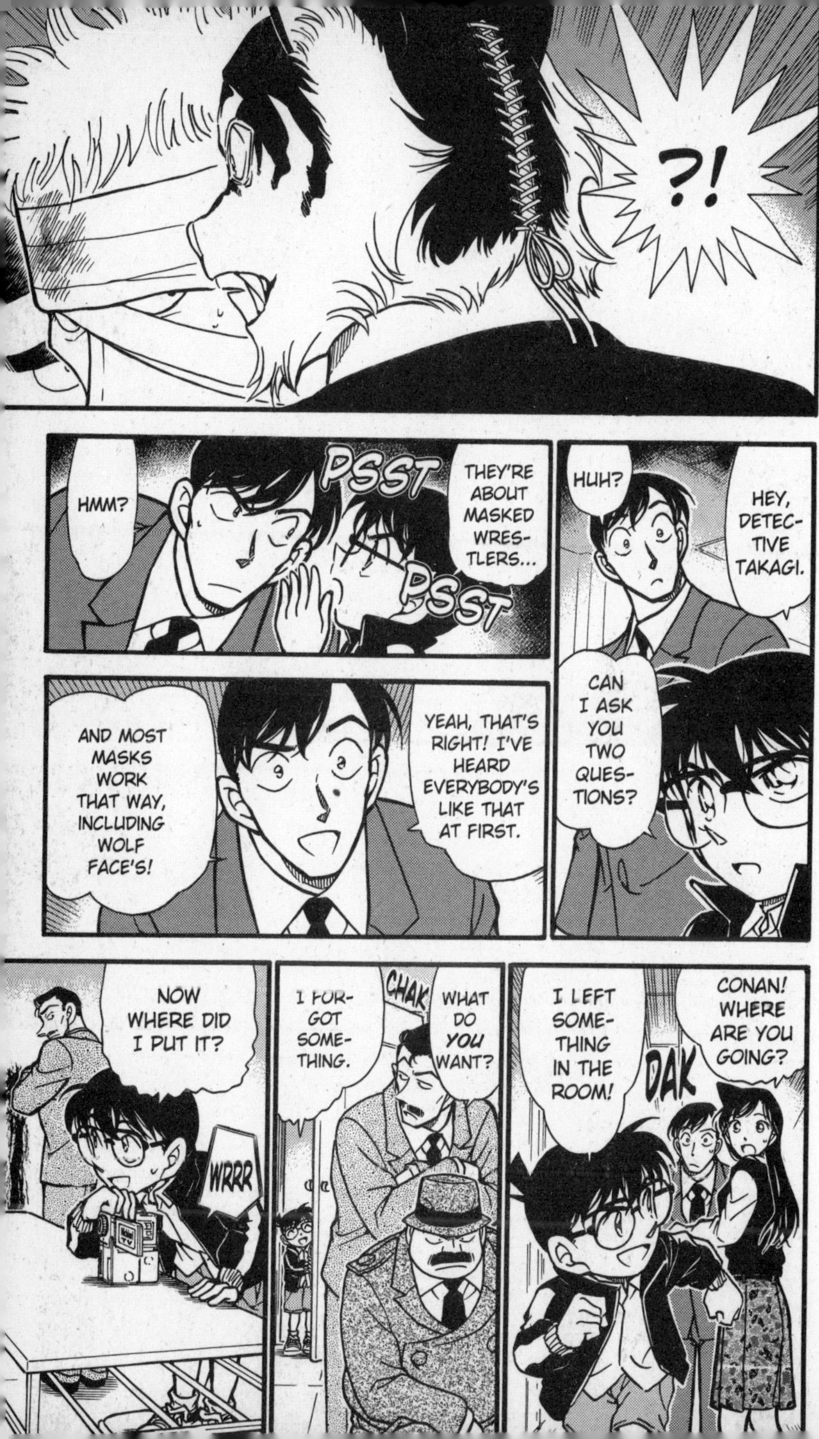
?!
HEY, DETECTIVE TAKAGI.
HUH?
THEY'RE ABOUT MASKED WRESTLERS...
PSST
PSST
HMM?
CAN I ASK YOU TWO QUESTIONS?
YEAH, THAT'S RIGHT! I'VE HEARD EVERYBODY'S LIKE THAT AT FIRST.
AND MOST MASKS WORK THAT WAY, INCLUDING WOLF FACE'S!
CONAN! WHERE ARE YOU GOING?
DAK
I LEFT SOMETHING IN THE ROOM!
CHAK
WHAT DO YOU WANT?
I FORGOT SOMETHING.
NOW WHERE DID I PUT IT?
WRRR

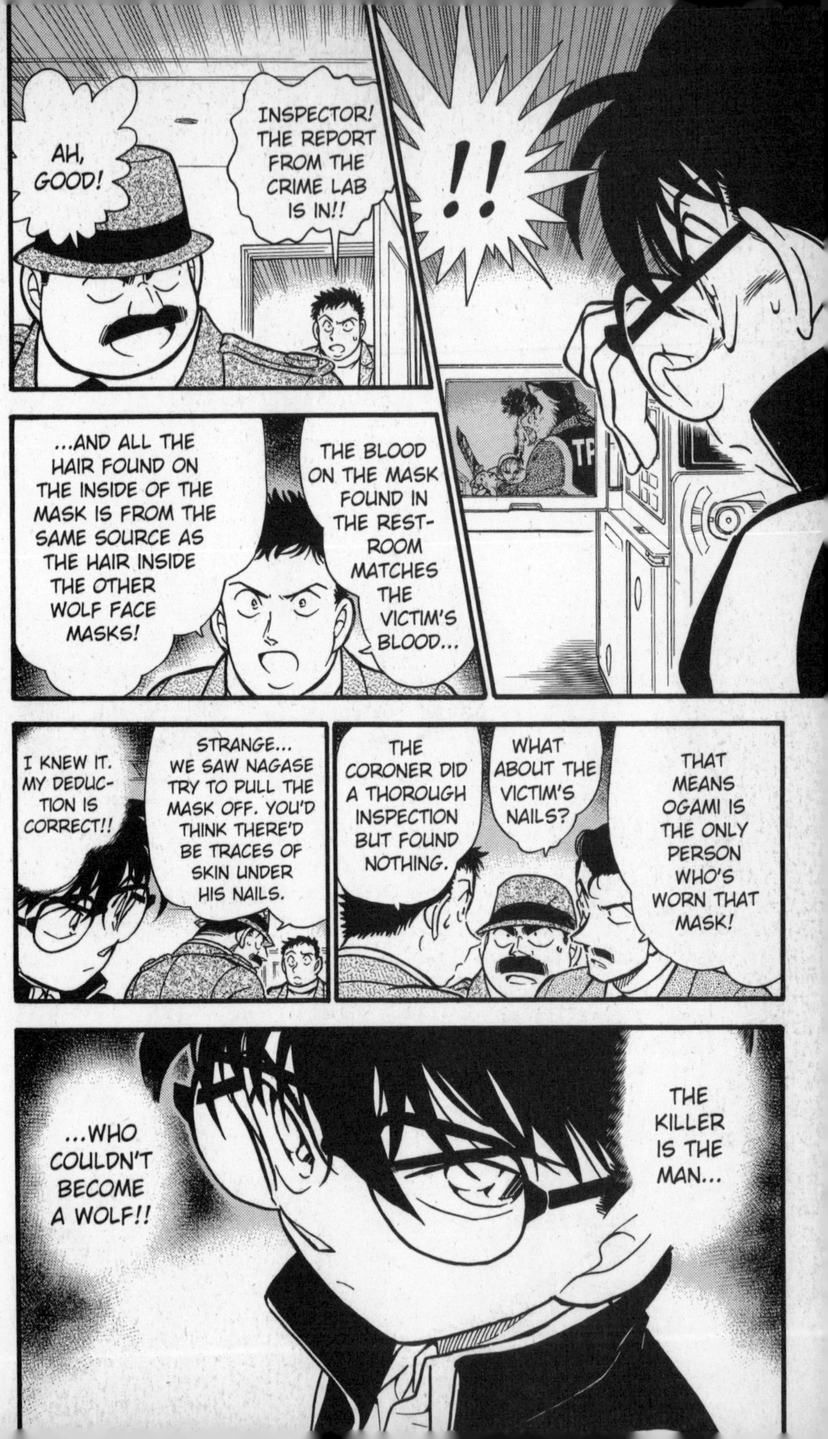
!!
INSPECTOR! THE REPORT FROM THE CRIME LAB IS IN!!
AH, GOOD!
THE BLOOD ON THE MASK FOUND IN THE REST-ROOM MATCHES THE VICTIM'S BLOOD...
...AND ALL THE HAIR FOUND ON THE INSIDE OF THE MASK IS FROM THE SAME SOURCE AS THE HAIR INSIDE THE OTHER WOLF FACE MASKS!
THAT MEANS OGAMI IS THE ONLY PERSON WHO'S WORN THAT MASK!
WHAT ABOUT THE VICTIM'S NAILS?
THE CORONER DID A THOROUGH INSPECTION BUT FOUND NOTHING.
STRANGE... WE SAW NAGASE TRY TO PULL THE MASK OFF. YOU'D THINK THERE'D BE TRACES OF SKIN UNDER HIS NAILS.
I KNEW IT. MY DEDUC-TION IS CORRECT!!
THE KILLER IS THE MAN...
...WHO COULDN'T BECOME A WOLF!!

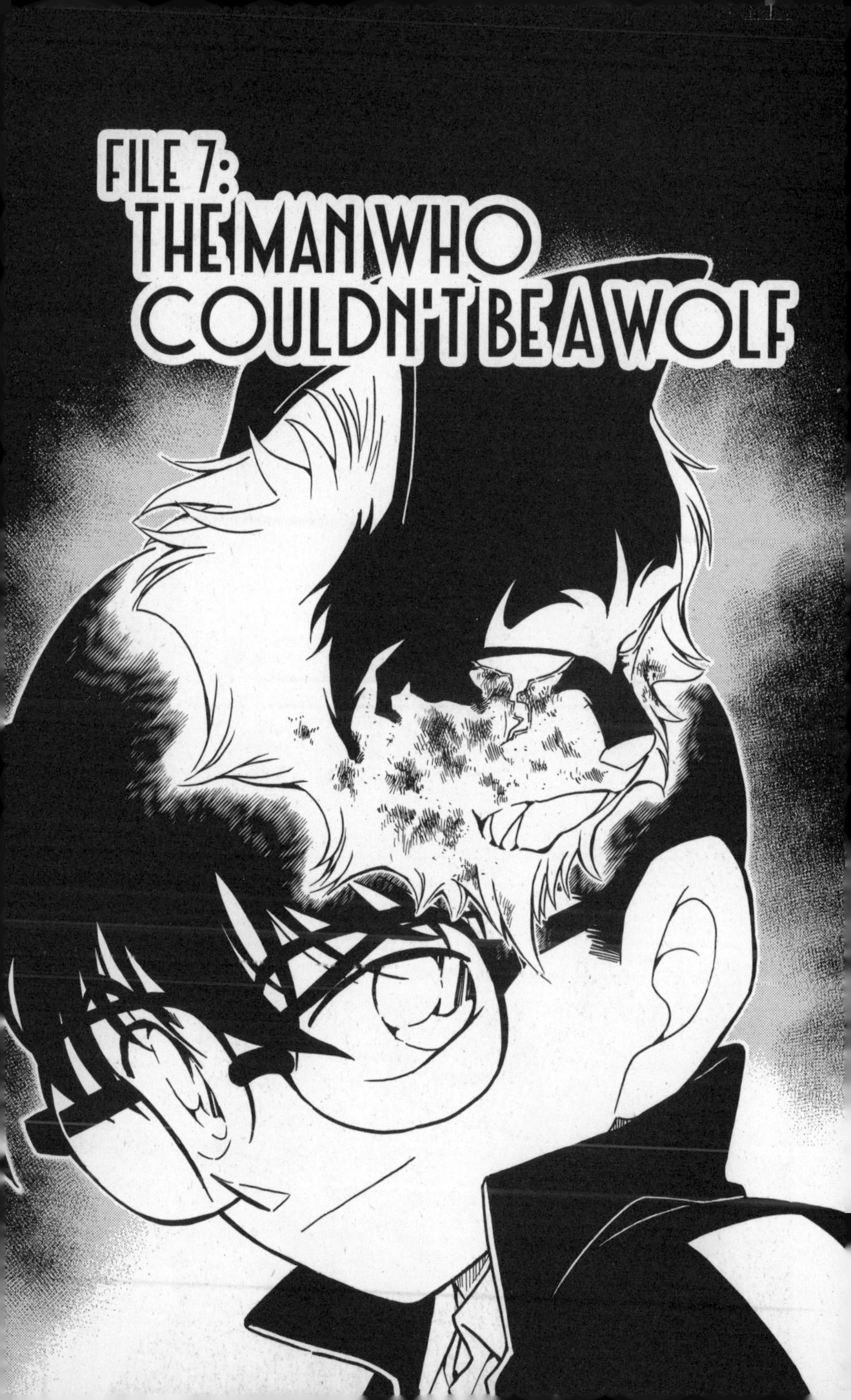
FILE 7:
THE MAN WHO COULDN'T BE A WOLF

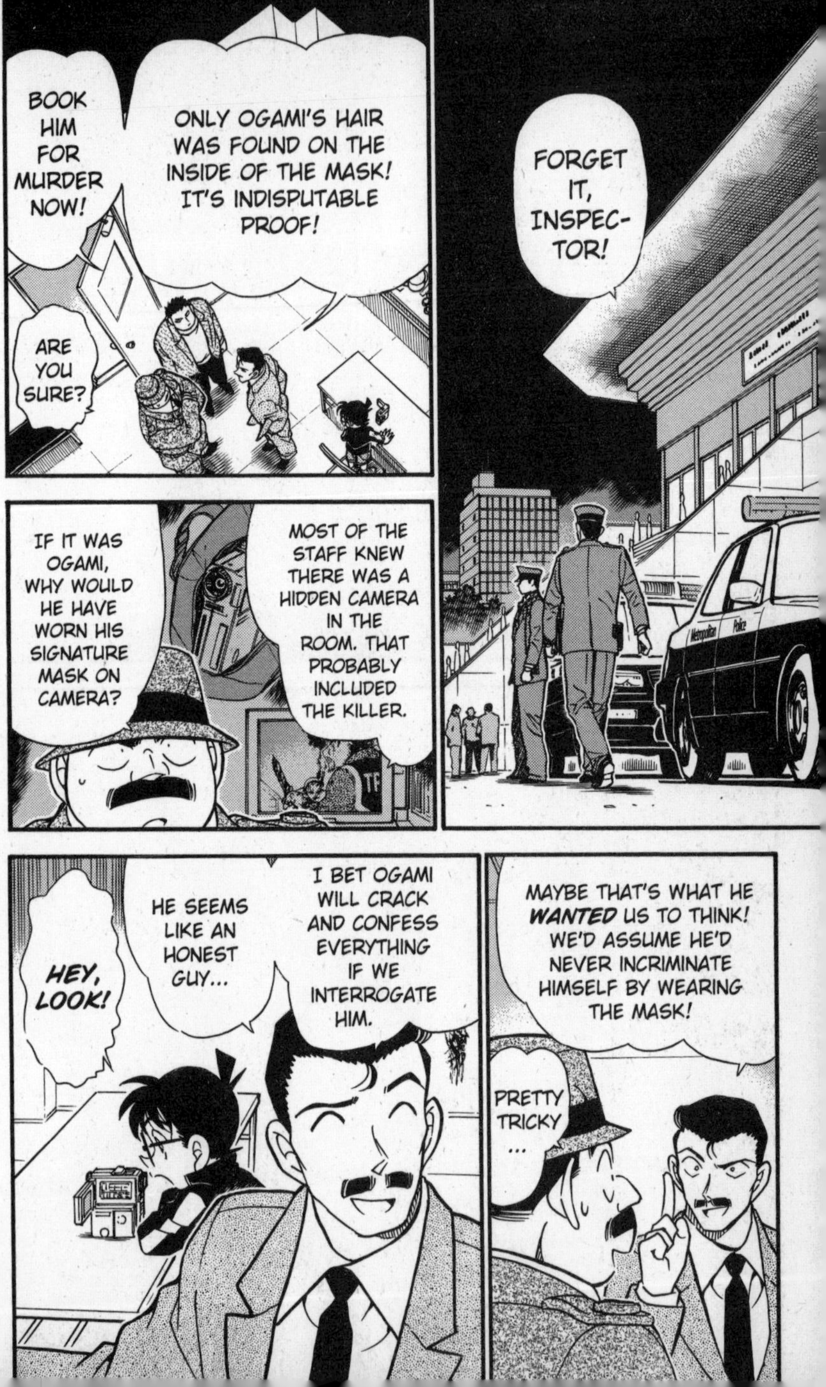
FORGET IT, INSPECTOR!
ONLY OGAMI'S HAIR WAS FOUND ON THE INSIDE OF THE MASK! IT'S INDISPUTABLE PROOF!
BOOK HIM FOR MURDER NOW!
ARE YOU SURE?
MOST OF THE STAFF KNEW THERE WAS A HIDDEN CAMERA IN THE ROOM. THAT PROBABLY INCLUDED THE KILLER.
IF IT WAS OGAMI, WHY WOULD HE HAVE WORN HIS SIGNATURE MASK ON CAMERA?
MAYBE THAT'S WHAT HE *WANTED* US TO THINK! WE'D ASSUME HE'D NEVER INCRIMINATE HIMSELF BY WEARING THE MASK!
PRETTY TRICKY ...
I BET OGAMI WILL CRACK AND CONFESS EVERYTHING IF WE INTERROGATE HIM.
HE SEEMS LIKE AN HONEST GUY...
HEY, LOOK!

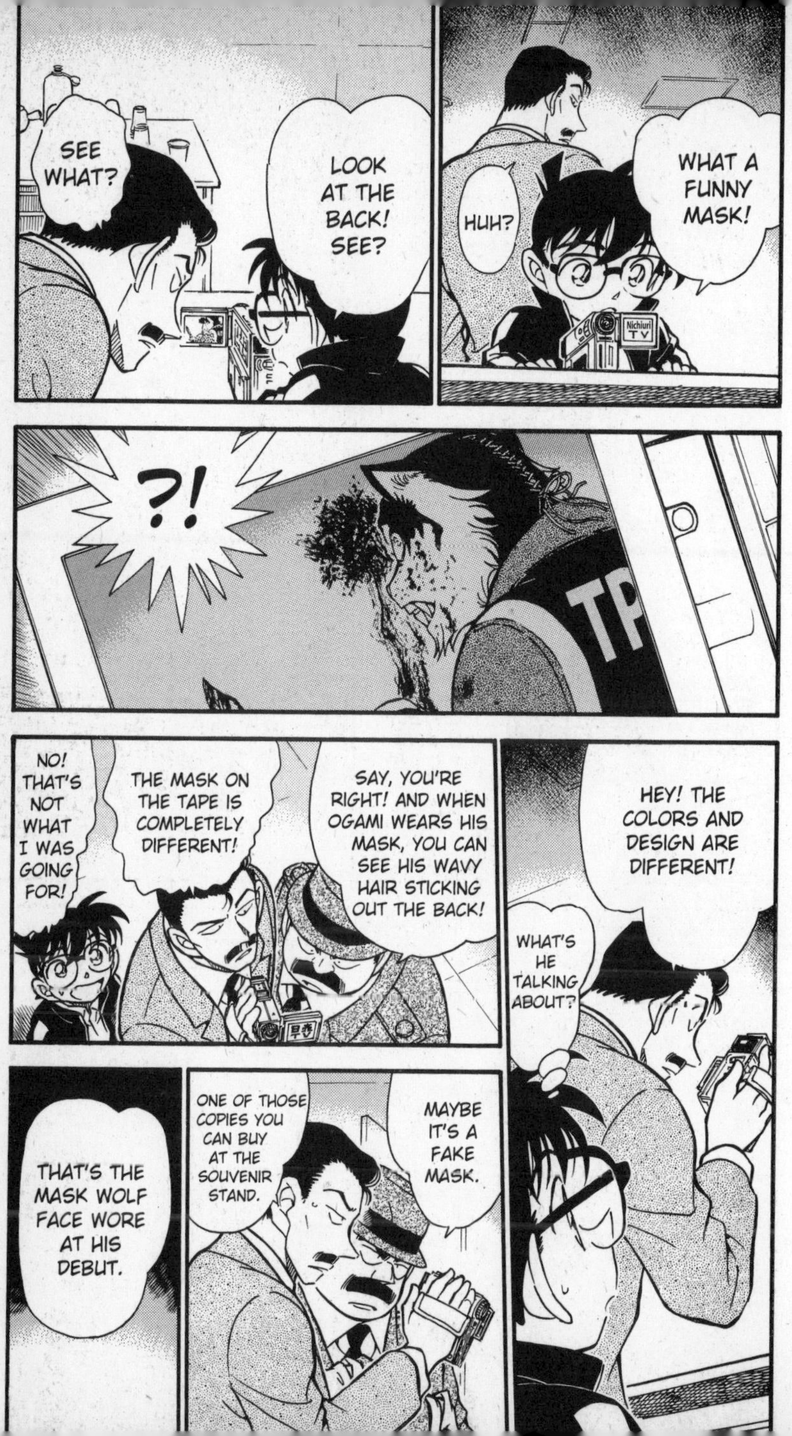
WHAT A FUNNY MASK!
HUH?
LOOK AT THE BACK! SEE?
SEE WHAT?
?!
TP
HEY! THE COLORS AND DESIGN ARE DIFFERENT!
WHAT'S HE TALKING ABOUT?
SAY, YOU'RE RIGHT! AND WHEN OGAMI WEARS HIS MASK, YOU CAN SEE HIS WAVY HAIR STICKING OUT THE BACK!
THE MASK ON THE TAPE IS COMPLETELY DIFFERENT!
NO! THAT'S NOT WHAT I WAS GOING FOR!
MAYBE IT'S A FAKE MASK.
ONE OF THOSE COPIES YOU CAN BUY AT THE SOUVENIR STAND.
THAT'S THE MASK WOLF FACE WORE AT HIS DEBUT.

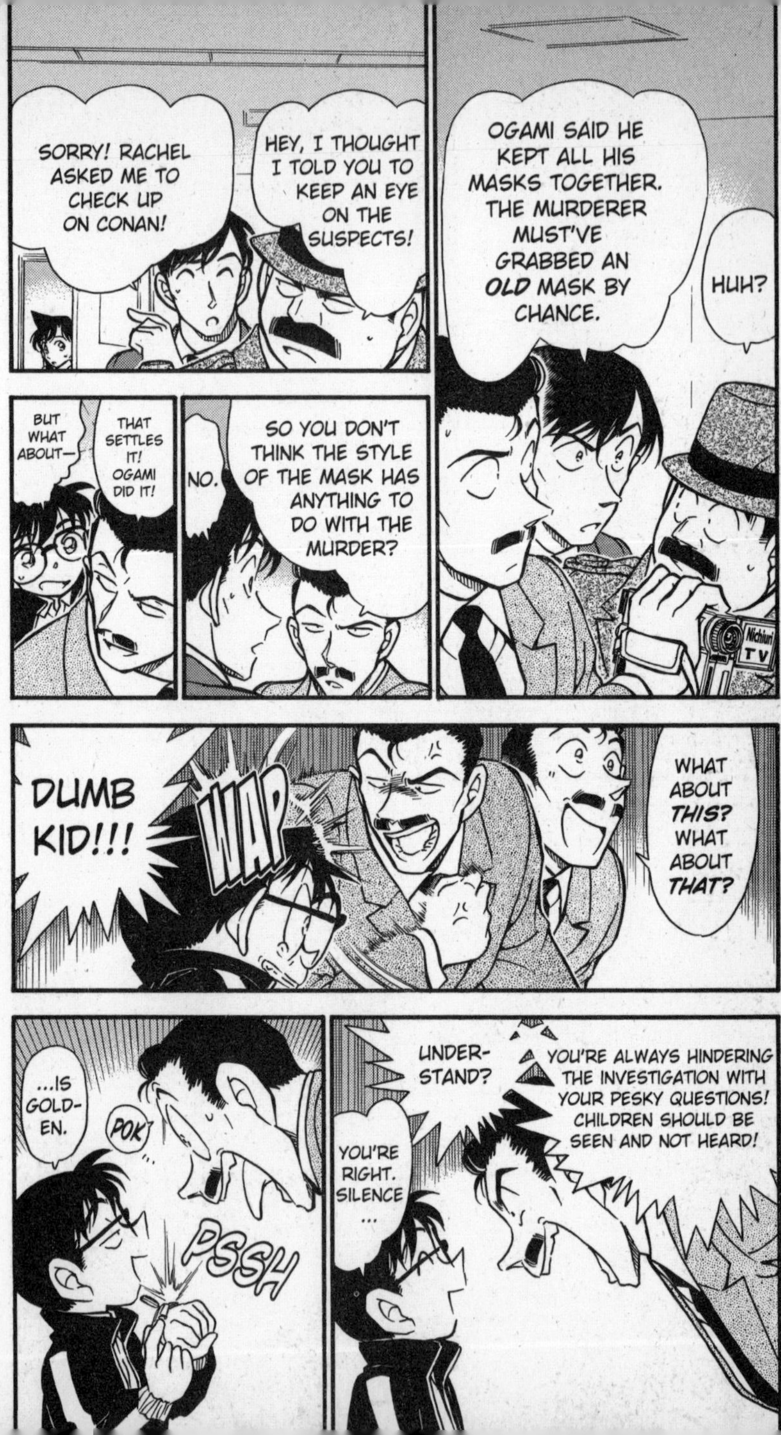
OGAMI SAID HE KEPT ALL HIS MASKS TOGETHER. THE MURDERER MUST'VE GRABBED AN *OLD* MASK BY CHANCE.
HUH?
HEY, I THOUGHT I TOLD YOU TO KEEP AN EYE ON THE SUSPECTS!
SORRY! RACHEL ASKED ME TO CHECK UP ON CONAN!
SO YOU DON'T THINK THE STYLE OF THE MASK HAS ANYTHING TO DO WITH THE MURDER?
NO.
THAT SETTLES IT! OGAMI DID IT!
BUT WHAT ABOUT—
WHAT ABOUT *THIS?* WHAT ABOUT *THAT?*
WAP
DUMB KID!!!
YOU'RE ALWAYS HINDERING THE INVESTIGATION WITH YOUR PESKY QUESTIONS! CHILDREN SHOULD BE SEEN AND NOT HEARD!
UNDER-STAND?
YOU'RE RIGHT. SILENCE ...
...IS GOLD-EN.
POK
PSSH

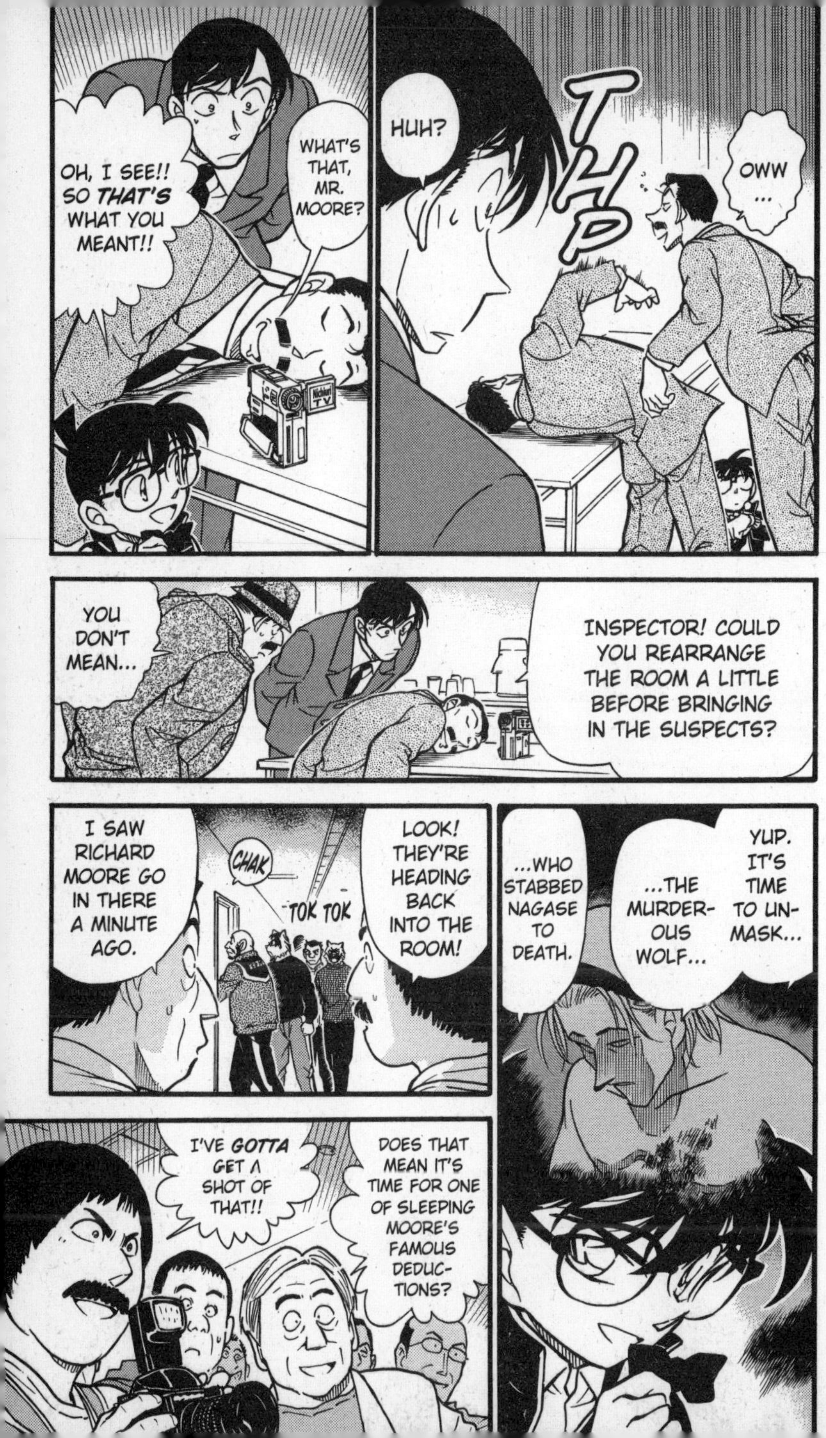
OWW ...
THP
HUH?
WHAT'S THAT, MR. MOORE?
OH, I SEE!! SO THAT'S WHAT YOU MEANT!!
INSPECTOR! COULD YOU REARRANGE THE ROOM A LITTLE BEFORE BRINGING IN THE SUSPECTS?
YOU DON'T MEAN...
YUP. IT'S TIME TO UN-MASK...
...THE MURDER-OUS WOLF...
...WHO STABBED NAGASE TO DEATH.
LOOK! THEY'RE HEADING BACK INTO THE ROOM!
CHAK
TOK TOK
I SAW RICHARD MOORE GO IN THERE A MINUTE AGO.
DOES THAT MEAN IT'S TIME FOR ONE OF SLEEPING MOORE'S FAMOUS DEDUC-TIONS?
I'VE GOTTA GET A SHOT OF THAT!!

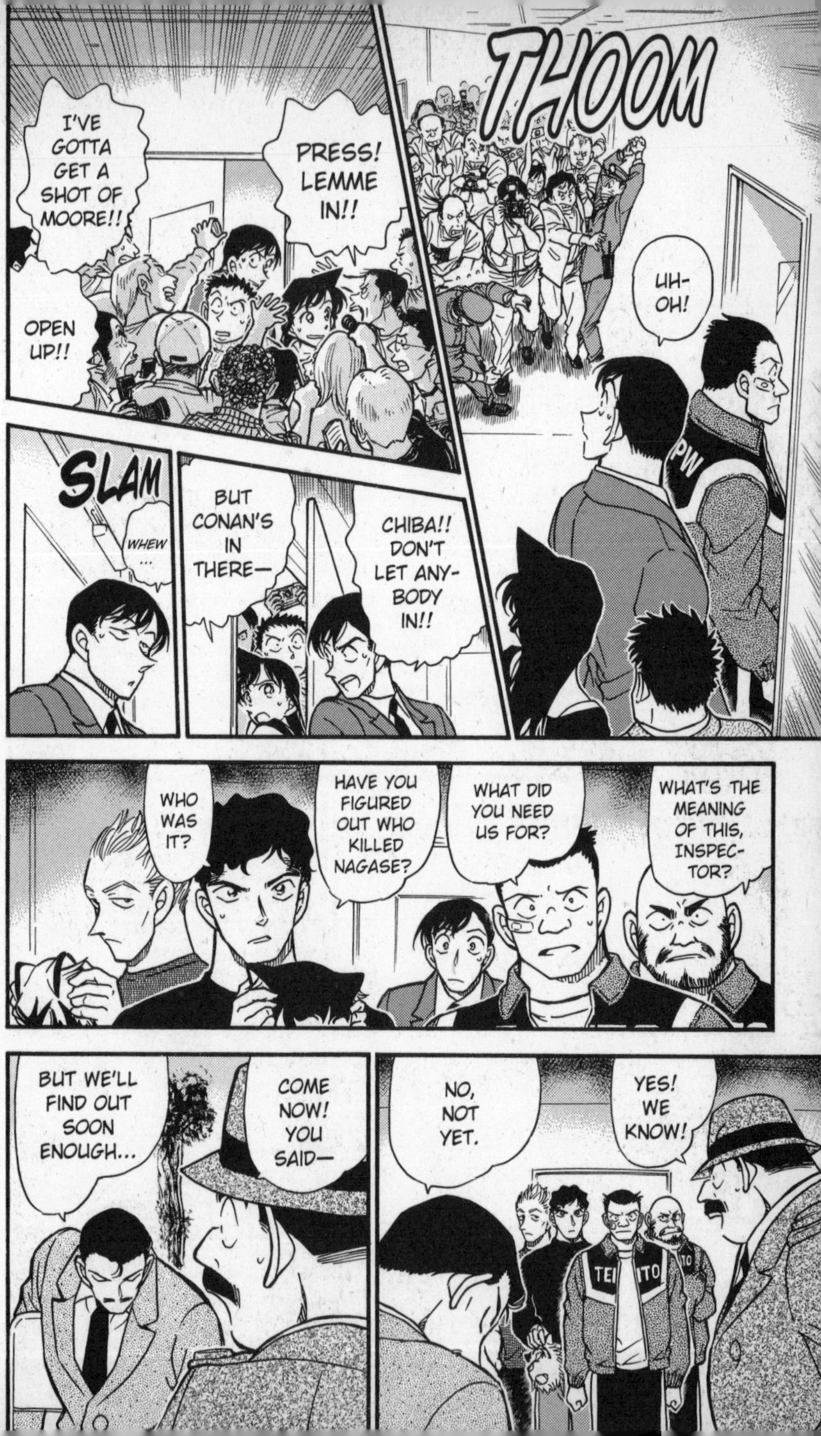
THOOM
UH-OH!
PRESS! LEMME IN!!
I'VE GOTTA GET A SHOT OF MOORE!!
OPEN UP!!
CHIBA!! DON'T LET ANYBODY IN!!
BUT CONAN'S IN THERE—
SLAM
WHEW...
WHAT'S THE MEANING OF THIS, INSPECTOR?
WHAT DID YOU NEED US FOR?
HAVE YOU FIGURED OUT WHO KILLED NAGASE?
WHO WAS IT?
YES! WE KNOW!
NO, NOT YET.
COME NOW! YOU SAID—
BUT WE'LL FIND OUT SOON ENOUGH...

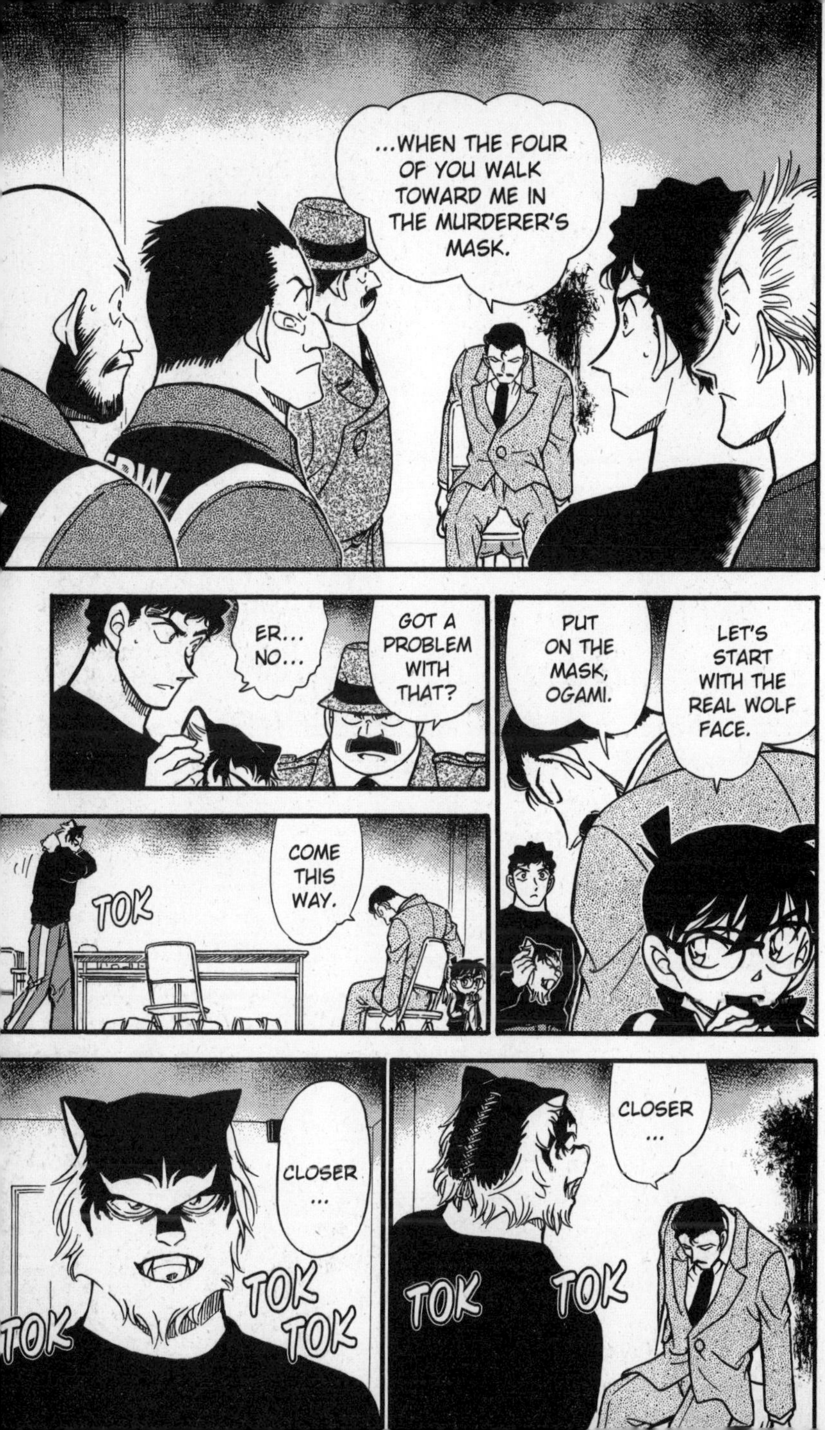
...WHEN THE FOUR OF YOU WALK TOWARD ME IN THE MURDERER'S MASK.
LET'S START WITH THE REAL WOLF FACE.
PUT ON THE MASK, OGAMI.
GOT A PROBLEM WITH THAT?
ER... NO...
COME THIS WAY.
TOK
CLOSER ...
TOK
TOK
CLOSER ...
TOK
TOK
TOK

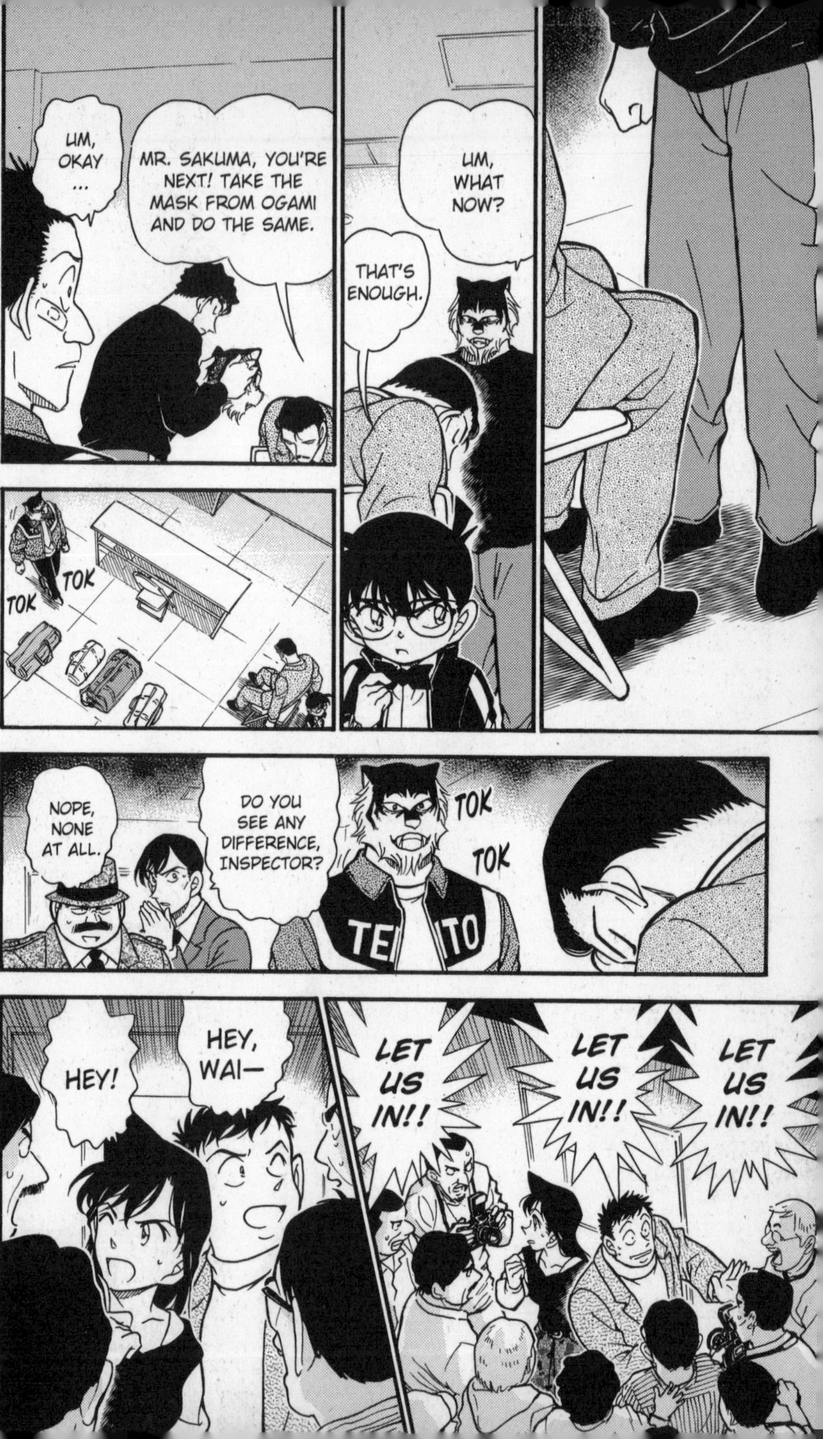
UM, WHAT NOW?
THAT'S ENOUGH.
MR. SAKUMA, YOU'RE NEXT! TAKE THE MASK FROM OGAMI AND DO THE SAME.
UM, OKAY ...
TOK
TOK
TOK
TOK
DO YOU SEE ANY DIFFERENCE, INSPECTOR?
NOPE, NONE AT ALL.
LET US IN!!
LET US IN!!
LET US IN!!
HEY, WAI—
HEY!

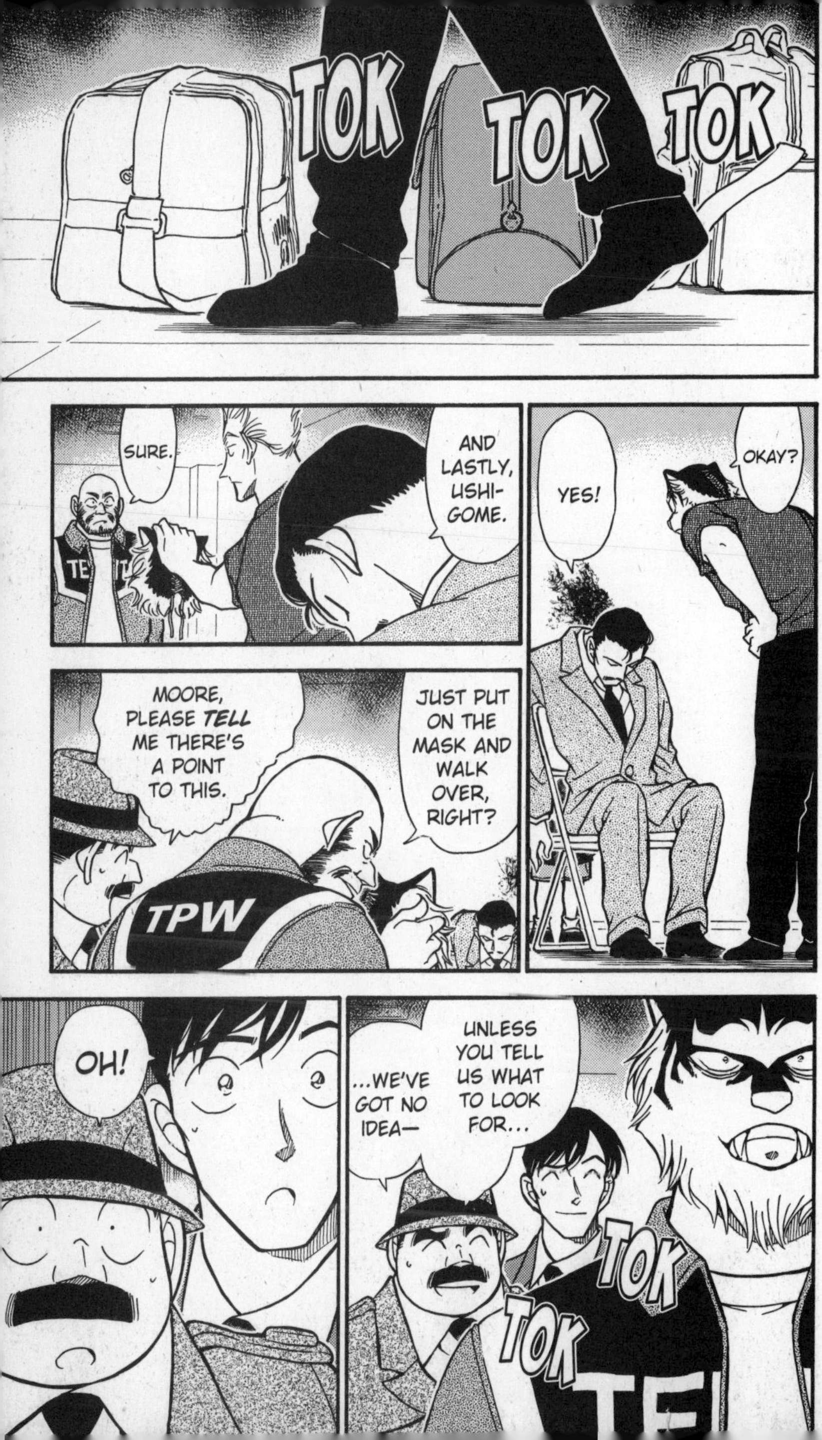
TOK
TOK
TOK
OKAY?
YES!
AND LASTLY, USHIGOME.
SURE.
JUST PUT ON THE MASK AND WALK OVER, RIGHT?
MOORE, PLEASE *TELL* ME THERE'S A POINT TO THIS.
TPW
UNLESS YOU TELL US WHAT TO LOOK FOR...
...WE'VE GOT NO IDEA—
TOK
TOK
OH!

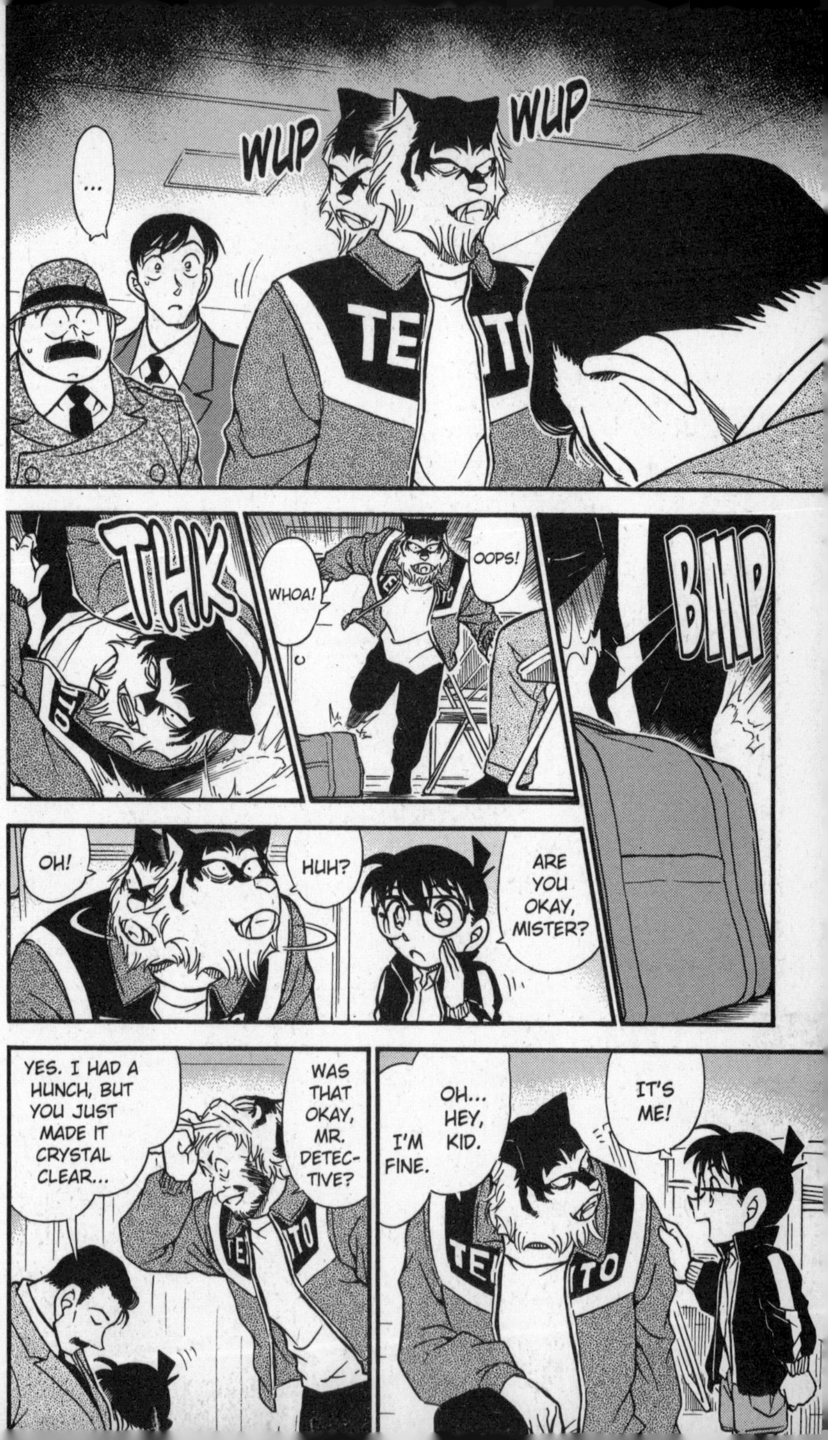
WLP
WLP
...
BMP
OOPS!
WHOA!
THK
ARE YOU OKAY, MISTER?
HUH?
OH!
IT'S ME!
OH... HEY, KID.
I'M FINE.
WAS THAT OKAY, MR. DETECTIVE?
YES. I HAD A HUNCH, BUT YOU JUST MADE IT CRYSTAL CLEAR...

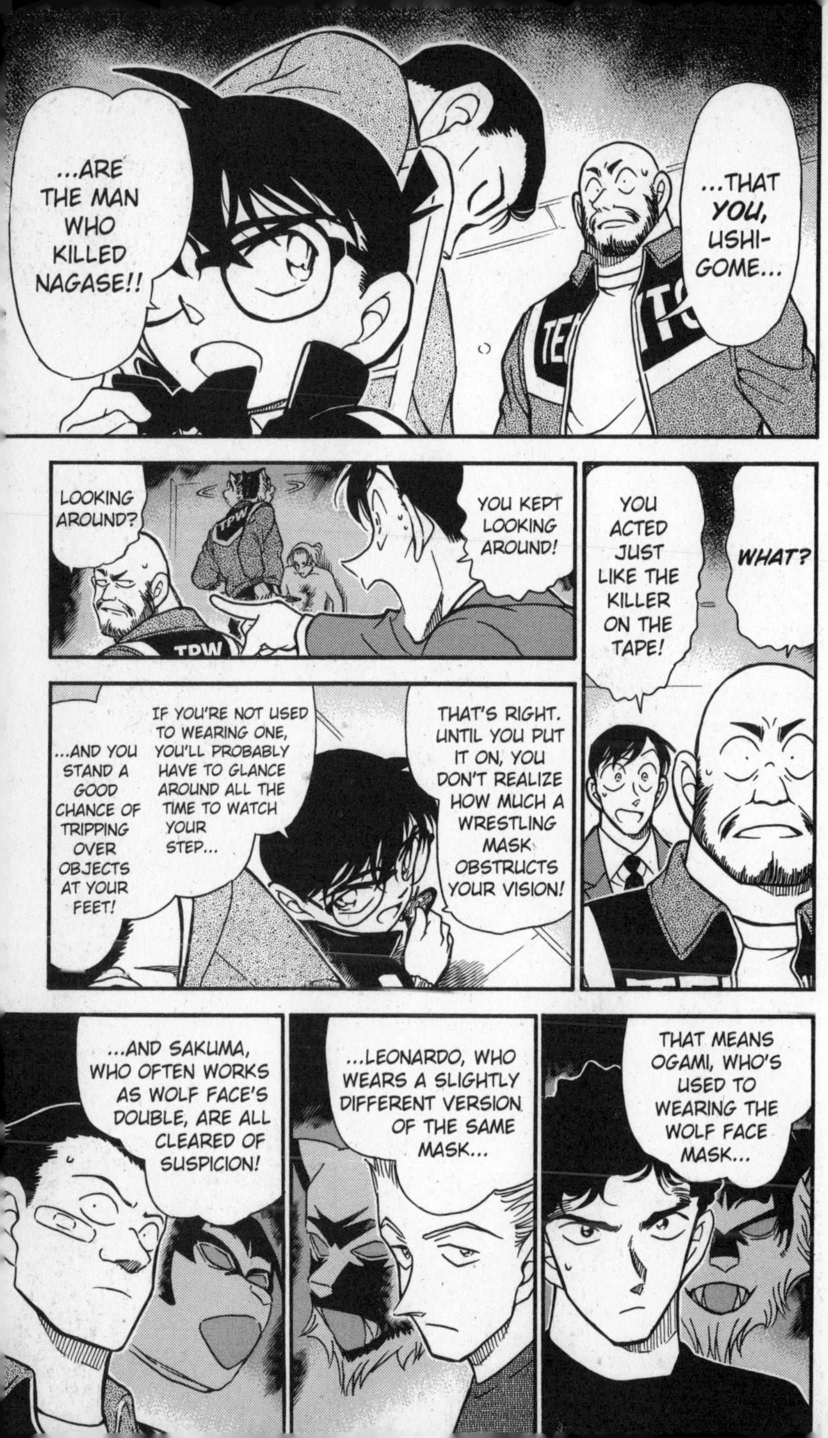
...THAT YOU, USHIGOME...
...ARE THE MAN WHO KILLED NAGASE!!
WHAT?
YOU ACTED JUST LIKE THE KILLER ON THE TAPE!
YOU KEPT LOOKING AROUND!
LOOKING AROUND?
THAT'S RIGHT. UNTIL YOU PUT IT ON, YOU DON'T REALIZE HOW MUCH A WRESTLING MASK OBSTRUCTS YOUR VISION!
IF YOU'RE NOT USED TO WEARING ONE, YOU'LL PROBABLY HAVE TO GLANCE AROUND ALL THE TIME TO WATCH YOUR STEP...
...AND YOU STAND A GOOD CHANCE OF TRIPPING OVER OBJECTS AT YOUR FEET!
THAT MEANS OGAMI, WHO'S USED TO WEARING THE WOLF FACE MASK...
...LEONARDO, WHO WEARS A SLIGHTLY DIFFERENT VERSION OF THE SAME MASK...
...AND SAKUMA, WHO OFTEN WORKS AS WOLF FACE'S DOUBLE, ARE ALL CLEARED OF SUSPICION!

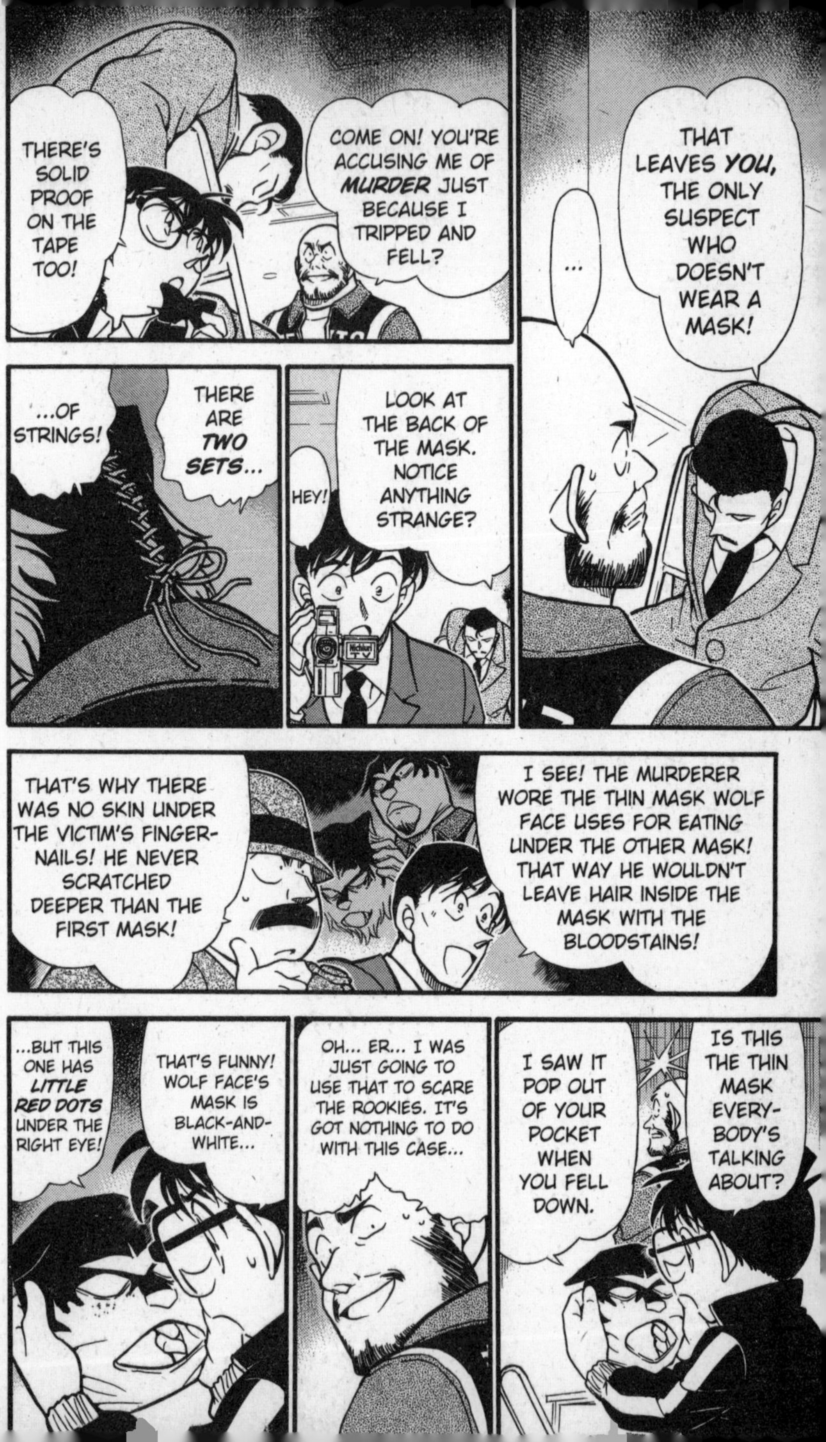
THAT LEAVES YOU, THE ONLY SUSPECT WHO DOESN'T WEAR A MASK!
...
COME ON! YOU'RE ACCUSING ME OF MURDER JUST BECAUSE I TRIPPED AND FELL?
THERE'S SOLID PROOF ON THE TAPE TOO!
LOOK AT THE BACK OF THE MASK. NOTICE ANYTHING STRANGE?
HEY!
THERE ARE TWO SETS...
...OF STRINGS!
I SEE! THE MURDERER WORE THE THIN MASK WOLF FACE USES FOR EATING UNDER THE OTHER MASK! THAT WAY HE WOULDN'T LEAVE HAIR INSIDE THE MASK WITH THE BLOODSTAINS!
THAT'S WHY THERE WAS NO SKIN UNDER THE VICTIM'S FINGER-NAILS! HE NEVER SCRATCHED DEEPER THAN THE FIRST MASK!
IS THIS THE THIN MASK EVERY-BODY'S TALKING ABOUT?
I SAW IT POP OUT OF YOUR POCKET WHEN YOU FELL DOWN.
OH... ER... I WAS JUST GOING TO USE THAT TO SCARE THE ROOKIES. IT'S GOT NOTHING TO DO WITH THIS CASE...
THAT'S FUNNY! WOLF FACE'S MASK IS BLACK-AND-WHITE...
...BUT THIS ONE HAS LITTLE RED DOTS UNDER THE RIGHT EYE!

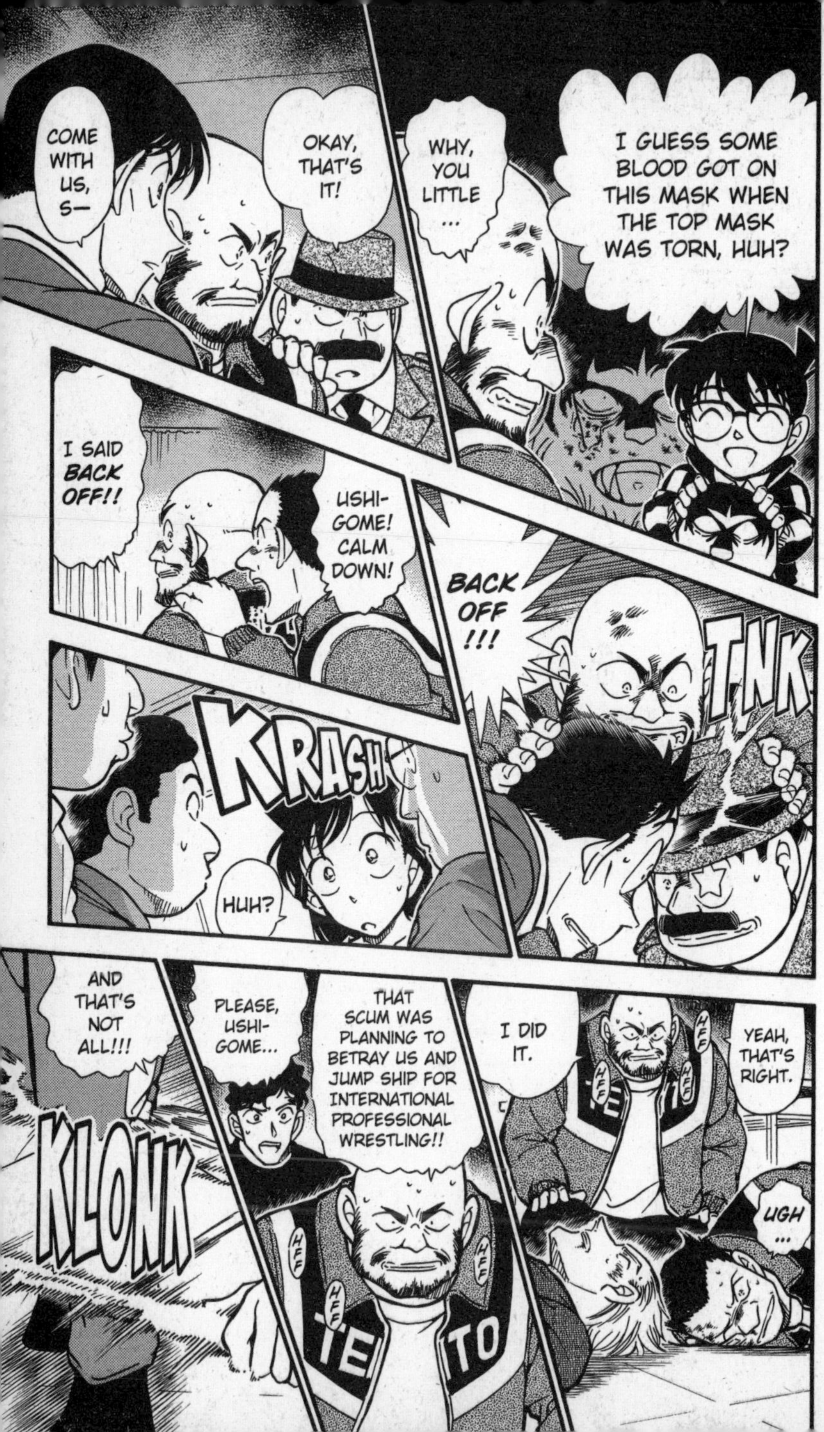
I GUESS SOME BLOOD GOT ON THIS MASK WHEN THE TOP MASK WAS TORN, HUH?
WHY, YOU LITTLE ...
OKAY, THAT'S IT!
COME WITH US, S—
BACK OFF !!!
TNK
USHI-GOME! CALM DOWN!
I SAID BACK OFF!!
KRASH
HUH?
YEAH, THAT'S RIGHT.
I DID IT.
UGH ...
THAT SCUM WAS PLANNING TO BETRAY US AND JUMP SHIP FOR INTERNATIONAL PROFESSIONAL WRESTLING!!
PLEASE, USHI-GOME...
AND THAT'S NOT ALL!!!
KLONK

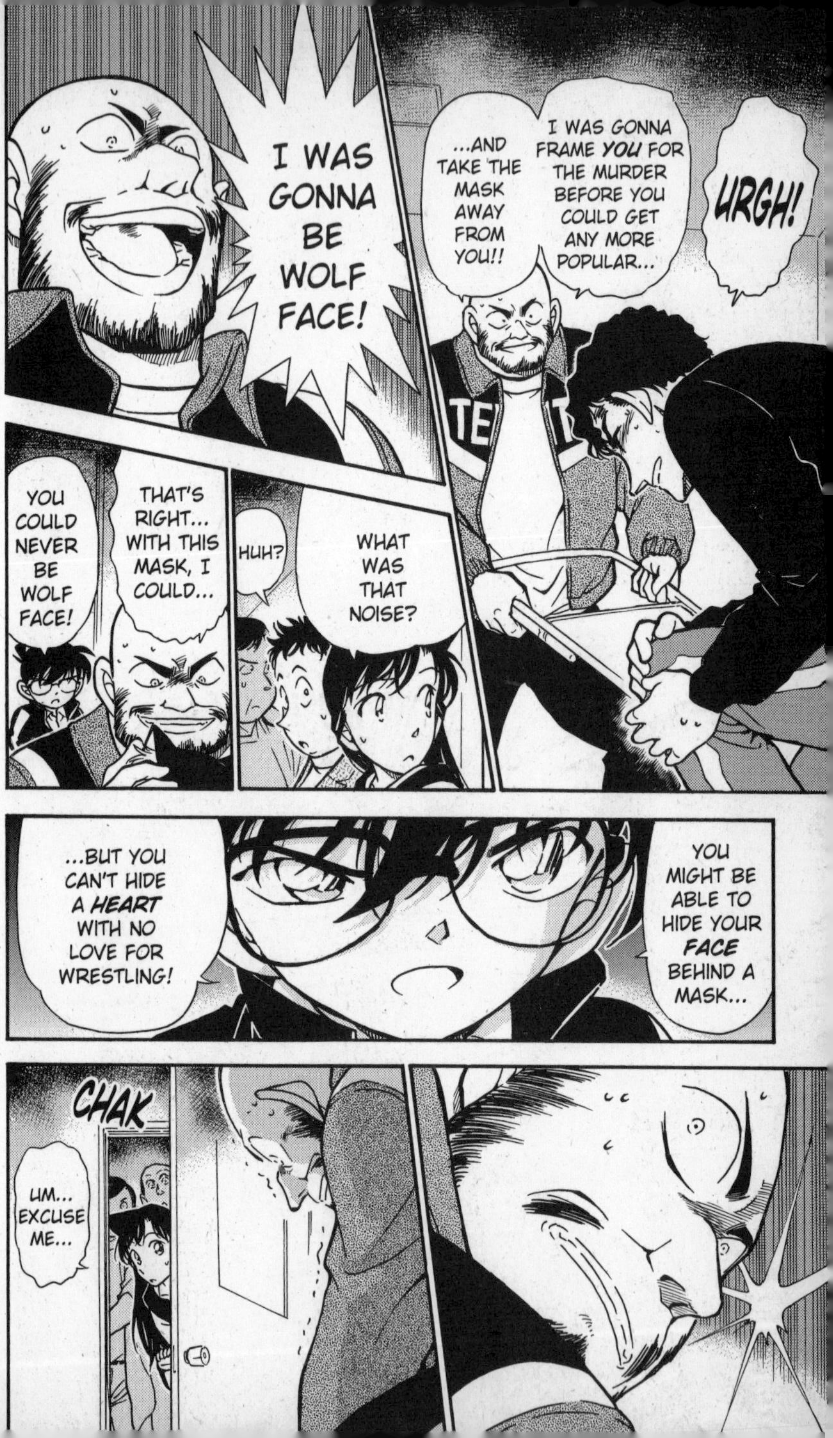
URGH!
I WAS GONNA FRAME YOU FOR THE MURDER BEFORE YOU COULD GET ANY MORE POPULAR...
...AND TAKE THE MASK AWAY FROM YOU!!
I WAS GONNA BE WOLF FACE!
WHAT WAS THAT NOISE?
HUH?
THAT'S RIGHT... WITH THIS MASK, I COULD...
YOU COULD NEVER BE WOLF FACE!
YOU MIGHT BE ABLE TO HIDE YOUR FACE BEHIND A MASK...
...BUT YOU CAN'T HIDE A HEART WITH NO LOVE FOR WRESTLING!
CHAK
UM... EXCUSE ME...

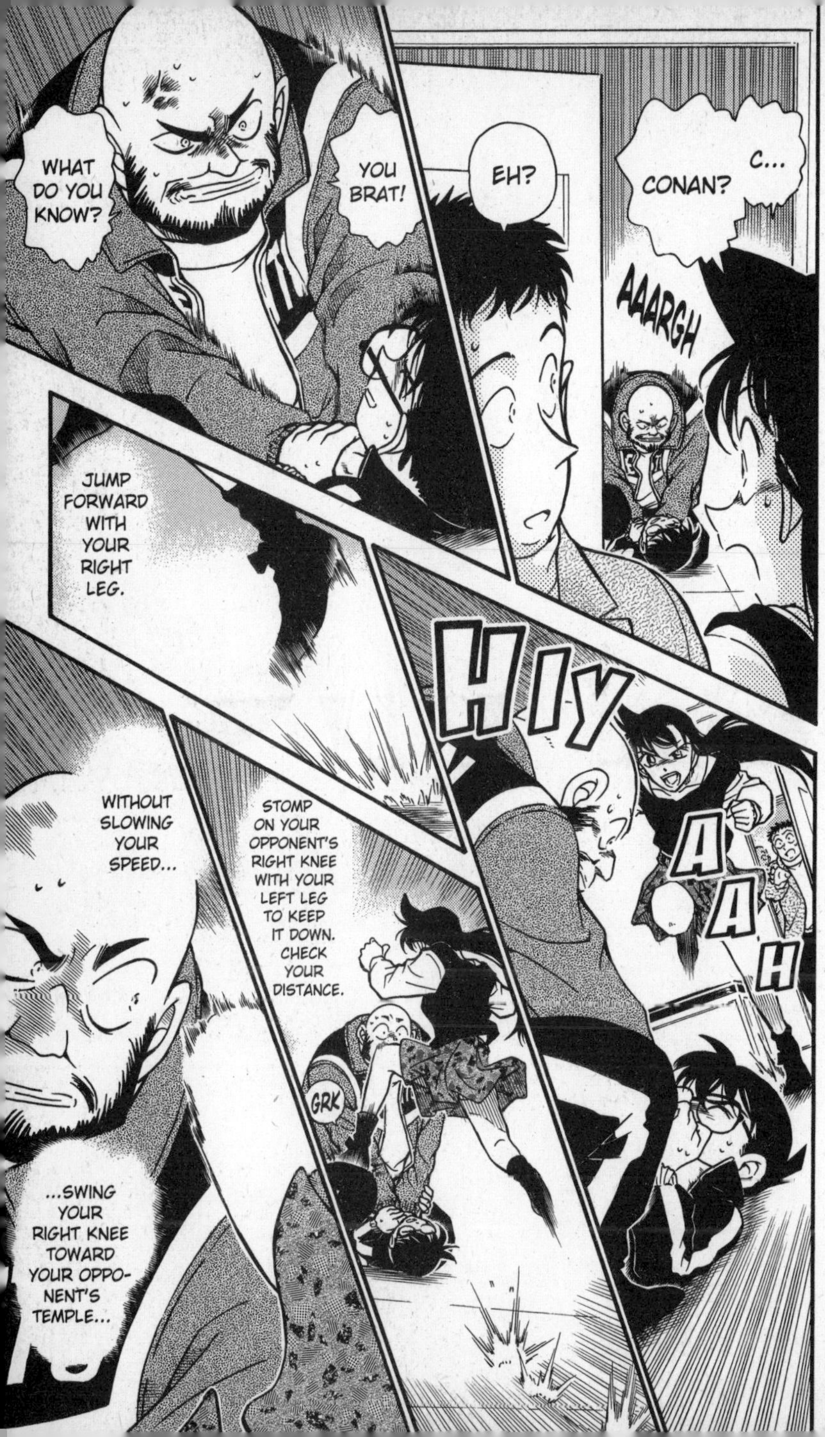
C... CONAN?
AAARGH
EH?
YOU BRAT!
WHAT DO YOU KNOW?
HIYAAAH
JUMP FORWARD WITH YOUR RIGHT LEG.
STOMP ON YOUR OPPONENT'S RIGHT KNEE WITH YOUR LEFT LEG TO KEEP IT DOWN. CHECK YOUR DISTANCE.
GRK
WITHOUT SLOWING YOUR SPEED...
...SWING YOUR RIGHT KNEE TOWARD YOUR OPPO-NENT'S TEMPLE...

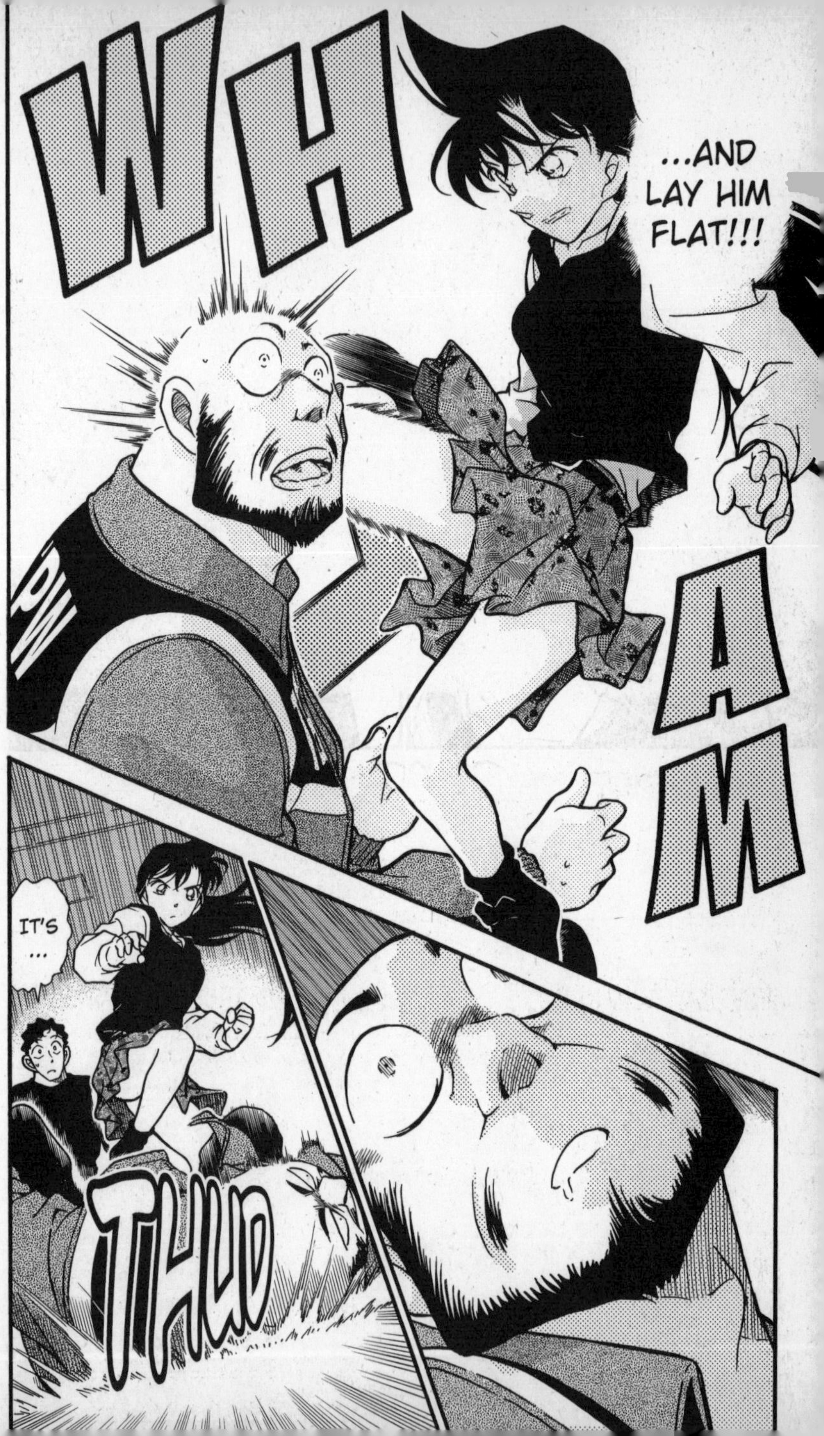
...AND LAY HIM FLAT!!!
WHAM
IT'S ...
THUD

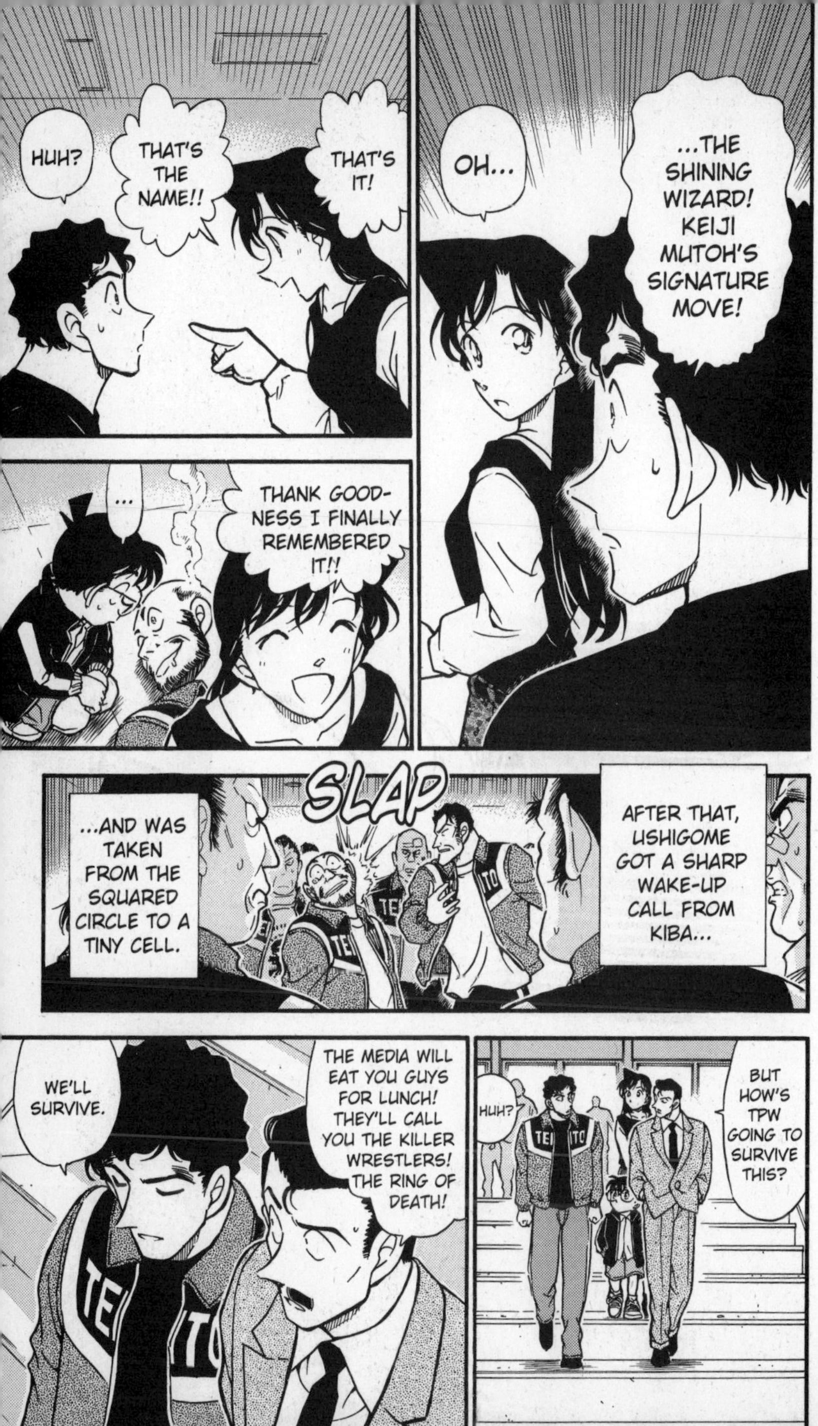
...THE SHINING WIZARD! KEIJI MUTOH'S SIGNATURE MOVE!
OH...
THAT'S IT!
THAT'S THE NAME!!
HUH?
THANK GOOD-NESS I FINALLY REMEMBERED IT!!
...
AFTER THAT, USHIGOME GOT A SHARP WAKE-UP CALL FROM KIBA...
SLAP
...AND WAS TAKEN FROM THE SQUARED CIRCLE TO A TINY CELL.
BUT HOW'S TPW GOING TO SURVIVE THIS?
HUH?
THE MEDIA WILL EAT YOU GUYS FOR LUNCH! THEY'LL CALL YOU THE KILLER WRESTLERS! THE RING OF DEATH!
WE'LL SURVIVE.

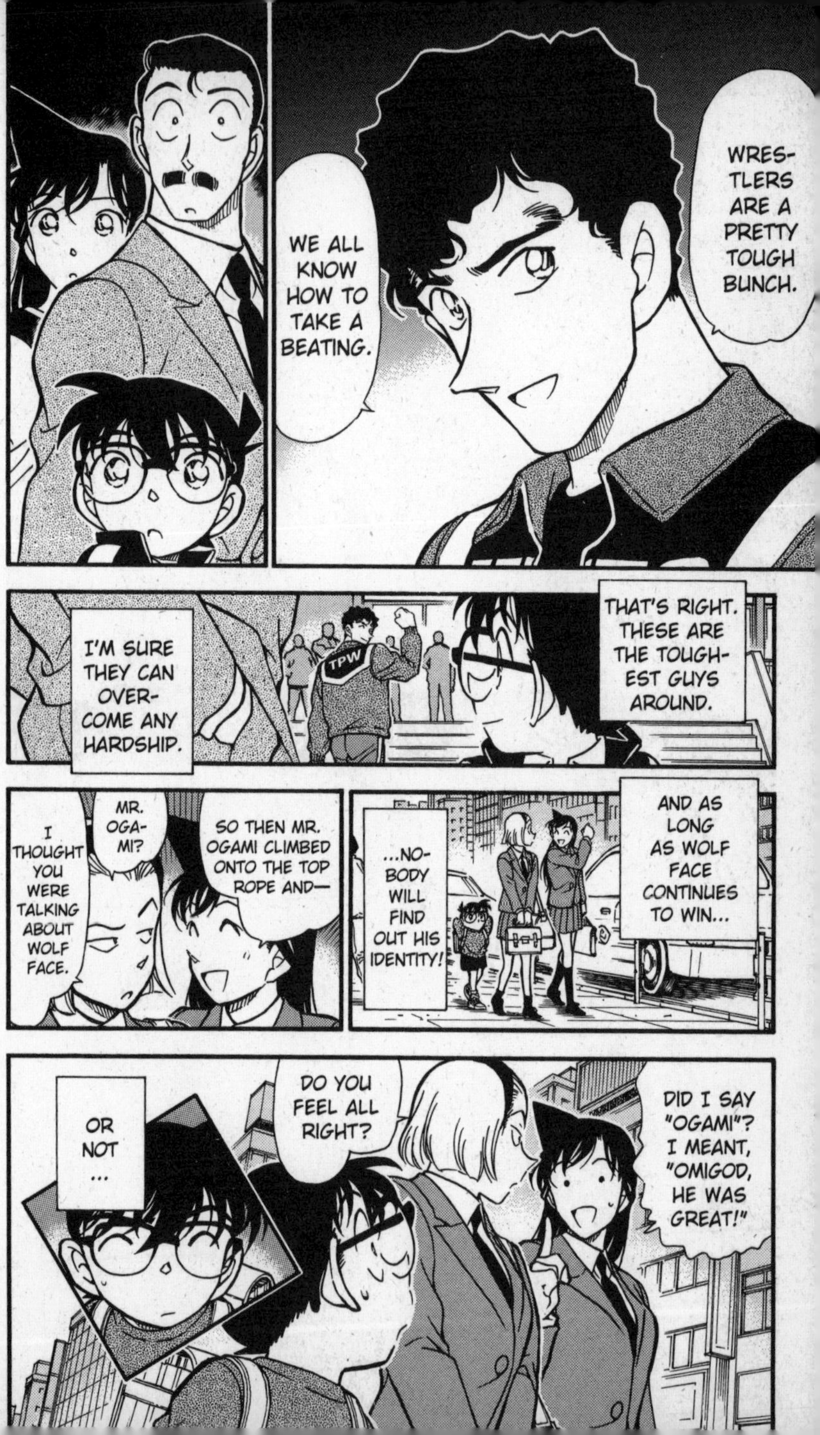
WRESTLERS ARE A PRETTY TOUGH BUNCH.
WE ALL KNOW HOW TO TAKE A BEATING.
THAT'S RIGHT. THESE ARE THE TOUGHEST GUYS AROUND.
I'M SURE THEY CAN OVERCOME ANY HARDSHIP.
AND AS LONG AS WOLF FACE CONTINUES TO WIN...
...NOBODY WILL FIND OUT HIS IDENTITY!
SO THEN MR. OGAMI CLIMBED ONTO THE TOP ROPE AND—
MR. OGAMI?
I THOUGHT YOU WERE TALKING ABOUT WOLF FACE.
DID I SAY "OGAMI"? I MEANT, "OMIGOD, HE WAS GREAT!"
DO YOU FEEL ALL RIGHT?
OR NOT ...

FILE 8: HARLEY'S STRUGGLE ①

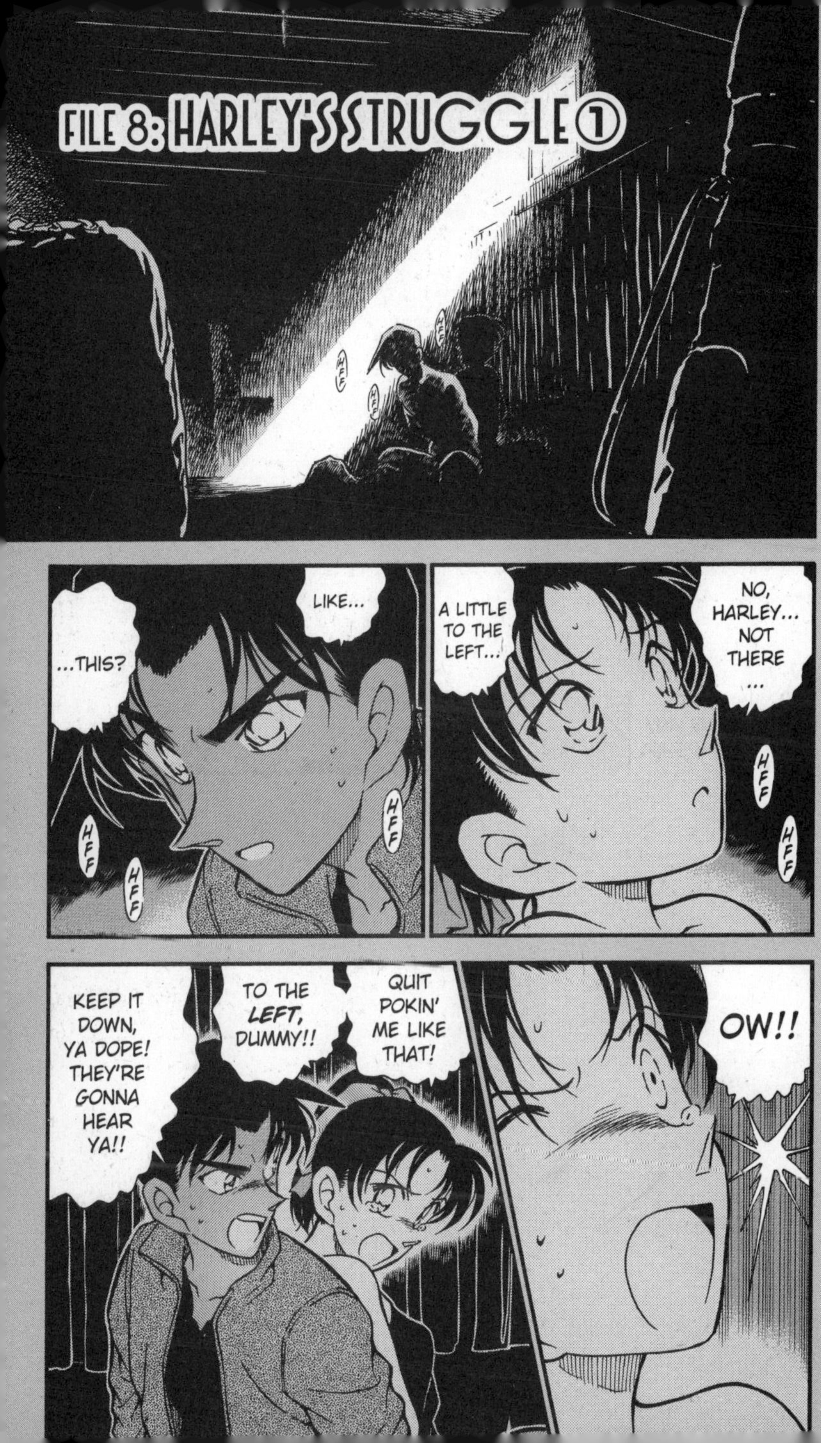
HFF
HFF
HFF
NO, HARLEY... NOT THERE ...
A LITTLE TO THE LEFT...
HFF
HFF
LIKE...
...THIS?
HFF
HFF
HFF
OW!!
QUIT POKIN' ME LIKE THAT!
TO THE *LEFT*, DUMMY!!
KEEP IT DOWN, YA DOPE! THEY'RE GONNA HEAR YA!!

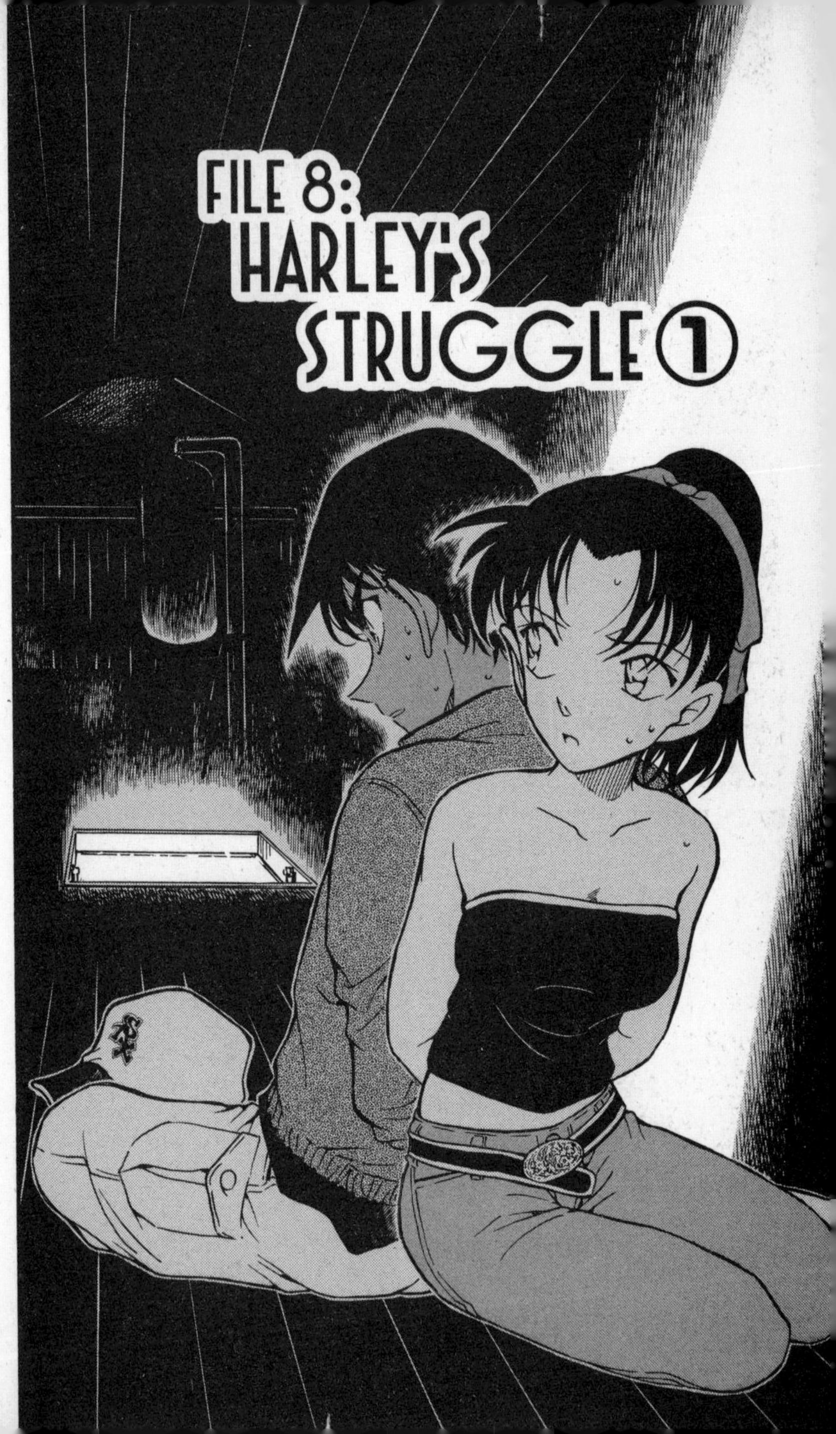
FILE 8:
HARLEY'S
STRUGGLE ①

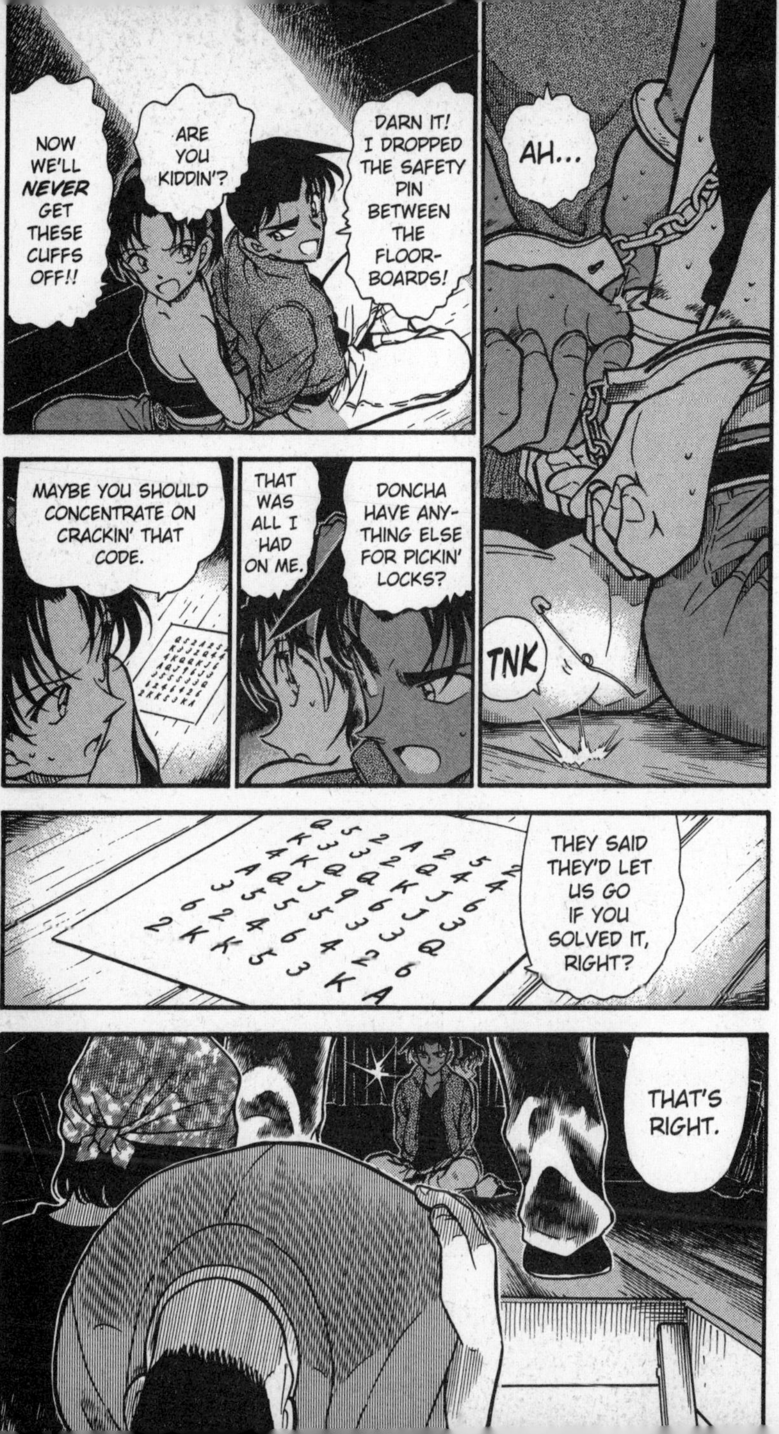
AH...
TNK
DARN IT! I DROPPED THE SAFETY PIN BETWEEN THE FLOOR-BOARDS!
ARE YOU KIDDIN'?
NOW WE'LL **NEVER** GET THESE CUFFS OFF!!
DONCHA HAVE ANY-THING ELSE FOR PICKIN' LOCKS?
THAT WAS ALL I HAD ON ME.
MAYBE YOU SHOULD CONCENTRATE ON CRACKIN' THAT CODE.
THEY SAID THEY'D LET US GO IF YOU SOLVED IT, RIGHT?
THAT'S RIGHT.

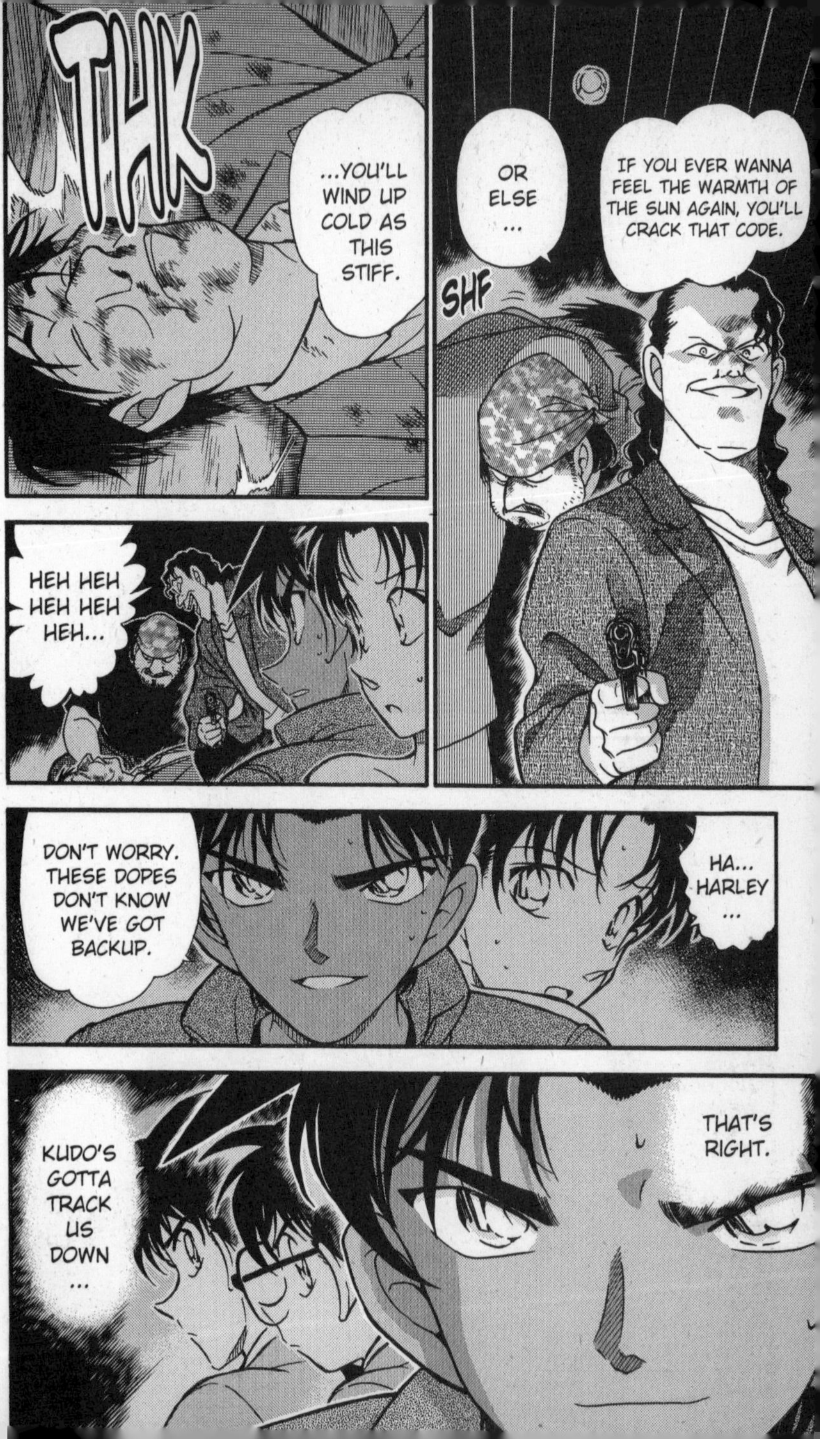
IF YOU EVER WANNA FEEL THE WARMTH OF THE SUN AGAIN, YOU'LL CRACK THAT CODE.
OR ELSE ...
SHF
THK
...YOU'LL WIND UP COLD AS THIS STIFF.
HEH HEH HEH HEH HEH...
HA... HARLEY ...
DON'T WORRY. THESE DOPES DON'T KNOW WE'VE GOT BACKUP.
THAT'S RIGHT.
KUDO'S GOTTA TRACK US DOWN ...

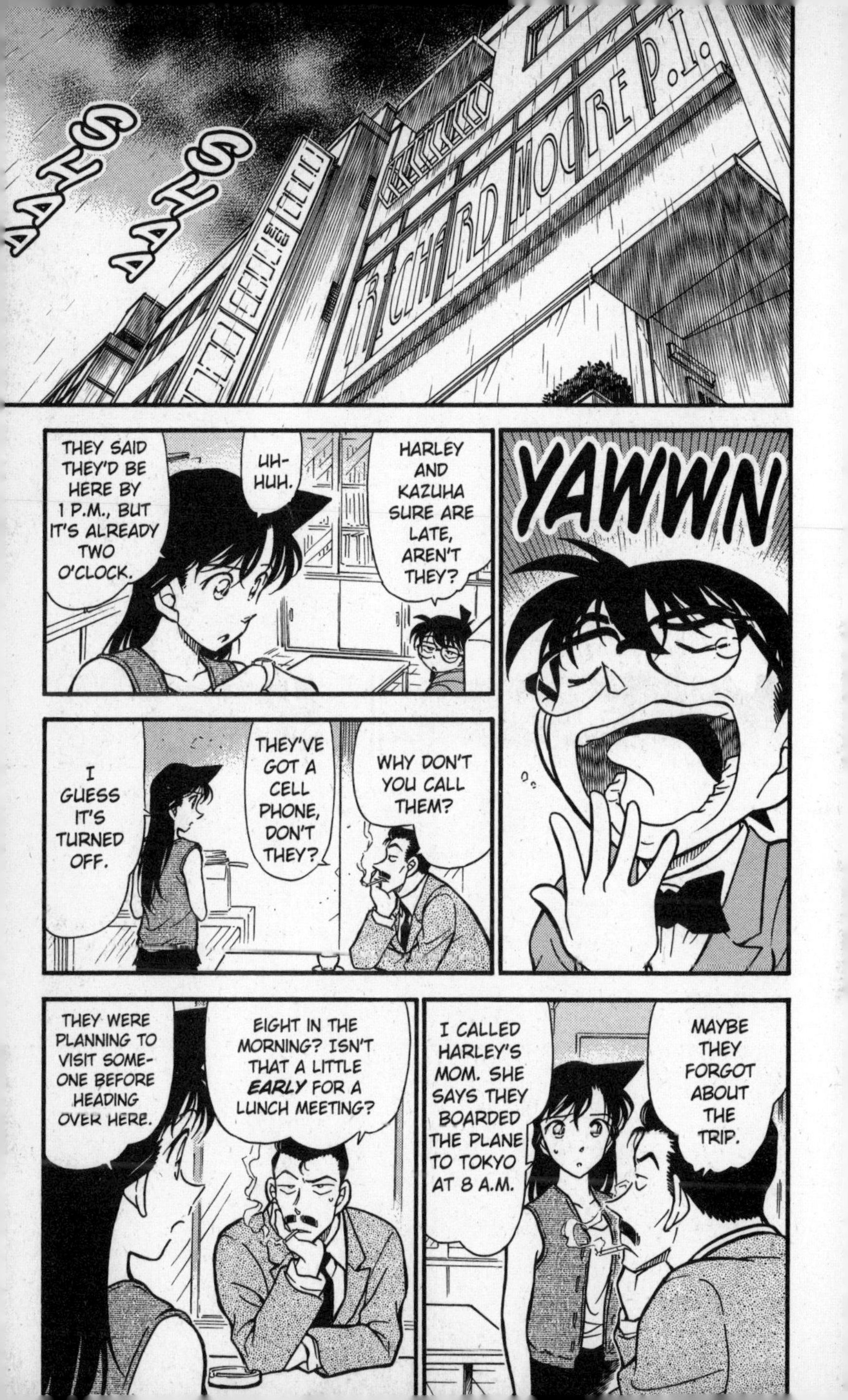
SHAA
SHAA
RICHARD MOORE P.I.
YAWWN
HARLEY AND KAZUHA SURE ARE LATE, AREN'T THEY?
UH-HUH.
THEY SAID THEY'D BE HERE BY 1 P.M., BUT IT'S ALREADY TWO O'CLOCK.
WHY DON'T YOU CALL THEM?
THEY'VE GOT A CELL PHONE, DON'T THEY?
I GUESS IT'S TURNED OFF.
MAYBE THEY FORGOT ABOUT THE TRIP.
I CALLED HARLEY'S MOM. SHE SAYS THEY BOARDED THE PLANE TO TOKYO AT 8 A.M.
EIGHT IN THE MORNING? ISN'T THAT A LITTLE ***EARLY*** FOR A LUNCH MEETING?
THEY WERE PLANNING TO VISIT SOMEONE BEFORE HEADING OVER HERE.

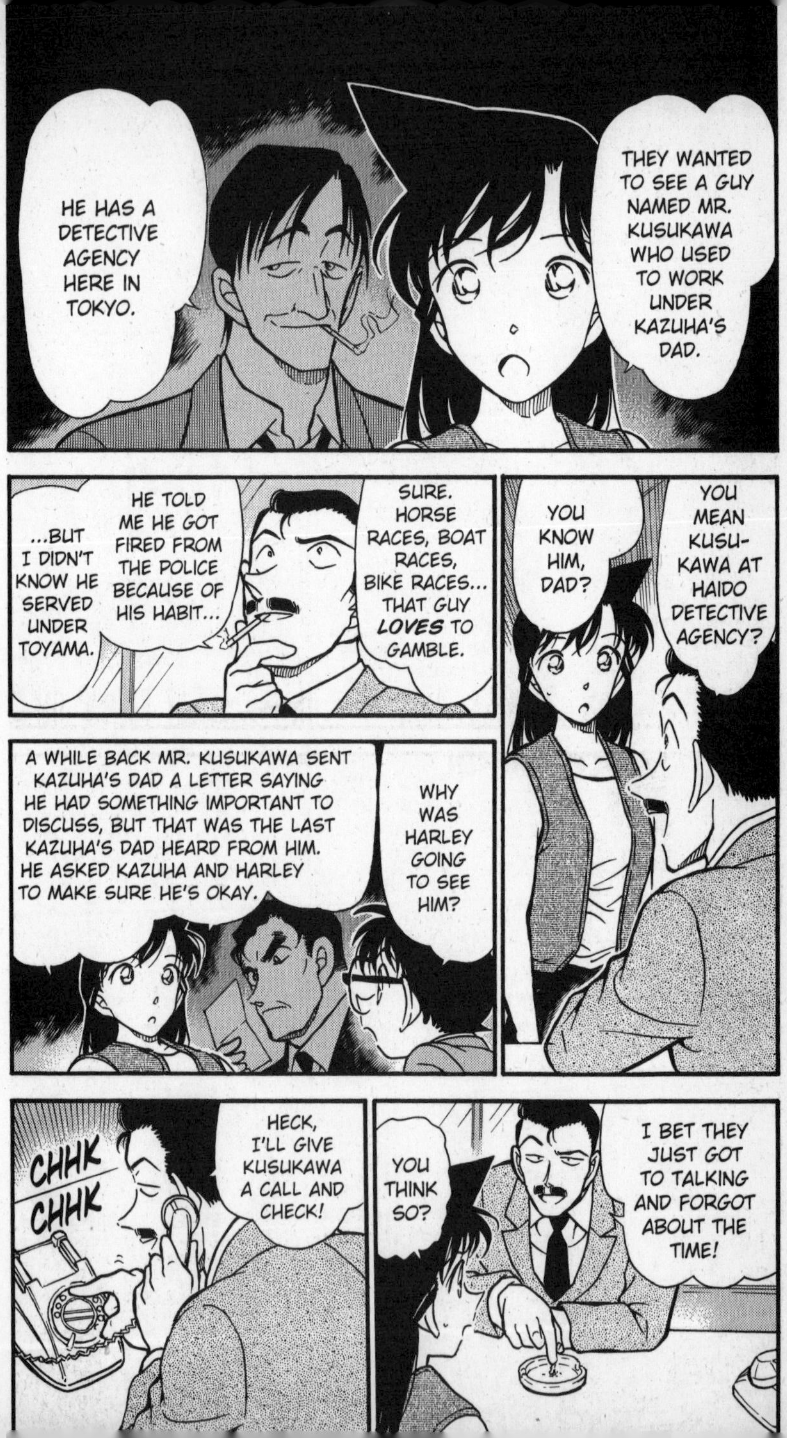
THEY WANTED TO SEE A GUY NAMED MR. KUSUKAWA WHO USED TO WORK UNDER KAZUHA'S DAD.
HE HAS A DETECTIVE AGENCY HERE IN TOKYO.
YOU MEAN KUSU-KAWA AT HAIDO DETECTIVE AGENCY?
YOU KNOW HIM, DAD?
SURE. HORSE RACES, BOAT RACES, BIKE RACES... THAT GUY *LOVES* TO GAMBLE.
HE TOLD ME HE GOT FIRED FROM THE POLICE BECAUSE OF HIS HABIT...
...BUT I DIDN'T KNOW HE SERVED UNDER TOYAMA.
WHY WAS HARLEY GOING TO SEE HIM?
A WHILE BACK MR. KUSUKAWA SENT KAZUHA'S DAD A LETTER SAYING HE HAD SOMETHING IMPORTANT TO DISCUSS, BUT THAT WAS THE LAST KAZUHA'S DAD HEARD FROM HIM. HE ASKED KAZUHA AND HARLEY TO MAKE SURE HE'S OKAY.
I BET THEY JUST GOT TO TALKING AND FORGOT ABOUT THE TIME!
YOU THINK SO?
HECK, I'LL GIVE KUSUKAWA A CALL AND CHECK!
CHHK
CHHK

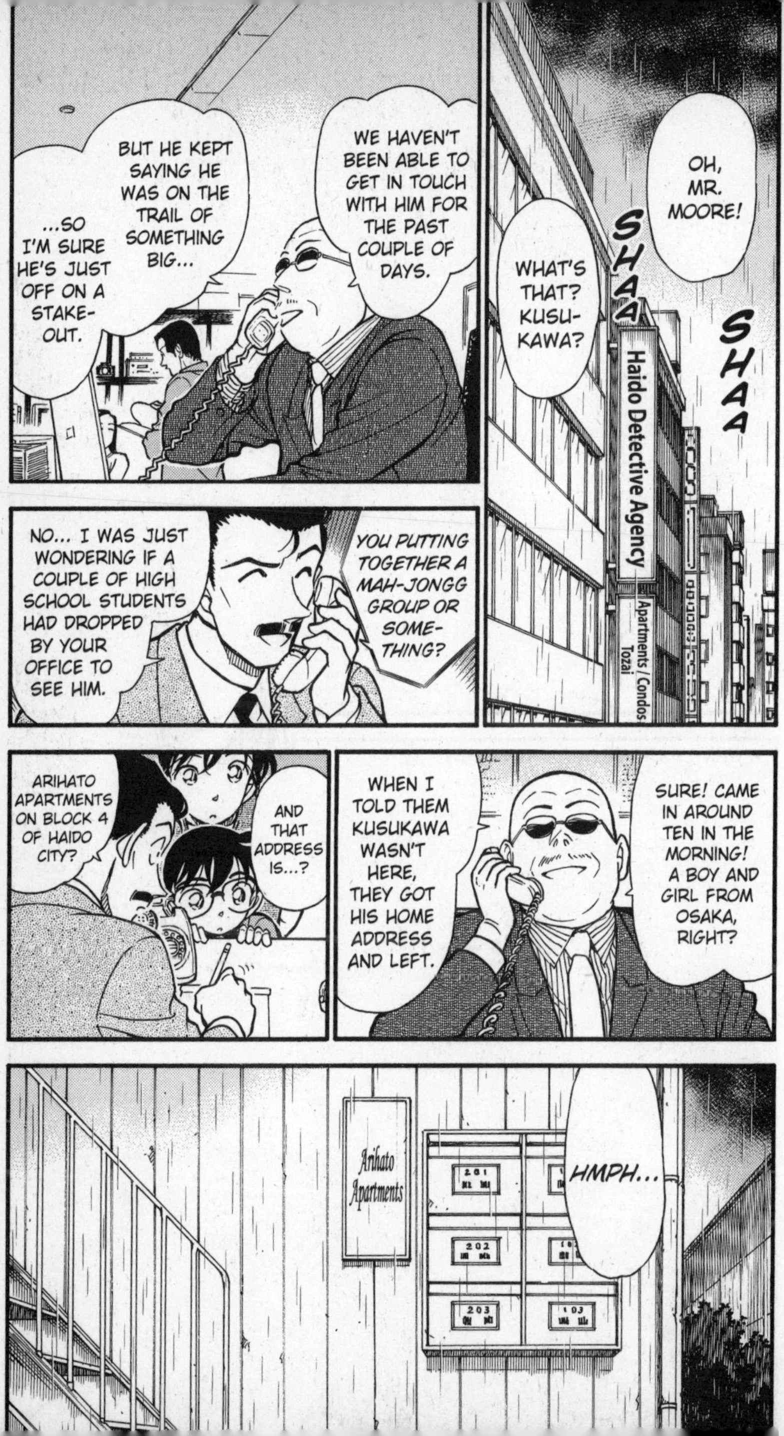

OH, MR. MOORE!
WHAT'S THAT? KUSU-KAWA?
SHAA
SHAA
Haido Detective Agency
Apartments / Condos Tozai
WE HAVEN'T BEEN ABLE TO GET IN TOUCH WITH HIM FOR THE PAST COUPLE OF DAYS.
BUT HE KEPT SAYING HE WAS ON THE TRAIL OF SOMETHING BIG...
...SO I'M SURE HE'S JUST OFF ON A STAKE-OUT.
YOU PUTTING TOGETHER A MAH-JONGG GROUP OR SOME-THING?
NO... I WAS JUST WONDERING IF A COUPLE OF HIGH SCHOOL STUDENTS HAD DROPPED BY YOUR OFFICE TO SEE HIM.
SURE! CAME IN AROUND TEN IN THE MORNING! A BOY AND GIRL FROM OSAKA, RIGHT?
WHEN I TOLD THEM KUSUKAWA WASN'T HERE, THEY GOT HIS HOME ADDRESS AND LEFT.
AND THAT ADDRESS IS...?
ARIHATO APARTMENTS ON BLOCK 4 OF HAIDO CITY?
HMPH...
Arihato Apartments
201
202
203
103

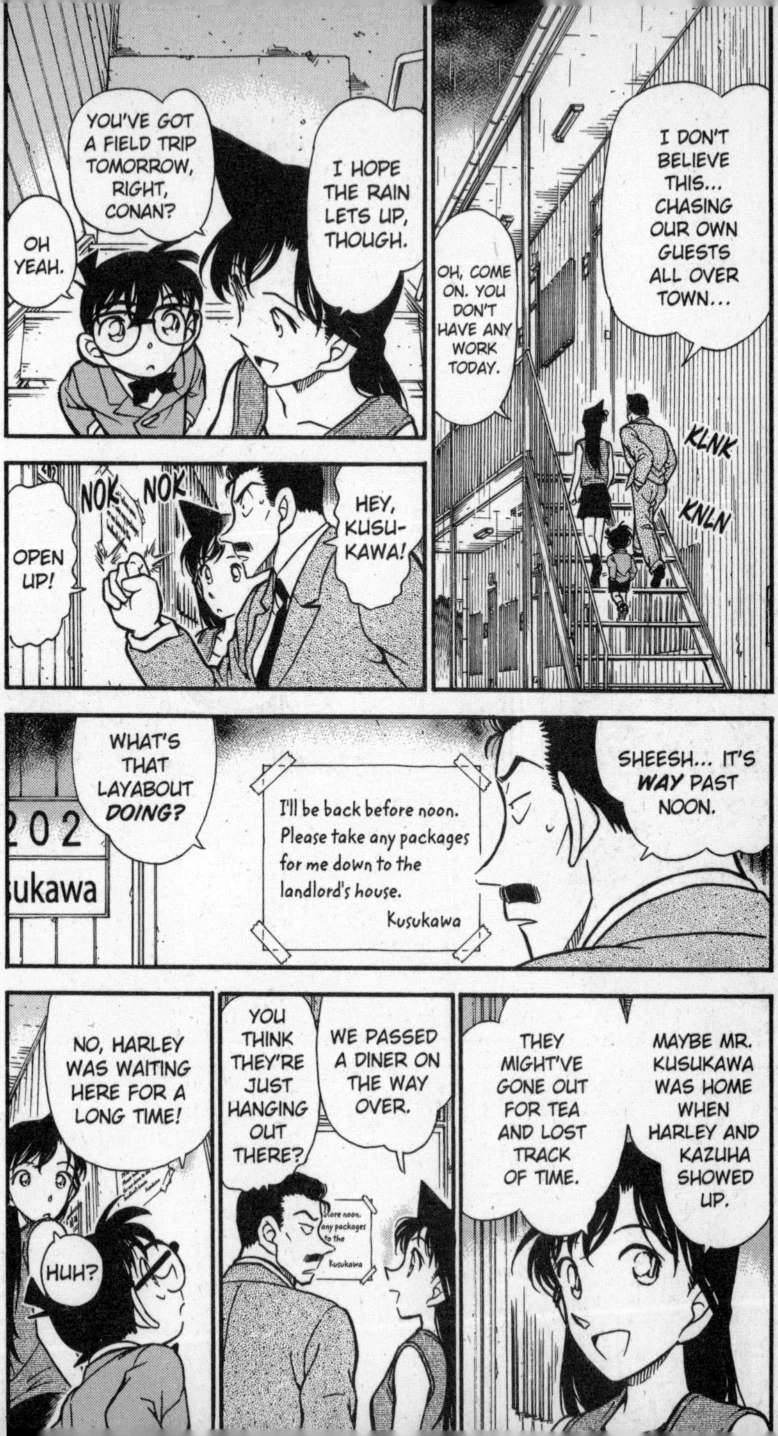
I DON'T BELIEVE THIS... CHASING OUR OWN GUESTS ALL OVER TOWN...
OH, COME ON. YOU DON'T HAVE ANY WORK TODAY.
KLNK
KNLN
I HOPE THE RAIN LETS UP, THOUGH.
YOU'VE GOT A FIELD TRIP TOMORROW, RIGHT, CONAN?
OH YEAH.
HEY, KUSU-KAWA!
NOK NOK
OPEN UP!
SHEESH... IT'S WAY PAST NOON.
I'll be back before noon. Please take any packages for me down to the landlord's house.
Kusukawa
WHAT'S THAT LAYABOUT DOING?
202
ukawa
MAYBE MR. KUSUKAWA WAS HOME WHEN HARLEY AND KAZUHA SHOWED UP.
THEY MIGHT'VE GONE OUT FOR TEA AND LOST TRACK OF TIME.
WE PASSED A DINER ON THE WAY OVER.
YOU THINK THEY'RE JUST HANGING OUT THERE?
NO, HARLEY WAS WAITING HERE FOR A LONG TIME!
HUH?

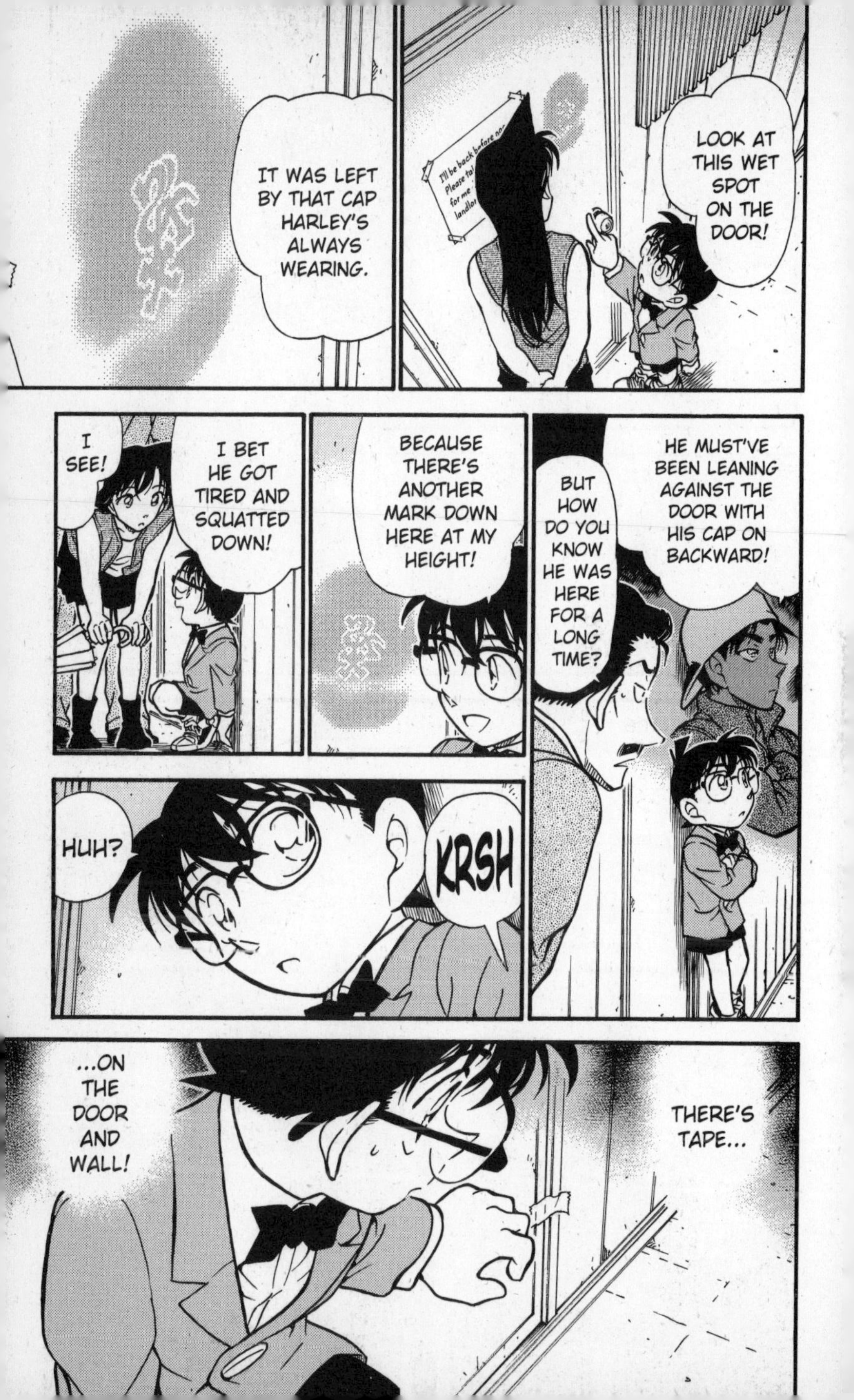
LOOK AT THIS WET SPOT ON THE DOOR!
IT WAS LEFT BY THAT CAP HARLEY'S ALWAYS WEARING.
HE MUST'VE BEEN LEANING AGAINST THE DOOR WITH HIS CAP ON BACKWARD!
BUT HOW DO YOU KNOW HE WAS HERE FOR A LONG TIME?
BECAUSE THERE'S ANOTHER MARK DOWN HERE AT MY HEIGHT!
I BET HE GOT TIRED AND SQUATTED DOWN!
I SEE!
KRSH
HUH?
THERE'S TAPE...
...ON THE DOOR AND WALL!

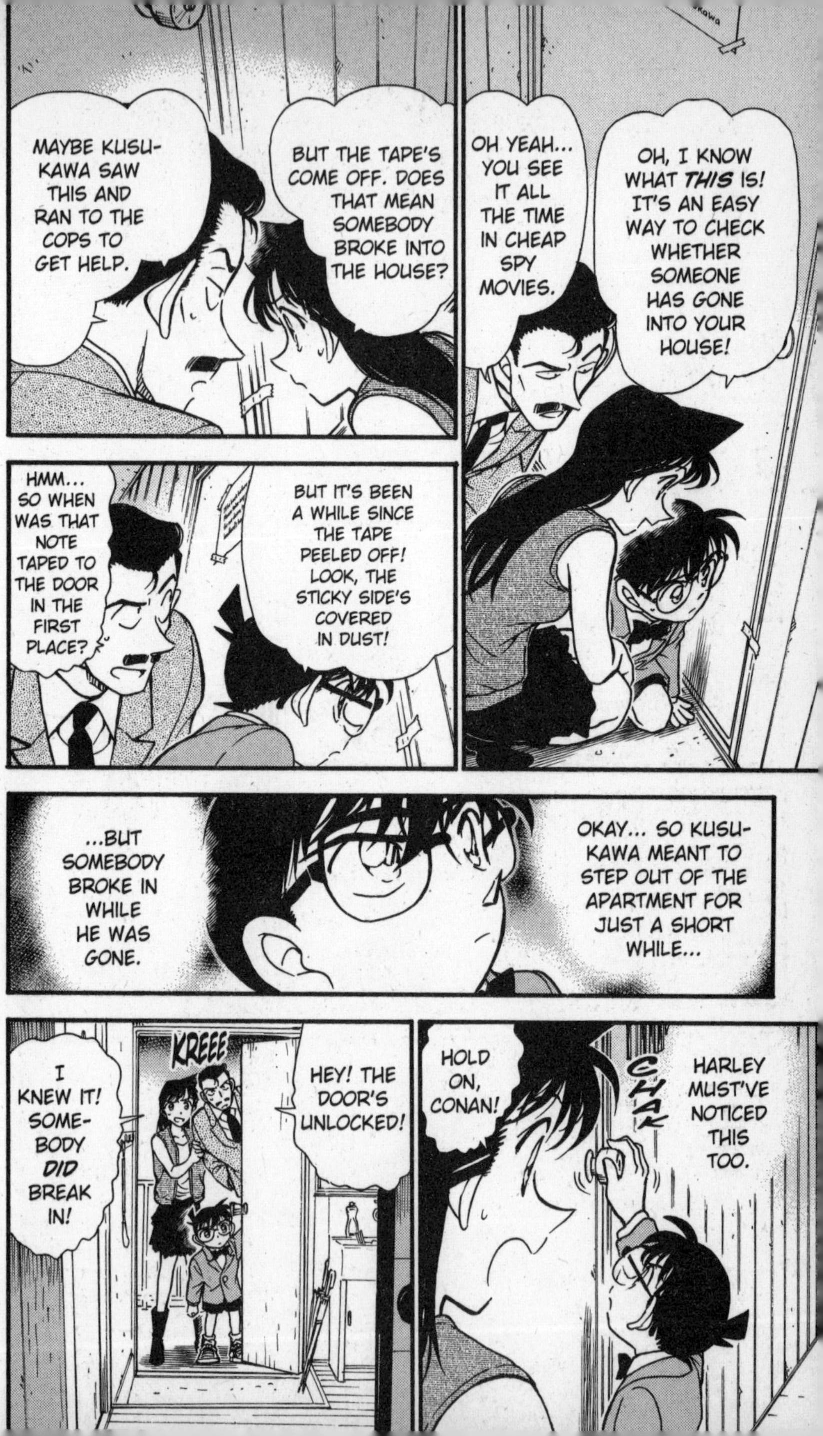
OH, I KNOW WHAT *THIS* IS! IT'S AN EASY WAY TO CHECK WHETHER SOMEONE HAS GONE INTO YOUR HOUSE!
OH YEAH... YOU SEE IT ALL THE TIME IN CHEAP SPY MOVIES.
BUT THE TAPE'S COME OFF. DOES THAT MEAN SOMEBODY BROKE INTO THE HOUSE?
MAYBE KUSU-KAWA SAW THIS AND RAN TO THE COPS TO GET HELP.
HMM... SO WHEN WAS THAT NOTE TAPED TO THE DOOR IN THE FIRST PLACE?
BUT IT'S BEEN A WHILE SINCE THE TAPE PEELED OFF! LOOK, THE STICKY SIDE'S COVERED IN DUST!
OKAY... SO KUSU-KAWA MEANT TO STEP OUT OF THE APARTMENT FOR JUST A SHORT WHILE...
...BUT SOMEBODY BROKE IN WHILE HE WAS GONE.
HARLEY MUST'VE NOTICED THIS TOO.
CHAK
HOLD ON, CONAN!
HEY! THE DOOR'S UNLOCKED!
KREEE
I KNEW IT! SOME-BODY *DID* BREAK IN!

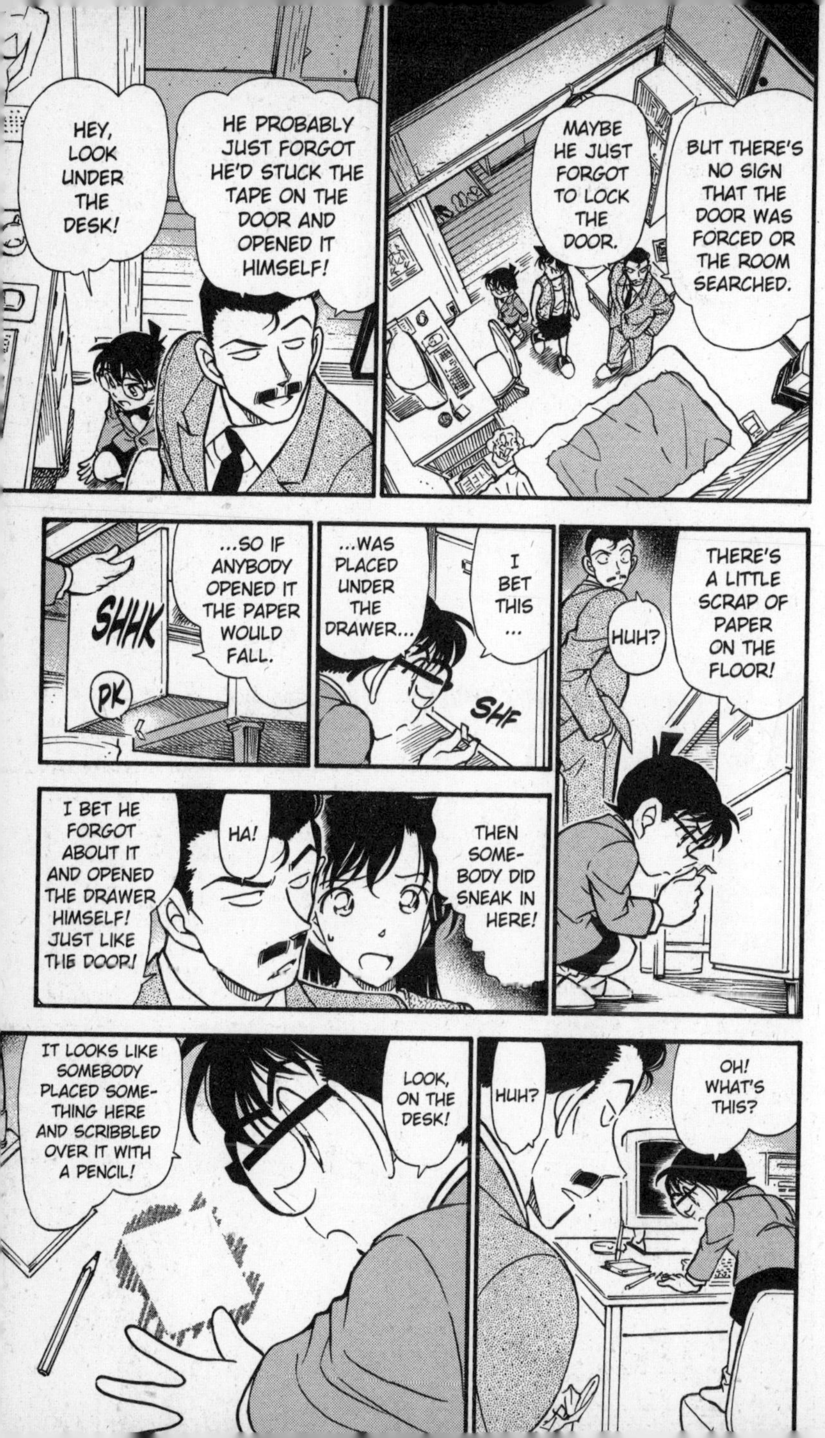
BUT THERE'S NO SIGN THAT THE DOOR WAS FORCED OR THE ROOM SEARCHED.
MAYBE HE JUST FORGOT TO LOCK THE DOOR.
HE PROBABLY JUST FORGOT HE'D STUCK THE TAPE ON THE DOOR AND OPENED IT HIMSELF!
HEY, LOOK UNDER THE DESK!
THERE'S A LITTLE SCRAP OF PAPER ON THE FLOOR!
HUH?
I BET THIS ...
...WAS PLACED UNDER THE DRAWER...
SHF
...SO IF ANYBODY OPENED IT THE PAPER WOULD FALL.
SHHK
PK
THEN SOME-BODY DID SNEAK IN HERE!
HA!
I BET HE FORGOT ABOUT IT AND OPENED THE DRAWER HIMSELF! JUST LIKE THE DOOR!
OH! WHAT'S THIS?
HUH?
LOOK, ON THE DESK!
IT LOOKS LIKE SOMEBODY PLACED SOME-THING HERE AND SCRIBBLED OVER IT WITH A PENCIL!

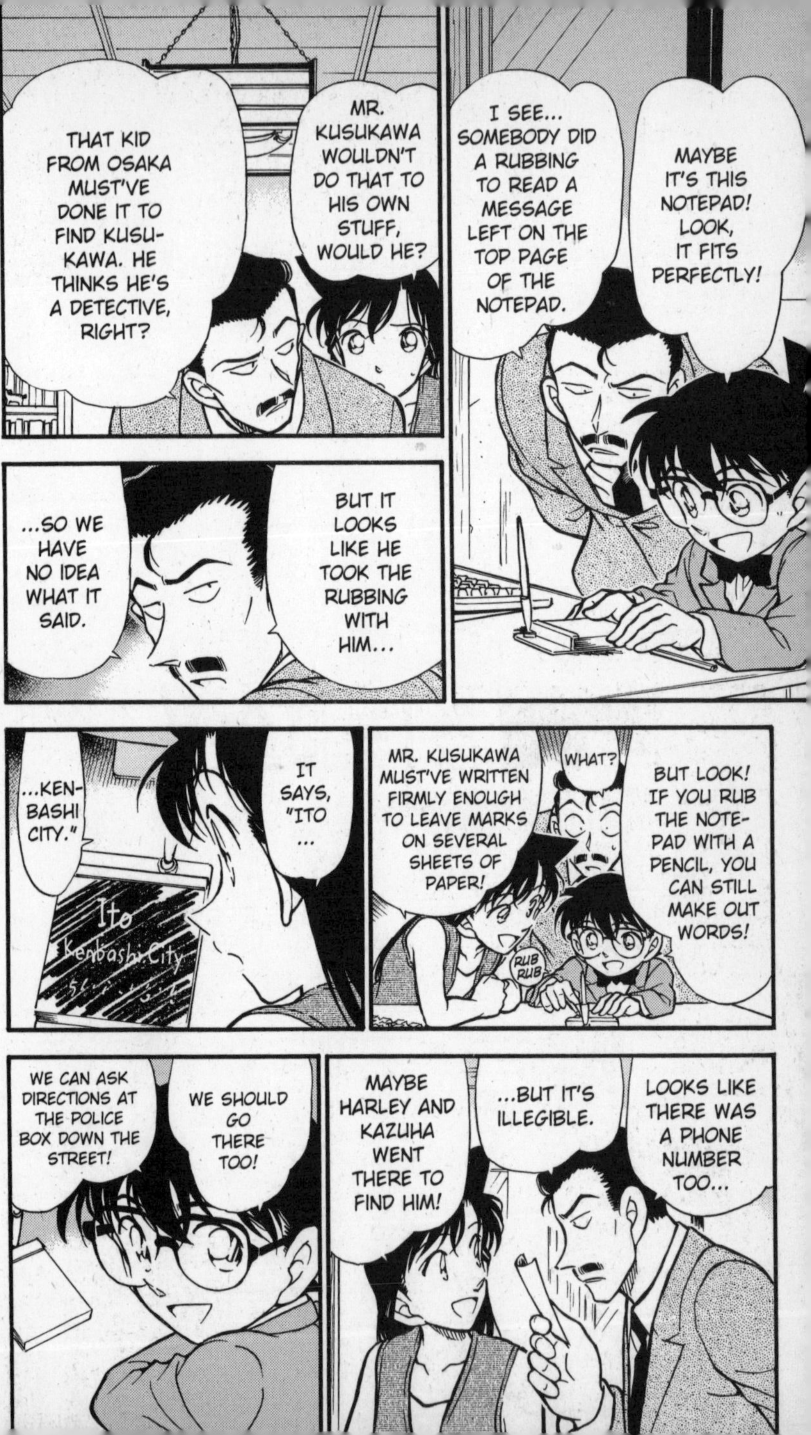
MAYBE IT'S THIS NOTEPAD! LOOK, IT FITS PERFECTLY!
I SEE... SOMEBODY DID A RUBBING TO READ A MESSAGE LEFT ON THE TOP PAGE OF THE NOTEPAD.
MR. KUSUKAWA WOULDN'T DO THAT TO HIS OWN STUFF, WOULD HE?
THAT KID FROM OSAKA MUST'VE DONE IT TO FIND KUSU-KAWA. HE THINKS HE'S A DETECTIVE, RIGHT?
BUT IT LOOKS LIKE HE TOOK THE RUBBING WITH HIM...
...SO WE HAVE NO IDEA WHAT IT SAID.
BUT LOOK! IF YOU RUB THE NOTE-PAD WITH A PENCIL, YOU CAN STILL MAKE OUT WORDS!
WHAT?
MR. KUSUKAWA MUST'VE WRITTEN FIRMLY ENOUGH TO LEAVE MARKS ON SEVERAL SHEETS OF PAPER!
RUB RUB
IT SAYS, "ITO ...
...KEN-BASHI CITY."
Ito
Kenbashi City
LOOKS LIKE THERE WAS A PHONE NUMBER TOO...
...BUT IT'S ILLEGIBLE.
MAYBE HARLEY AND KAZUHA WENT THERE TO FIND HIM!
WE SHOULD GO THERE TOO!
WE CAN ASK DIRECTIONS AT THE POLICE BOX DOWN THE STREET!

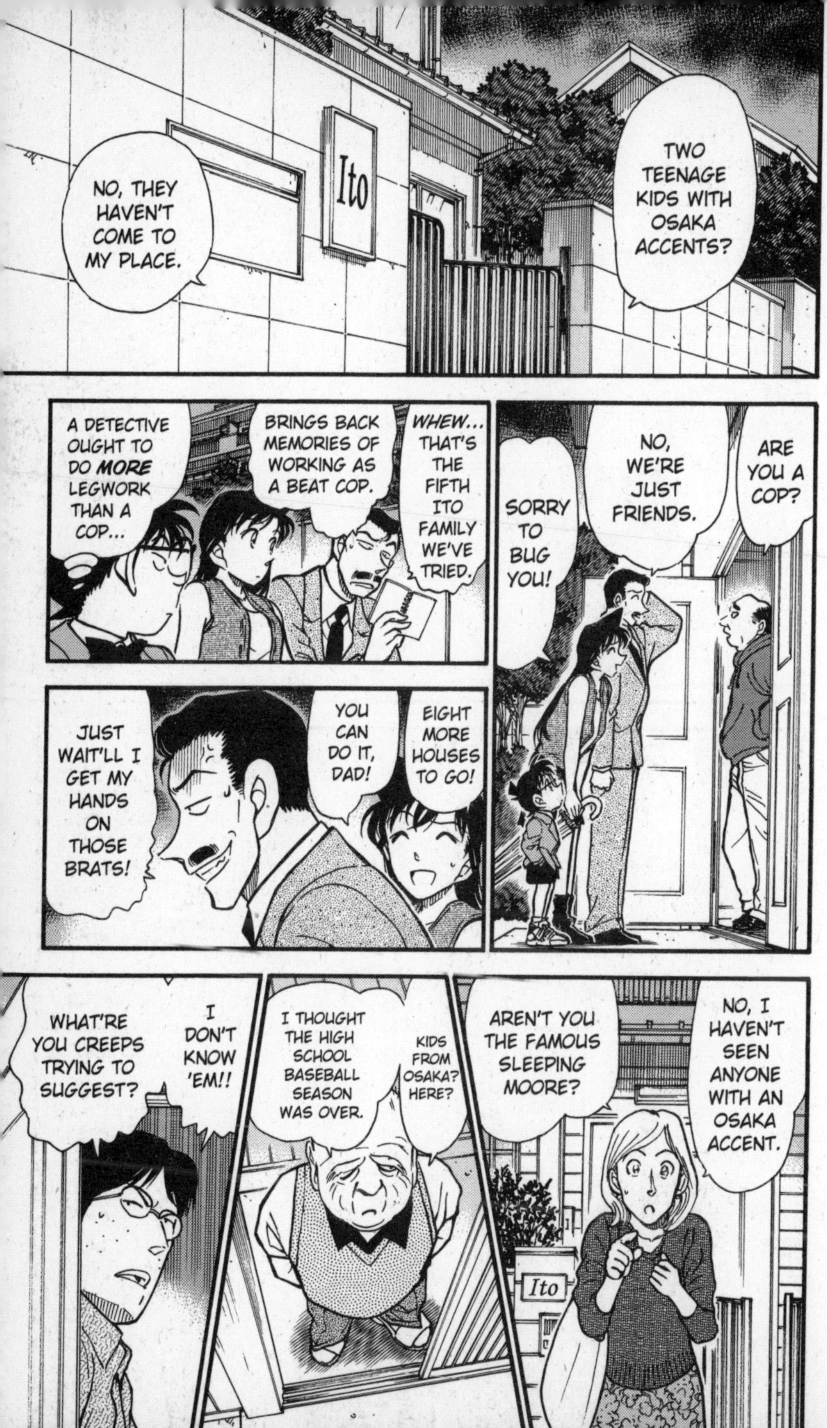
TWO TEENAGE KIDS WITH OSAKA ACCENTS?
NO, THEY HAVEN'T COME TO MY PLACE.
Ito
ARE YOU A COP?
NO, WE'RE JUST FRIENDS.
SORRY TO BUG YOU!
WHEW... THAT'S THE FIFTH ITO FAMILY WE'VE TRIED.
BRINGS BACK MEMORIES OF WORKING AS A BEAT COP.
A DETECTIVE OUGHT TO DO MORE LEGWORK THAN A COP...
EIGHT MORE HOUSES TO GO!
YOU CAN DO IT, DAD!
JUST WAIT'LL I GET MY HANDS ON THOSE BRATS!
NO, I HAVEN'T SEEN ANYONE WITH AN OSAKA ACCENT.
AREN'T YOU THE FAMOUS SLEEPING MOORE?
Ito
KIDS FROM OSAKA? HERE?
I THOUGHT THE HIGH SCHOOL BASEBALL SEASON WAS OVER.
I DON'T KNOW 'EM!!
WHAT'RE YOU CREEPS TRYING TO SUGGEST?

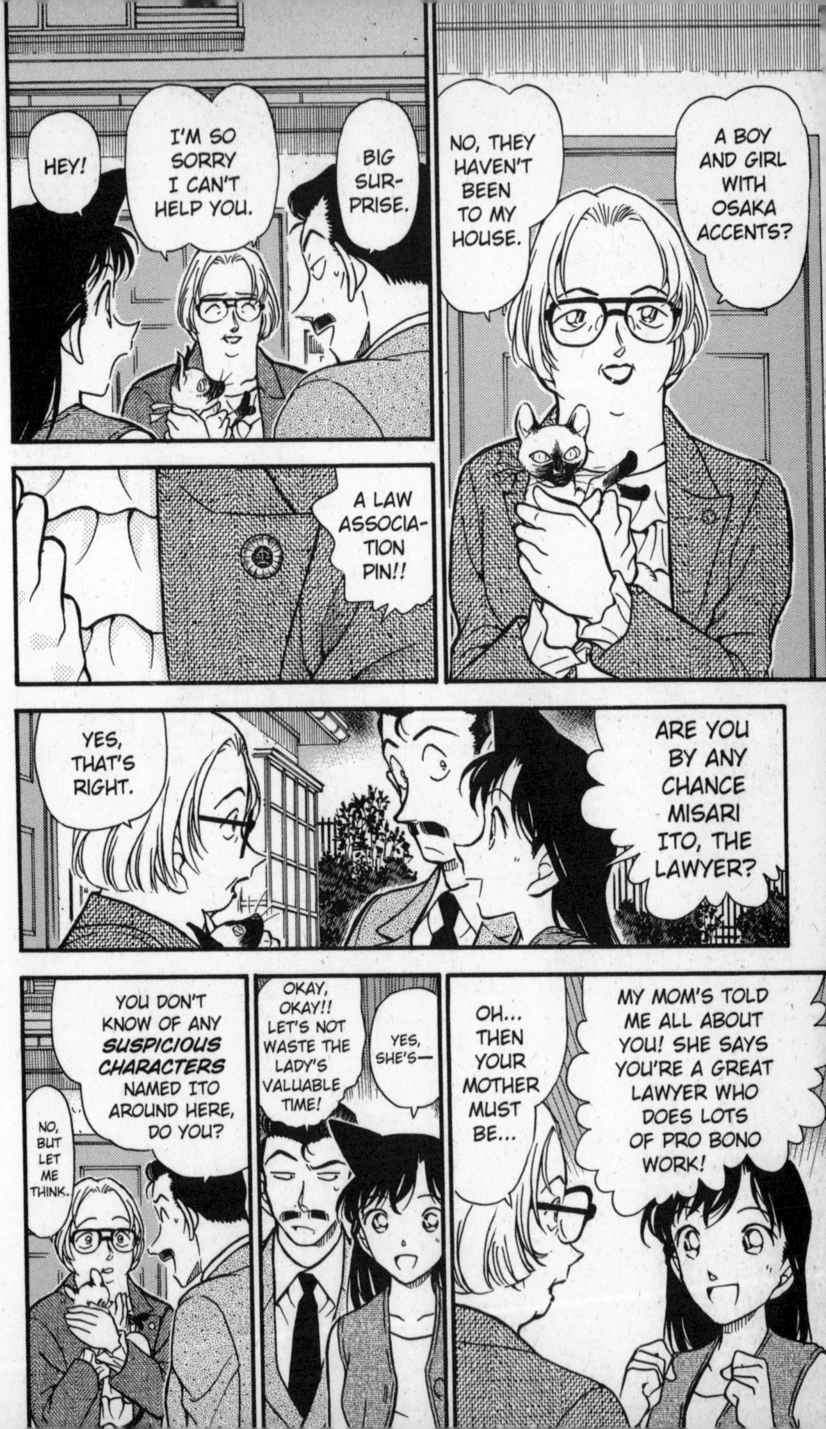
A BOY AND GIRL WITH OSAKA ACCENTS?
NO, THEY HAVEN'T BEEN TO MY HOUSE.
BIG SURPRISE.
I'M SO SORRY I CAN'T HELP YOU.
HEY!
A LAW ASSOCIATION PIN!!
ARE YOU BY ANY CHANCE MISARI ITO, THE LAWYER?
YES, THAT'S RIGHT.
MY MOM'S TOLD ME ALL ABOUT YOU! SHE SAYS YOU'RE A GREAT LAWYER WHO DOES LOTS OF PRO BONO WORK!
OH... THEN YOUR MOTHER MUST BE...
YES, SHE'S—
OKAY, OKAY!! LET'S NOT WASTE THE LADY'S VALUABLE TIME!
YOU DON'T KNOW OF ANY SUSPICIOUS CHARACTERS NAMED ITO AROUND HERE, DO YOU?
NO, BUT LET ME THINK.

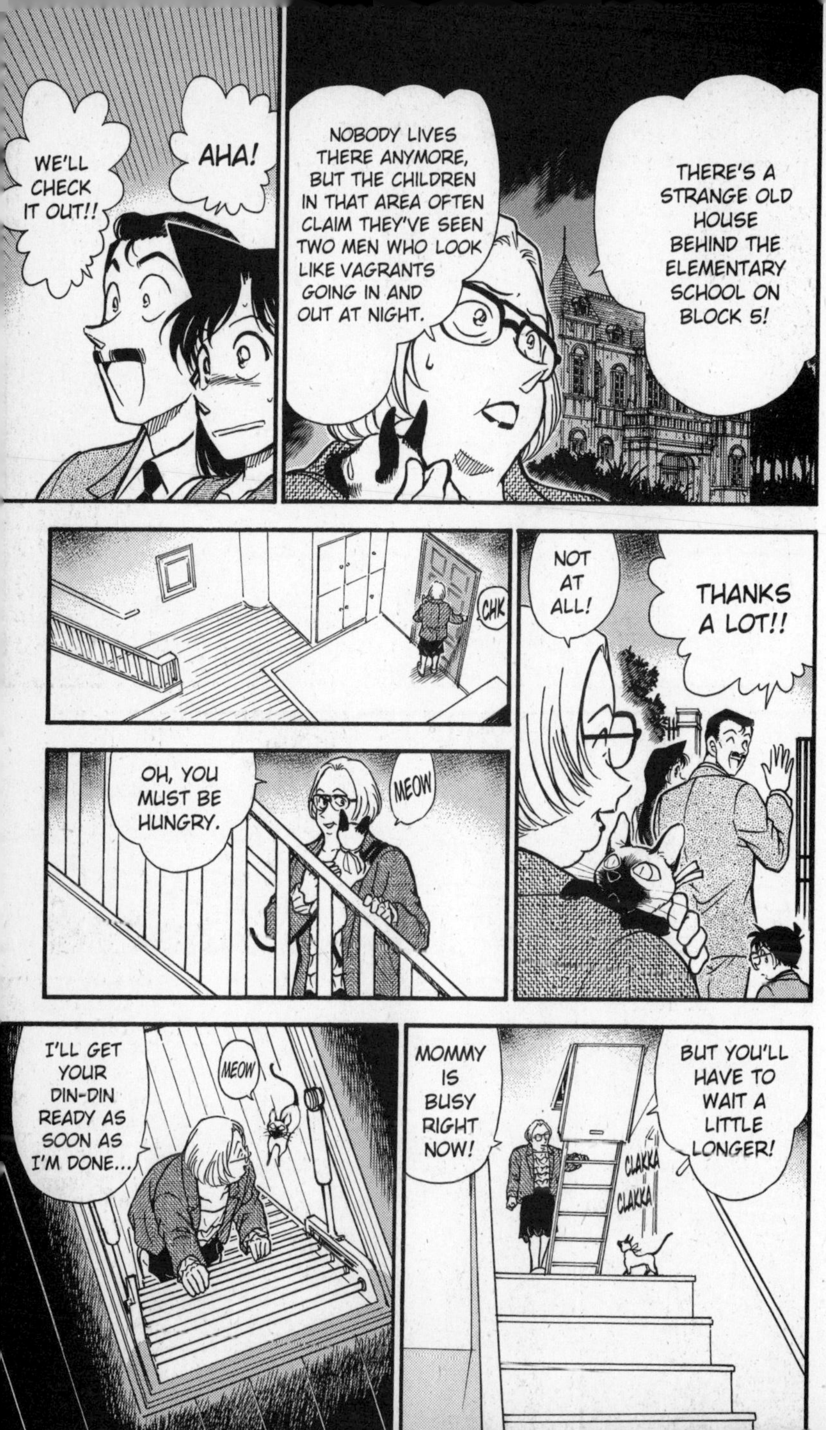
THERE'S A STRANGE OLD HOUSE BEHIND THE ELEMENTARY SCHOOL ON BLOCK 5!
NOBODY LIVES THERE ANYMORE, BUT THE CHILDREN IN THAT AREA OFTEN CLAIM THEY'VE SEEN TWO MEN WHO LOOK LIKE VAGRANTS GOING IN AND OUT AT NIGHT.
AHA!
WE'LL CHECK IT OUT!!
THANKS A LOT!!
NOT AT ALL!
CHK
MEOW
OH, YOU MUST BE HUNGRY.
BUT YOU'LL HAVE TO WAIT A LITTLE LONGER!
CLAKKA CLAKKA
MOMMY IS BUSY RIGHT NOW!
MEOW
I'LL GET YOUR DIN-DIN READY AS SOON AS I'M DONE...

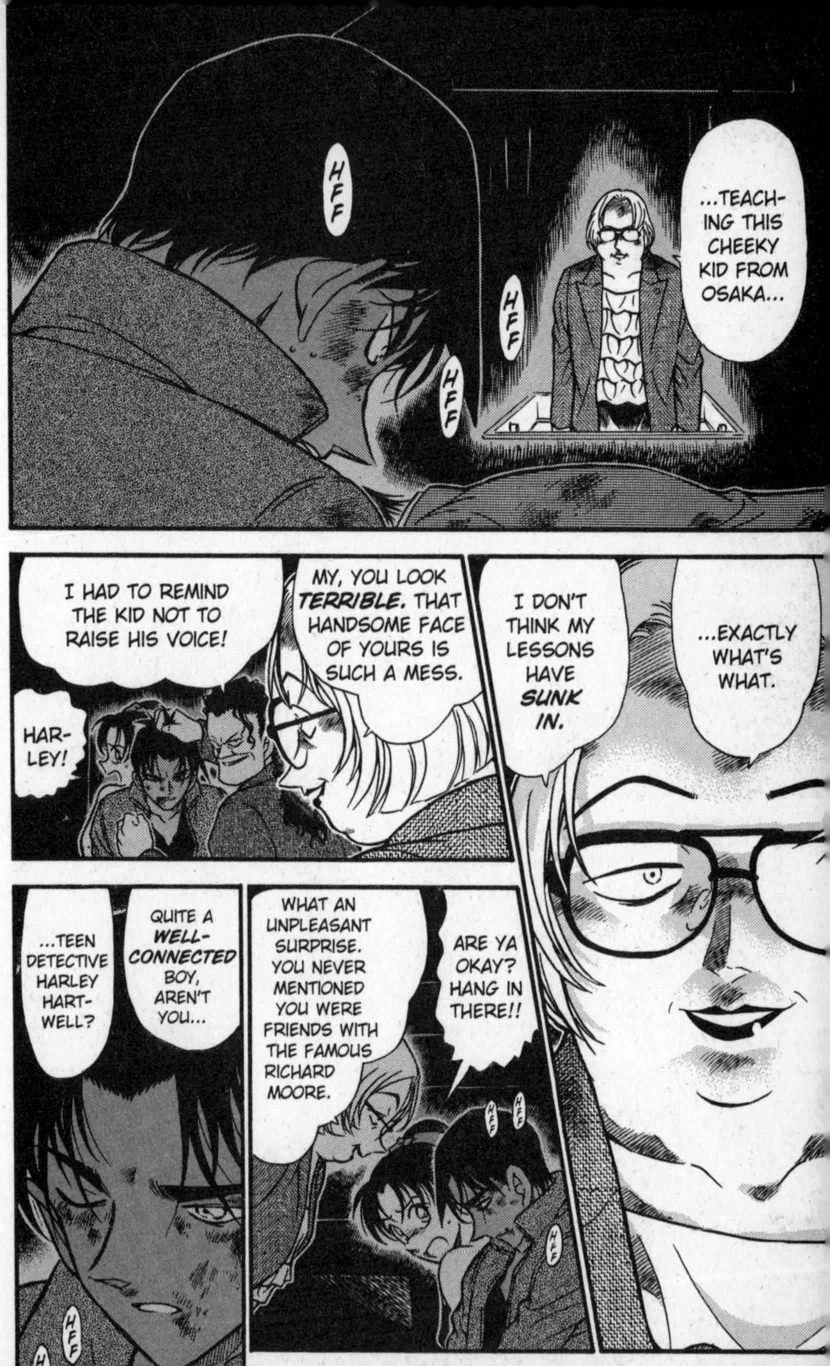
...TEACH-
ING THIS
CHEEKY
KID FROM
OSAKA...
HFF
HFF
HFF
...EXACTLY
WHAT'S
WHAT.
I DON'T
THINK MY
LESSONS
HAVE
*SUNK
IN.*
MY, YOU LOOK
TERRIBLE. THAT
HANDSOME FACE
OF YOURS IS
SUCH A MESS.
I HAD TO REMIND
THE KID NOT TO
RAISE HIS VOICE!
HAR-
LEY!
ARE YA
OKAY?
HANG IN
THERE!!
WHAT AN
UNPLEASANT
SURPRISE.
YOU NEVER
MENTIONED
YOU WERE
FRIENDS WITH
THE FAMOUS
RICHARD
MOORE.
HFF
HFF
HFF
QUITE A
*WELL-
CONNECTED*
BOY,
AREN'T
YOU...
...TEEN
DETECTIVE
HARLEY
HART-
WELL?
HFF
HFF

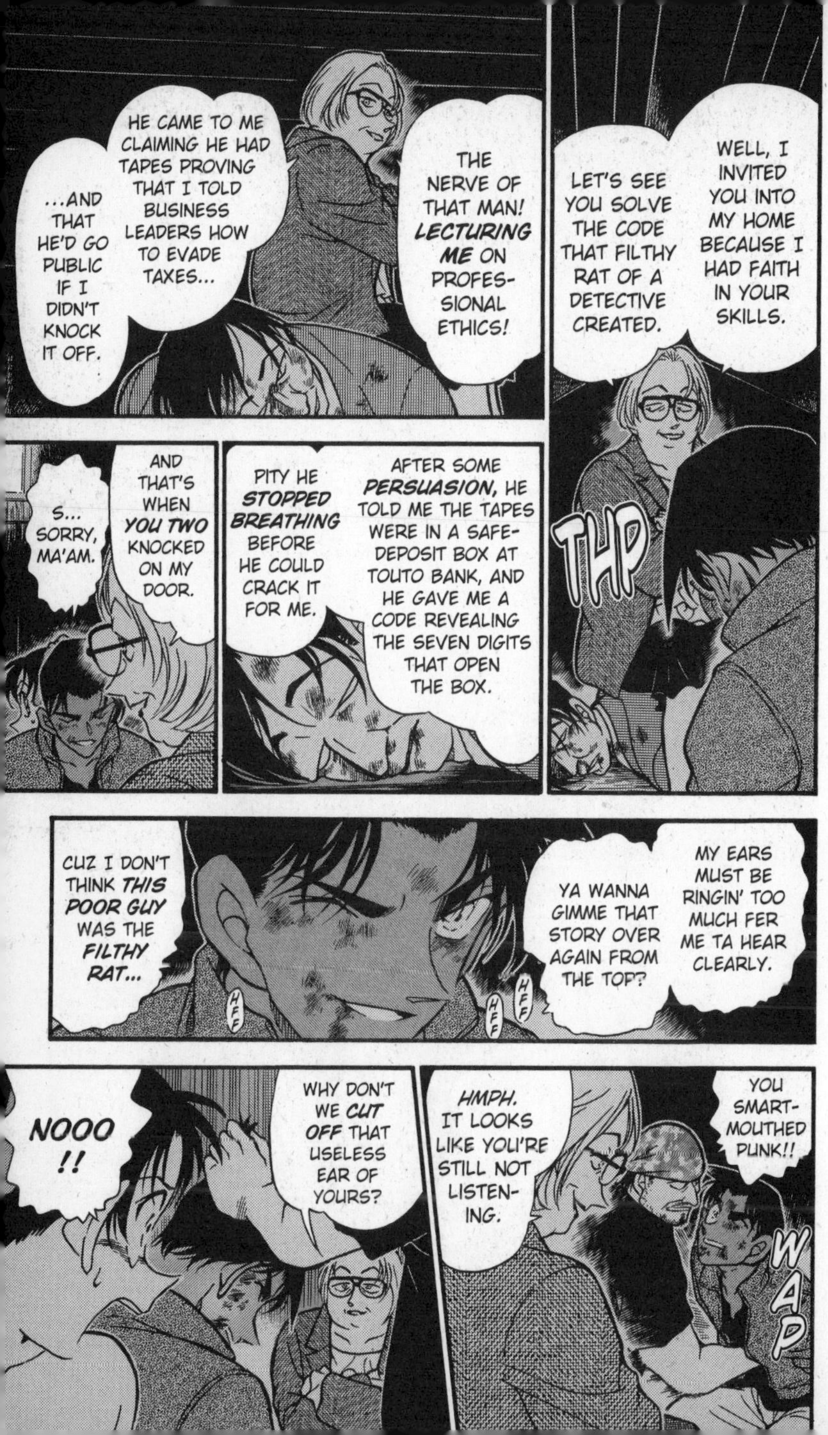
WELL, I INVITED YOU INTO MY HOME BECAUSE I HAD FAITH IN YOUR SKILLS.
LET'S SEE YOU SOLVE THE CODE THAT FILTHY RAT OF A DETECTIVE CREATED.
THP
THE NERVE OF THAT MAN! **LECTURING ME** ON PROFESSIONAL ETHICS!
HE CAME TO ME CLAIMING HE HAD TAPES PROVING THAT I TOLD BUSINESS LEADERS HOW TO EVADE TAXES...
...AND THAT HE'D GO PUBLIC IF I DIDN'T KNOCK IT OFF.
AFTER SOME **PERSUASION,** HE TOLD ME THE TAPES WERE IN A SAFE-DEPOSIT BOX AT TOUTO BANK, AND HE GAVE ME A CODE REVEALING THE SEVEN DIGITS THAT OPEN THE BOX.
PITY HE **STOPPED BREATHING** BEFORE HE COULD CRACK IT FOR ME.
AND THAT'S WHEN **YOU TWO** KNOCKED ON MY DOOR.
S... SORRY, MA'AM.
MY EARS MUST BE RINGIN' TOO MUCH FER ME TA HEAR CLEARLY.
YA WANNA GIMME THAT STORY OVER AGAIN FROM THE TOP?
HFF
HFF
CUZ I DON'T THINK **THIS POOR GUY** WAS THE **FILTHY RAT...**
YOU SMART-MOUTHED PUNK!!
WAP
HMPH. IT LOOKS LIKE YOU'RE STILL NOT LISTENING.
WHY DON'T WE **CUT OFF** THAT USELESS EAR OF YOURS?
NOOO!!

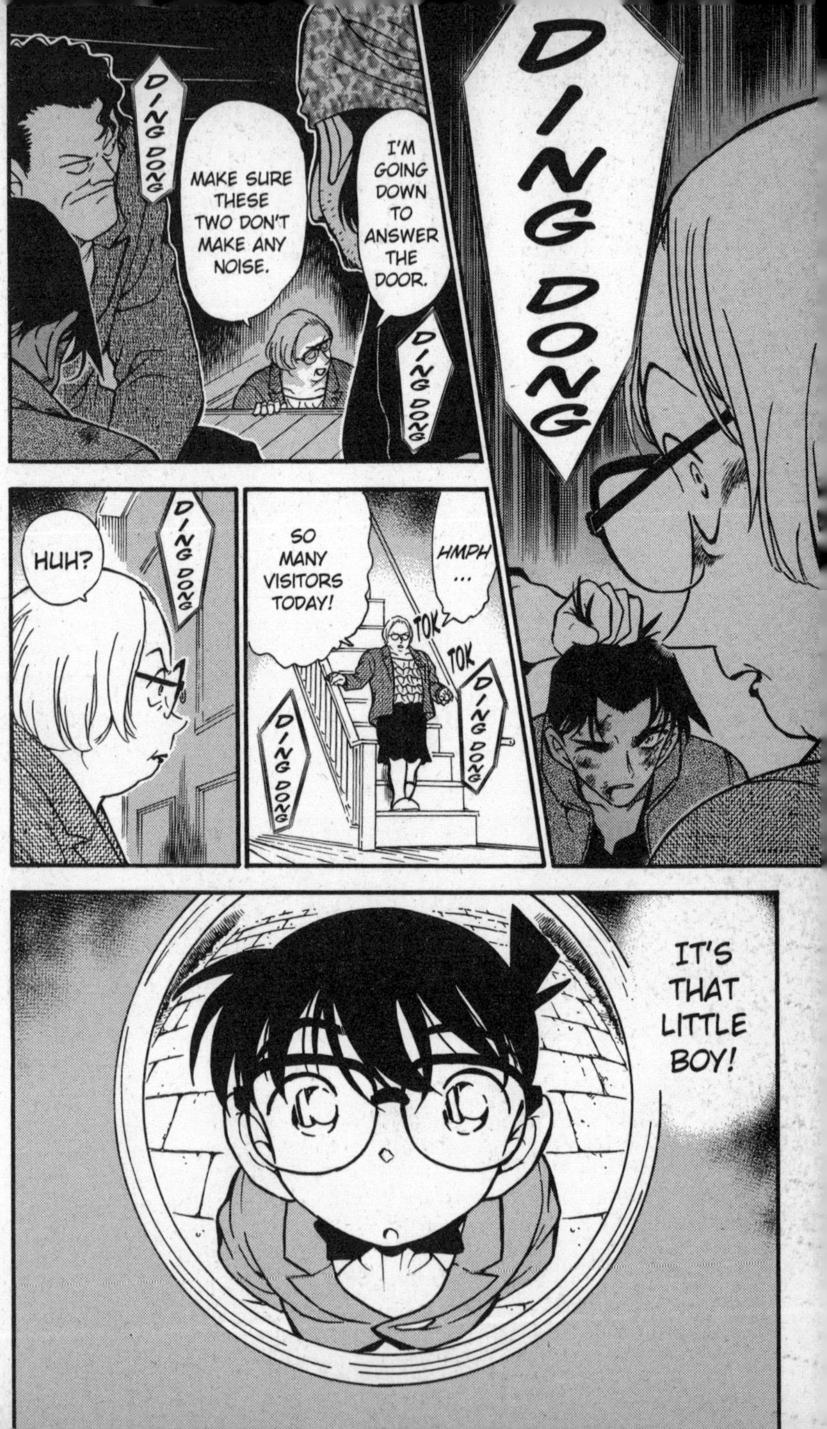
DING DONG
I'M GOING DOWN TO ANSWER THE DOOR.
DING DONG
DING DONG
MAKE SURE THESE TWO DON'T MAKE ANY NOISE.
HMPH ...
SO MANY VISITORS TODAY!
TOK
TOK
DING DONG
DING DONG
DING DONG
HUH?
IT'S THAT LITTLE BOY!

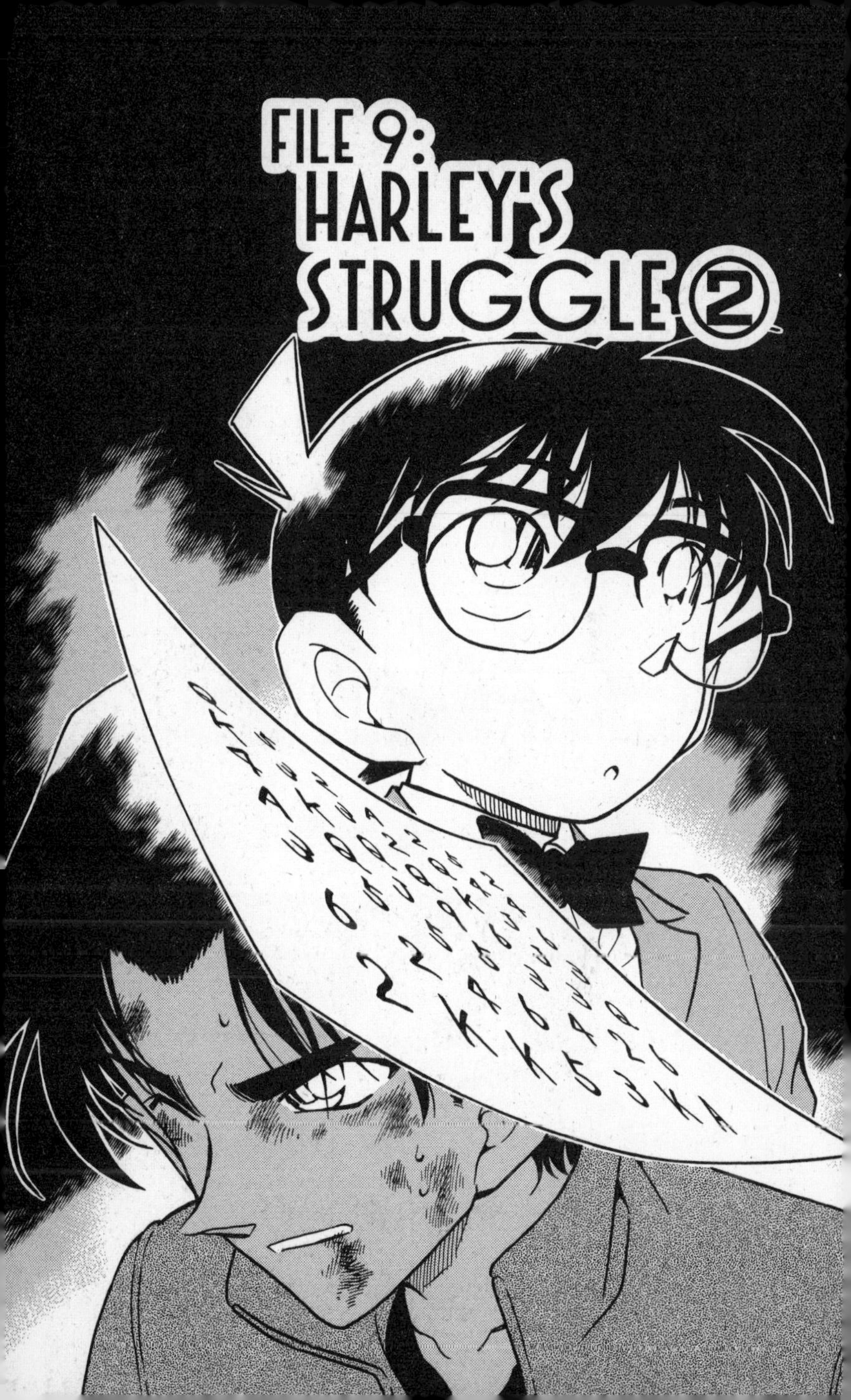
FILE 9:
HARLEY'S
STRUGGLE ②

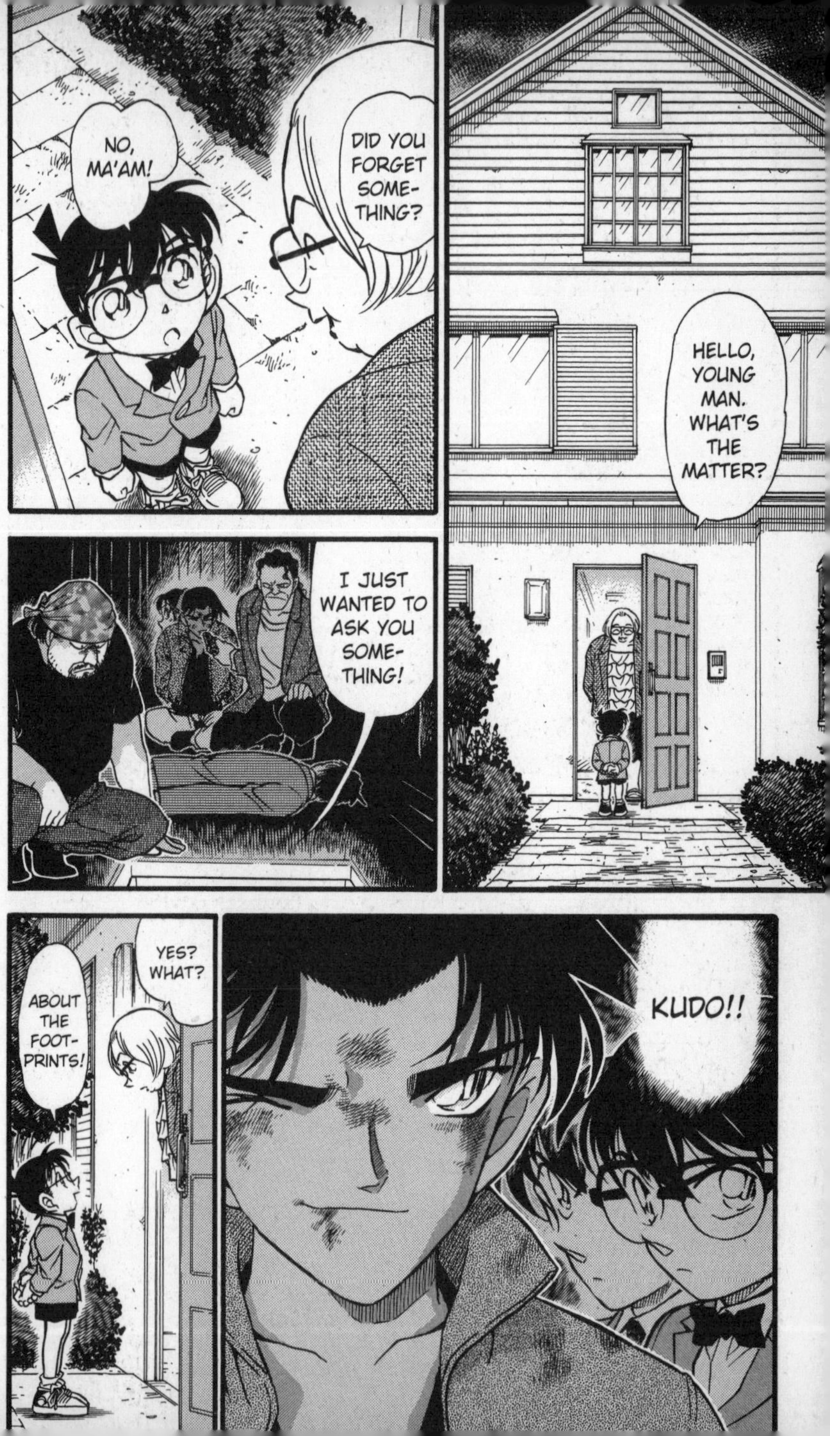
HELLO, YOUNG MAN. WHAT'S THE MATTER?
DID YOU FORGET SOMETHING?
NO, MA'AM!
I JUST WANTED TO ASK YOU SOMETHING!
KUDO!!
YES? WHAT?
ABOUT THE FOOTPRINTS!

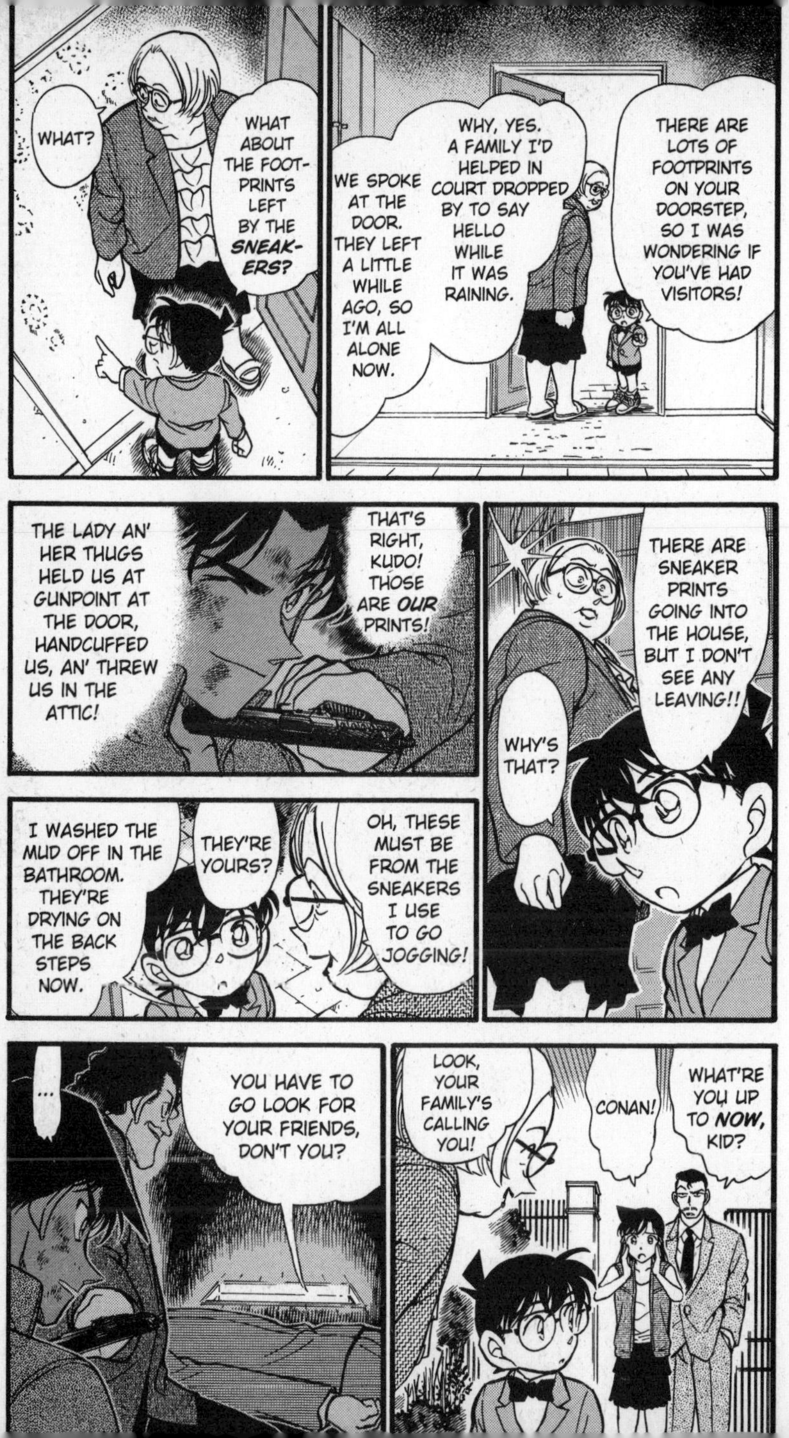
THERE ARE LOTS OF FOOTPRINTS ON YOUR DOORSTEP, SO I WAS WONDERING IF YOU'VE HAD VISITORS!
WHY, YES. A FAMILY I'D HELPED IN COURT DROPPED BY TO SAY HELLO WHILE IT WAS RAINING.
WE SPOKE AT THE DOOR. THEY LEFT A LITTLE WHILE AGO, SO I'M ALL ALONE NOW.
WHAT ABOUT THE FOOTPRINTS LEFT BY THE ***SNEAKERS?***
WHAT?
THERE ARE SNEAKER PRINTS GOING INTO THE HOUSE, BUT I DON'T SEE ANY LEAVING!!
WHY'S THAT?
THAT'S RIGHT, KUDO! THOSE ARE ***OUR*** PRINTS!
THE LADY AN' HER THUGS HELD US AT GUNPOINT AT THE DOOR, HANDCUFFED US, AN' THREW US IN THE ATTIC!
OH, THESE MUST BE FROM THE SNEAKERS I USE TO GO JOGGING!
THEY'RE YOURS?
I WASHED THE MUD OFF IN THE BATHROOM. THEY'RE DRYING ON THE BACK STEPS NOW.
WHAT'RE YOU UP TO ***NOW,*** KID?
CONAN!
LOOK, YOUR FAMILY'S CALLING YOU!
YOU HAVE TO GO LOOK FOR YOUR FRIENDS, DON'T YOU?
...

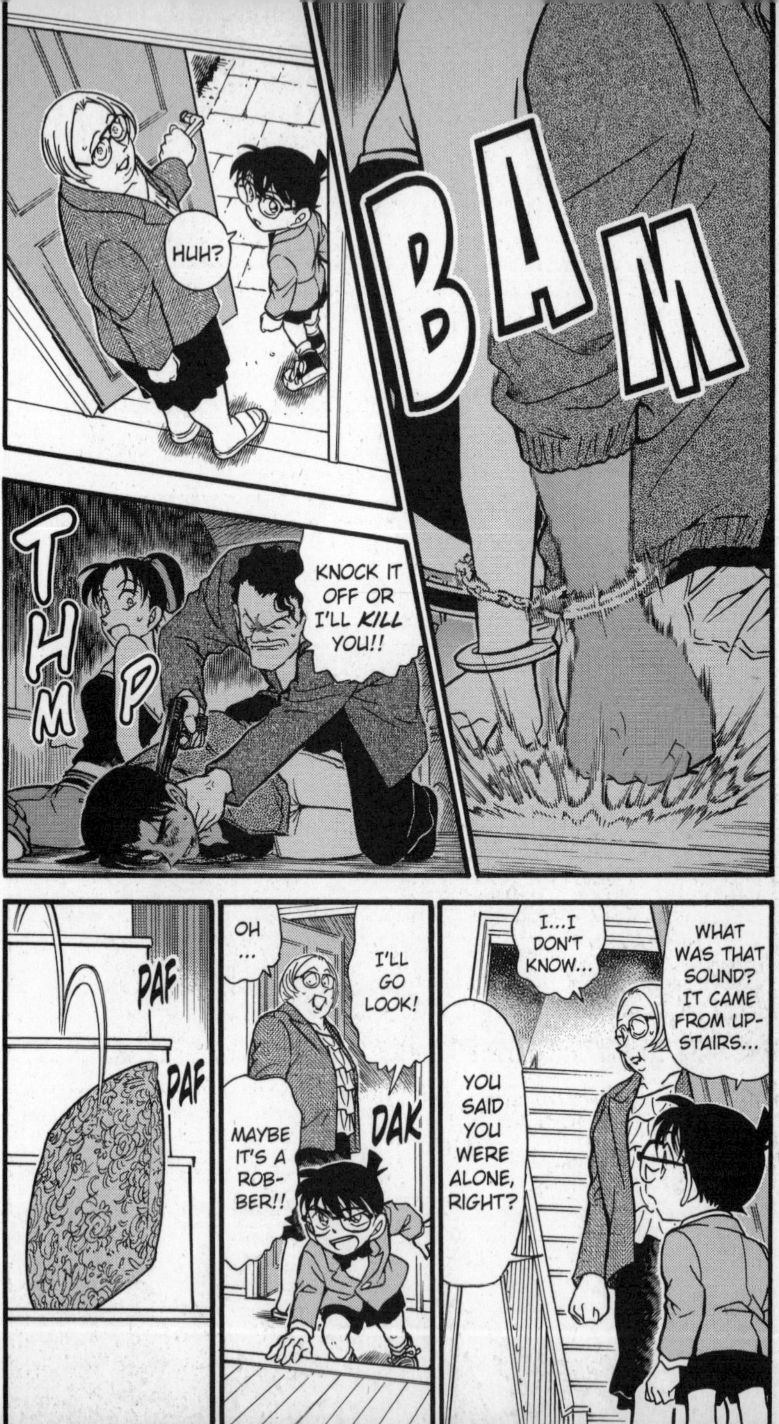
BAM
HUH?
THUMP
KNOCK IT OFF OR I'LL *KILL* YOU!!
WHAT WAS THAT SOUND? IT CAME FROM UP-STAIRS...
I...I DON'T KNOW...
YOU SAID YOU WERE ALONE, RIGHT?
I'LL GO LOOK!
OH ...
DAK
MAYBE IT'S A ROB-BER!!
PAF
PAF

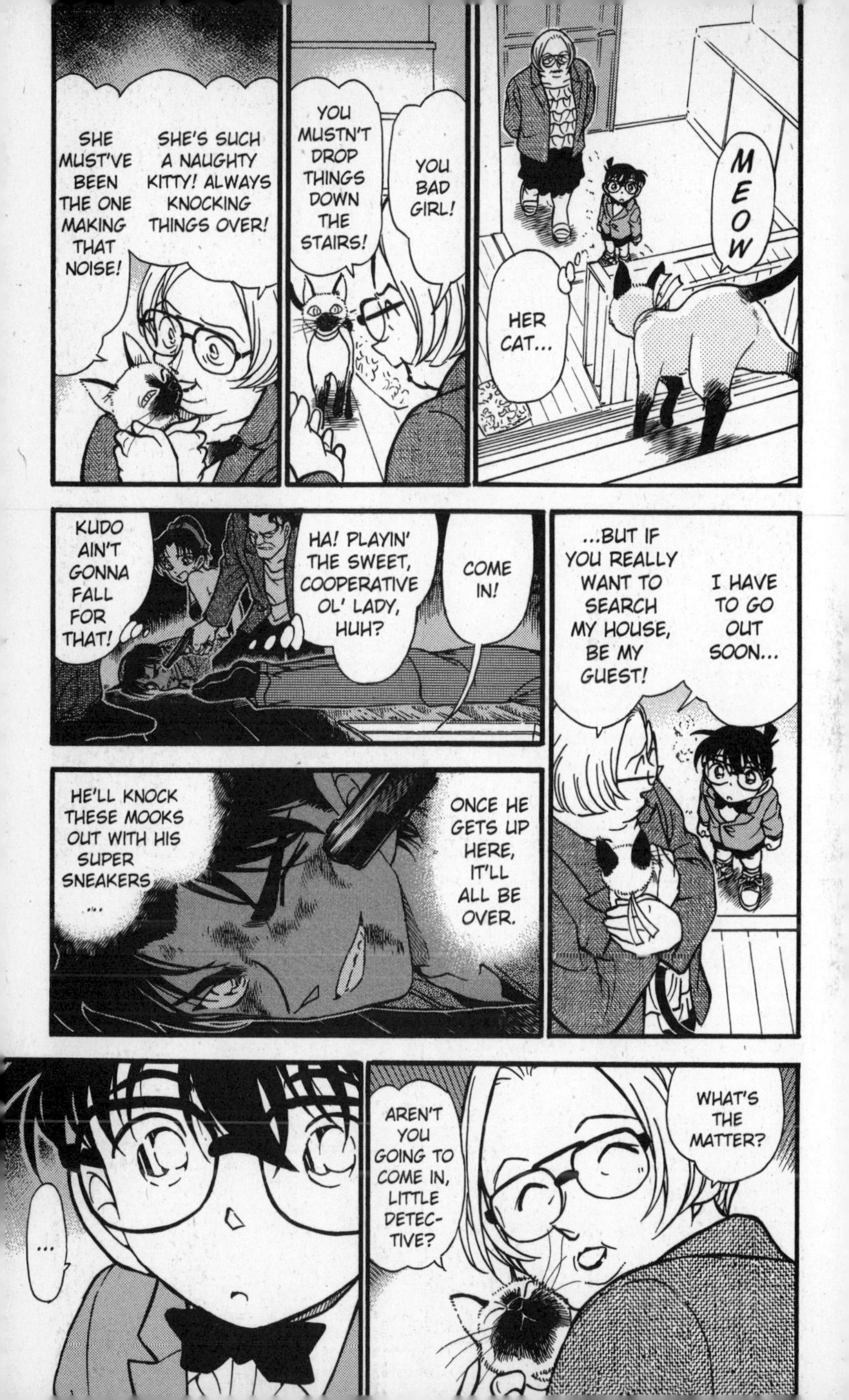
MEOW
HER CAT...
YOU BAD GIRL!
YOU MUSTN'T DROP THINGS DOWN THE STAIRS!
SHE'S SUCH A NAUGHTY KITTY! ALWAYS KNOCKING THINGS OVER!
SHE MUST'VE BEEN THE ONE MAKING THAT NOISE!
I HAVE TO GO OUT SOON...
...BUT IF YOU REALLY WANT TO SEARCH MY HOUSE, BE MY GUEST!
COME IN!
HA! PLAYIN' THE SWEET, COOPERATIVE OL' LADY, HUH?
KUDO AIN'T GONNA FALL FOR THAT!
ONCE HE GETS UP HERE, IT'LL ALL BE OVER.
HE'LL KNOCK THESE MOOKS OUT WITH HIS SUPER SNEAKERS ...
WHAT'S THE MATTER?
AREN'T YOU GOING TO COME IN, LITTLE DETECTIVE?
...

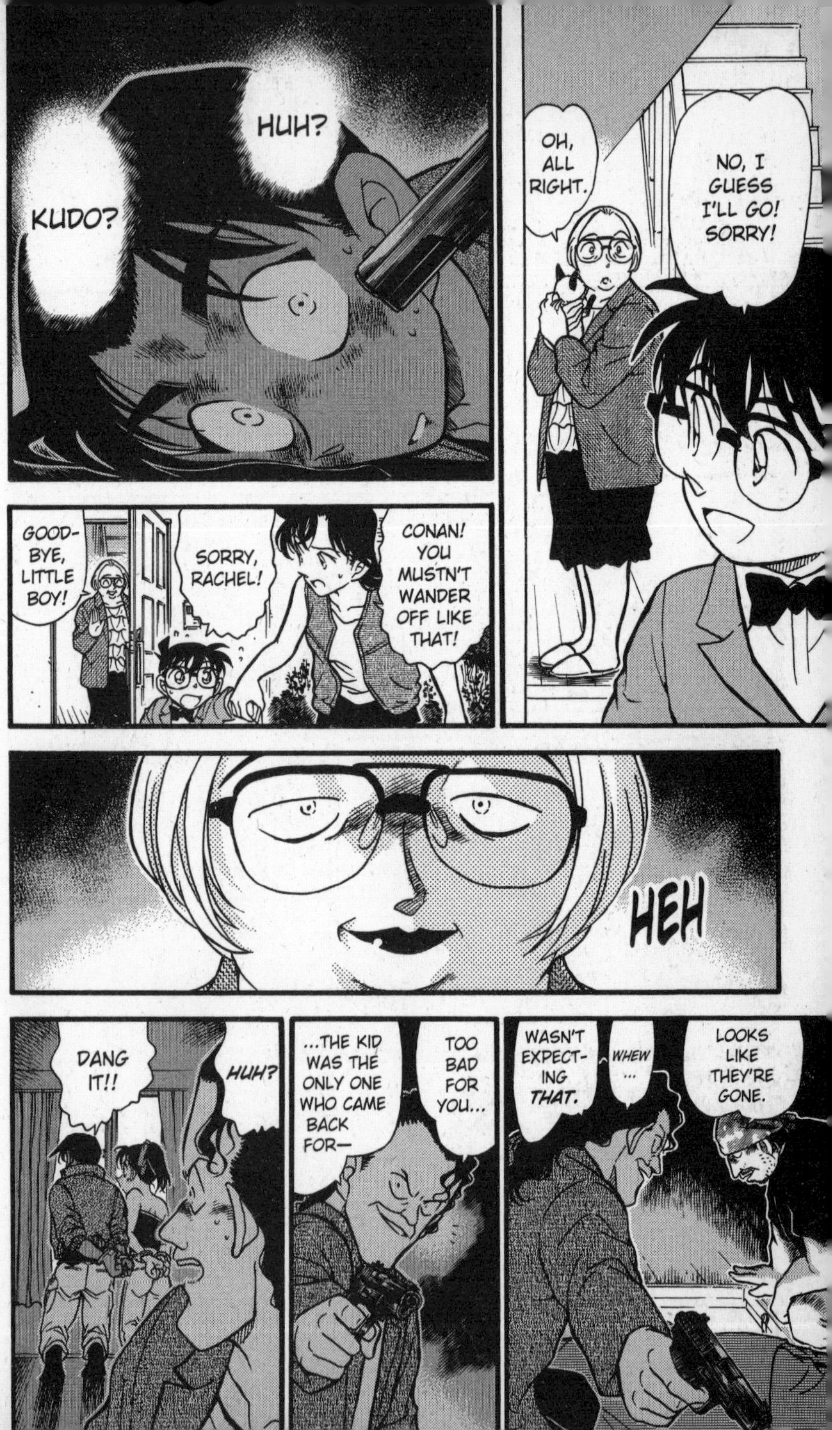
NO, I GUESS I'LL GO! SORRY!
OH, ALL RIGHT.
HUH?
KUDO?
CONAN! YOU MUSTN'T WANDER OFF LIKE THAT!
SORRY, RACHEL!
GOOD-BYE, LITTLE BOY!
HEH
LOOKS LIKE THEY'RE GONE.
WHEW...
WASN'T EXPECTING THAT.
TOO BAD FOR YOU...
...THE KID WAS THE ONLY ONE WHO CAME BACK FOR—
HUH?
DANG IT!!

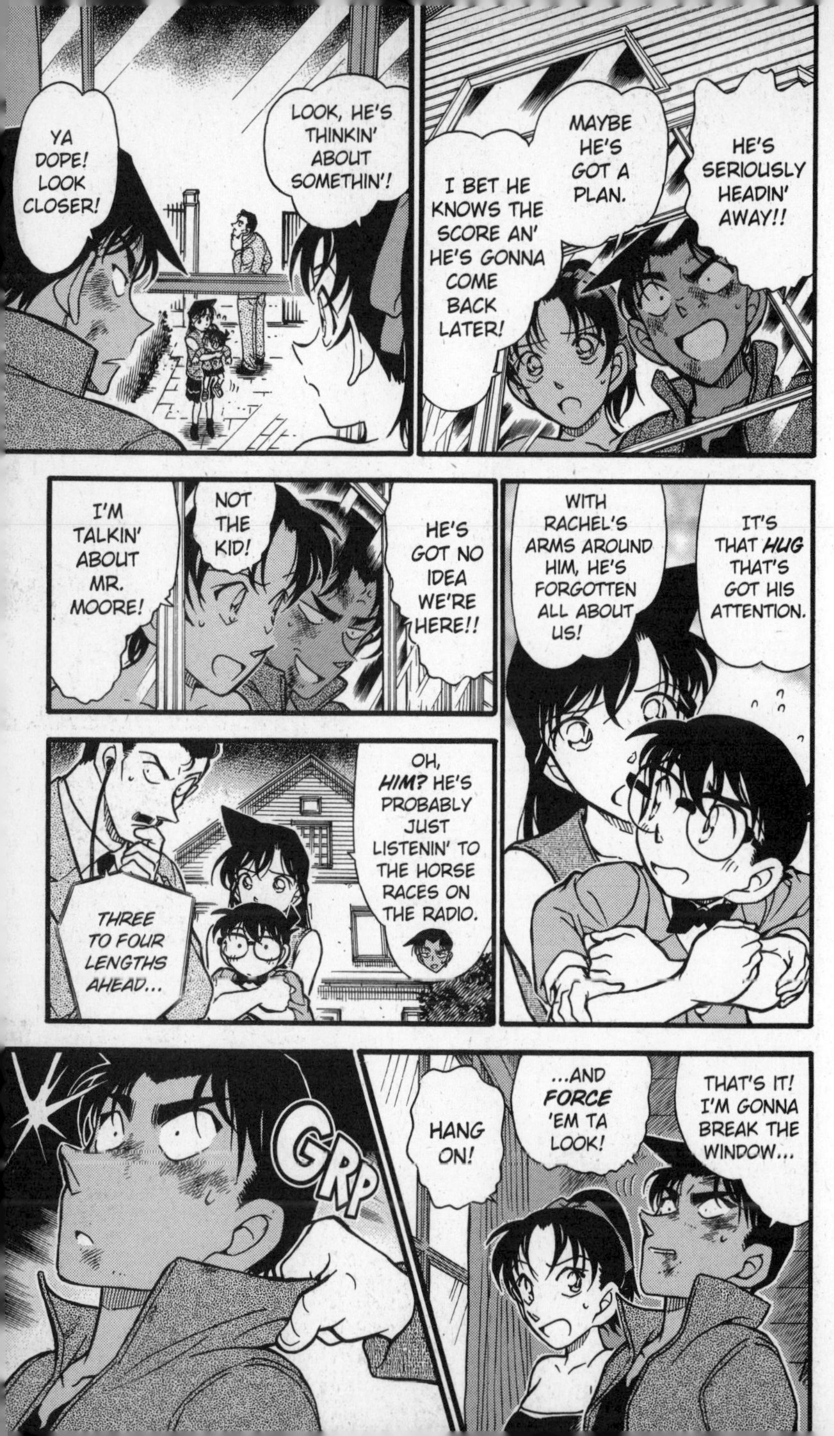
HE'S SERIOUSLY HEADIN' AWAY!!
MAYBE HE'S GOT A PLAN.
I BET HE KNOWS THE SCORE AN' HE'S GONNA COME BACK LATER!
LOOK, HE'S THINKIN' ABOUT SOMETHIN'!
YA DOPE! LOOK CLOSER!
IT'S THAT HUG THAT'S GOT HIS ATTENTION.
WITH RACHEL'S ARMS AROUND HIM, HE'S FORGOTTEN ALL ABOUT US!
HE'S GOT NO IDEA WE'RE HERE!!
NOT THE KID!
I'M TALKIN' ABOUT MR. MOORE!
OH, HIM? HE'S PROBABLY JUST LISTENIN' TO THE HORSE RACES ON THE RADIO.
THREE TO FOUR LENGTHS AHEAD...
THAT'S IT! I'M GONNA BREAK THE WINDOW...
...AND FORCE 'EM TA LOOK!
HANG ON!
GRP

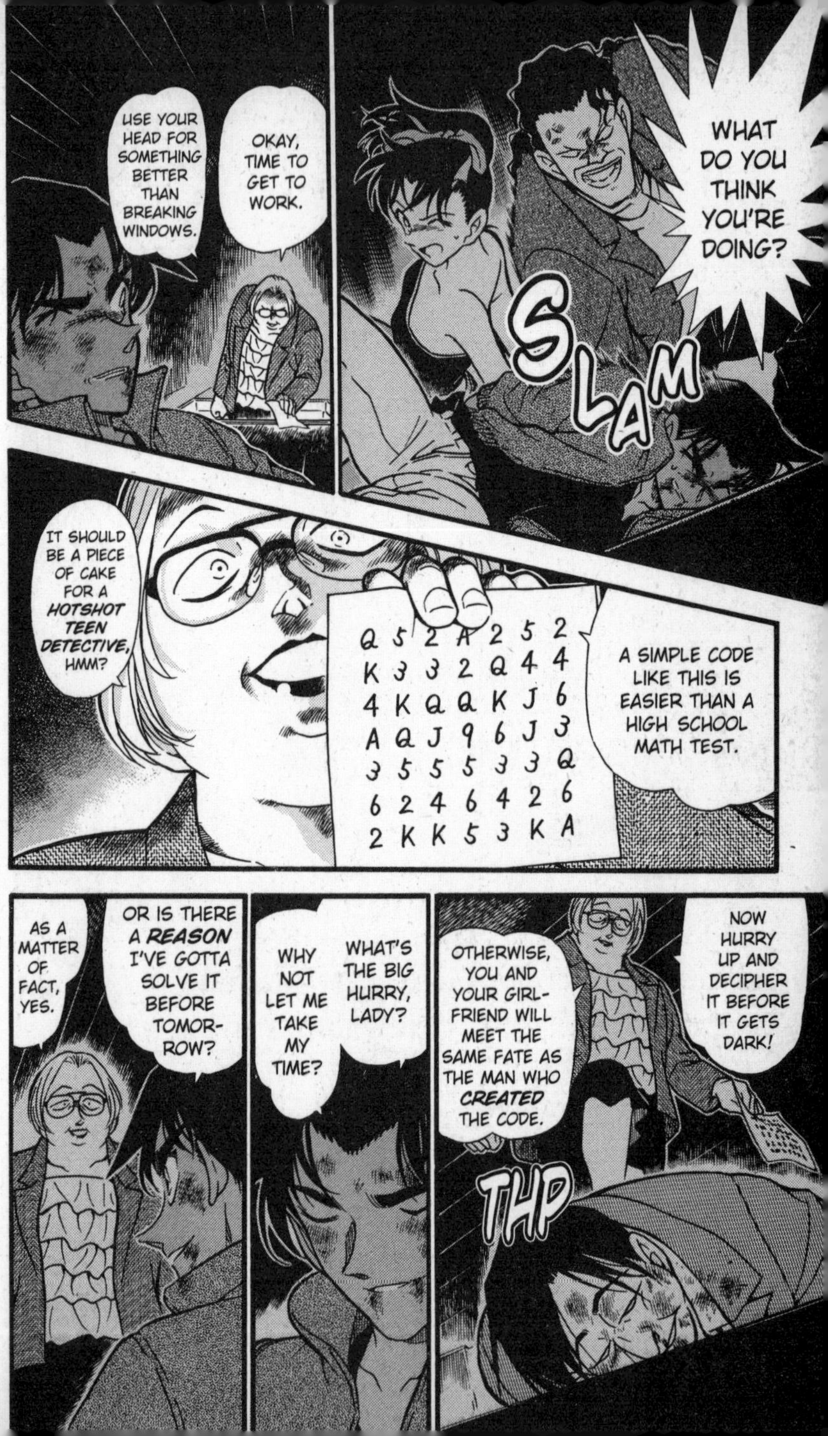
WHAT DO YOU THINK YOU'RE DOING?
SLAM
OKAY, TIME TO GET TO WORK.
USE YOUR HEAD FOR SOMETHING BETTER THAN BREAKING WINDOWS.
A SIMPLE CODE LIKE THIS IS EASIER THAN A HIGH SCHOOL MATH TEST.
Q 5 2 A 2 5 2
K 3 3 2 Q 4 4
4 K Q Q K J 6
A Q J 9 6 J 3
3 5 5 5 3 3 Q
6 2 4 6 4 2 6
2 K K 5 3 K A
IT SHOULD BE A PIECE OF CAKE FOR A **HOTSHOT TEEN DETECTIVE,** HMM?
NOW HURRY UP AND DECIPHER IT BEFORE IT GETS DARK!
OTHERWISE, YOU AND YOUR GIRL-FRIEND WILL MEET THE SAME FATE AS THE MAN WHO **CREATED** THE CODE.
THP
WHAT'S THE BIG HURRY, LADY?
WHY NOT LET ME TAKE MY TIME?
OR IS THERE A **REASON** I'VE GOTTA SOLVE IT BEFORE TOMORROW?
AS A MATTER OF FACT, YES.

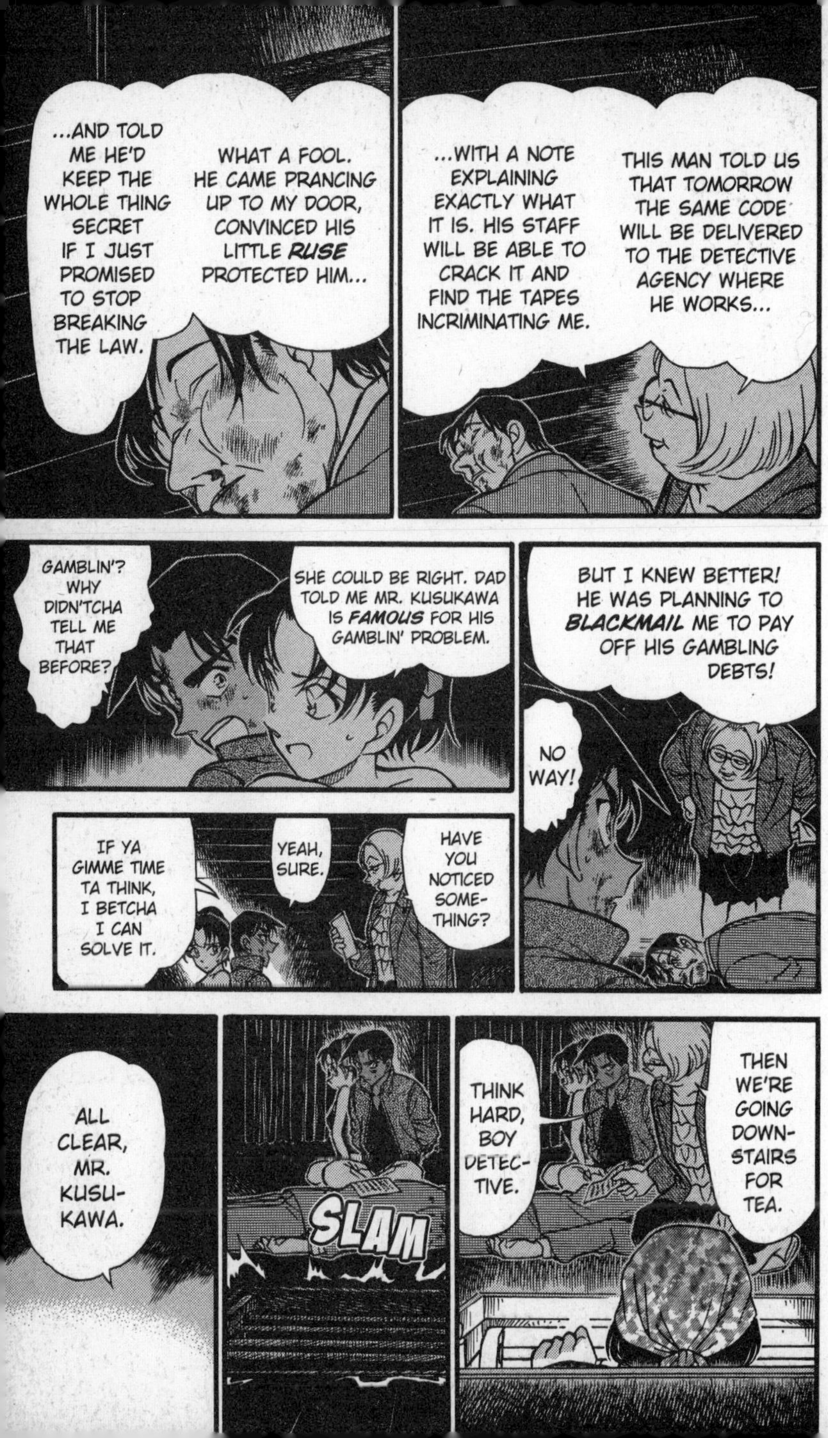
THIS MAN TOLD US THAT TOMORROW THE SAME CODE WILL BE DELIVERED TO THE DETECTIVE AGENCY WHERE HE WORKS...
...WITH A NOTE EXPLAINING EXACTLY WHAT IT IS. HIS STAFF WILL BE ABLE TO CRACK IT AND FIND THE TAPES INCRIMINATING ME.
WHAT A FOOL. HE CAME PRANCING UP TO MY DOOR, CONVINCED HIS LITTLE *RUSE* PROTECTED HIM...
...AND TOLD ME HE'D KEEP THE WHOLE THING SECRET IF I JUST PROMISED TO STOP BREAKING THE LAW.
BUT I KNEW BETTER! HE WAS PLANNING TO *BLACKMAIL* ME TO PAY OFF HIS GAMBLING DEBTS!
NO WAY!
SHE COULD BE RIGHT. DAD TOLD ME MR. KUSUKAWA IS *FAMOUS* FOR HIS GAMBLIN' PROBLEM.
GAMBLIN'? WHY DIDN'TCHA TELL ME THAT BEFORE?
HAVE YOU NOTICED SOMETHING?
YEAH, SURE.
IF YA GIMME TIME TA THINK, I BETCHA I CAN SOLVE IT.
THEN WE'RE GOING DOWNSTAIRS FOR TEA.
THINK HARD, BOY DETECTIVE.
SLAM
ALL CLEAR, MR. KUSUKAWA.

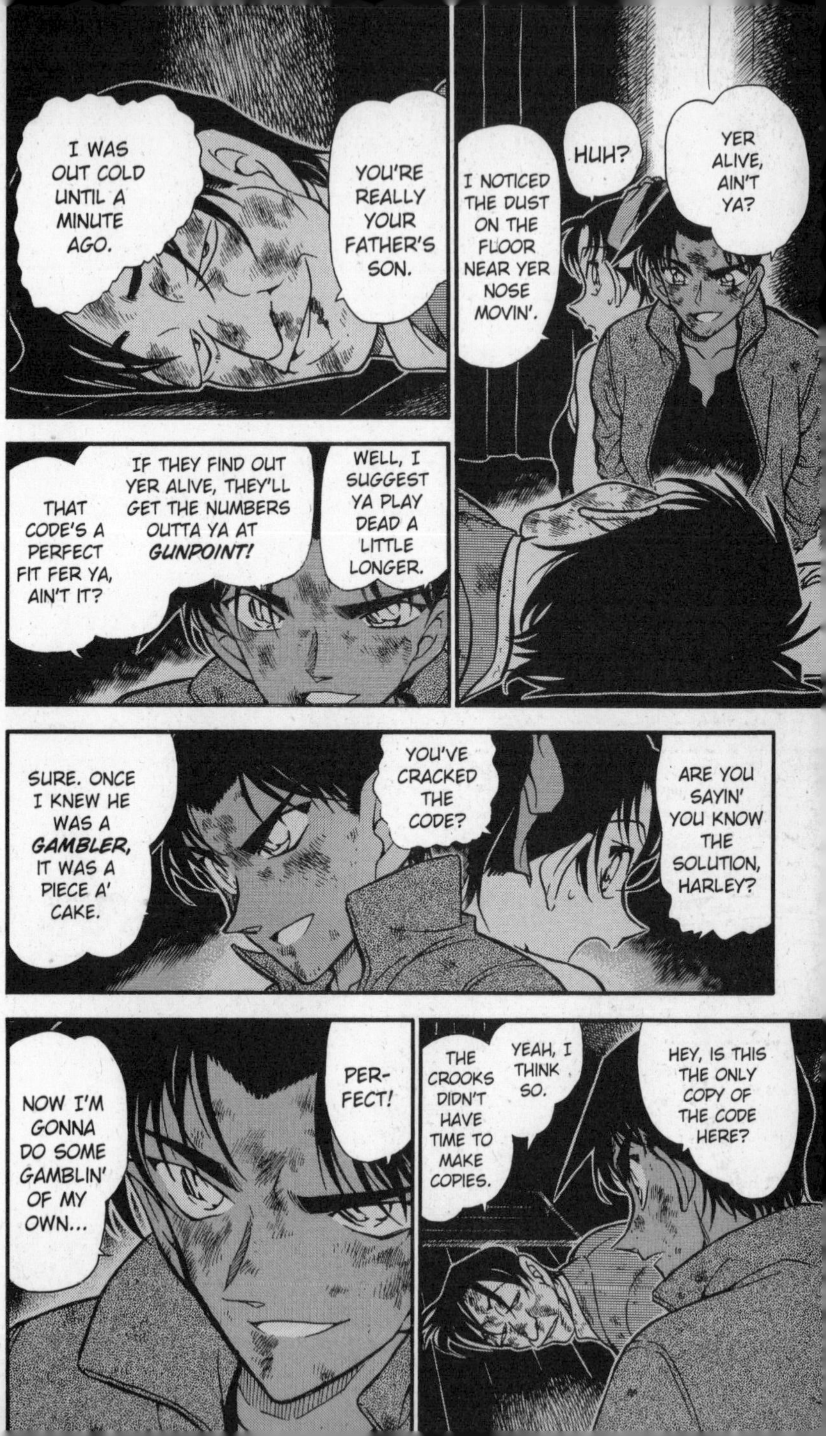
YER ALIVE, AIN'T YA?
HUH?
I NOTICED THE DUST ON THE FLOOR NEAR YER NOSE MOVIN'.
YOU'RE REALLY YOUR FATHER'S SON.
I WAS OUT COLD UNTIL A MINUTE AGO.
WELL, I SUGGEST YA PLAY DEAD A LITTLE LONGER.
IF THEY FIND OUT YER ALIVE, THEY'LL GET THE NUMBERS OUTTA YA AT **GUNPOINT!**
THAT CODE'S A PERFECT FIT FER YA, AIN'T IT?
ARE YOU SAYIN' YOU KNOW THE SOLUTION, HARLEY?
YOU'VE CRACKED THE CODE?
SURE. ONCE I KNEW HE WAS A **GAMBLER,** IT WAS A PIECE A' CAKE.
HEY, IS THIS THE ONLY COPY OF THE CODE HERE?
YEAH, I THINK SO.
THE CROOKS DIDN'T HAVE TIME TO MAKE COPIES.
PER-FECT!
NOW I'M GONNA DO SOME GAMBLIN' OF MY OWN...

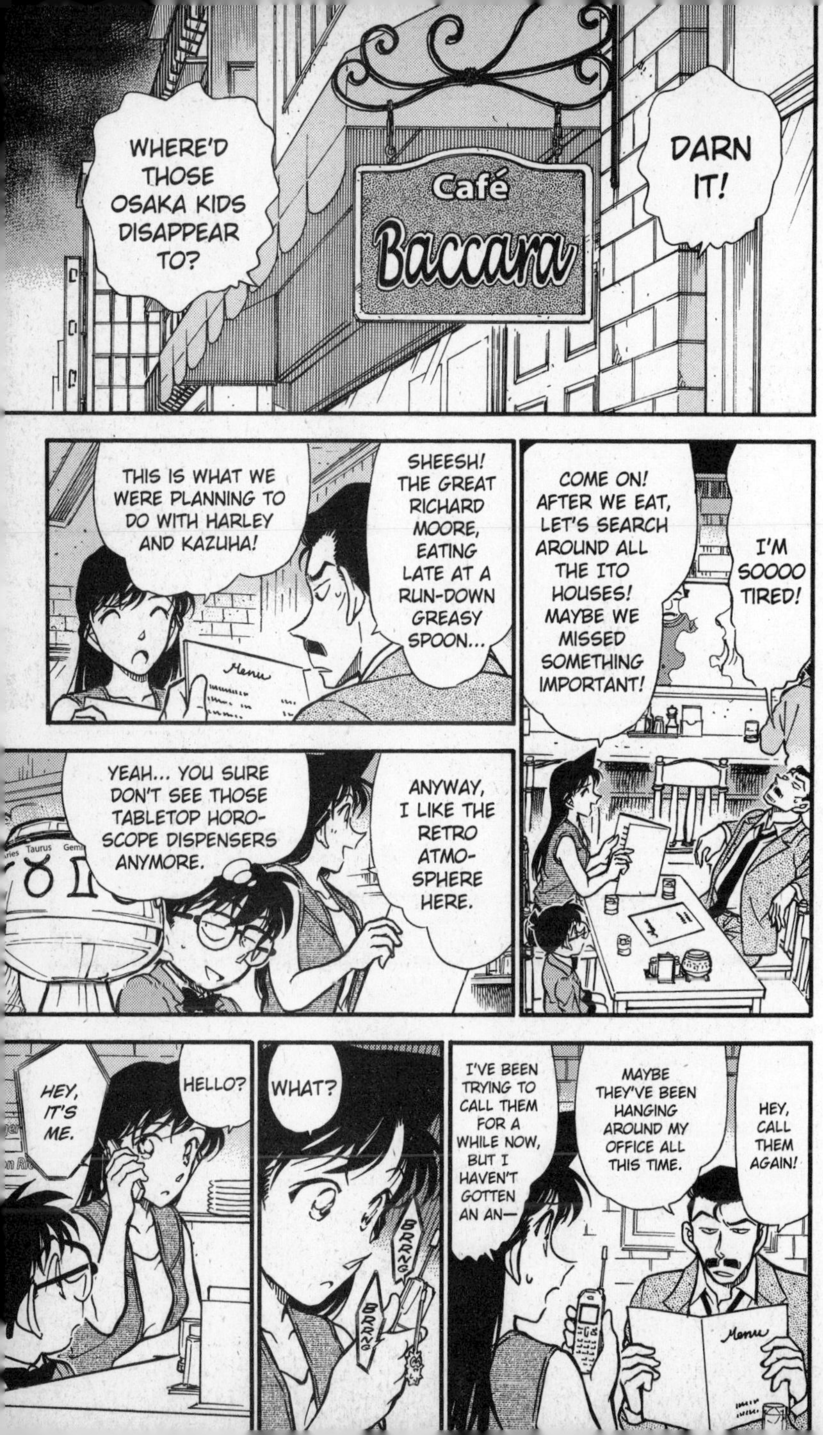
DARN IT!
WHERE'D THOSE OSAKA KIDS DISAPPEAR TO?
Café Baccara
I'M SOOOO TIRED!
COME ON! AFTER WE EAT, LET'S SEARCH AROUND ALL THE ITO HOUSES! MAYBE WE MISSED SOMETHING IMPORTANT!
SHEESH! THE GREAT RICHARD MOORE, EATING LATE AT A RUN-DOWN GREASY SPOON...
THIS IS WHAT WE WERE PLANNING TO DO WITH HARLEY AND KAZUHA!
Menu
ANYWAY, I LIKE THE RETRO ATMO-SPHERE HERE.
YEAH... YOU SURE DON'T SEE THOSE TABLETOP HORO-SCOPE DISPENSERS ANYMORE.
Taurus
HEY, CALL THEM AGAIN!
MAYBE THEY'VE BEEN HANGING AROUND MY OFFICE ALL THIS TIME.
I'VE BEEN TRYING TO CALL THEM FOR A WHILE NOW, BUT I HAVEN'T GOTTEN AN AN—
Menu
WHAT?
BRRNG
BRRNG
HELLO?
HEY, IT'S ME.

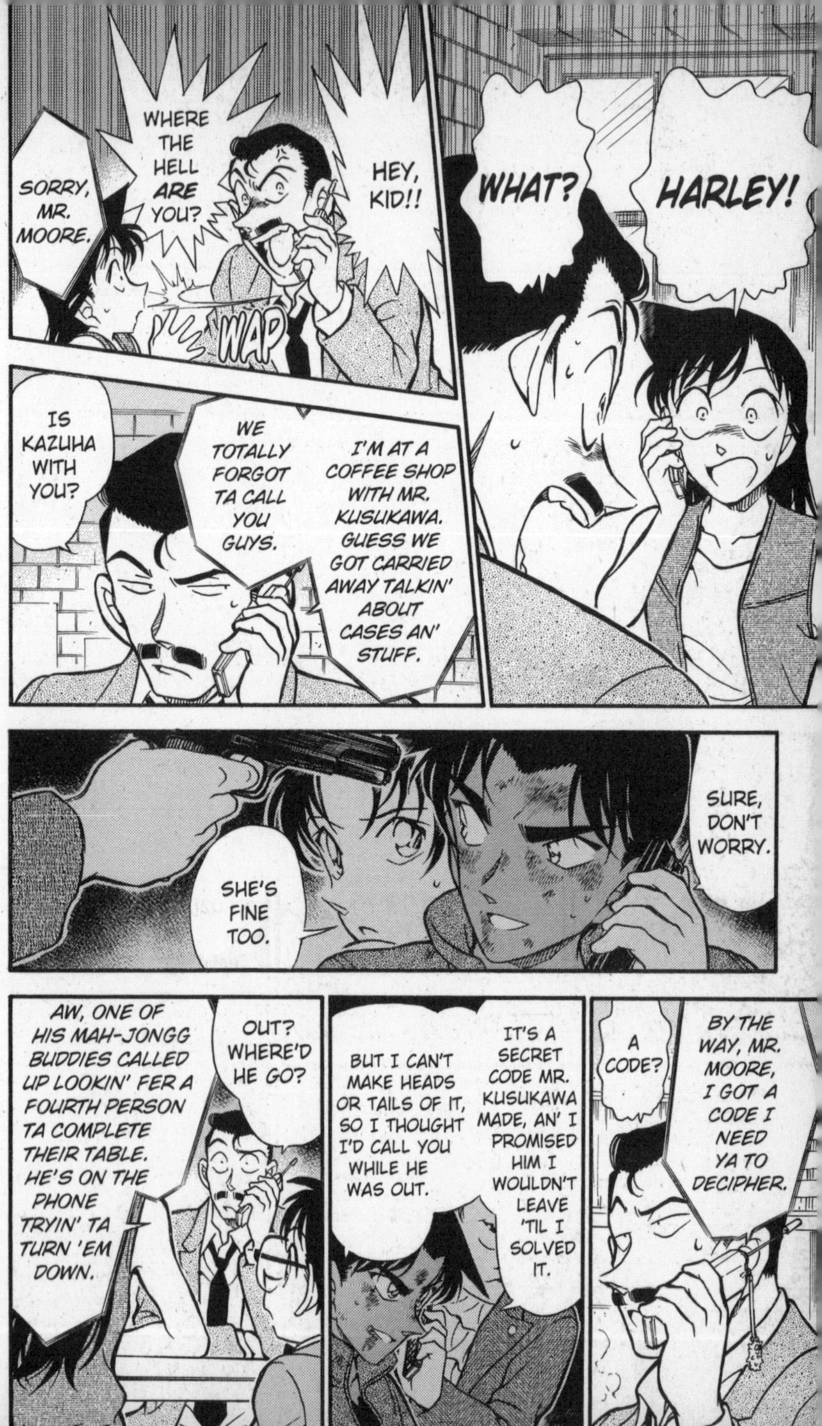
HARLEY!
WHAT?
HEY, KID!!
WHERE THE HELL ARE YOU?
WAP
SORRY, MR. MOORE.
I'M AT A COFFEE SHOP WITH MR. KUSUKAWA. GUESS WE GOT CARRIED AWAY TALKIN' ABOUT CASES AN' STUFF.
WE TOTALLY FORGOT TA CALL YOU GUYS.
IS KAZUHA WITH YOU?
SURE, DON'T WORRY.
SHE'S FINE TOO.
BY THE WAY, MR. MOORE, I GOT A CODE I NEED YA TO DECIPHER.
A CODE?
IT'S A SECRET CODE MR. KUSUKAWA MADE, AN' I PROMISED HIM I WOULDN'T LEAVE 'TIL I SOLVED IT.
BUT I CAN'T MAKE HEADS OR TAILS OF IT, SO I THOUGHT I'D CALL YOU WHILE HE WAS OUT.
OUT? WHERE'D HE GO?
AW, ONE OF HIS MAH-JONGG BUDDIES CALLED UP LOOKIN' FER A FOURTH PERSON TA COMPLETE THEIR TABLE. HE'S ON THE PHONE TRYIN' TA TURN 'EM DOWN.

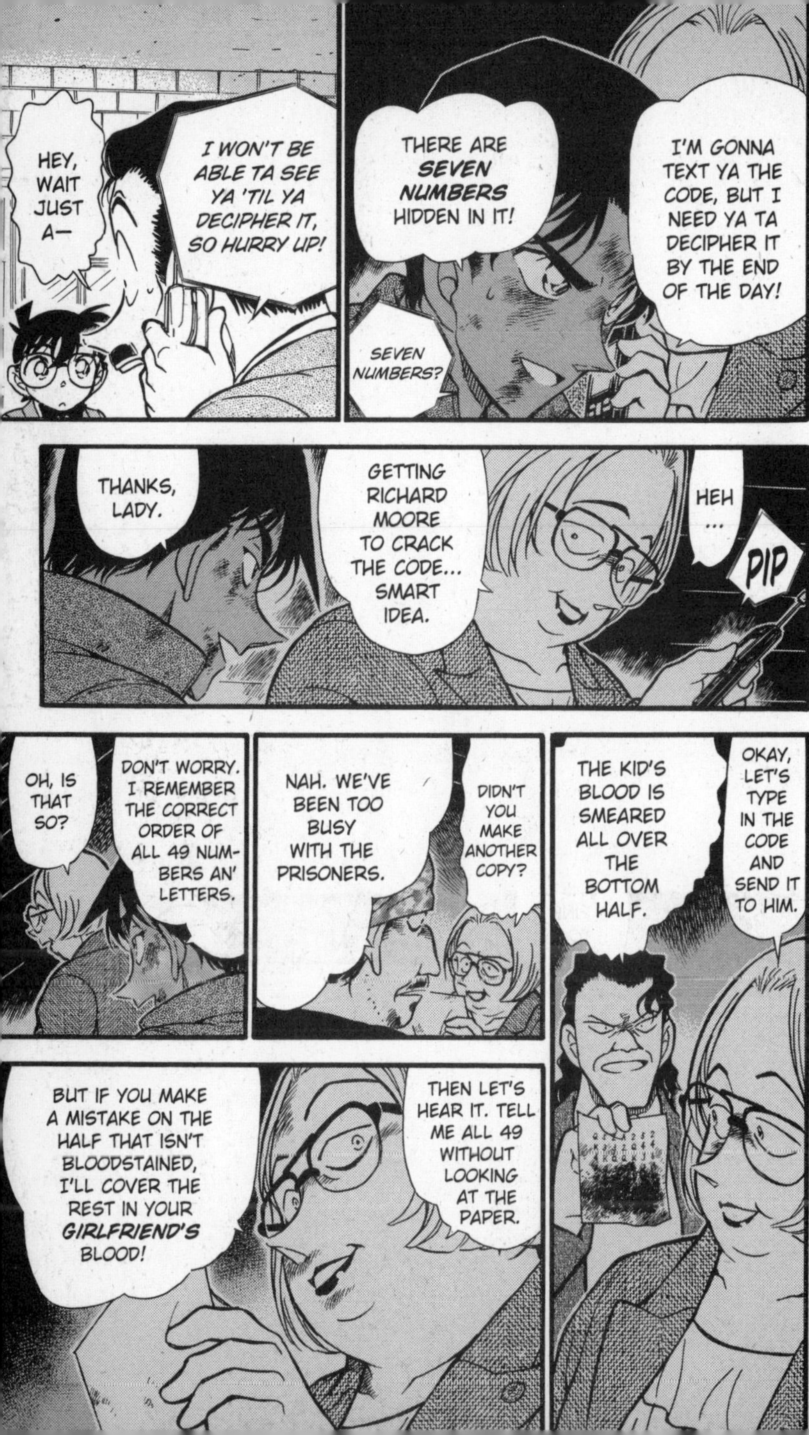
I'M GONNA TEXT YA THE CODE, BUT I NEED YA TA DECIPHER IT BY THE END OF THE DAY!
THERE ARE **SEVEN NUMBERS** HIDDEN IN IT!
SEVEN NUMBERS?
I WON'T BE ABLE TA SEE YA 'TIL YA DECIPHER IT, SO HURRY UP!
HEY, WAIT JUST A—
HEH ...
PIP
GETTING RICHARD MOORE TO CRACK THE CODE... SMART IDEA.
THANKS, LADY.
OKAY, LET'S TYPE IN THE CODE AND SEND IT TO HIM.
THE KID'S BLOOD IS SMEARED ALL OVER THE BOTTOM HALF.
DIDN'T YOU MAKE ANOTHER COPY?
NAH. WE'VE BEEN TOO BUSY WITH THE PRISONERS.
DON'T WORRY. I REMEMBER THE CORRECT ORDER OF ALL 49 NUM-BERS AN' LETTERS.
OH, IS THAT SO?
THEN LET'S HEAR IT. TELL ME ALL 49 WITHOUT LOOKING AT THE PAPER.
BUT IF YOU MAKE A MISTAKE ON THE HALF THAT ISN'T BLOODSTAINED, I'LL COVER THE REST IN YOUR ***GIRLFRIEND'S*** BLOOD!

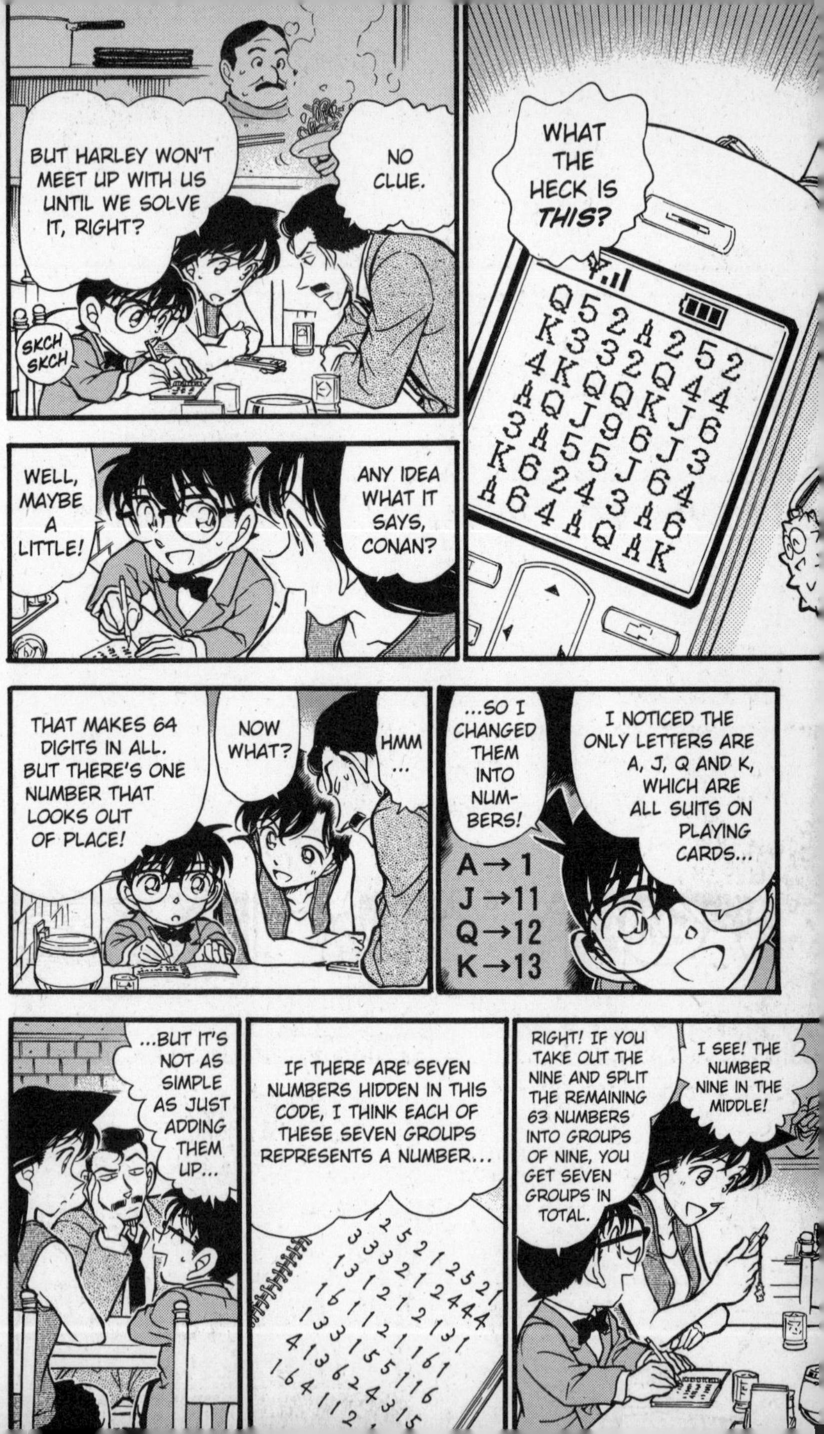
WHAT THE HECK IS THIS?
NO CLUE.
BUT HARLEY WON'T MEET UP WITH US UNTIL WE SOLVE IT, RIGHT?
SKCH SKCH
ANY IDEA WHAT IT SAYS, CONAN?
WELL, MAYBE A LITTLE!
I NOTICED THE ONLY LETTERS ARE A, J, Q AND K, WHICH ARE ALL SUITS ON PLAYING CARDS...
...SO I CHANGED THEM INTO NUMBERS!
A→1
J→11
Q→12
K→13
HMM ...
NOW WHAT?
THAT MAKES 64 DIGITS IN ALL. BUT THERE'S ONE NUMBER THAT LOOKS OUT OF PLACE!
I SEE! THE NUMBER NINE IN THE MIDDLE!
RIGHT! IF YOU TAKE OUT THE NINE AND SPLIT THE REMAINING 63 NUMBERS INTO GROUPS OF NINE, YOU GET SEVEN GROUPS IN TOTAL.
IF THERE ARE SEVEN NUMBERS HIDDEN IN THIS CODE, I THINK EACH OF THESE SEVEN GROUPS REPRESENTS A NUMBER...
...BUT IT'S NOT AS SIMPLE AS JUST ADDING THEM UP...

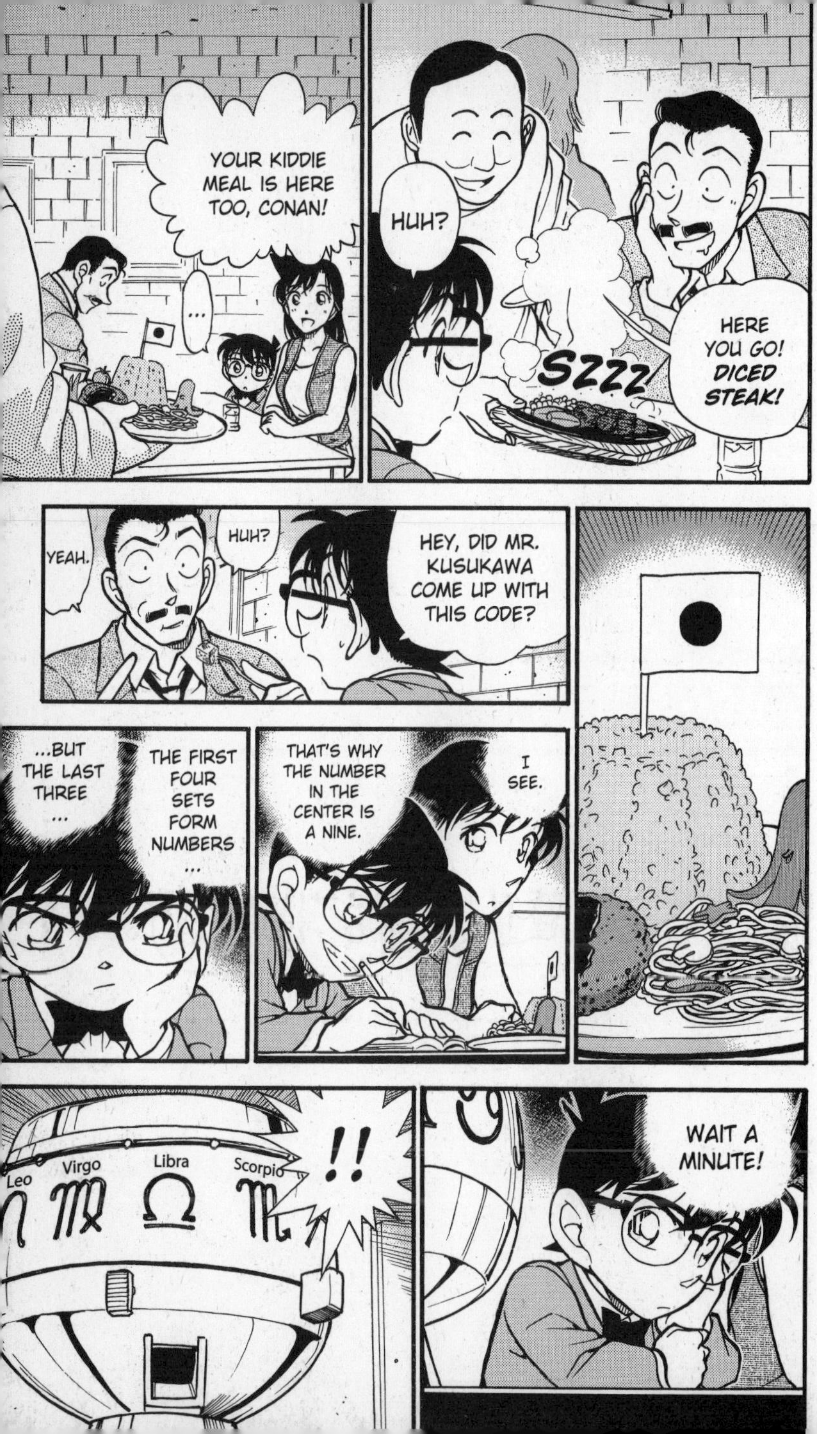
HERE YOU GO! DICED STEAK!
SZZZ
HUH?
YOUR KIDDIE MEAL IS HERE TOO, CONAN!
...
HEY, DID MR. KUSUKAWA COME UP WITH THIS CODE?
HUH?
YEAH.
I SEE.
THAT'S WHY THE NUMBER IN THE CENTER IS A NINE.
THE FIRST FOUR SETS FORM NUMBERS ...
...BUT THE LAST THREE ...
WAIT A MINUTE!
!!
Scorpio
Libra
Virgo
Leo

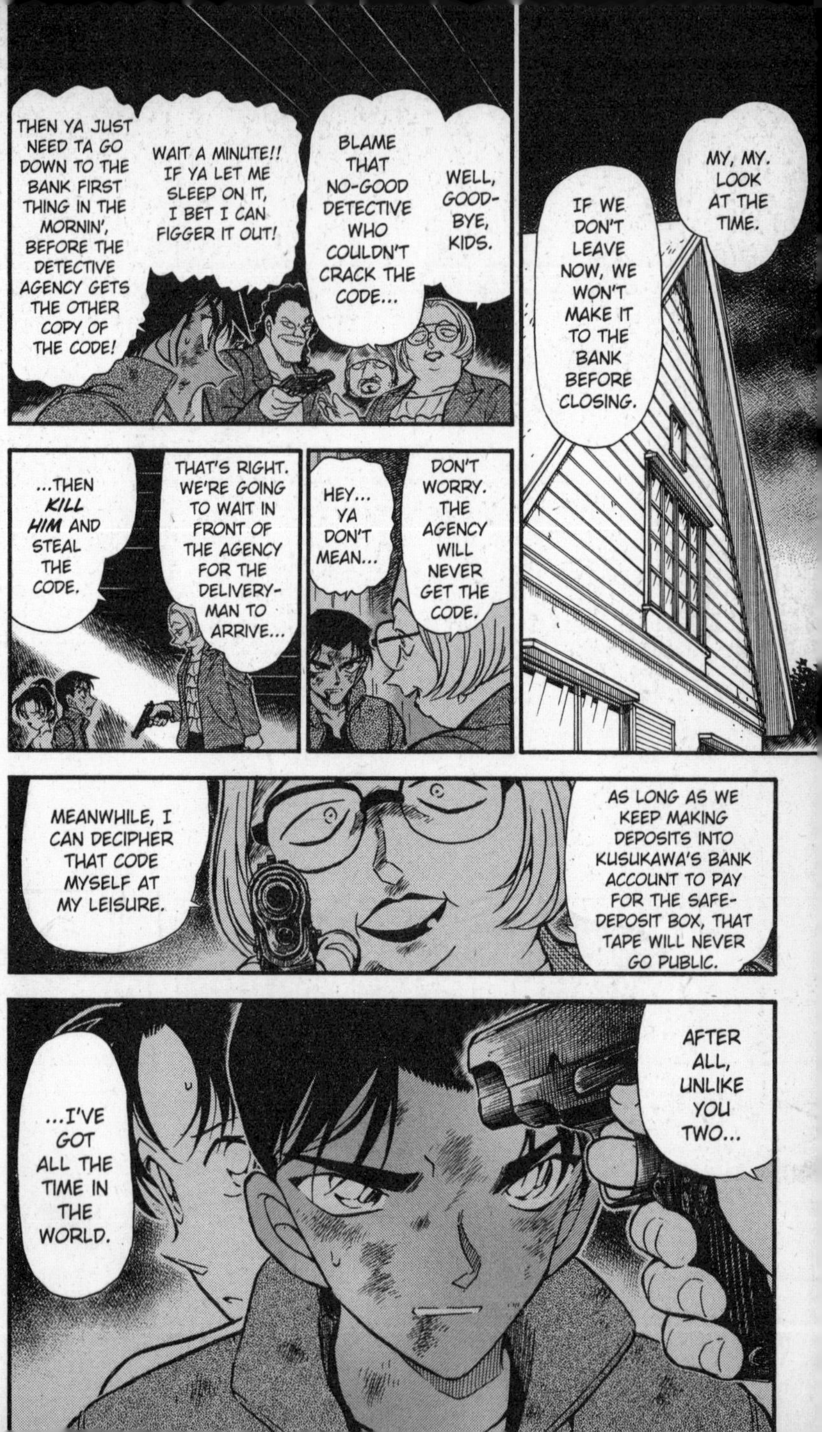
MY, MY. LOOK AT THE TIME.
IF WE DON'T LEAVE NOW, WE WON'T MAKE IT TO THE BANK BEFORE CLOSING.
WELL, GOOD-BYE, KIDS.
BLAME THAT NO-GOOD DETECTIVE WHO COULDN'T CRACK THE CODE...
WAIT A MINUTE!! IF YA LET ME SLEEP ON IT, I BET I CAN FIGGER IT OUT!
THEN YA JUST NEED TA GO DOWN TO THE BANK FIRST THING IN THE MORNIN', BEFORE THE DETECTIVE AGENCY GETS THE OTHER COPY OF THE CODE!
DON'T WORRY. THE AGENCY WILL NEVER GET THE CODE.
HEY... YA DON'T MEAN...
THAT'S RIGHT. WE'RE GOING TO WAIT IN FRONT OF THE AGENCY FOR THE DELIVERYMAN TO ARRIVE...
...THEN *KILL HIM* AND STEAL THE CODE.
AS LONG AS WE KEEP MAKING DEPOSITS INTO KUSUKAWA'S BANK ACCOUNT TO PAY FOR THE SAFE-DEPOSIT BOX, THAT TAPE WILL NEVER GO PUBLIC.
MEANWHILE, I CAN DECIPHER THAT CODE MYSELF AT MY LEISURE.
AFTER ALL, UNLIKE YOU TWO...
...I'VE GOT ALL THE TIME IN THE WORLD.

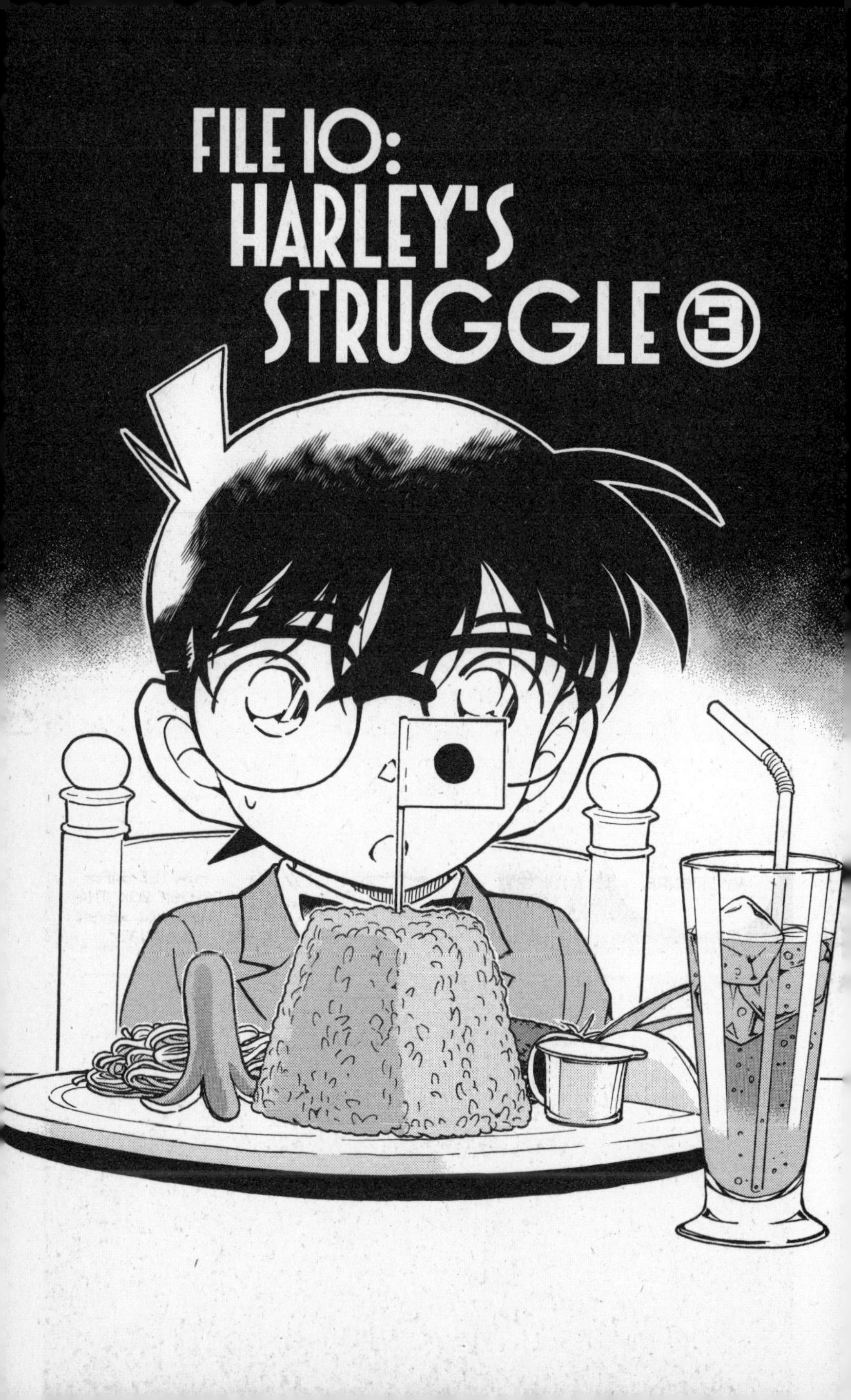
FILE 10:
HARLEY'S
STRUGGLE ③

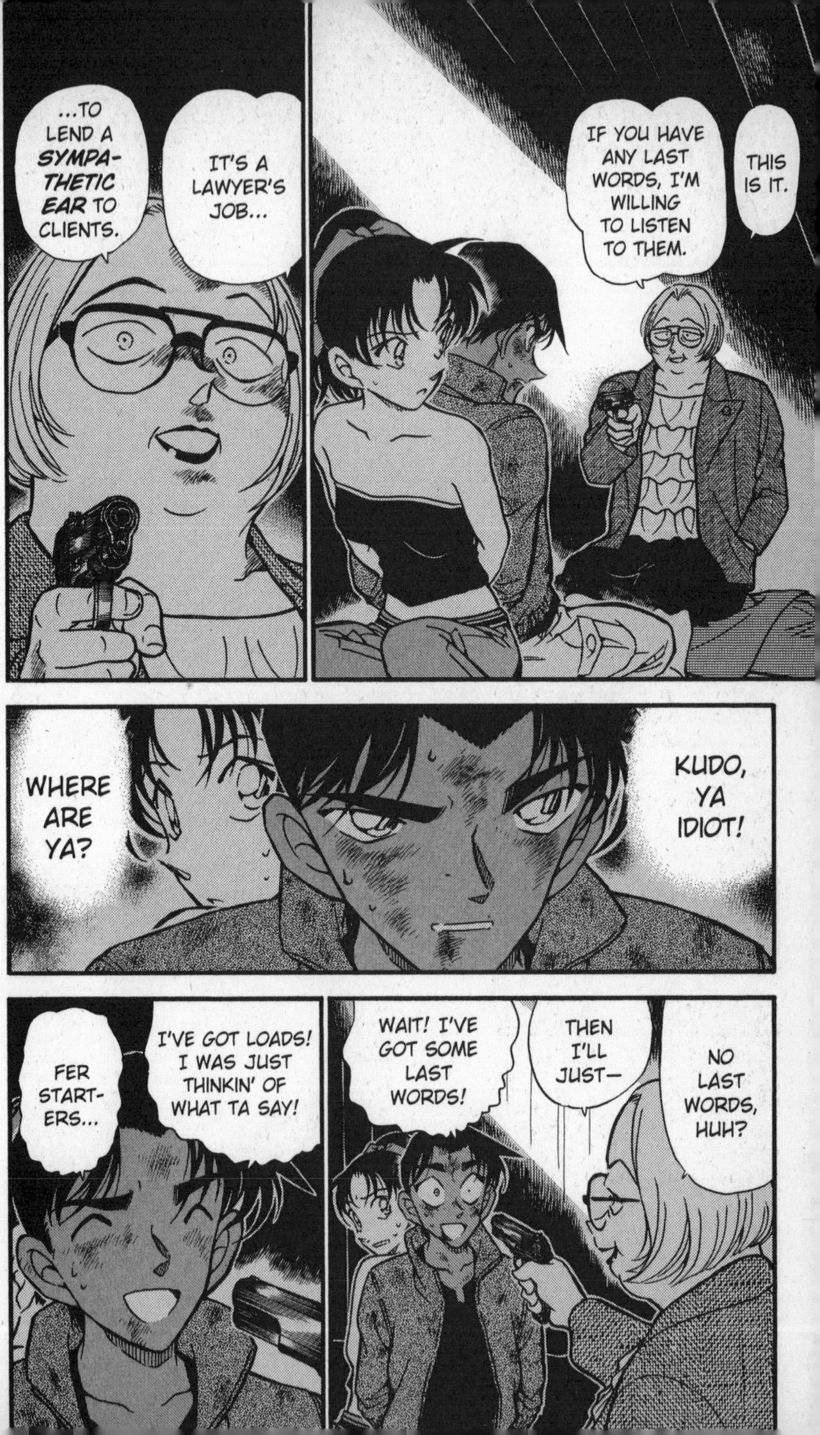
THIS IS IT.
IF YOU HAVE ANY LAST WORDS, I'M WILLING TO LISTEN TO THEM.
IT'S A LAWYER'S JOB...
...TO LEND A SYMPATHETIC EAR TO CLIENTS.
KUDO, YA IDIOT!
WHERE ARE YA?
NO LAST WORDS, HUH?
THEN I'LL JUST—
WAIT! I'VE GOT SOME LAST WORDS!
I'VE GOT LOADS! I WAS JUST THINKIN' OF WHAT TA SAY!
FER STARTERS...

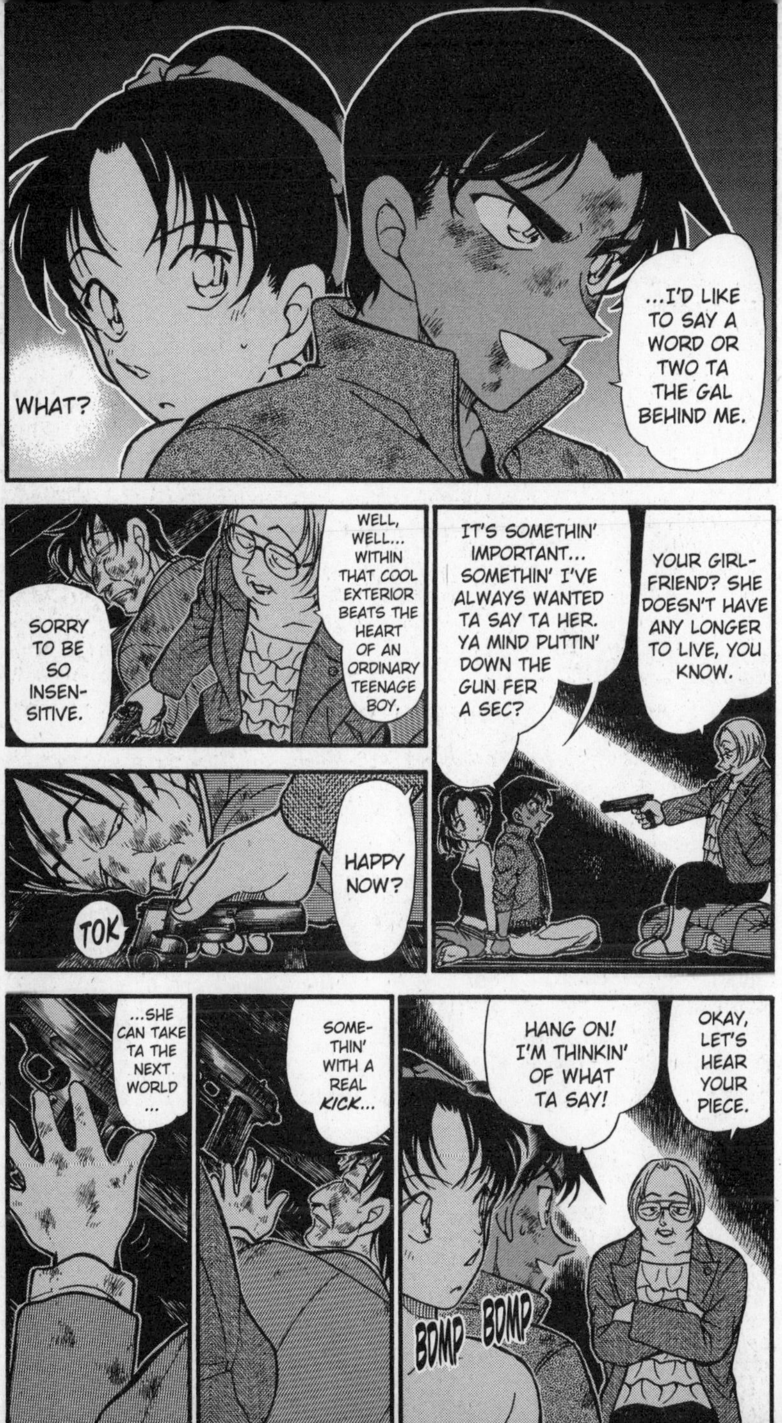
...I'D LIKE TO SAY A WORD OR TWO TA THE GAL BEHIND ME.
WHAT?
YOUR GIRL-FRIEND? SHE DOESN'T HAVE ANY LONGER TO LIVE, YOU KNOW.
IT'S SOMETHIN' IMPORTANT... SOMETHIN' I'VE ALWAYS WANTED TA SAY TA HER. YA MIND PUTTIN' DOWN THE GUN FER A SEC?
WELL, WELL... WITHIN THAT COOL EXTERIOR BEATS THE HEART OF AN ORDINARY TEENAGE BOY.
SORRY TO BE SO INSEN-SITIVE.
HAPPY NOW?
TOK
OKAY, LET'S HEAR YOUR PIECE.
HANG ON! I'M THINKIN' OF WHAT TA SAY!
BDMP
BDMP
SOME-THIN' WITH A REAL *KICK*...
...SHE CAN TAKE TA THE NEXT WORLD ...

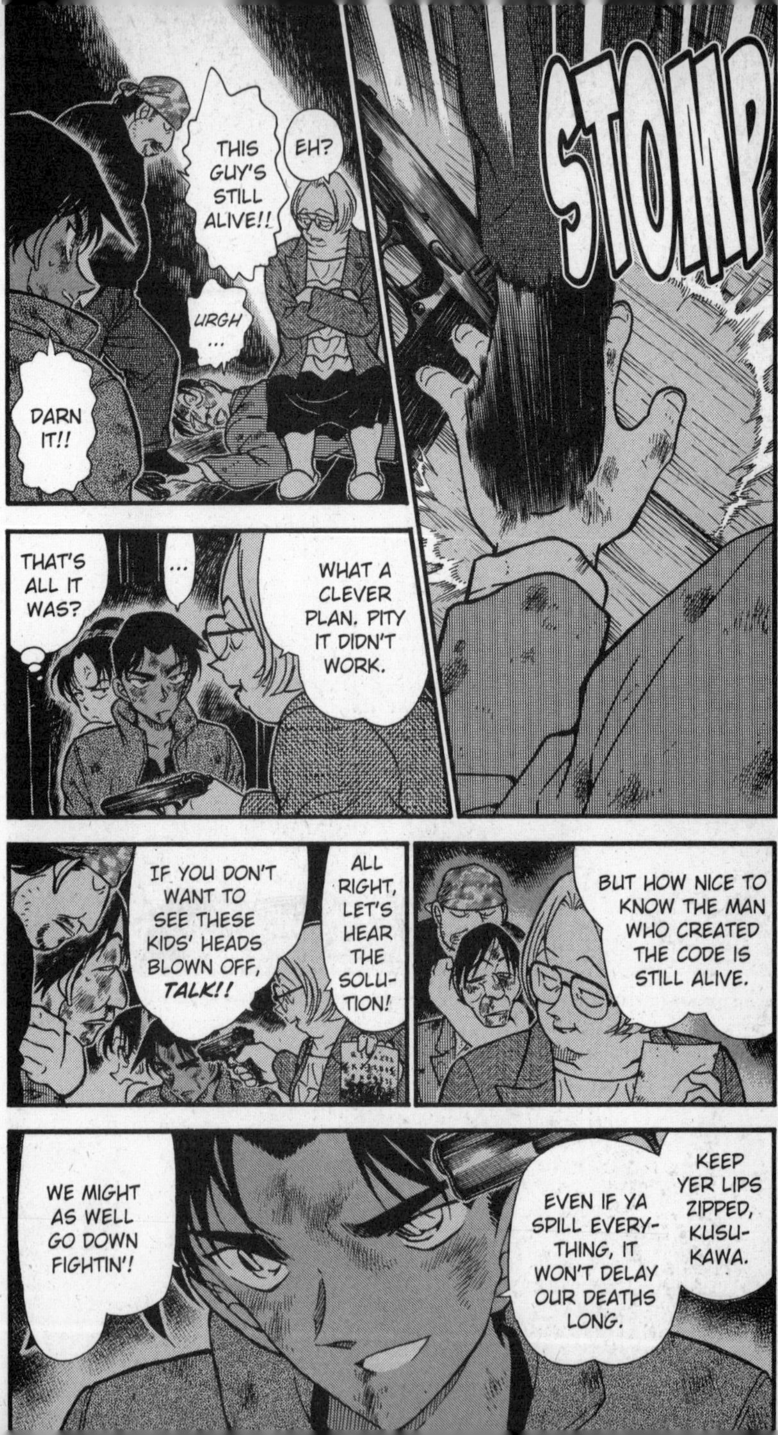
STOMP
EH?
THIS GUY'S STILL ALIVE!!
URGH ...
DARN IT!!
WHAT A CLEVER PLAN. PITY IT DIDN'T WORK.
...
THAT'S ALL IT WAS?
BUT HOW NICE TO KNOW THE MAN WHO CREATED THE CODE IS STILL ALIVE.
ALL RIGHT, LET'S HEAR THE SOLU-TION!
IF YOU DON'T WANT TO SEE THESE KIDS' HEADS BLOWN OFF, TALK!!
KEEP YER LIPS ZIPPED, KUSU-KAWA.
EVEN IF YA SPILL EVERY-THING, IT WON'T DELAY OUR DEATHS LONG.
WE MIGHT AS WELL GO DOWN FIGHTIN'!

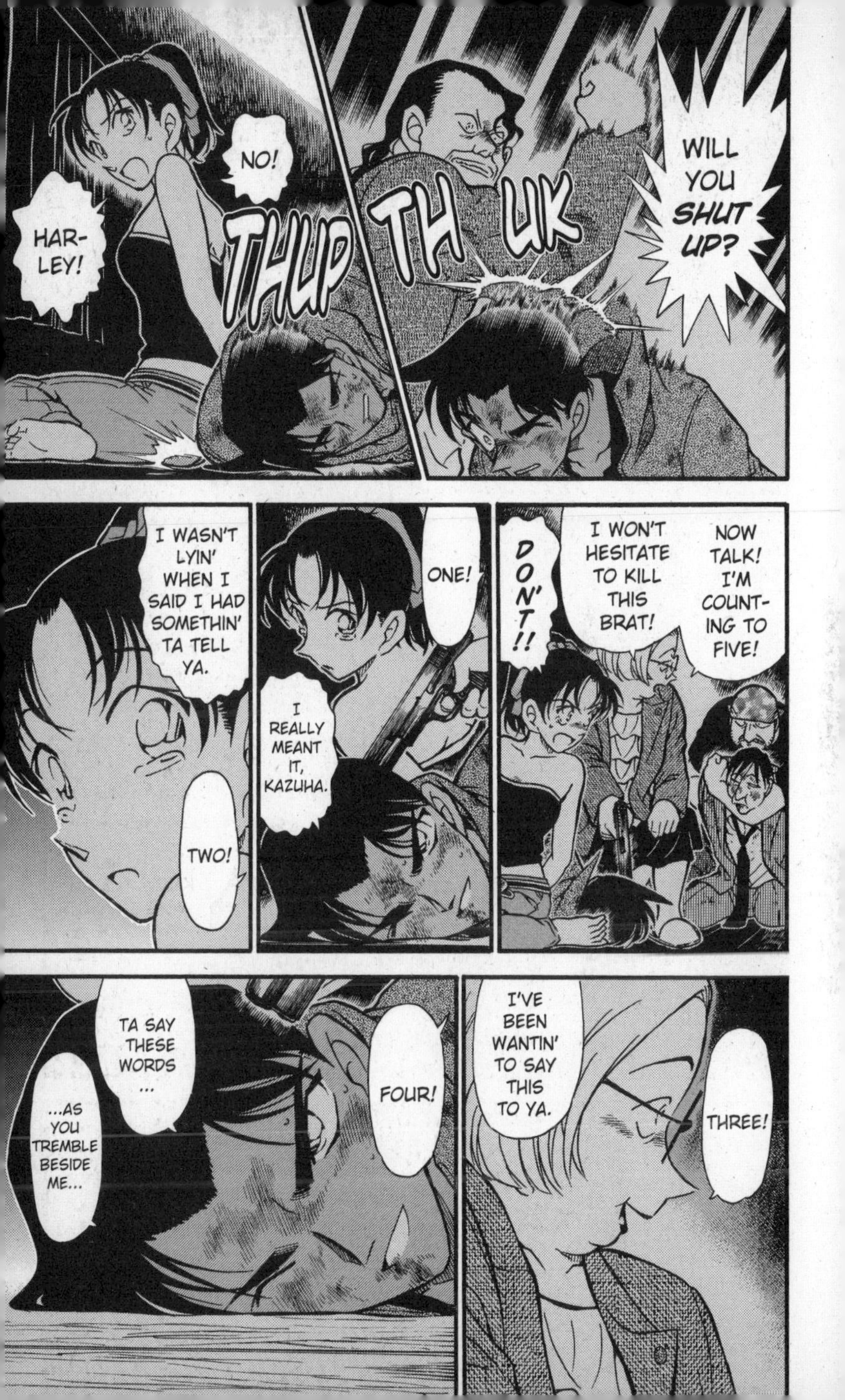
WILL YOU SHUT UP?
TH UK
THUP
NO!
HAR-LEY!
NOW TALK! I'M COUNT-ING TO FIVE!
I WON'T HESITATE TO KILL THIS BRAT!
DON'T!!
ONE!
I REALLY MEANT IT, KAZUHA.
I WASN'T LYIN' WHEN I SAID I HAD SOMETHIN' TA TELL YA.
TWO!
THREE!
I'VE BEEN WANTIN' TO SAY THIS TO YA.
FOUR!
TA SAY THESE WORDS ...
...AS YOU TREMBLE BESIDE ME...

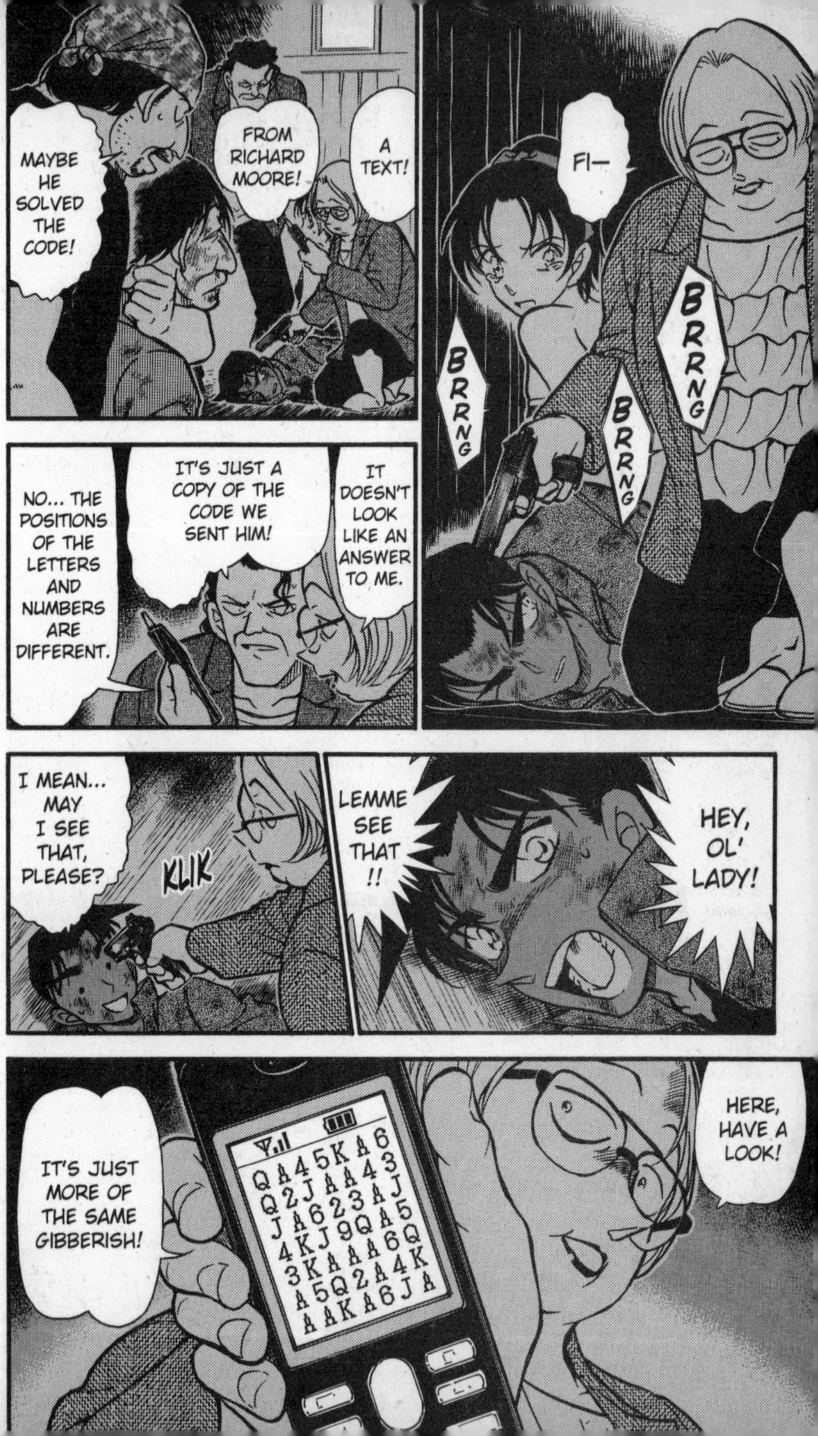
FI—
BRRNG
BRRNG
BRRNG
A TEXT!
FROM RICHARD MOORE!
MAYBE HE SOLVED THE CODE!
IT DOESN'T LOOK LIKE AN ANSWER TO ME.
IT'S JUST A COPY OF THE CODE WE SENT HIM!
NO... THE POSITIONS OF THE LETTERS AND NUMBERS ARE DIFFERENT.
HEY, OL' LADY!
LEMME SEE THAT !!
KLIK
I MEAN... MAY I SEE THAT, PLEASE?
HERE, HAVE A LOOK!
QA45KA6
Q2JAA43
JA623AJ
4KJ9QA5
3KAAA6Q
A5Q2A4K
AAKA6JA
IT'S JUST MORE OF THE SAME GIBBERISH!

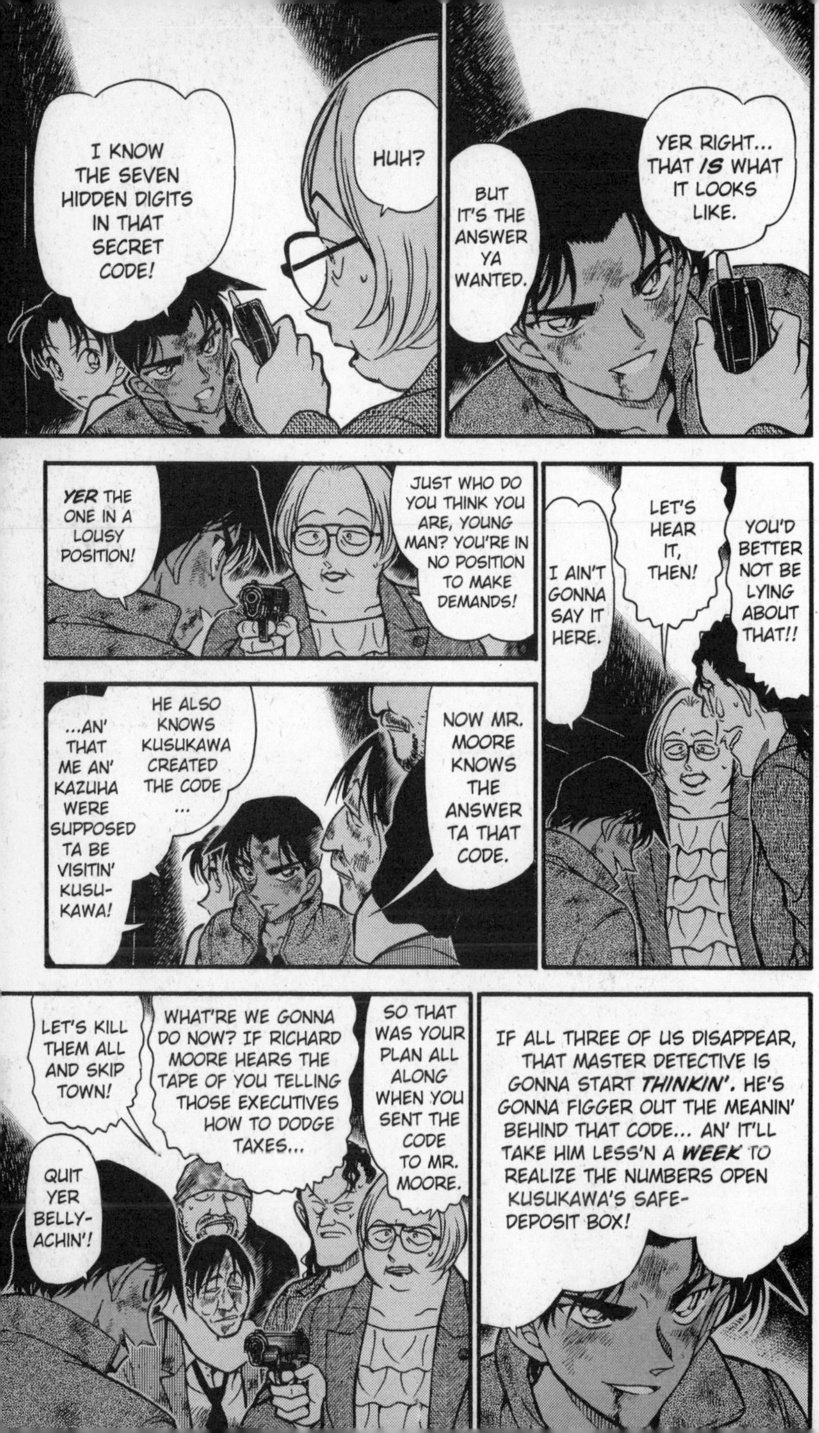

YER RIGHT... THAT *IS* WHAT IT LOOKS LIKE.
BUT IT'S THE ANSWER YA WANTED.
HUH?
I KNOW THE SEVEN HIDDEN DIGITS IN THAT SECRET CODE!
YOU'D BETTER NOT BE LYING ABOUT THAT!!
LET'S HEAR IT, THEN!
I AIN'T GONNA SAY IT HERE.
JUST WHO DO YOU THINK YOU ARE, YOUNG MAN? YOU'RE IN NO POSITION TO MAKE DEMANDS!
YER THE ONE IN A LOUSY POSITION!
NOW MR. MOORE KNOWS THE ANSWER TA THAT CODE.
HE ALSO KNOWS KUSUKAWA CREATED THE CODE ...
...AN' THAT ME AN' KAZUHA WERE SUPPOSED TA BE VISITIN' KUSUKAWA!
IF ALL THREE OF US DISAPPEAR, THAT MASTER DETECTIVE IS GONNA START *THINKIN'*. HE'S GONNA FIGGER OUT THE MEANIN' BEHIND THAT CODE... AN' IT'LL TAKE HIM LESS'N A *WEEK* TO REALIZE THE NUMBERS OPEN KUSUKAWA'S SAFE-DEPOSIT BOX!
SO THAT WAS YOUR PLAN ALL ALONG WHEN YOU SENT THE CODE TO MR. MOORE.
WHAT'RE WE GONNA DO NOW? IF RICHARD MOORE HEARS THE TAPE OF YOU TELLING THOSE EXECUTIVES HOW TO DODGE TAXES...
LET'S KILL THEM ALL AND SKIP TOWN!
QUIT YER BELLY-ACHIN'!

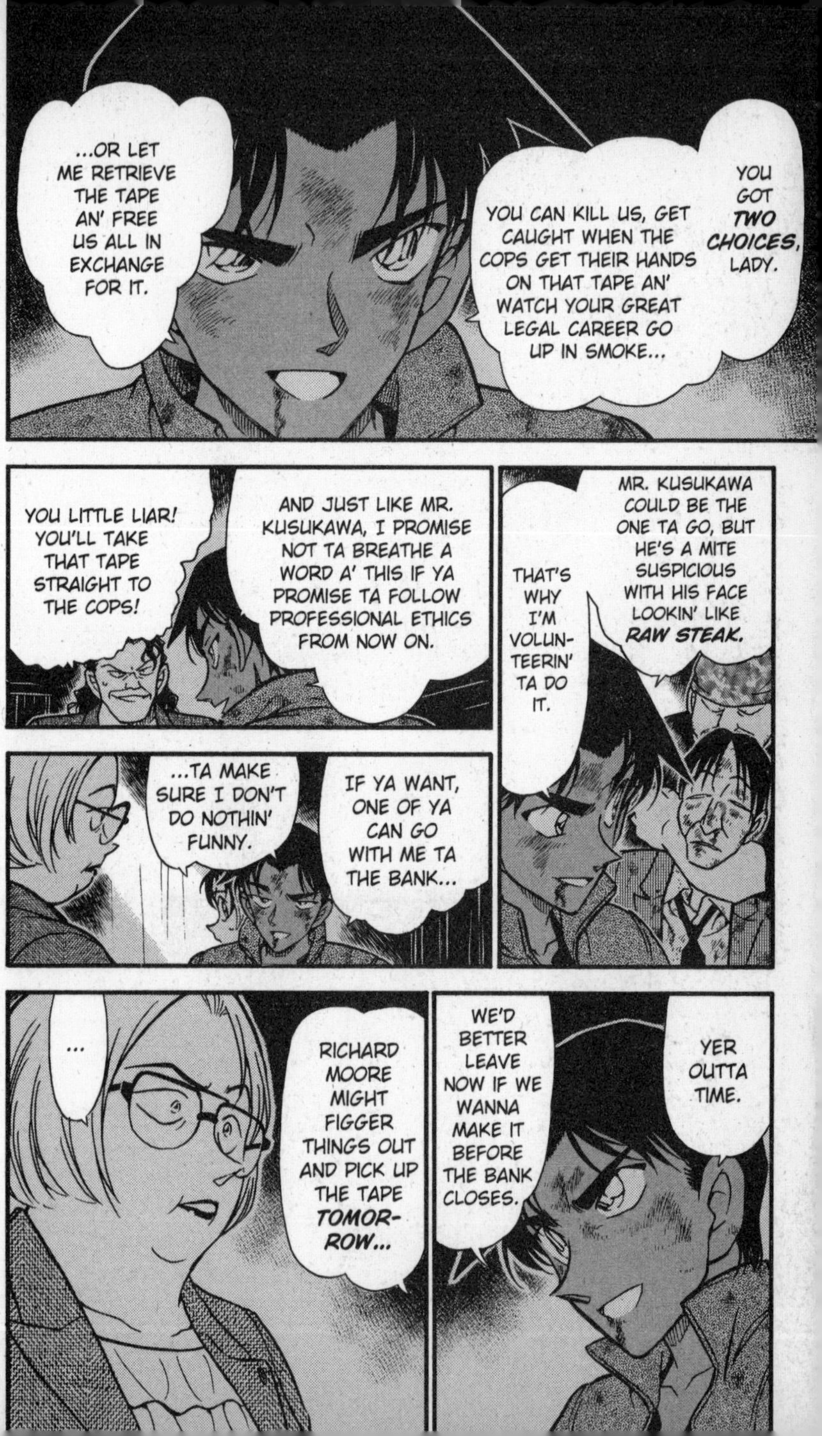
YOU GOT TWO CHOICES, LADY.
YOU CAN KILL US, GET CAUGHT WHEN THE COPS GET THEIR HANDS ON THAT TAPE AN' WATCH YOUR GREAT LEGAL CAREER GO UP IN SMOKE...
...OR LET ME RETRIEVE THE TAPE AN' FREE US ALL IN EXCHANGE FOR IT.
MR. KUSUKAWA COULD BE THE ONE TA GO, BUT HE'S A MITE SUSPICIOUS WITH HIS FACE LOOKIN' LIKE RAW STEAK.
THAT'S WHY I'M VOLUNTEERIN' TA DO IT.
AND JUST LIKE MR. KUSUKAWA, I PROMISE NOT TA BREATHE A WORD A' THIS IF YA PROMISE TA FOLLOW PROFESSIONAL ETHICS FROM NOW ON.
YOU LITTLE LIAR! YOU'LL TAKE THAT TAPE STRAIGHT TO THE COPS!
IF YA WANT, ONE OF YA CAN GO WITH ME TA THE BANK...
...TA MAKE SURE I DON'T DO NOTHIN' FUNNY.
YER OUTTA TIME.
WE'D BETTER LEAVE NOW IF WE WANNA MAKE IT BEFORE THE BANK CLOSES.
RICHARD MOORE MIGHT FIGGER THINGS OUT AND PICK UP THE TAPE TOMORROW...
...

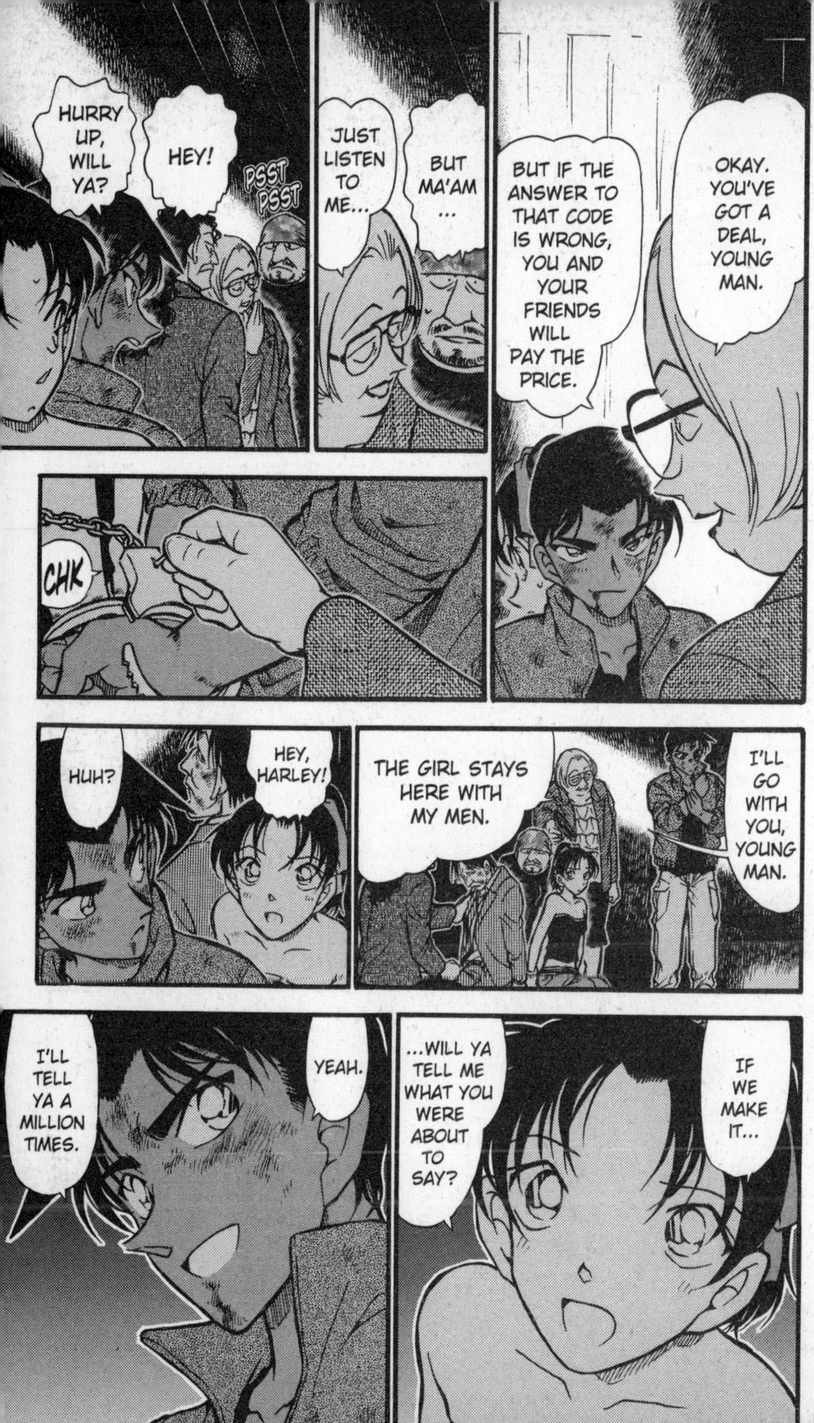
OKAY. YOU'VE GOT A DEAL, YOUNG MAN.
BUT IF THE ANSWER TO THAT CODE IS WRONG, YOU AND YOUR FRIENDS WILL PAY THE PRICE.
BUT MA'AM ...
JUST LISTEN TO ME...
PSST PSST
HEY!
HURRY UP, WILL YA?
CHK
I'LL GO WITH YOU, YOUNG MAN.
THE GIRL STAYS HERE WITH MY MEN.
HEY, HARLEY!
HUH?
IF WE MAKE IT...
...WILL YA TELL ME WHAT YOU WERE ABOUT TO SAY?
YEAH.
I'LL TELL YA A MILLION TIMES.

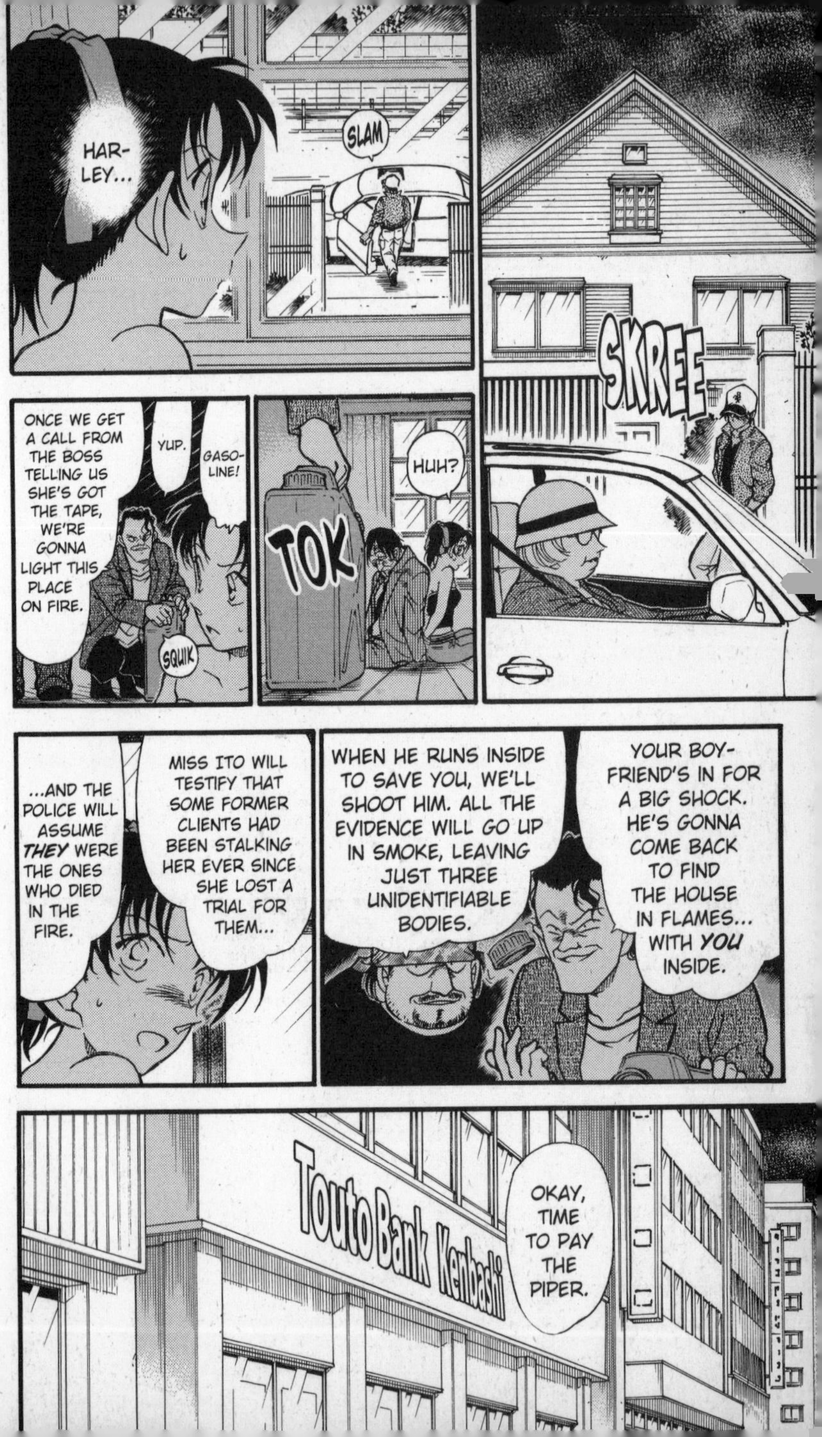
SKREE
SLAM
HAR-LEY...
HUH?
TOK
GASO-LINE!
YUP.
ONCE WE GET A CALL FROM THE BOSS TELLING US SHE'S GOT THE TAPE, WE'RE GONNA LIGHT THIS PLACE ON FIRE.
SQUIK
YOUR BOY-FRIEND'S IN FOR A BIG SHOCK. HE'S GONNA COME BACK TO FIND THE HOUSE IN FLAMES... WITH *YOU* INSIDE.
WHEN HE RUNS INSIDE TO SAVE YOU, WE'LL SHOOT HIM. ALL THE EVIDENCE WILL GO UP IN SMOKE, LEAVING JUST THREE UNIDENTIFIABLE BODIES.
MISS ITO WILL TESTIFY THAT SOME FORMER CLIENTS HAD BEEN STALKING HER EVER SINCE SHE LOST A TRIAL FOR THEM...
...AND THE POLICE WILL ASSUME *THEY* WERE THE ONES WHO DIED IN THE FIRE.
OKAY, TIME TO PAY THE PIPER.
Touto Bank Kenbashi

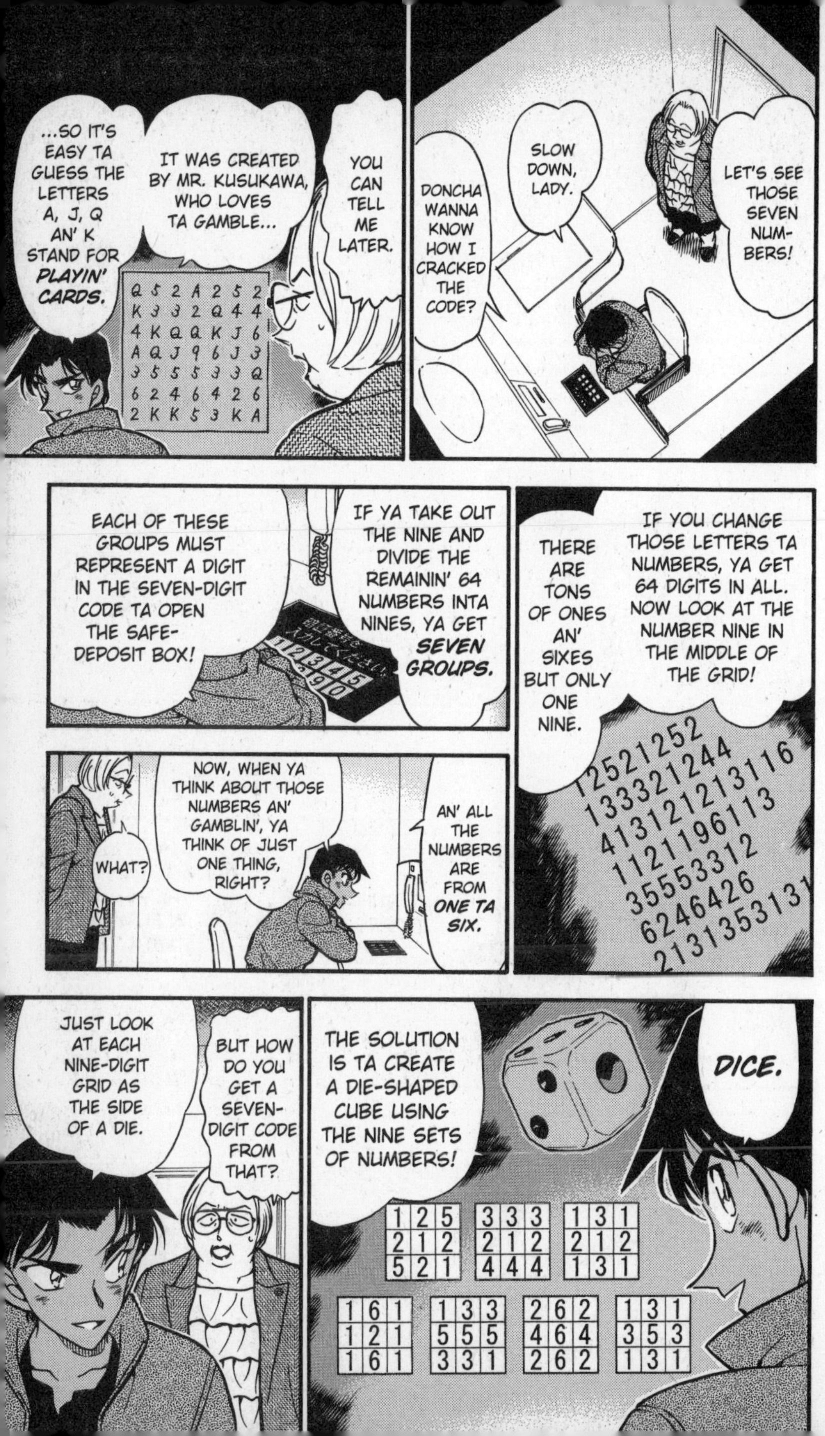
LET'S SEE THOSE SEVEN NUMBERS!
SLOW DOWN, LADY.
DONCHA WANNA KNOW HOW I CRACKED THE CODE?
YOU CAN TELL ME LATER.
IT WAS CREATED BY MR. KUSUKAWA, WHO LOVES TA GAMBLE...
...SO IT'S EASY TA GUESS THE LETTERS A, J, Q AN' K STAND FOR *PLAYIN' CARDS.*
Q 5 2 A 2 5 2
K 3 3 2 Q 4 4
4 K Q Q K J 6
A Q J 9 6 J 3
3 5 5 5 3 3 Q
6 2 4 6 4 2 6
2 K K 5 3 K A
IF YOU CHANGE THOSE LETTERS TA NUMBERS, YA GET 64 DIGITS IN ALL. NOW LOOK AT THE NUMBER NINE IN THE MIDDLE OF THE GRID!
THERE ARE TONS OF ONES AN' SIXES BUT ONLY ONE NINE.
12521252
133321244
413121213116
1121196113
35553312
6246426
213135313
IF YA TAKE OUT THE NINE AND DIVIDE THE REMAININ' 64 NUMBERS INTA NINES, YA GET *SEVEN GROUPS.*
EACH OF THESE GROUPS MUST REPRESENT A DIGIT IN THE SEVEN-DIGIT CODE TA OPEN THE SAFE-DEPOSIT BOX!
AN' ALL THE NUMBERS ARE FROM *ONE TA SIX.*
NOW, WHEN YA THINK ABOUT THOSE NUMBERS AN' GAMBLIN', YA THINK OF JUST ONE THING, RIGHT?
WHAT?
DICE.
THE SOLUTION IS TA CREATE A DIE-SHAPED CUBE USING THE NINE SETS OF NUMBERS!
125 212 521
333 212 444
131 212 131
161 121 161
133 555 331
262 464 262
131 353 131
BUT HOW DO YOU GET A SEVEN-DIGIT CODE FROM THAT?
JUST LOOK AT EACH NINE-DIGIT GRID AS THE SIDE OF A DIE.

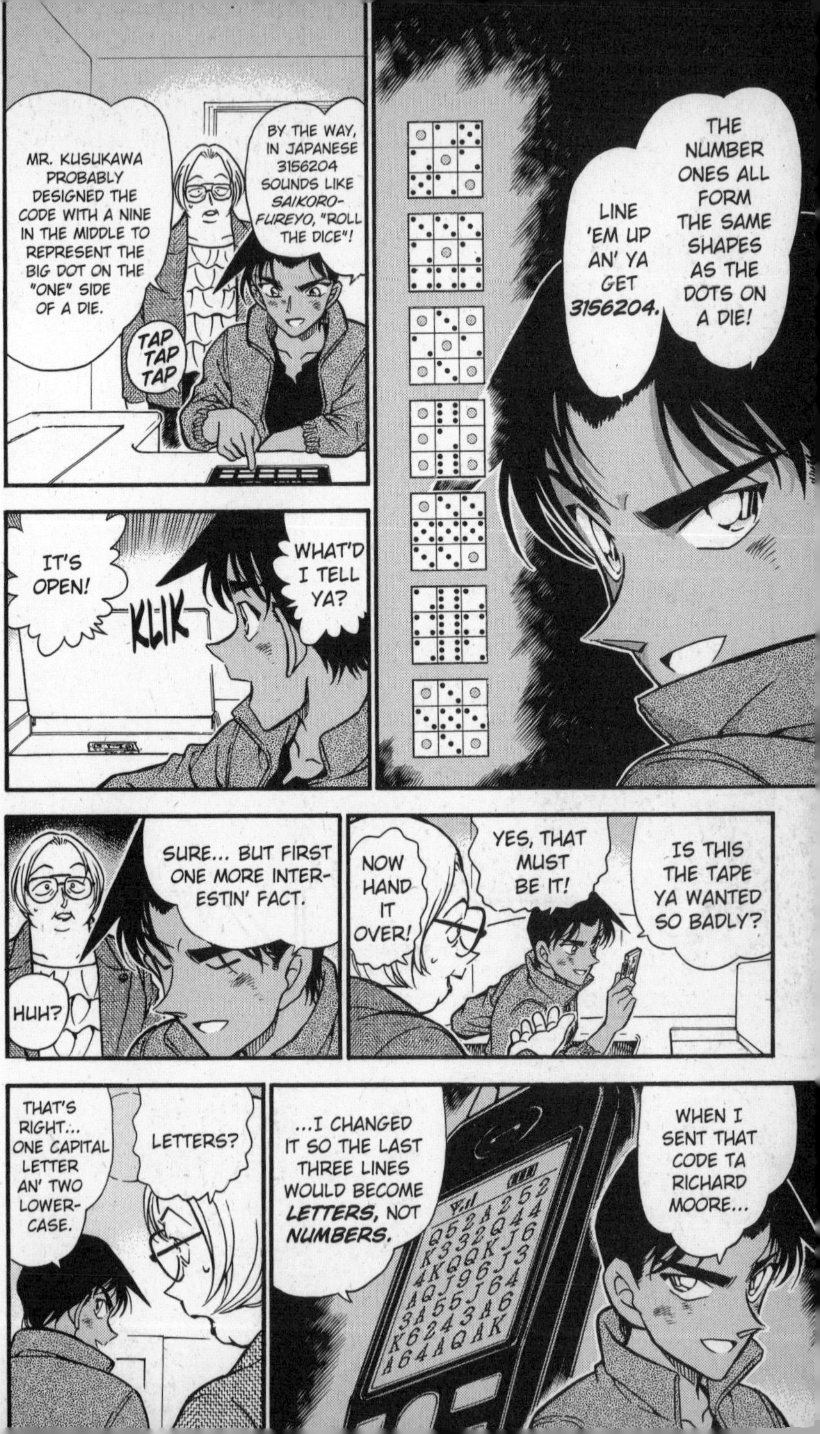
THE NUMBER ONES ALL FORM THE SAME SHAPES AS THE DOTS ON A DIE!
LINE 'EM UP AN' YA GET 3156204.
BY THE WAY, IN JAPANESE 3156204 SOUNDS LIKE SAIKORO-FUREYO, "ROLL THE DICE"!
MR. KUSUKAWA PROBABLY DESIGNED THE CODE WITH A NINE IN THE MIDDLE TO REPRESENT THE BIG DOT ON THE "ONE" SIDE OF A DIE.
TAP TAP TAP
WHAT'D I TELL YA?
IT'S OPEN!
KLIK
IS THIS THE TAPE YA WANTED SO BADLY?
YES, THAT MUST BE IT!
NOW HAND IT OVER!
SURE... BUT FIRST ONE MORE INTER-ESTIN' FACT.
HUH?
WHEN I SENT THAT CODE TA RICHARD MOORE...
...I CHANGED IT SO THE LAST THREE LINES WOULD BECOME LETTERS, NOT NUMBERS.
LETTERS?
THAT'S RIGHT... ONE CAPITAL LETTER AN' TWO LOWER-CASE.

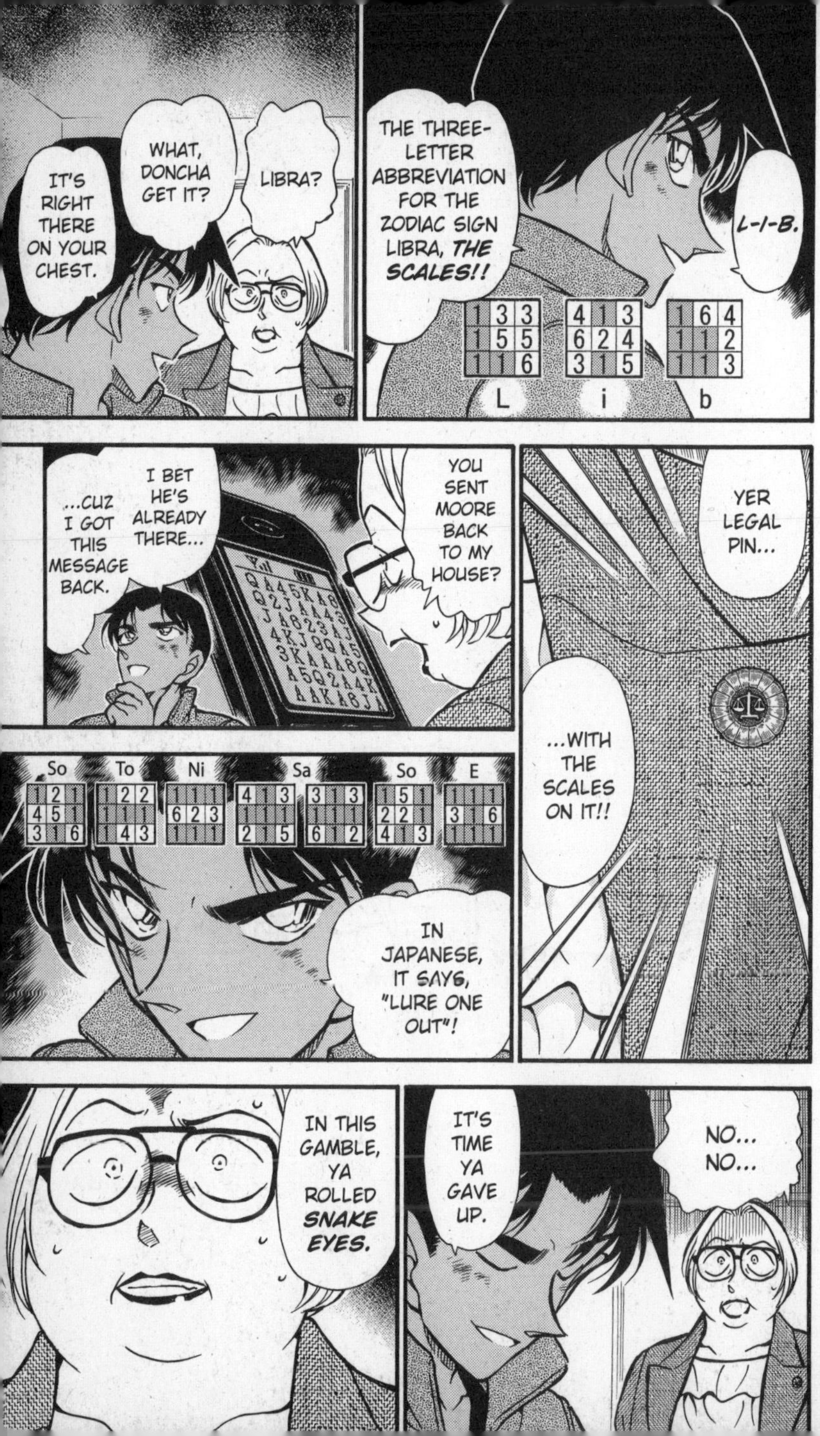
L-I-B.
THE THREE-LETTER ABBREVIATION FOR THE ZODIAC SIGN LIBRA, *THE SCALES!!*
133 155 116
413 624 315
164 112 113
L i b
LIBRA?
WHAT, DONCHA GET IT?
IT'S RIGHT THERE ON YOUR CHEST.
YER LEGAL PIN...
...WITH THE SCALES ON IT!!
YOU SENT MOORE BACK TO MY HOUSE?
I BET HE'S ALREADY THERE...
...CUZ I GOT THIS MESSAGE BACK.
So To Ni Sa So E
121 451 316
122 111 143
111 623 111
413 111 215
313 111 612
151 221 413
111 316 111
IN JAPANESE, IT SAYS, "LURE ONE OUT"!
NO... NO...
IT'S TIME YA GAVE UP.
IN THIS GAMBLE, YA ROLLED *SNAKE EYES.*

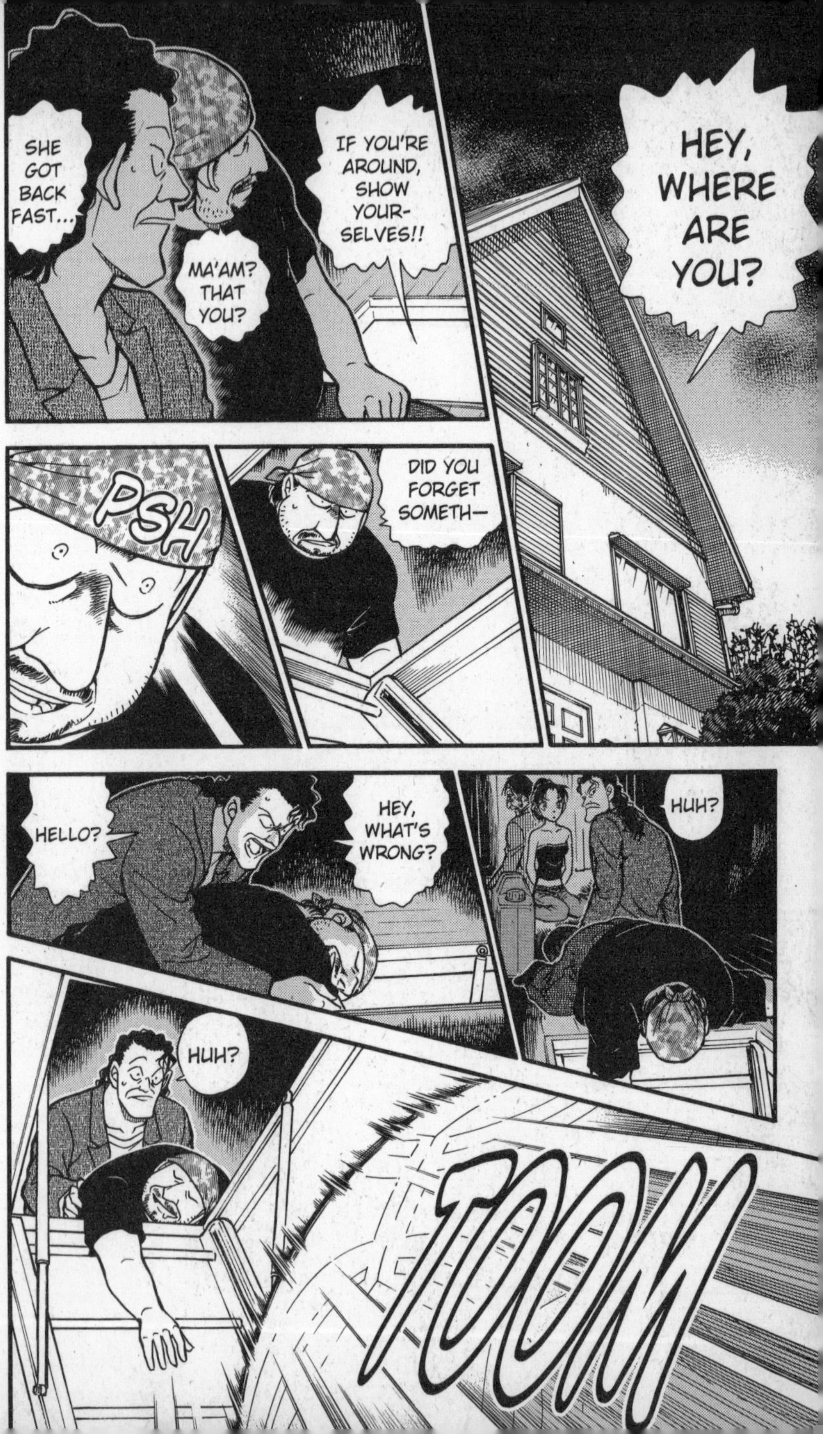
HEY, WHERE ARE YOU?
IF YOU'RE AROUND, SHOW YOUR-SELVES!!
MA'AM? THAT YOU?
SHE GOT BACK FAST...
DID YOU FORGET SOMETH—
PSH
HUH?
HEY, WHAT'S WRONG?
HELLO?
HUH?
TOOM

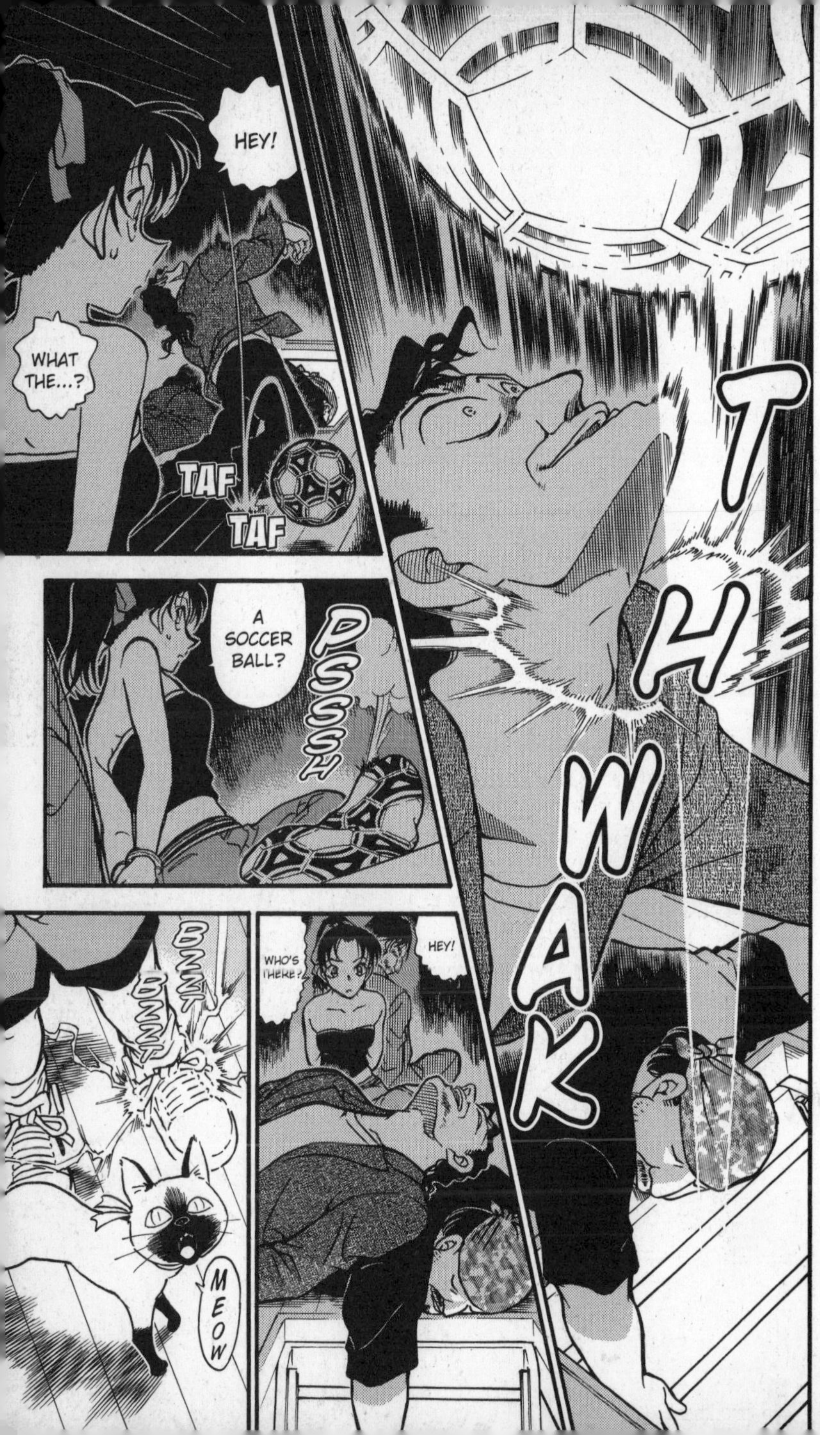
THWAK
HEY!
WHAT THE...?
TAF
TAF
A SOCCER BALL?
PSSSH
HEY!
WHO'S THERE?
BZZT
BZZT
MEOW

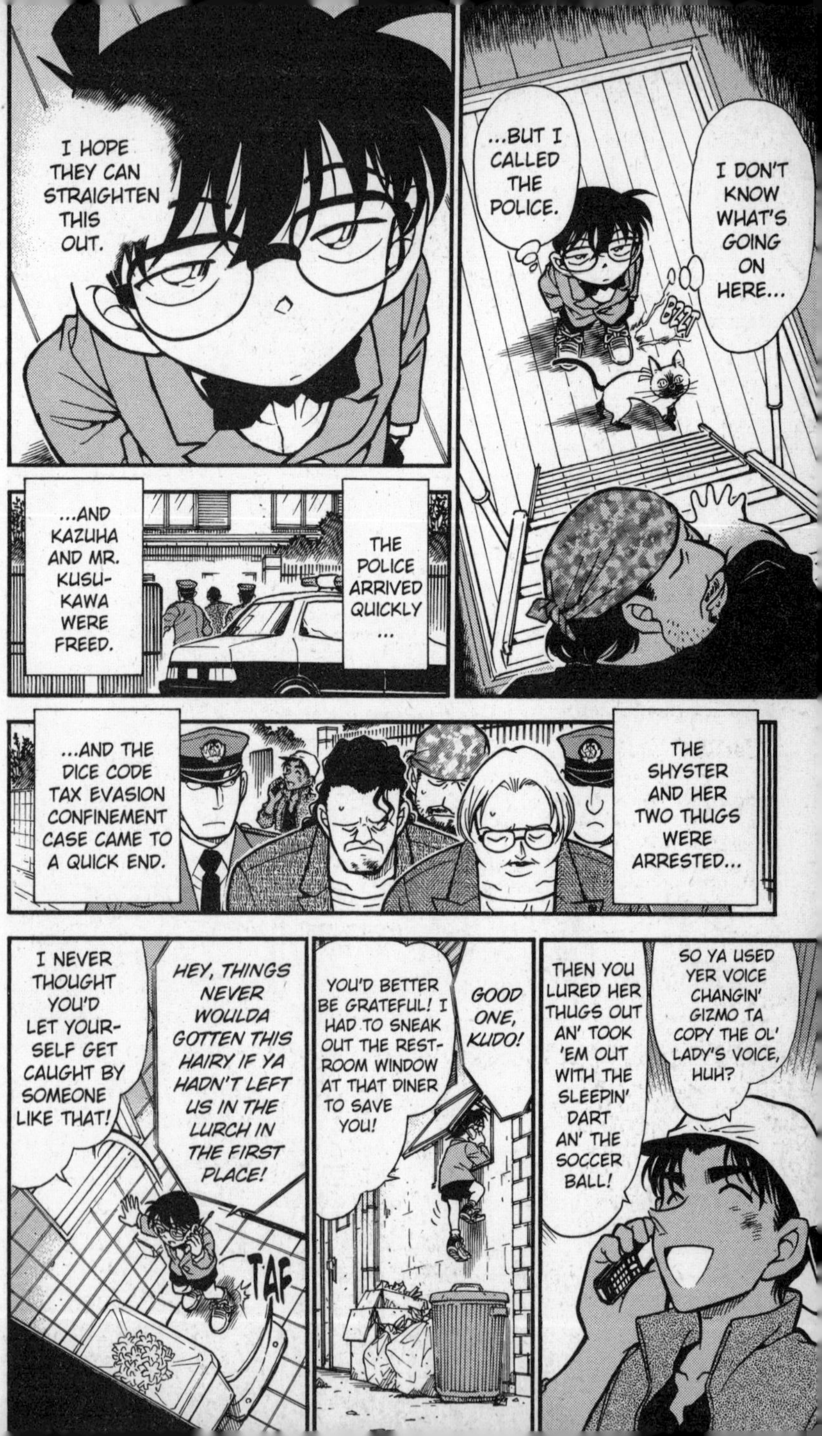
I DON'T KNOW WHAT'S GOING ON HERE...
...BUT I CALLED THE POLICE.
BZZT
I HOPE THEY CAN STRAIGHTEN THIS OUT.
THE POLICE ARRIVED QUICKLY...
...AND KAZUHA AND MR. KUSUKAWA WERE FREED.
THE SHYSTER AND HER TWO THUGS WERE ARRESTED...
...AND THE DICE CODE TAX EVASION CONFINEMENT CASE CAME TO A QUICK END.
SO YA USED YER VOICE CHANGIN' GIZMO TA COPY THE OL' LADY'S VOICE, HUH?
THEN YOU LURED HER THUGS OUT AN' TOOK 'EM OUT WITH THE SLEEPIN' DART AN' THE SOCCER BALL!
GOOD ONE, KUDO!
YOU'D BETTER BE GRATEFUL! I HAD TO SNEAK OUT THE RESTROOM WINDOW AT THAT DINER TO SAVE YOU!
HEY, THINGS NEVER WOULDA GOTTEN THIS HAIRY IF YA HADN'T LEFT US IN THE LURCH IN THE FIRST PLACE!
I NEVER THOUGHT YOU'D LET YOURSELF GET CAUGHT BY SOMEONE LIKE THAT!
TAF

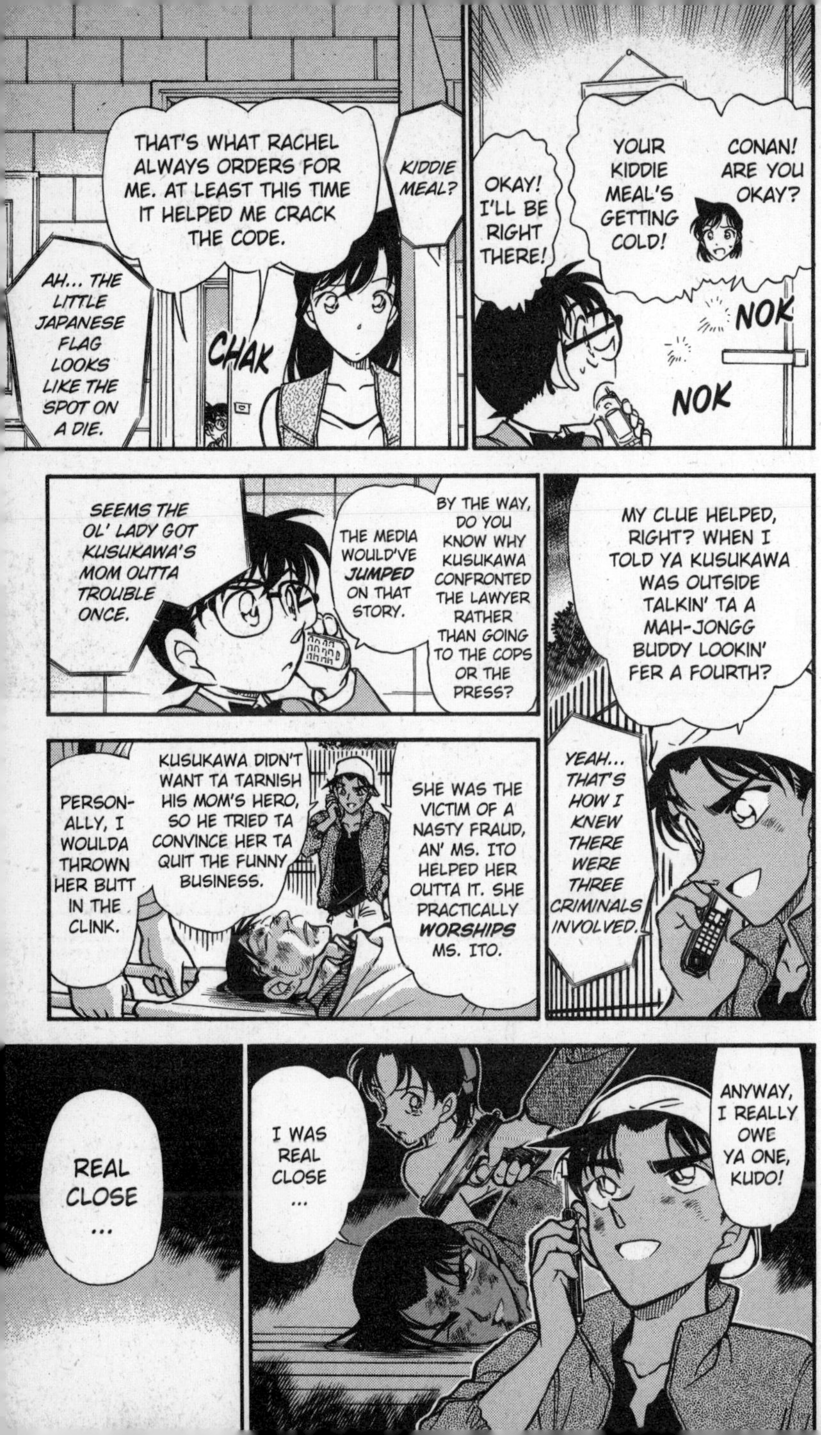
CONAN! ARE YOU OKAY?
YOUR KIDDIE MEAL'S GETTING COLD!
NOK
NOK
OKAY! I'LL BE RIGHT THERE!
KIDDIE MEAL?
THAT'S WHAT RACHEL ALWAYS ORDERS FOR ME. AT LEAST THIS TIME IT HELPED ME CRACK THE CODE.
CHAK
AH... THE LITTLE JAPANESE FLAG LOOKS LIKE THE SPOT ON A DIE.
MY CLUE HELPED, RIGHT? WHEN I TOLD YA KUSUKAWA WAS OUTSIDE TALKIN' TA A MAH-JONGG BUDDY LOOKIN' FER A FOURTH?
YEAH... THAT'S HOW I KNEW THERE WERE THREE CRIMINALS INVOLVED.
BY THE WAY, DO YOU KNOW WHY KUSUKAWA CONFRONTED THE LAWYER RATHER THAN GOING TO THE COPS OR THE PRESS?
THE MEDIA WOULD'VE JUMPED ON THAT STORY.
SEEMS THE OL' LADY GOT KUSUKAWA'S MOM OUTTA TROUBLE ONCE.
SHE WAS THE VICTIM OF A NASTY FRAUD, AN' MS. ITO HELPED HER OUTTA IT. SHE PRACTICALLY WORSHIPS MS. ITO.
KUSUKAWA DIDN'T WANT TA TARNISH HIS MOM'S HERO, SO HE TRIED TA CONVINCE HER TA QUIT THE FUNNY BUSINESS.
PERSON-ALLY, I WOULDA THROWN HER BUTT IN THE CLINK.
ANYWAY, I REALLY OWE YA ONE, KUDO!
I WAS REAL CLOSE ...
REAL CLOSE ...

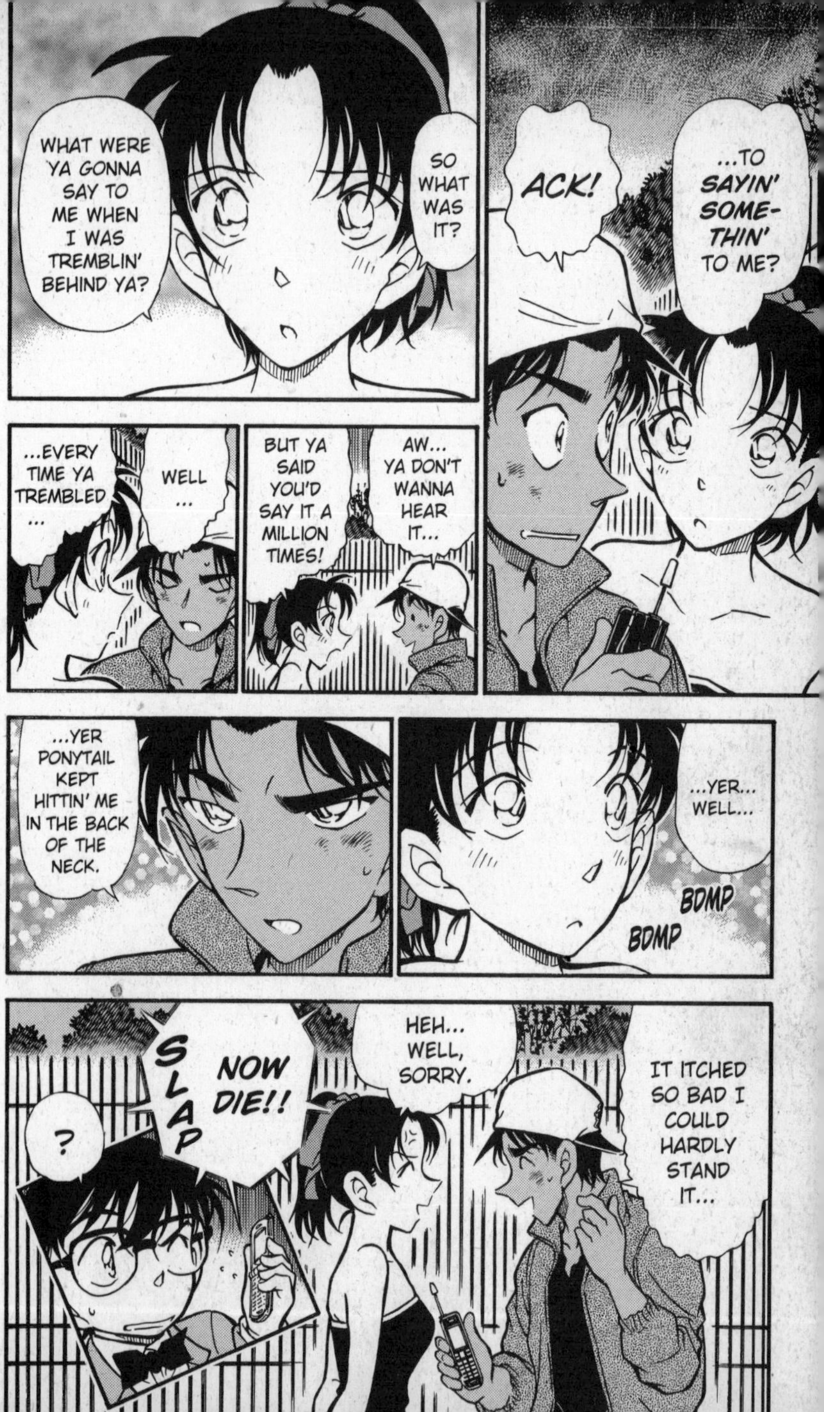
...TO SAYIN' SOMETHIN' TO ME?
ACK!
SO WHAT WAS IT?
WHAT WERE YA GONNA SAY TO ME WHEN I WAS TREMBLIN' BEHIND YA?
AW... YA DON'T WANNA HEAR IT...
BUT YA SAID YOU'D SAY IT A MILLION TIMES!
WELL...
...EVERY TIME YA TREMBLED...
...YER... WELL...
BDMP
BDMP
...YER PONYTAIL KEPT HITTIN' ME IN THE BACK OF THE NECK.
IT ITCHED SO BAD I COULD HARDLY STAND IT...
HEH... WELL, SORRY.
NOW DIE!!
SLAP
?

Hello, Aoyama here.

For those of you wondering about Conan's outfit on the front cover...

That's the costume Stan Hansen, my favorite wrestler from back when I was a student, wore when he entered the ring! Ooh, the time he made a surprise appearance at an All Japan Pro Wrestling match was an even bigger shock than the time my bridgework fell out. Heh...

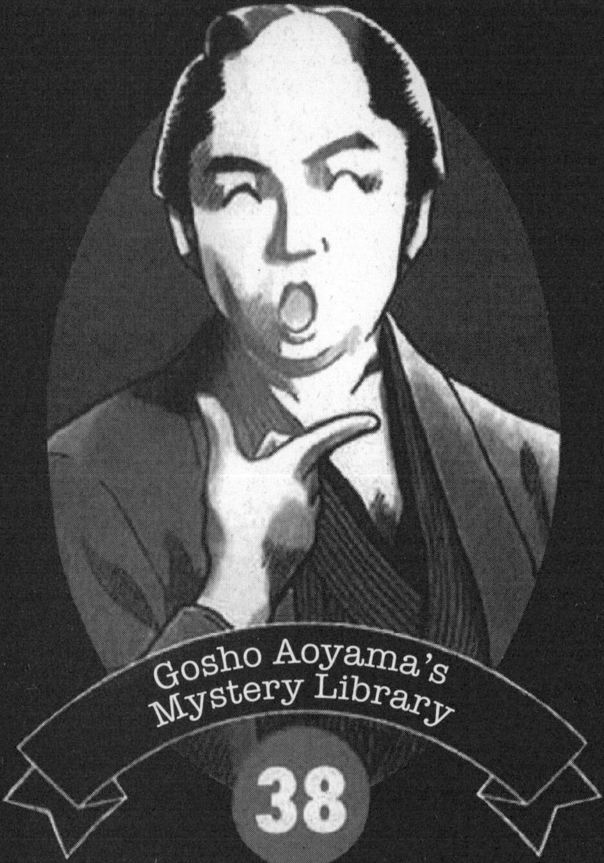
Gosho Aoyama's
Mystery Library
38

DENSHICHI

"Yo yo yoi, yo yo yoi, yo yo yoi yoi, this is so great!" That's the catchphrase of Denshichi of Kuromon, the great Edo-period detective who always celebrates the closing of a case with rhythmic finger clapping! Denshichi is a police detective who lives in the town of Shimoya Kuromon with his wife, Oshun. He takes orders from his boss Toyama Saemonnojo, sends his men to gather information and brilliantly uncovers the truth behind each case. Denshichi is a very humane man, but he is unforgiving to the evils of the world. He captures suspects with his trusty weighted chain and shouts, "Give it up!" as he points his *jutte* with the purple rope, a special weapon only he is permitted to carry, at them.

Denshichi's author, Tatsuro Jinta, is the pen name for a group called the Police Detective Club. Life would be so easy if I had a group like that to come up with Conan's stories...

I recommend *Yashabotan* (The Demon Peony).

[Editor's Note: A *jutte* is a pronged weapon used today in martial arts but originally developed for law enforcement.]

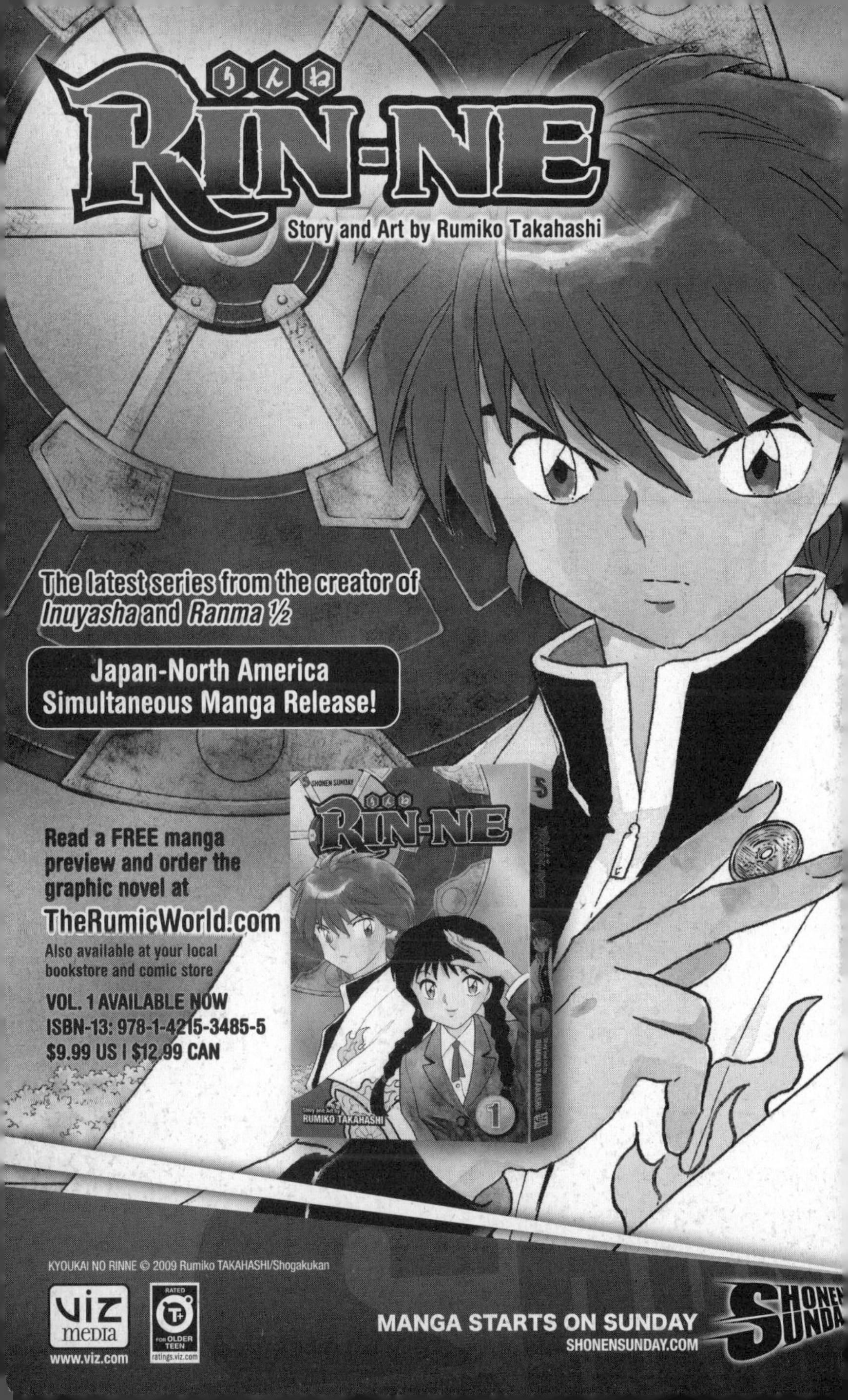

りんね
RIN-NE
Story and Art by Rumiko Takahashi
The latest series from the creator of
Inuyasha and *Ranma ½*
Japan-North America
Simultaneous Manga Release!
SHONEN SUNDAY
RIN-NE
Story and Art by
RUMIKO TAKAHASHI
1
Read a FREE manga
preview and order the
graphic novel at
TheRumicWorld.com
Also available at your local
bookstore and comic store
VOL. 1 AVAILABLE NOW
ISBN-13: 978-1-4215-3485-5
$9.99 US | $12.99 CAN
KYOUKAI NO RINNE © 2009 Rumiko TAKAHASHI/Shogakukan
viz media
www.viz.com
RATED T+ FOR OLDER TEEN
ratings.viz.com
MANGA STARTS ON SUNDAY
SHONENSUNDAY.COM
SHONEN SUNDAY

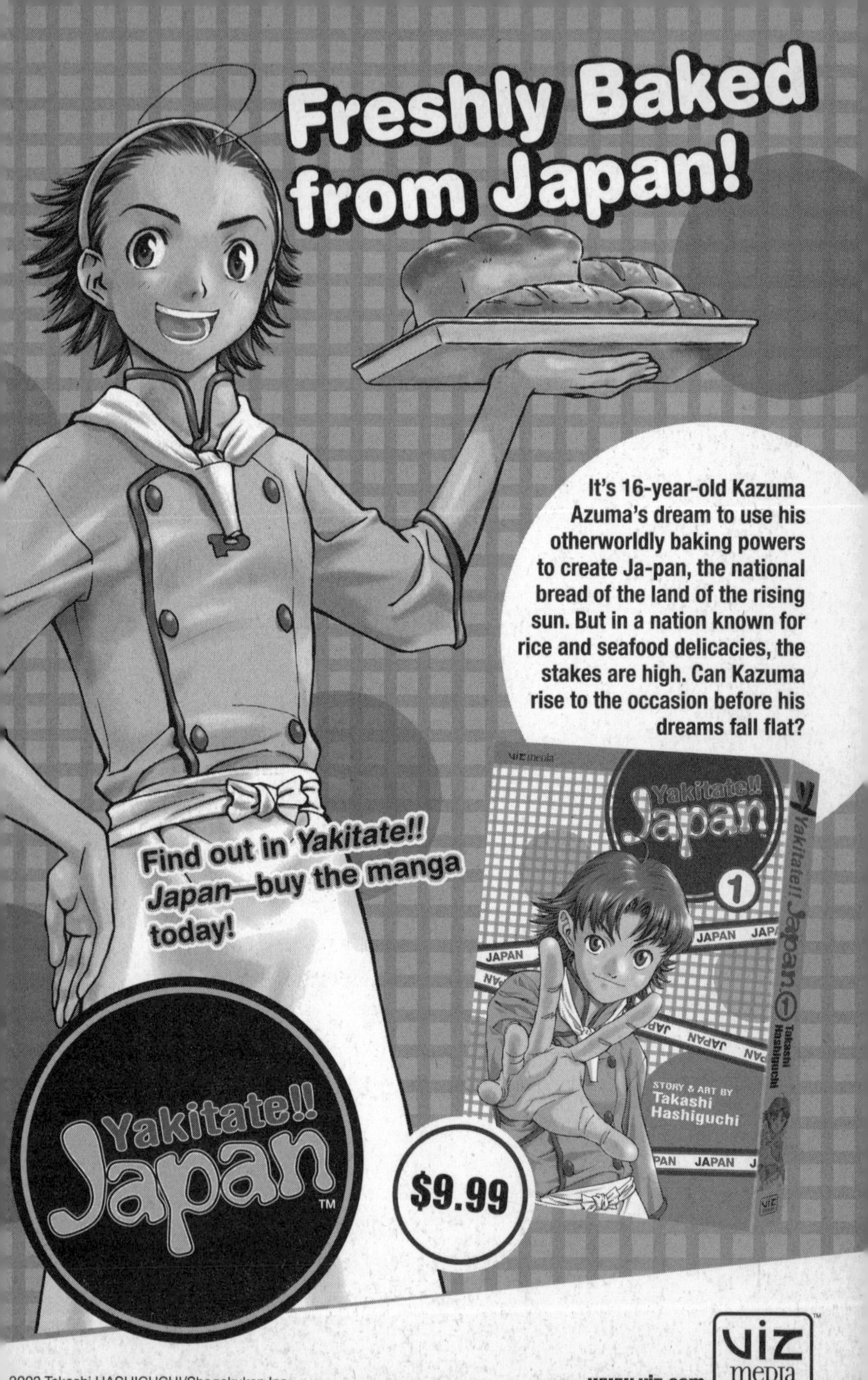
Freshly Baked from Japan!
It's 16-year-old Kazuma Azuma's dream to use his otherworldly baking powers to create Ja-pan, the national bread of the land of the rising sun. But in a nation known for rice and seafood delicacies, the stakes are high. Can Kazuma rise to the occasion before his dreams fall flat?
Find out in Yakitate!! Japan—buy the manga today!
Yakitate!! Japan
1
STORY & ART BY
Takashi Hashiguchi
$9.99
Yakitate!! Japan™